A Handbook of Dates

A Handbook of Dates is an unrivalled reference book for historians. It provides in clear, user-friendly form, tables which allow the calculation of the dates (and days) on which historical events have fallen or will fall, from AD 400 to 2100. It describes the calendars and other systems used for dating purposes in England from Roman times to the present, including regnal years. Lists of Easter dates, saints' days, popes, rulers of England and the Roman calendar are also given. In this updated and expanded edition, edited by Professor Michael Jones, the introductory materials for each set of tables have been revised. New tables for legal chronology, old and new style dates, Celtic Easter, adoption of Gregorian style, and the French Revolutionary calendar have been added, while the existing Anglo-Saxon regnal lists have been significantly revised. *A Handbook of Dates* is an essential tool for all researchers in British history.

The late **C. R. CHENEY** was Professor of Medieval History at the Universities of Manchester and Cambridge; among his books are *From Becket to Langton* (Manchester, 1956) and (with Sir Maurice Powick) *Councils and Synods and other Documents relating to the English Church, 1205–1313* (Oxford, 1964).

MICHAEL JONES is Professor of Medieval French History at the University of Nottingham. He is a former Literary Director of the Royal Historical Society, and the editor of *Nottingham Medieval Studies*, and of volume VI of the *New Cambridge Medieval History*, *c. 1300–c. 1415*.

ROYAL
HISTORICAL SOCIETY
GUIDES
AND HANDBOOKS
NO. 4

A Handbook
of Dates

For students of British history

EDITED BY

C.R. CHENEY

NEW EDITION

REVISED BY

MICHAEL JONES

CAMBRIDGE
UNIVERSITY PRESS

PUBLISHED BY THE PRESS SYNDICATE OF THE UNIVERSITY OF CAMBRIDGE
The Pitt Building, Trumpington Street, Cambridge, United Kingdom

CAMBRIDGE UNIVERSITY PRESS
The Edinburgh Building, Cambridge CB2 2RU, UK   www.cup.cam.ac.uk
40 West 20th Street, New York, NY 10011–4211, USA   www.cup.org
10 Stamford Road, Oakleigh, Melbourne 3166, Australia
Ruiz de Alarcón 13, 28014 Madrid, Spain

First published 1945
Revised edition 2000

Printed in the United Kingdom at the University Press, Cambridge

Typeface TEFFLexicon 9¼/13 pt   *System* QuarkXPress® [SE]

A catalogue record for this book is available from the British Library

Library of Congress cataloguing-in-publication data
A handbook of dates/edited by C. R. Cheney, Michael Jones. – 2nd edn.
p.   cm.
(Royal Historical Society guides and handbooks: no. 4)
Rev. edn. of: Handbook of dates for students of English history. 1945.
Includes index.
ISBN 0 521 77095 5 hardback
1. Great Britain – History – Chronology.
2. Church history – Chronology.
3. Great Britain – Calendars.
I. Cheney, C. R. (Christopher Robert). 1906–   .
II. Jones, Michael, 1940–   .
III. Handbook of dates for students of English history.
IV. Title
V. Series: Guides and handbooks: no. 4.
DA34.H29   1999   941′.002′02 – dc21   99–27383 CIP

ISBN 0 521 77095 5 hardback
ISBN 0 521 77845 x paperback

Contents

Contents

Preface to the new edition

Christopher Cheney's *Handbook of Dates for Students of English History* established itself as a minor classic from the moment of its first publication (1945). It has been reprinted at regular intervals ever since, latterly in an increasingly smudgy form, though it continues to sell well to successive generations of students. Although corrected and partially updated, it has never been thoroughly overhauled in the light of new knowledge, nor has its information been checked against that provided in other handbooks of the Royal Historical Society, like the third edition of the *Handbook of British Chronology* (1986). The urgent need to revise some tables as we pass into a new millennium now presents an opportunity not only to review its contents yet again, but also to reflect some changes in the study of English history since 1945. There has, however, been no attempt at such radical revision or enlargement of scope that it would turn Cheney's original work into something very different.

Originally intended (and admirably fulfilling its purpose) as a short, handy reference tool which could be used daily by practising historians, this new edition is intended to preserve, even enhance, the main features of the *Handbook*, above all its clarity, concision and practicality which so eminently serves to make it a model of its kind. For while it does not pretend to include the mass of information found in some of its continental cousins, it easily surpasses them for ease of use and uncluttered presentation. In resetting or re-ordering tables, these criteria have above all been borne in mind.

Unrepentantly, it remains very much an 'Anglo-centric' work, and one perhaps inevitably biased more towards the needs of medievalists than modernists. It is, for instance, the early sections of the table of 'Rulers of England' that has undergone the most obvious revision in this edition, both to reflect major advances in the critical study of charter evidence and the now generally accepted standard forms of Anglo-Saxon and Scandinavian names. Unfortunately, lack of space has prevented the inclusion of lists of rulers of other parts of the British Isles, for whom some information is available in the *Handbook of British Chronology*, 3rd edn (1986), though this also requires major surgery in the light of modern scholarship.

The provision of more information on the adoption of the Gregorian Calendar by European States and the inclusion of the French Revolutionary Calendar are meant to assist those concerned with English (and later British) diplomatic history, while for legal historians, it has seemed appropriate to provide full tables of law terms. Clarification, new graphics and additional material have been inserted into the introductory remarks for several of the tables, which have now been numbered throughout. General and miscellaneous works and those on Diplomatic are listed immediately after the end of the original preface below (pp. xiv–xvii), whilst other revised bibliographies have been added to the end of the most appropriate sections of the *Handbook*.

In coordinating this revised edition, I have been particularly helped by colleagues who have written or revised particular sections or contributed new material: Professor J. H. Baker and Dr Paul Brand (legal chronology); Professor Christopher Brooke (dating of episcopal *acta*); Professor Nicholas Brooks, Professor David Dumville and Dr Simon Keynes (rulers of England); Professor Gordon Campbell (Gregorian calendar); Dr Elizabeth Hallam Smith (law terms); Dr Judith Jesch (rulers of Scandinavian York); Dr Richard Sharp (reckonings of time); Professor Diana Greenway (bibliography), Professor David Smith and Dr David Crook (bibliography; saints' days); Professor Ronald Hutton (Protestant calendar). Dr Brian Yallop, Superintendent, H. M. Nautical Almanac Office, The Royal Observatories, provided the tables for Easter AD 2001–2100, and Amanda Hill, Rhodes House, Oxford, drew attention to an algorithm or calculating the Gregorian calendar Easter date. Matters of detail have been brought to my attention by Dr Julia Barrow, Leofranc Holford-Strevens, Graham P. Lewis, Omer Rocoux and Dr Derek Spring. Among those who have proffered much valuable advice, I am particularly grateful to Dr Daniel P. McCarthy for suggesting graphics and other ways of re-tabulating information for 'Reckonings of time'. Elizabeth Howard (and before her, Ruth Parr and Vicky Cuthill) and Richard Fisher at Cambridge University Press have been extremely helpful in advising on presentation.

The *Handbook* has long been the Royal Historical Society's 'best seller' accessible to amateurs and professionals, many historians use it daily; copies of it allegedly disappeared from the Round Room of the old Public Record Office in Chancery Lane more frequently than any other work of reference. Whilst some of its material can now be found in electronic form, there is nevertheless continuing and overwhelming demand for it as a conventional book; I am sure that this new edition, despite its imperfections, will receive a ready welcome and continue to serve students of English history well into the twenty-first century.

MICHAEL JONES
Literary Director, Royal Historical Society, 1990–7
Candlemas 1999

Preface to the original edition (1945)

The plan of this book is the direct result of a suggestion made in January 1944 by Mr D. L. Evans, of the Public Record Office. Mr Evans observed that the older English handbooks of dates (notably E. A. Fry's *Almanacks for students of English history*, 1915) were out of print, and that a new volume containing some of the same tables was urgently required. He suggested, moreover, that a new compilation need not follow slavishly the form of the existing books and that it might well include the more strictly chronological parts of Professor F. M. Powicke's *Handbook of British Chronology* (1939, cf. below, p. xiv). The Council of the Royal Historical Society approved the project and the present volume is the result. In its planning the editor has had the advantage of help and advice from many quarters. The chapters on reckonings of time and saints' days are essentially the work of Professor Hilda Johnstone and were published in their original form in the *Handbook of British Chronology*; as they now appear, they embody revision and addition by the editor, made with the author's consent. Professor Johnstone's list of saints' days and festivals has been republished practically as it stands in the former handbook. Professor T. F. T. Plucknett has likewise contributed a revised version of the chapter on legal chronology which first appeared in the *Handbook of British Chronology*. The same book has been laid under contribution for the list of rulers of England before A D 1154; here Professor R. R. Darlington has given his advice on the presentation of material which is extracted wholly from this section of the earlier handbook. The editor is deeply obliged to these contributors and also to all those other scholars who have given help; he wishes to thank especially Mr D. Bonner-Smith, Professor V. H. Galbraith, Mr A. V. Judges, Mr I. G. Philip, Mr H. G. Richardson, Professor M. A. Thomson and Dr M. Tyson.

The plan of the book has of necessity been rigorously exclusive, and those who wish to use it deserve to be warned about the things it does not contain. In the first place, one must emphasize the fact that it does not set up to be a systematic treatise on chronology. It is intended, rather, to provide a compact and convenient means of verifying dates, a work of ready reference which is required as much by the expert as the novice in the daily handling and check-ing of historical material. But the lists and tables which form the greater part of the book cannot safely be used unless the reader constantly remembers that at different times and in different places and in the minds of different people a single date may mean different things. Thus 28 December 1190 would be reckoned by the English chancery clerk of that day as falling in the second year of King Richard I, but for a clerk of the exchequer the accounts covering this date belonged to the Pipe Roll of 3 Richard I, and a Benedictine chronicler would include the events of that day in the year of grace 1191. Cervantes and Shakespeare did not die on the same day, although each died on 23 April 1616, according to the computation of his country. An English document dated 28 January 1620 would be written on the same day as a docu-ment dated in Scotland 28 January 1621 or a document dated in France 7 February 1621. These examples indicate some of the pitfalls. To afford some guidance in the difficult paths of chronology the book provides chapters on reckonings of time, festivals, regnal years, and so forth. But varieties of prac-tice, both in the reckoning of time and in the presentation of chronological data, are innumerable. For further details of a subject far too complex to be completely covered in a volume of this size and character, the reader is referred to the works cited in the select bibliography which follows this preface.

The book is strictly limited to the dating of records which a student of English history will commonly encounter. Even so, it cannot claim to be com-plete, since the student will sometimes handle documents dated according to a French or German or Russian calendar, or may even be called upon to translate a date from the Jewish or Muhammadan to the Christian era. Moreover, the year of an episcopate, mayoralty, or shrievalty may be intro-duced into a document to perplex the historian. Any historical fact imagin-able may be not only a clue to the date of a record, but an element deliberately introduced by the writer to date it; so, for instance, we have a charter dated 'in the seventh year of the translation of the blessed Thomas the martyr', and a mortgage reckoned from 'the Easter after Henry the son of the king of England espoused the daughter of the king of France'.[1] Clearly, a handbook of this kind can only include the commonest chronological material, together with such general directions as will help the student to use other material for dating.

Nor is it within the scope of this work to discuss how undated or imper-

---

1. Brit. Mus., Add. charter 7593; *Essays in history presented to R. L. Poole* (Oxford, 1927), p. 205.

fectly dated documents may be dated accurately by the application of paleographical or diplomatic tests. Even when the student is not able, by handling the original, to draw inferences from handwriting, he learns to distinguish between the royal styles employed by the various Henries of England, to distinguish between one Pope Innocent and another by reference to their itineraries, and he can date an undated London private charter by finding among its witnesses the mayor and sheriffs of a particular year. These are but instances of a principle which applies to all documentary records: that a comparison with other records of the same class almost always produces at least an approximate date. And the student will often find that work of assembling these records and of fitting them into the chronological scheme has been done for him already; he must simply learn his way about a library. All this, however, pertains not to chronology but to diplomatic. The reader must be referred once and for all to the classics of that subject, with the advice that where these fail to provide infallible tests, he must have recourse to the great collections of *Regesta*, to cartularies of private charters, and so on.[2] Nor is this method applicable only to the records of the Middle Ages. In modern times the undated or incompletely dated letter is as common as it ever was; but, to quote Professor L. B. Namier, 'there is hardly an undated document which, given reasonable care, cannot be dated, at least approximately, from internal evidence'. The reader may be directed to this scholar's *Additions and corrections to Sir John Fortescue's edition of the correspondence of George III (vol. I)* (Manchester, 1937) for examples of deficient dating and models of method in the establishing of dates.

It will be observed that this handbook contains no detailed discussion of the *significance* of dates in official documents. Yet it behoves the historian to bear this matter well in mind. The fact that a charter of King Henry VI is dated at a certain place on a certain day does not mean that the king (or, indeed, any of the witnesses named) was at that place on that day. The date has a meaning, but not the obvious one, and to understand it we must understand the workings of the royal chancery and the privy seal and signet offices. So also with the written products of any highly organized government: when the student (with the help of this book) has translated the dates of the documents into modern terms, he has still to find out what the dates signify.[3]

---

2. For books on diplomatic, etc., see below, p. xiv–xvii; for the *regesta* of kings and popes, see pp. 46–7 and 57–8. [In the present edition (2000), bibliographical information has usually been added at the end of its appropriate section.]

3. The work of Maxwell-Lyte on the great seal (see p. xv) is particularly important for this question, so far as the English chancery is concerned.

Not only are we able by diplomatic tests to date the undated document and appreciate the significance of dates; it sometimes happens that the dating clause of a document provides an important diplomatic test of authenticity. For the forger can be detected by the use of anachronistic forms of date. He may add a date to a soi-disant writ of William the Conqueror, whose writs were undated, or he may give the year of grace instead of the imperial year in fabricating an early papal bull. But this, after all, is only one among many tests of authenticity and is more fittingly discussed in a treatise on diplomatic than in a handbook of dates.

Finally, to come to an end of warnings, the reader must consider the causes of errors in dating. He will certainly encounter in the course of his work inconsistencies and downright impossibilities in the dates before him. As regards inconsistencies, a word may not be amiss. Where a date is expressed with a wealth of detail, as in the solemn diplomas of the later Anglo-Saxon kings, those elements in the date which are most remote from ordinary usage are the elements most likely to be wrong. Let no one suppose that these errors necessarily bespeak the forger's work. Even the chancery of Pope Innocent III was at sea in the reckoning of indictions in A D 1206 and A D 1207, whereas it never made a mistake in calculating the year of the pontificate. When we are presented with a date in which the day of the week and the day of the month do not harmonize, it is generally the day of the week which is right. Thus, Lord Halifax dated a letter to George III Friday 3 April 1765, but 3 April 1765 fell on Wednesday and the date of the letter was Friday 3 May.[4] The student must also be prepared to find whole statements of date which for one reason or another are inadmissible. He will make due allowance for human error, remembering how he has occasionally misdated his own correspondence, especially at the beginning of a month or year. But he will do more than this if he wants to make constructive criticism; he will consider the conditions in which the date is transmitted, whether in an original document or in a later copy, whether expressed in word or in roman or arabic numerals, whether written in good faith or with the intention to deceive. Of all these points he must take account; but they do not concern us in this handbook of dates.

Throughout this work the terms of Old Style and New Style are used with the primary meanings attached to them by the *Oxford English Dictionary*; that is to say, by Old Style we mean the Julian calendar and by New Style the Gregorian, irrespective of the date adopted for the beginning of the year

4. Namier, *Additions and corrections*, p. 23, cf. *ibid.*, p. 63 (nos. 384–5).

where these systems are in use. The practice of historians, both in England and on the Continent, has varied in the past, and the result is confusion. To use 'New Style', as is often done, to denote simply the historical year, which begins on 1 January is, strictly speaking, incorrect and to be avoided. If the reader will consider the variations in the practice of England, Scotland and France between the years 1600 and 1752, he will realize at once the danger of laxity in this matter.

Select bibliography

This list and others added at the end of each section may serve to direct students to further reading on chronological matters, and to indicate where material may be found for the interpretation of dates and the dating of undated documents. Works which are particularly useful are marked with an asterisk (*).

General and miscellaneous works

L'art de vérifier les dates et les faits historiques, par un religieux de la congrégation de St Maur. 4th edn, by N. V. de St. Allais and others. 44 vols. (Paris, 1818–44).

    A great repository of detailed information, sometimes inaccurate but not altogether superseded. Mainly of use to the student of continental history.

Borst, Arno, *The ordering of time: from the ancient compotus to the modern computer*, trans. A. Winnard (Oxford, 1993).

Burnaby, S. B., *Elements of the Jewish and Muhammadan calendars with rules and tables and explanatory notes on the Julian and Gregorian calendars* (London, 1901).

    A full and useful treatise. Tables of corresponding Jewish-Christian dates (A D 610–3003) and Muhammadan-Christian dates (A D 622–3008). For a simple concordance of Muslim and Christian years Sir Wolseley Haig, *Comparative tables of Muhammadan and Christian dates* (London, 1932).

Cappelli, A., *Cronologia e calendario perpetuo*, 'Manuali Hoepli' series (Milan, 1906, 6th edn 1988).

Duncan, D. E., *The calendar* (London, 1998).

Fry, Edward Alexander, *Almanacks for students of English history* (London, 1915).

Ginzel, F. K., *Handbuch der mathematischen und technischen Chronologie. Das Zeitrechnungswesen der Völker*, 3 vols. (Leipzig, 1906–14).

    Vol. III contains a valuable chapter of nearly 200 pp. on medieval reckonings of time, and a series of detailed tables.

*Giry, A., *Manuel de diplomatique* (Paris, 1894, reprinted 1925).

    Livre II Chronologie technique (pp. 79–314) is an elaborate and valuable study, with lists and tables.

Greenway, Diana E., 'Dates in history: chronology and memory', *Historical Research*, 72 (1999), 127–39.

Gregorian reform of the calendar: proceedings of the Vatican conference to commemorate its 400th anniversary, ed. G. V. Coyne, M. A. Hoskin and O. Pedersen (Vatican City, 1983).

*Grotefend, H., *Taschenbuch der Zeitrechnung des deutschen Mittelalters und der Neuzeit* (Hannover, 1898; 12th edition, 1991).

    An excellent manual, accurate and full, based on Grotefend's larger *Zeitrechnung des deutschen Mittelalters und der Neuzeit*, 2 vols. in 3 (Hannover, 1891–8).

Handbook of British Chronology, ed. E. B. Fryde, D. E. Greenway, S. Porter and I. Roy, 3rd edn (Royal Hist. Soc., Guides and Handbooks no. 2, London, 1986).

This omits the sections on Reckonings of Time and Saints' Days and Legal Chronology and the Table of Regnal Years all contained in the first edition of 1939 ed. F. M. Powicke. The third edition greatly enlarges the lists of office-holders and gives more bibliographical matter.

Handbook of Oriental History, ed. C. H. Philips (Royal Hist. Soc., Guides and Handbooks no. 6, London, 1951 and reprinted).

Mas Latrie, J. M. L. de, *Trésor de chronologie, d'histoire et de géographie pour l'étude et l'emploi des documents du moyen âge* (Paris, 1889).

    A vast work, chiefly of use for French history.

*de Morgan, Augustus, *The book of almanacs* (London, 1851; 3rd edn, 1907).

    The work of a great mathematician, with admirable tables and the material for calculating phases of the moon.

Nicolas, Sir Nicholas Harris, *Chronology of history* (London, 1833; 2nd edn (quoted in this work) 1838, and later reprints).

    A deservedly popular handbook, now somewhat out of date and not always accurate in detail.

*Poole, Reginald Lane, *Medieval reckonings of time*, SPCK, 'Helps for students of history', no. 3 (London, 1921).

    A lucid little guide by a great scholar.

    Studies in chronology and history (Oxford, 1934).

Schram, Robert, *Kalendariographische und Chronologische Tafeln* (Leipzig, 1908) (contains Jewish and Muslim calendars, as well as the Gregorian and Julian calendars, with tables carried forward to 31 December 2399).

Stamp, A. E., *Methods of chronology*. Historical Association pamphlet no. 92 (London, 1933).

    Designed as a series of practical hints and warnings for historical students, by a former Deputy Keeper of the Public Records.

Stevens, W. M., *Cycles of time and scientific learning in medieval Europe* (London, Variorum, 1995).

Ware, R. D., 'Medieval chronology: theory and practice', in *Medieval studies: an introduction*, ed. J. M. Powell (2nd edn, Syracuse, 1992), pp. 252–77.

Wilcox, D. J., *The measure of times past: pre-Newtonian chronologies and the rhetoric of relative time* (Chicago and London, 1987).

Wüstenfeld, F., *Vergleichungstabellen der muhammedanischen und christlichen Zeitrechnungen*. 2nd edn, revised by E. Mahler (Leipzig, 1926).

For the calendar used by the Society of Friends see Harris Nicolas, *Chronology of history*, pp. 180–1.

For the reckoning by mayoral years in London judicial records of the seventeenth and eighteenth centuries see Hugh Bowler in *Publications of the Catholic Record Soc.*, 34 (1934), pp. xix–xx, and P. E. Jones in *Notes and Queries*, 189 (1945), 278.

For eclipses of the sun and moon:

Schove, D. J. and Fletcher, A., *Chronology of eclipses and comets AD1–1000* (Woodbridge, 1984).

Schroeter, J. Fr., *Spezieller Kanon der zentralen Sonnen- und Mondfinsternisse, welche innerhalb des Zeitraums von 600 bis 1800 n. Chr. in Europa sichtbar waren* (Kristiania, 1923).

For storms, droughts and famines:

Britton, C. E., *A meteorological chronology to A.D. 1450*. Meteorological Office, Geophysical Memoirs no. 70 (London, Stationery Office, 1937).

Jordan, W. C., *The Great Famine. Northern Europe in the early fourteenth century* (Princeton, N. J., 1996). Excellent bibliography.

Lamb, H. H., *Climate, History and the Modern World* (London, 1982).

Titow, J. 'Evidence of weather in the account rolls of the Bishopric of Winchester, 1209–1350', *Economic History Review*, 2nd series, xii (1960), 360–407.

Diplomatic, etc.

(a) The following list only gives a few of the most important general works and essays of outstanding value.

Bishop, T. A. M., *Scriptores regis: facsimiles to identify and illustrate the hands of royal scribes in original charters of Henry I, Stephen, and Henry II* (Oxford, 1961).

Bishop, T. A. M. and Chaplais, P., *Facsimiles of English writs to A.D. 1100* (Oxford, 1957).

de Boüard, A., *Manuel de diplomatique française et pontificale*, Tomes I and II, with plates (Paris, 1929–52).

*Bresslau, Harry, *Handbuch der Urkundenlehre für Deutschland und Italien*. 2nd edn, 2 vols. (Leipzig, 1912–31).
  The most solid and trustworthy modern guide.

Chaplais, P., *English royal documents: King John to Henry VI, 1199–1461* (Oxford, 1971).
  'The origin and authenticity of the royal Anglo-Saxon diploma', *Journal of the Society of Archivists*, vol. 3, no. 2 (October 1965), 48–61, reprinted in *Prisca Munimenta*, ed. F. Ranger (London, 1973), pp. 28–42.
  'The Anglo-Saxon chancery: from diploma to the writ', *Journal of the Society of Archivists*, vol. 3, no. 4 (October 1966), 160–76, reprinted in *Prisca Munimenta*, ed. F. Ranger (London, 1973), pp. 43–62.
  'Who introduced charters into England? The case for Augustine', *Journal of the Society of Archivists*, vol. 3, no. 10 (October 1969), 526–42, reprinted in *Prisca Munimenta*, ed. F. Ranger (London, 1973), pp. 88–107.
  'The letter from Bishop Wealdhere of London to Archbishop Brihtwold of Canterbury: the earliest original "letter close" extant in the West', *Medieval scribes, manuscripts and libraries: essays presented to N. R. Ker*, ed. M. B. Parkes and A. G. Watson (London, 1978), pp. 3–23, reprinted in his *Essays in medieval diplomacy and administration* (London, 1981), ch. 14, with same pagination.
  'Master John de Branketre and the office of notary in chancery, 1355–1375', *Journal of the Society of Archivists*, vol. 4, no. 3 (April 1971), 169–99, reprinted in his *Essays in medieval diplomacy and administration*, (London, 1981), ch. 22, with same pagination.
  'The royal Anglo-Saxon "chancery" of the tenth century revisited', *Studies in medieval history presented to R. H. C. Davis*, ed. Henry Mayr-Harting and R. I. Moore (London, 1985), pp. 41–51.

Cheney, C. R., *English bishops' chanceries, 1100–1250* (Manchester, 1950).
  Notaries public in England in thirteenth and fourteenth centuries (Oxford, 1972).

*Giry, Arthur, *Manuel de diplomatique* (Paris, 1894, reprinted 1925).
  Out of date in many details, but still the clearest and most elaborate treatise.

Hall, Hubert, *A formula book of English official historical documents*, 2 parts (Cambridge, 1908–9).
  A useful collection, rather confusedly presented and full of hazards!

Insley, C., 'Charters and episcopal scriptoria in the Anglo-Saxon south-west', *Early Medieval Europe*, 7 (1998), 173–97.

Keynes, Simon, *The diplomas of King Æthelred 'the unready', 978–1016: a study in their use as historical evidence* (Cambridge, 1980).
  A handlist of Anglo-Saxon charters: archives and single sheets (London, 1991).

*[Madox, Thomas], *Formulare anglicanum* (London, 1702).
  An important collection of documents, preceded by an important introduction.

Maxwell-Lyte, Sir Henry C., *Historical notes on the use of the Great Seal of England* (London, 1926).

    Discusses in great detail the significance of dates in documents of the English chancery, etc.

*Stenton, F. M., *Transcripts of charters relating to Gilbertine houses* (Lincoln Record Society Publications, vol. 18, 1922).

    The introduction contains a valuable note on the diplomatic of private charters.

Tessier, Georges, *Diplomatique royale française* (Paris, 1962). Lucidly updates de Boüard.

(b) For dating by study of handwriting the following amply illustrated works are recommended:

Aris, R., *Explicatio formarum litterarum: the unfolding of letterforms* (Minnesota College of Calligraphy, 1990).

Bishop, T. A. M., *English Carolingian miniscule* (Oxford, 1971).

Bischoff, B., *Latin palaeography*, trans. D. O. Cronin and D. Ganz (Cambridge, 1990).

Dumville, David, 'English square miniscule script: the background and earliest phase', *Anglo-Saxon England* xvi (1987), 147–79.

Facsimilies of Anglo-Saxon charters, ed. Simon Keynes (Oxford for the British Academy 1991).

Jenkinson, Hilary, *The later court hands in England*, 2 vols. (Cambridge, 1927).

Johnson, Charles, and Jenkinson, Hilary, *English court hand A.D. 1066 to 1500*, 2 vols. (Oxford, 1915).

Lowe, E. A., *English uncial* (Oxford, 1960).

Parkes, M. B., *English cursive book hands 1250–1500* (Oxford, 1969).

Robinson, Pamela R., *Catalogue of dated and datable manuscripts c. 737–1600 in Cambridge Libraries* (Oxford, 1988).

Temple, E., *Anglo-Saxon manuscripts, 900–1066* (London, 1976).

Watson, Andrew, *Catalogue of dated and datable manuscripts c. 700–1600 in the Department of Manuscripts, the British Library* (Oxford, 1979).

    Catalogue of dated and datable manuscripts c. 435–1600 in Oxford libraries (Oxford, 1984).

(c) For the possibilities of dating by tests applied to paper and ink, see:

Harrison, W. R., *Suspect documents: their scientific examination* (London, 1968).

Mitchell, C. Ainsworth, *Documents and their scientific examination* (London, 1922, new edition, 1935).

An admirable demonstration of detecting forgeries by applying dating tests to paper and printers' founts is to be be found in:

Carter, John, and Pollard, Graham, *An enquiry into the nature of certain nineteenth century pamphlets* (London, 1934).

(d) For paper in general, and for watermarks, see:

Briquet, C. M, *Les filigranes: dictionnaire historique des marques du papier*. 2nd edn, 4 vols. (Leipzig, 1923; repr. New York, 1968) [for period to 1600].

Churchill, W. A., *Watermarks in paper in Holland, England, France in the 17th and 18th centuries* (Amsterdam, 1935).

Heawood, E., *Watermarks mainly of the 17th and 18th centuries* (Hilversum, 1950).

Stevenson, A., 'Paper as bibliographic evidence', *The Library*, 5th ser. 17 (1962), 197–212.

1

Reckonings of time[*]

I The Julian calendar: Old Style

Throughout the Middle Ages, and in some countries for much longer, the calendar in use was that known as the Julian, because it was originally introduced by Julius Caesar in 45 BC. This way of reckoning is now known as the Old Style, in contradistinction to the New Style, that is to say reckoning by the Gregorian calendar, introduced by Pope Gregory XIII in 1582.

The Julian calendar set up a common year consisting of 365 days, while every fourth year was to contain an extra day, the sixth calends of March (24 February) being doubled and the year therefore being described as *annus bissextilis*. This latter device was intended to rectify, at regular intervals, the accumulated discrepancy between the calendar year of 365 days and the solar year, calculated by the astronomers at 365¼ days. The mistake was made, however, of counting in the current year when deciding which was 'every fourth year', and in practice the bissextile years occurred in what we should call every third year. Thus an error rapidly accumulated, until the Emperor Augustus got rid of it by ordaining that twelve successive years should consist of 365 days only. The next bissextile or leap year was AD 4, and thereafter, as long as the Old Style lasted, every fourth year, in the modern sense, was a leap year.

II The year

The Christian era

The use for dating purposes of the Christian year (*annus domini, annus ab incarnatione domini, annus gratiæ*) arose somewhat unexpectedly through the compilation of a table for calculating the date of Easter, made by the monk Dionysius Exiguus in AD 525. This was intended to continue to AD 626 the Easter Table then in use, of which the cycle would end in 531. Dionysius, a Scythian by birth, but living in Rome and *moribus omnino*

*Chiefly revised by Dr Richard Sharpe.

1

romanus, constructed a list of years calculated not from the prevailing era of Diocletian, the pagan emperor, but from the Incarnation of Our Lord. A continuator carried on the table to AD 721. At the synod of Whitby, in AD 664, Wilfred, as part of his advocacy of all things Roman, secured the acceptance in Northumbria of the Dionysian Easter Table. Dionysius himself had had no thought of establishing a new era, but now his device was adopted for chronological purposes by Bede. Starting from English usage in the eighth century, the new era gradually spread to the Continent until in every country of Western Europe except Spain (see below), Christians reckoned from AD 1.

In England this method was used for the dating of official documents long before it was adopted by continental chanceries. The year *ab incarnatione* is found in Anglo-Saxon diplomas very soon after the death of Bede to replace or supplement dating by indiction, and was commonly used for such royal documents as bore dates (even when they also used the regnal year) until late in the twelfth century. Outside the royal chancery the reckoning is to be found in English legal instruments of all sorts in the exceptional cases in which a date of any kind is vouchsafed. Later in the Middle Ages documents of ecclesiastical provenance generally, and private charters occasionally, are dated by the year of grace. The era of the incarnation also regularly provided the chronological framework of English chronicles and annals.

The Spanish era

In Spain, Portugal, and those southeastern parts of Gaul which were for a time under the rule of the Visigoths, an era was used which had been taken over by the latter from the Christians of Roman Spain. According to some authorities, the era originated in an Easter Table of which the first cycle began, not at the year of incarnation, but at 38 BC, and it was reckoned from 1 January 38 BC, though the reasons for this remain unresolved. The era was in use in Catalonia to 1180, in Aragon to 1350, in Valencia to 1358, in Castile to 1382, in Portugal to 1420. The date is always given in the form 'era millesima octava' not 'anno millesimo octavo', and to find the equivalent year of the Christian era one must subtract 38 from the date in the Spanish era.

The indiction

Unlike the Christian and Spanish eras, the indiction was originally a civil reckoning of time. It is a cycle of fifteen years, counted as *indictio prima*, *secunda,* and so on, to 15, reverting then to 1. The first cycle was counted from AD 312, but there were three chief methods of reckoning the opening date:

(a) The Greek, or Constantinopolitan, Indiction, beginning on
     1 September. The popes seem to have used this fairly regularly till 1087,
     after which the practice of the papal chancery varied till Alexander III
     (1159–81).
(b) The Bedan, or Cæsarean, or Imperial Indiction, or the Indiction of
     Constantine, beginning on 24 September. This was probably intro-
     duced by Bede into England, where it became usual, and was adopted
     by the papacy under Alexander III.
(c) The Roman, or Pontifical, Indiction, beginning on 25 December (or
     sometimes on 1 January), was in fact only occasionally used in the papal
     chancery, but is found in other places at various periods.

The use of the indiction-year as an element in the dating of documents goes back to imperial Rome, when it was added to statements of the consular and imperial years. It continued to be used by the papacy and the royal chanceries of the West in the early Middle Ages for the more solemn privileges and legal records. It is also found in some private charters. But by the end of the thirteenth century it was generally ignored except in one class of document: the instruments drawn up by public notaries continue to exhibit the indiction together with other dating elements until the sixteenth century.

The dating formula, *indictio prima,* etc., simply shows the place which the year occupies in an unspecified cycle of fifteen years. The rule for calculating it is to subtract 312 from the number of the year of grace and divide by fifteen: the remainder will correspond with the number of the year in indiction and the quotient will be one less than the number of the indiction (but the latter is seldom mentioned in documents). Since the beginning of the year of grace does not, in most systems of reckoning, coincide with the beginning of the indiction, the equation must take account of the day of the year. As an example, take a document dated 1 November 1094: $1094 - 312 = 782$; $782 \div 15 = 52$ with a remainder of 2. Therefore, the number of the indiction *for the greater part of* 1094 is 2. But the date in question (1 November) falls in the lesser part of the year according to the Greek and Bedan indictions: it is therefore *indictio tertia* by these reckonings, *indictio secunda* by the Roman reckoning. This is illustrated in figure 1.

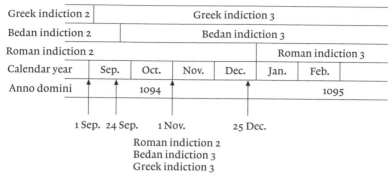

Figure 1 Calendars for 1094–1095

The regnal year

From ancient up to modern times it has been a common practice to date official documents by the year of the rulers or magistrates from whom the documents emanated or within whose jurisdiction they were issued. Roman law demanded that certain classes of documents should bear the names of the consuls for the year; and, in the absence of exact information, dating by reference to past consuls was sometimes preferred (e.g. *post consulatum Flavi Fausti iunioris*). In AD 537 Justinian provided that the years of the emperor's reign should be added and thereafter the *post-consulatum* element, though it lingered on in various forms, ceased to be of practical importance. But the system which had been used by the consuls of the Roman people and the emperors was copied by popes, bishops, kings, dukes, and lesser men. It found its way, moreover, from official documents to literary narratives. Sometimes the regnal year was used to the exclusion of the indiction or year of grace, sometimes it accompanied these elements. For the method of its use in the English chancery and the papal chancery the reader is referred to the notes which precede the lists of kings and popes (pp. 21–2 and 48–50).

III The date of Easter

As noted above (p. 1), it was the calculation of Easter that led Dionysius to devise the numbering of years that we now use, and, incidentally explains the necessity of this *Handbook*, since it is because of the movable character of Easter that the annual calendar has also to accommodate other movable feasts. Easter was 'movable' in the sense that it was fixed in relation to the moon's phases and the day of the week, and these do not recur at the same point in successive calendar years. After many disputes, which produced divergences in other parts of Christendom,[1] the Latin Church determined that Easter should be celebrated on the Sunday following the first full moon on or after 21 March.[2] The result, in short, is this: that Easter never falls on the same day of the month in two successive years and it may fall on any of the thirty-five days between 22 March and 25 April (both included.[3] The ecclesiastical calendar for the entire year is controlled by this fact of a movable Easter. To enable students to see clearly the ecclesiastical calendar for any given year from AD 400 to AD 2100, a series of tables is provided later in this volume (8/1–35). Confronted, for example, with a document dated on the Tuesday after Trinity, AD 1288, the student first discovers from the chronological table on p. 229 that Easter fell on the 28 March in 1288; then on turning to Table 8/7, it will be found that the date in question is, in modern terms, 25 May 1288.

The medieval computists, faced with similar problems of calculating the incidence of movable feasts, adopted various devices for relating the days of the week and the lunar month to the calendar. The scaffolding of the tables they compiled provided material for elaborating statements of date which for ordinary purposes were quite long enough already. Thus the Anglo-Saxon solemn diploma might set out not only the indiction

1. Some of these are indicated in table 7; for more detail on Easter in the Celtic British Church, see also D. McCarthy and Dáibhí Ó Cróinín, 'The "lost" Irish 84-year Easter Table rediscovered', *Peritia*, 6–7 (1987–8), 227–42.
2. Because 21 March was taken to be invariably the date of the vernal equinox. In fact it is not; and therefore some accurate astronomical calculations of the paschal moon differ from the approximate historical reckonings. But generally only the latter is in question when Easter is concerned. The Protestant states of Germany observed Easter according to an improved calculation in 1724 and 1744. The divergence of Swedish usage in the eighteenth and nineteenth centuries is more complicated (see Grotefend, *Taschenbuch*, 12th edn (1982), pp. 27–8).
3. It is a relatively simple matter now, with a computer, to use an algorithm to calculate the date of Easter, since the cycles on which the ecclesiastical moon is based can be easily programmed. The following algorithm can be used to compute the date of Easter in the Gregorian calendar. All variables are integers and all remainders from division are dropped. The algorithm takes the year (y) and yields the month (m), and day (d) of Easter. The symbol * means multiply:

$$c = y/100$$
$$n = y - 19 * (y/19)$$
$$k = (c-17)/25$$
$$i = c - c/4 - (c-k)/3 + 19 * n + 15$$
$$i = i - 30 * (i/30)$$
$$i = i - (i/28) * (1 - (i/28) * (29/(i+1)) * ((21-n)/11))$$
$$j = y + y/4 + i + 2 - c + c/4$$
$$j = j - 7 * (j/7)$$
$$l = i - j$$
$$m = 3 + (1 + 40)/44$$
$$d = 1 + 28 - 31 * (m/4)$$

This algorithm is due to J.-M. Oudin (1940), is reprinted in the *Explanatory Supplement to the Astronomical Almanac*, ed. P. K. Seidelmann (London, 1992), ch. 12, 'Calendars' [by L. E. Doggett], and was kindly brought to the editor's notice by Amanda Hill, Archivist, Rhodes House, Oxford.

year, the regnal year, and the day of the month in Roman form, but also the golden number, the epact, the dominical letter, and the concurrents. These elements also find their way into dating clauses of documents at other times and places during the Middle Ages. Used in this way, as parts of a dating clause, they indicate the position of the year in cycles of years, and thus might fittingly have found a place in the preceding section of this chapter; but their original purpose was purely to establish the place of the Church's festivals in the calendar, and so they may logically be described at this point. We shall make no attempt to do more that state how they are computed. For a more complete discussion the reader is referred to Giry's *Manuel*, on which this brief account is chiefly based.

Golden number (*numerus aureus, cyclus decemnovennalis*). For calculating the date of the paschal moon, which in turn governed the date of Easter, computists have made use of the close approximation of the lunar and solar cycles after a lapse of nineteen solar years. The slight inexactitude of their calculation has had no effect on the fixing of dates: the cycle of nineteen years has been generally accepted. The years of the cycle are numbered from I to XIX in direct series and the number for each year is known as the Golden Number. The cycle is computed from the year 1 BC and is usually held to begin 1 January in that year. To find the golden number of a year of grace, add 1 to a year of grace and divide by 19. The remainder is the golden number, unless the remainder is 0, when the golden number is XIX.

Epact (*Epact lunaris*). The position of the year in the nineteen-year cycle is also represented in another way for the purpose of calculating the date of Easter. For this purpose it is necessary to establish the relationship between the solar year and the phase of the moon at 22 March, the earliest date for Easter. Since the solar year was estimated to have eleven days in excess of twelve complete lunar cycles, this relationship changed by eleven days annually; the moon begins each year eleven days older than it was a year ago. When a new moon falls on 22 March the golden number is 1 (e.g., AD 1482: 1483 divided by 19 leaves a remainder of 1), and the epact, which represents the age of the moon, is nil (*epacta nulla*). In the next year the epact is eleven, and the next year twenty-two. The progression through the nineteen-year is straightforward, except that thirty is deducted from numbers in excess of thirty.[4]

---

4. The cycle thus becomes 0, 11, 22, 3, 14, 25, 6, 17, 28, 9, 20, 1, 12, 23, 4, 15, 26, 7, 18. This cycle, and the above description, only hold good for the Old Style calendar. It seems unnecessary to enter into the complexities of the New Style reckoning of epacts, since the epact only appears as an element in the dating of documents during the Middle Ages.

To find the epact of any year of grace, divide the year of grace by 19, multiply the remainder by 11, and divide by 30: the remainder is the number of the epact.

While the annual mutation of the epact occurred, according to some medieval computists, on 1 January, it seems that other reckonings were also employed. When the calendar year began on 25 March or 1 September, the epact probably changed at that point.

Dominical letter (littera dominicalis). To determine the date of Easter one must know the sequence of the days of the week following the paschal full moon, and for this purpose special tables were devised in early Christian times. There are seven possible relationships of the days of the week to the calendar of the year, and the letters A to G were used to indicate the cycle of seven days beginning at 1 January. The dominical letter for the year is the letter allocated, according to this system, to the first Sunday in the year. Thus, Sunday fell on 4 January 1545 and the dominical letter for the year is the fourth letter, D; in 1549 it fell on 6 January and the dominical letter is F, and so on. In the sequence of years the dominical letters run in retrograde series, for the year beginning on Monday (dominical letter G) is commonly succeeded by a year beginning on Tuesday (dominical letter F). A complication is introduced in the leap year. The extra day, or *dies bissextus*, has the same letter assigned to it as the day which it doubles. This produces a change in the cycle during February, so that the dominical letter for the period after *bis vi kal. Mar.* (24 February) – or after 29 February, if the modern system of dating is employed – differs from that for the preceding period. Thus the dominical letter for 1 January–29 February 1944 (a leap year) is B (1 January was Saturday), while for the remainder of the year it is A. The dominical letter for the next year 1945 (a common year) is G (1 January was Monday). It follows from the existence of leap years that the dominical letters move in cycles of twenty-eight, not seven, years.

Concurrents (concurrentes septimanæ). To each year was allotted by the computists a number (1 to 7) which represents the concurrents, or number of days between the last Sunday in the preceding year and 1 January. Since the concurrents are designed to serve the same purpose as the dominical letters, there is a regular correspondence between the two reckonings. This can be simply expressed as follows:

Dominical letter	F	E	D	C	B	A	G
Concurrents	1	2	3	4	5	6	7

It will be noticed that the concurrents are counted as 7 when the preceding year ends on a Sunday. It should also be observed that in leap years the concurrents correspond to the dominical letter for the *latter* part of the year.

Christian festivals in a leap year

An anomaly arising from the Church's adoption of the Roman calendar requires brief consideration. Using the Roman calendar, The Intercalary Day (*bis VI Kal. Mart.*) preceded the common *VI Kal. Mart.* When the simple numbering of days was adopted, the intercalary day *appeared* to be 29 February, but canonically it was 24 February, the exact equivalent of *bis VI Kal. Mart.* In leap years therefore St Mathias was commemorated on 25 February rather than 24 February, which was counted as *Vigilia S. Matthei apostoli*. This came to be regarded as a popish custom in England, and in the 1680s St Mathias came to be kept on 24 February, and the saints of the remaining days of February were not postponed; 29 February became *de facto* the intercalary day.

iv The beginning of the year of grace

Historians' errors in translating dates are most often due to carelessness about the various starting-points of the year of grace. Half a dozen different reckonings have been used at one time or another, and it is not uncommon to find two reckonings simultaneously used in adjacent countries or even in one country in different types of record. This has long been a matter for remark among historians. Gervase, the twelfth-century monk of Canterbury, bewailed the confusion arising from various computations: he himself had wavered between the systems of Christmas and the Annunciation before finally adopting the former for his chronicle and even then he made a concession to the more popular system for one famous event, the death of Thomas Becket on 29 December 1170. R. L. Poole furnishes an excellent illustration of the varieties in use in the Middle Ages: 'If we suppose [he says] a traveller to set out from Venice on 1 March 1245, the first day of the Venetian year, he would find himself in 1244 when he reached Florence: and if after a short stay he went on to Pisa, the year 1246 would already have begun there. Continuing his journey westward, he would find himself again in 1245 when he entered Provence, and on arriving in France before Easter (16 April) he would be once more in 1244.' To take a case from the simpler conditions of the eighteenth century, a traveller who left England in January 1720 would arrive in France to discover that the French had begun the year 1721.

Students must therefore do their best to discover what reckonings their authorities employ before they accept their chronology as it stands. Two graphics for the years 1099–1101 and 1153–5 can be used to illustrate the range of possibilities for the start of various different 'years' simultaneously in use in the central Middle Ages; their significance is explained in more detail below.

The reckoning of years still used, that of Dionysius, counts the number of years since the Incarnation, and Dionysius estimated when Jesus Christ was born. Other ideas of the Christian era existed. It became a Christian convention to view the past in three eras: the first, Nature, began with Adam; the second, Law, began with the delivery of the Law to Moses; the third era, the divine dispensation which through Christ superseded the Law, was named Grace.[5] When did Grace come into the world? Different answers were the birth of Christ, the beginning of his mother's pregnancy, and the redemption achieved by his death and resurrection. Hence different views existed as to when the year of grace began.

Christmas Day

Bede, following Dionysius, took for granted that the year of Grace must begin with the Nativity, Christmas Day, though in his *Ecclesiastical History*, since he was dealing with documents dated by the earlier reckoning from the Indiction of September, he started his own year in September also.[6] The reckoning from Christmas was soon in general vogue. It was used in the Empire until the second quarter of the thirteenth century, by the popes from 962 to 1098 (and even later in letters, as distinct from *privilegia*), in France and most of western Europe, except Spain, till the twelfth century. The Anglo-Saxon and Norman kings of England used it and Benedictine writers, with characteristic conservatism, still employed it after it had been abandoned in most quarters of Plantagenet England; as late even as the fourteenth century, the *Chronicon de Lanercost* still used the Nativity style. This fact has too often been overlooked by later historians. Thus, for example, Edmund of Cornwall, cousin of Edward I, is very commonly said – on the authority of Matthew Paris – to have been born on 26 December 1250. But Matthew Paris used the Christmas reckoning, and the historical date is therefore 26 December 1249. The whole octave of the

---

5. See *Dictionary of Medieval Latin from British sources*, s. v. gratia 5; the term derives from Romans 6:14–15.
6. In his technical treatises on chronology, of course, he used the solar year of twelve months from 1 January as the basis of all dates.

1099–1101

	Dec.	Jan.	Feb.	Mar.	Apr.	May.	Jun.	Jul.	Aug.	Sept.	Oct.	Nov.	Dec.	Jan.	Feb.	Mar.	Apr.
MODERN YEARS	1099	1 Jan.					1100							1 Jan.		1101	
NATIVITY		25 Dec.					1100						25 Dec.			1101	
ANNUNCIATION (Conventional)		1099		25 Mar.					1100							25 Mar.	1101
ANNUNCIATION (Pisanus)		1100		25 Mar.					1101							25 Mar.	1102
EASTER (Mos Gallicanus)		1099			Easter 1 Apr.				1100								Easter 1101 21 Apr.
REGNAL YEAR (Chancery)		13 WILLIAM II 26 Sept. 1099 – 2 Aug. 1100							2 Aug. ‖ 5 Aug.				1 HENRY I 5 Aug. 1100 – 5 Aug. 1101				
EXCHEQUER YEAR		1 HENRY I 29 Sep. 1099 – 28 Sep. 1100								29 Sept.			2 HENRY I 29 Sep. 1100 – 28 Sep. 1101				
PONTIFICAL YEAR		1 PASCHAL II 14 Aug. 1099 – 13 Aug. 1100											2 PASCHAL II 14 Aug. 1100 – 13 Aug. 1101				

Figure 2 Calendars for 1099–1101

1153–5

	Sept.	Oct.	Nov.	Dec.	Jan.	Feb.	Mar.	Apr.
MODERN YEARS	1153					1155		
				1154				
NATIVITY	1153			25 Dec.		1155		
				1154			25 Dec.	
ANNUNCIATION		1153					25 Mar.	1155
					1154			25 Mar.
ANNUNCIATION (Pisanus)		1154					25 Mar.	1156
					1155			25 Mar.
EASTER (Mos Gallicanus)		1153					4 Apr.	1155
					1154			27 Mar.
REGNAL YEAR	18 STEPHEN 22 Dec. 1152 – 21 Dec. 1153			22 Dec.	19 STEPHEN 22 Dec. 1153 – 25 Oct. 1154			25 Oct.	1 HENRY II 19 Dec. 1154 – 18 Dec. 1155	19 Dec.
EXCHEQUER YEAR	18 STEPHEN 29 Sept.	19 STEPHEN						29 Sept.	1 HENRY I
PONTIFICAL YEAR	1 ANASTASIUS IV 12 Jul. 1153 – 11 Jul. 1154						12 Jul.	2 ANASTASIUS IV 12 Jul. – 4 Dec. 1154	5 Dec.	1 ADRIAN IV 5 Dec. 1154 – 4 Dec. 1155

Figure 3 Calendars for 1153–1155

Nativity was, of course, a time of high festival, so that in practice the new beginning on 25 December and the older reckoning from 1 January sometimes shaded into each other.

The Annunciation

Lady Day, the feast of the Annunciation on 25 March, came to be considered the more correct starting-point from a theological point of view of years reckoned from the Incarnation. This was first used in the ninth and tenth centuries, but during the twelfth and thirteenth centuries it replaced reckoning from the Nativity. It is often extremely difficult to know whether a source in this period was counting years from the Nativity or the Incarnation, and the historian's predicament is made worse by the use of two conventions in counting from the Annunciation. Logically it preceded the first Christmas Day, so that the year AD 1 had to be put back nine months. This practice had only limited use, and the more common use was to begin the era from 25 March following the first Christmas Day.[7]

Reckoning from 25 March preceding started at Arles late in the ninth century and spread in Burgundy and northern Italy; it was used, though with growing infrequency, in the papal chancery between 1088 and 1145, but remained a local practice in some regions. It survived at Pisa till 1750, and has therefore been named the *calculus pisanus*. It is of little importance to students of English documents, though R. L. Poole found an isolated case of its use in a charter of Richard I. The grant, however, was to Pisan merchants in the Holy Land, so that the occasion was exceptional.

Less logical, but far more convenient, widespread, and important to the English historian was the use of 25 March *after* Christmas as the opening of the year. The origin of this practice is obscure, but may perhaps be traced to the influence of the abbey of Fleury, itself under Cluniac influence, and largely responsible for the increased emphasis laid upon devotions to the Virgin Mary in the early eleventh century.[8] In 1030 the style was in use at Fleury, and perhaps a few years earlier at Poitiers, which had connections with Fleury. Thus it long preceded the foundation of Cîteaux (1098), and cannot be due, as has often been suggested, to

7. Cf. D. P. McCarthy, 'The chronological apparatus of the annals of Ulster', *Peritia*, 8 (1994), 57 for an example of Annunciation dates based on 25 March *following* rather than *preceding* Christmas.

8. For full discussion, see Poole, *Studies*, pp. 13–17.

the Cistercians. The latter, however, gladly adopted the practice, as one more feature among many differentiating them from the earlier Benedictines. From a sense of a different kind of rivalry, Florence preferred the method as the opposite to that in vogue in Pisa, and so the new practice came to be called the *calculus florentinus*. It spread freely in France, though mainly in ecclesiastical circles, and from 1098 the papal chancery generally used it in its more solemn documents. In England it is found as early as the middle of the eleventh century, when certain annals of the *Anglo-Saxon chronicle* were apparently dated by this reckoning, but it only came into common English use late in the twelfth century and so continued to 1752.

From about the middle of the seventeenth century the practice of those continental countries, which had gone over to a year beginning with 1 January must inevitably have had an effect on England.[9] This influence was probably strengthened by English exiles abroad in the period of the Commonwealth. For official purposes, Englishmen continued till 1751 to use the old reckoning from 25 March, but they were wavering in their allegiance and found it convenient to give a double indication for the period between 1 January and 24 March; we commonly meet this in the form 29 February 1675/6 and we find it in all manner of official records and private papers of the period. Where no double indication is given, it is usually safe for the historian to assume that an Englishman writing in England reckons from 25 March, but it is worth remark that like medieval church calendars, the printed almanacks started their year with 1 January and used the modern historical year, and so did some, at least, of the early periodicals and newspapers.[10]

Easter day

The *mos gallicanus*, which reckoned the year from the movable feast of Easter,[11] was introduced into the French chancery by Philip Augustus (1180–1223). It spread to some regions, such as Holland and Cologne, where there were direct family or trading connections, but it never

9. The Oxford bookseller John Dorne already used the 1 January style in his accounts in 1520 (Oxford Hist. Soc., *Collectanea*, i (1885)), as did Thomas Wilson, *The art of rhetoric*, printed by Richard Grafton, which is dated 'M. D. LIII. Mense Januarij', but manifestly published under Edward VI (*ex inf.* Leofranc Holford-Strevens).
10. Thus *The Spectator* begins in the historical year 1711 and bears the date '1 January 1711' on its first page; so also *The Gentleman's Magazine* begins the historical year 'January 1751' without any double indication of date.
11. Those who used the Easter reckoning sometimes started their year on Good Friday (whence the term 'a Passione') or Holy Saturday.

became uniform for the whole of France, or popular outside court circles. Its disadvantages were obvious, and if, as Poole has suggested, Philip chose it because he 'desired to mark his conquest of the English possessions in France by the use of a style different from those which had been current in them',[12] he could hardly have made a gesture more disconcerting to his own subjects.

1 January

The historical year of what is now more often known as the Common Era rather than the Christian Era begins on 1 January. Modern chronological practice thus corresponds with the beginning of the Roman civil year adopted for the Julian Calendar.[13] January was always regarded as the first month of the calendar; the movable feasts were calculated on the basis of a solar year beginning on 1 January, the calendar of Saints' days followed the twelve Roman months, but the cycle of months was not homologous with counting years of Grace.[14] The year of Grace measured time from the Incarnation rather than counting cycles of twelve months.

There is no evidence that anyone was perturbed by this anomaly, even when the adoption of the Annunciation rather than the Nativity increased it from one week to three months or nine months. Yet it was one of three changes made by the reform of the calendar authorized by Pope Gregory XIII in 1582 (see p. 18). Italy, Spain and France began the year on 1 January. In Scotland it became the official beginning of the year in 1600 following 31 December 1599. In England, Wales and Ireland the change was not effected until the day after 31 December 1751 which became 1 January 1752.

The persistence of the calendar of months, the calculation of Easter based on a solar year beginning 1 January, and simple convenience prevailed over theological correctness. Moreover 1 January had everywhere been associated with the New Year in popular estimation. Thus Samuel Pepys, who reckoned the years of his diary from 25 March, always made mention of New Year's Day when he reached 1 January. In Shetland the New Year's Eve festival continued to follow Old Style and is still kept on 11 January.

---

12. Poole, *Studies*, p. 23.
13. Older Roman practice began the year at 1 March; this is reflected in the names for the months September, October, November and December.
14. 1 January was observed as the Feast of the Circumcision at least as early as the sixth century, and still earlier as the octave of the Nativity. Cf. *Decretum*, II, 26, 7, 14, and 16.

v Divisions of the year

The Roman calendar

The division of the Julian year into months, as revised by the Emperor Augustus, has prevailed up to the present day. The Julian method of counting the days within the months also persisted for many centuries and was unaffected by the Gregorian reform. This calendar of the year is set out in Table 6 below (pp. 145–6).

The modern way of numbering the days of the month in one continuous series is found occasionally in very early times and gradually won widespread acceptance during the Middle Ages, though it never fully ousted the Roman system.

The Bolognese calendar

Another method of counting the days is known as the *consuetudo bononiensis*, or custom of Bologna. So far as concerns England it may be termed the notarial method, for it is scarcely found outside documents drafted by public notaries. According to this reckoning, the day of the month was indicated by its position in the first sixteen days (or fifteen days in months of thirty days) reckoning forwards, or in the last fifteen days, reckoning backwards. Thus, *quarto die intrante Madio* indicates 4 May, and *quarto die exeunte* (or *stante*) *Madio* indicates 28 May.

The ecclesiastical calendar

While the Christian Church could not drive out use of the Roman calendar, it introduced into common practice other methods of reckoning and stating dates. In the first place, the ecclesiastical calendar divided the year by weeks in the manner now universal.[15] Sunday was the first day of the week (counted as *prima feria* but always called *dies dominicus*) and the chief day as regards liturgical observance. But the Church also consecrated certain days of the year (irrespective of their place in the week) to festivals of particular saints, and these became material for dating events (see below 4, pp. 64–93). Finally the Church attached special importance to commemorations connected with the life of Christ: Christmas, Good Friday, Easter Day, Ascension Day, and the like. Some of these, like the feasts of the saints were fixed points in the Roman year: Christmas, for

---

15. We are only concerned here of course with the week as an element in the dating of records. For the observance of the week in the pagan Roman world and in Jewry, see F. H. Colson, *The Week* (Cambridge, 1926).

example, was always celebrated on *viii kal. Jan.* otherwise 25 December. But Easter Day was a 'movable' feast, and on Easter, as explained above (pp. 4–8) depended a whole series of other commemorations.

VI Fractions of the day

Roman custom divided the day into two periods, running from sunset to sunrise and from sunrise to sunset respectively. Within each period were twelve hours, the length of which necessarily varied with the season. The hour which formed 1/12 of the winter night, for example would be longer than a similar fraction of the summer night.[16] As a consequence of this, the seven 'canonical hours', or the times appointed for the services of the Church, similarly varied with the season until the introduction of hours 'of the clock'.[17]

By the thirteenth century clocks with bells began to be displayed in churches and other buildings, and by this means a system of hours uniform in length came gradually into use – a process encouraged by economic imperatives as employers and guilds also began to lay down hours of work.[18] The hours 'of the clock' have been usually counted in two series of twelve, from midnight and from noon respectively. But for many purposes the modern world uses a single 24-hour series beginning at midnight (a system perhaps most commonly encountered with railway or airline timetables). The development of telephony and wireless telegraphy in the nineteenth century and of more advanced methods of instant communication in the late twentieth century, including satellite links, global financial markets, and improvements in international transport facilities which enable more frequent meetings between government ministers and diplomats of different countries, have made it particularly necessary for the historian of modern times to pay attention to the exact hour of related events. In doing so the adjustments must of course be

16. Certain evidence suggests that for purposes of dating in the early Middle Ages the day began with sunset (cf. Anscombe, in *British Numismatic Journal*, 1st ser. IV, 284–92), and the liturgical observance of a feast might indubitably begin before sunrise. But cf. *Rogeri de Wendover Flores* (Rolls series), I, 299: 'diem dominicum cum noctu sequente, qui dies dicitur naturalis'.

17. See *Dictionary of medieval Latin from British sources*, s.v. hora. The canonical hours are Matins, Prime, Terce, Sect, None, Vespers and Compline. For clear and detailed accounts of the early monastic timetable, see Cuthbert Butler, *Benedictine monachism* (2nd edn, London, 1920), pp. 275–86, and Dom David Knowles, *The monastic order in England 943–1216* (Cambridge, 1941), pp. 448–53 and 714–15.

18. Cf. J. Le Goff, 'Merchant's time and the Church's time in the Middle Ages', *Time, work and culture in the Middle Ages*, trans. Arthur Goldhammer (Chicago and London, 1980), pp. 29–42.

made for discrepant methods of timing, just like those shaping events have to do. During World War II the cubicle in the Cabinet War Rooms from which Churchill telephoned President Roosevelt contained a clock showing Washington time; a local public house in Lincoln currently displays a series of clocks showing the time at the various other Lincolns scattered across the globe. Quite apart from the difference which arises from astronomical readings taken in different parts of the world (Zone Standard Times), there is also the difference between Greenwich Mean Time and Summer Time used in the British Isles (and their continental equivalents),[19] although there is intermittent pressure from some quarters to terminate this practice (an earlier experiment in doing so in Britain took place in the late 1960s).

Finally, the student of nautical records must take account of the system of reckoning found in ships' log-books from the seventeenth century until early in the nineteenth. Like the astronomer, the mariner determined his day by observation of the sun; and he recorded the events of twenty-four hours (on his log-board) from midday to midday. It was his practice to make the division of his log-book according to this scheme and to assign to each 24-hour period a date twelve hours in advance of the ordinary calendar-day. Thus, the battle of Trafalgar, fought in the afternoon of 21 October 1805, is recorded in the log-book of the *Victory* under 22 October. At about this very time, the Navy apparently began to date its log-book entries from midnight, following an Admiralty Order of October 1805; but in the merchant service it was still usual at a much later date for log-books to begin their day at noon.[20] This was, we may note, a chronological arrangement peculiar to one class of record. Throughout the period in which it prevailed, sailors used the ordinary calendar-day in their letters and journals.

VII The Gregorian calendar: New Style

In the course of the Middle Ages various scholars interested in chronology pointed out that the calendar year was increasingly divergent from the solar year. The reckoning of the latter at 365¼ days was a slight over-estimate, and by the sixteenth century this annual error had caused, cumulatively, a discrepancy of ten days. It was not, however, until

19. Summer Time was first introduced as 'daylight saving' during World War I, a measure renewed annually by Parliament until 1925 and made permanent thereafter.
20. H. Raper, *The practice of navigation and nautical astronomy* (1840), p. 93.

24 February 1582 that a bull of Pope Gregory XIII ordered the use of a reformed calendar. This met immediate trouble by cutting ten days out of the year 1582, so that 15 October followed immediately upon 4 October, while future difficulties were to be avoided by making only the fourth of the end-years of successive centuries a leap year. The bull allowed for AD 2000 to be a leap year, and this was adopted in later changes to the Gregorian calendar. The year was to begin on 1 January.

This desirable reform was proposed at an unfortunate date, when religious and political hostilities were so pronounced that even a measure so much to the general benefit was not regarded objectively as a mere matter of chronological accuracy, and was therefore at the time not accepted by any but states in the Roman obedience. The student of history from 1582 onwards, therefore, is in a worse plight than before, for he has to be sure, as he deals with the documents of Catholic, Orthodox, or Protestant states, whether at the date concerned that state was dating by the Gregorian calendar ('New Style') or by the Julian calendar ('Old Style'). Broadly speaking, Catholic states adopted the New Style in the sixteenth century, Protestant states early or late in the eighteenth century, Russia, the Balkan States, and Greece in the twentieth century, but as Table **12** below (pp. 236–41) shows, there is a very wide disparity of practice, especially in federal states like the Low Countries and Switzerland.

It must be remembered that in every country an interval necessarily followed between the acceptance of the reform and its being put into practice, and that the methods of introduction were not uniform. In Great Britain and Ireland the change was effected by 'Chesterfield's Act' (24 Geo. II, c. 23), passed in March 1751, which decreed that throughout the dominions of the British crown the following 1 January should be the first day of 1752 and 2 September 1752 should be followed by 14 September.[21] For purposes of taxation the change would have involved calculations for a year of abnormal length; to avoid this taxes continued to be based on the Old Style year, 25 March, and then the year 1752–3 continued until 5 April rather than only having 354 days. The Inland Revenue still uses 6 April as the beginning of the financial year. Nor must it be assumed that each European state, when it adopted the New Style calendar, acted like the

---

21. For the effect upon George II's twenty-sixth regnal year see below p. 233, and for the complete calendar for the year 1752 see Table **11**. Robert Poole, '"Give us back our eleven days": Calendar reform in Eighteenth-century England', *Past and Present*, no. 149 (November 1995), 95–139 sets the issue in a broad context.

Papacy and England in fixing 1 January as the beginning of the year. In some countries this preceded the change from the Julian to the Gregorian calendar, while in a few it only followed long afterwards.[22]

Because the adoption of New Style had not been synchronized in all countries, there came into being 'one of the most dangerous traps for students using original documents',[23] to be avoided only by careful consideration of the origin of any document in use and the habits of its writer. Because of leap years, a difference of dating may amount to 10, 11, 12 or 13 days according to whether the document is written after 1582, 1700, 1800 or 1900. Thus, when William of Orange had left Holland, where the New Style was in use, on 11 November 1688, he reached England, where it was not, on 5 November. In official communications with foreign powers and with its representatives abroad, the English government sought to obviate the confusion which might easily arise from the conflict of Styles. From Elizabeth's reign onwards English correspondence with the continent often gives both forms of date. Sir William Boswell writes from The Hague to Sir John Coke on '12/22 Dec. 1635'. Nearly three centuries later we find the same practice in a country which retained the Old Style: Isvolski, Russian minister of Foreign Affairs, dates a letter to the British ambassador '16/29 Août 1907'. At times when the writer does not give a double date, he may indicate the Style employed by adding os or ns; but more often the date bears no such indication and the historian must decide what was intended according to the nationality and the circumstances of the writer.

BIBLIOGRAPHY

Anscombe, Alfred, 'The Anglo-Saxon computation of historic time in the ninth century', *British Numismatic Journal*, 1st series, 4 (1908), 241–310; 5 (1909), 381–407.

Beavan, Murray L. R., 'The regnal dates of Alfred, Edward the Elder, and Athelstan', *English Historical Review*, 32 (1917), 516–31.

'The beginning of the year in the Alfredian chronicle (866–87)', *English Historical Review*, 33 (1918), 328–42.

Harrison, Kenneth, 'The *Annus Domini* in some early charters', *Journal of the Society of Archivists*, vol. 4, no. 7 (April 1973), 551–7 (but cf. Chaplais, Pierre. 'Some early Anglo-Saxon Diplomas on single sheets: Original or copies?', ibid., vol. 3 no. 7 (April 1968), at pp. 73–5, reprinted in *Prisca Munimenta. Studies in archival and administrative history presented to Dr. A. E. J. Hollaender*, ed. Felicity Ranger (London, 1973), pp. 63–87).

22. Details of the changes on the continent will be found in Table **12**. Despite the adoption of the Gregorian calendar by eastern European countries in modern times, the Orthodox Church still uses the Julian calendar in some places like Bulgaria.
23. Stamp, *Methods of Chronology*, p. 6.

'The beginning of the year in England, c. 500–900', *Anglo-Saxon England*, ed. Peter Clemoes and others, vol. II (Cambridge, 1973), 51–70.

The framework of Anglo-Saxon history (Cambridge, 1976).

Hodgkin, R. H., 'The beginning of the year in the English Chronicle', *English Historical Review*, 39 (1924), 497–510.

Levison, Wilhelm, *England and the continent in the eighth century* (Oxford, 1946).

Appendix vi: 'The beginning of the year of the incarnation of Bede's "Historia ecclesiastica"', criticizes Poole's study (see below). See also Paul Grosjean, 'La date du colloque de Whitby', *Analecta Bollandiana*, 78 (1960), 233–74.

Pollard, A. F., 'New Year's day and leap year in English history', *English Historical Review*, 55 (1940), 177–93.

Poole, R. L., 'The chronology of Bede's *Historia ecclesiastica* and the councils of 679–680', *Journal of Theological Studies*, 20 (1919), 24–40, reprinted in Poole's *Studies*, pp. 38–55.

'The beginning of the year in the Middle Ages', *Proceedings of the British Academy*, x (1921), reprinted in *Studies*, pp. 1–27.

Poole, Robert, ' "Give us back our eleven days"; Calendar reform in eighteenth-century England', *Past and Present*, no. 149 (November, 1995), 95–139.

Van de Vyver, A., 'L'évolution du comput Alexandrin et Romain du 3e au 5e siècle', *Revue d'histoire ecclésiastique*, 52 (1957), 1–25.

Vaughan, R., 'The chronology of the Parker Chronicle, 890–970', *English Historical Review*, 69 (1954), 59–66.

Wainwright, F. T., 'The chronology of the "Mercian Register"', *English Historical Review*, 60 (1945), 385–92.

Whitelock, Dorothy, 'On the commencement of the year in the Anglo-Saxon chronicles', in *Two Anglo-Saxon chronicles parallel*, ed. C. Plummer, reprinted Oxford, 1952, vol. II, pp. cxxxix–cxlii[c].

2

Rulers of England and regnal years

The regnal year is used in Anglo-Saxon royal charters early in the eighth century and the usage is based, one can hardly doubt, on contemporary Merovingian practice. The Anglo-Saxon kings continue to use this reckoning upon occasion until the tenth century, but thereafter it is only found exceptionally until the reign of Richard I.[1] From 1189 onwards it has been the approved method of expressing the year-date in documents of the civil government in England. Moreover, English private charters, which until Edward I's reign are usually undated, thereafter record the regnal year as a matter of course.

The scarcity of dated documents before the reign of Henry II prevents us from saying how the regnal year was reckoned in early days, i.e. at what point the reign was deemed to have begun. From Henry II to Henry III the regnal year was always reckoned from the day of the coronation. With the death of Henry III a change of system occurred. Edward I's reign was deemed to begin four days after his father died and 'before the tomb had even been closed', although he did not return from abroad until two years later. Thereafter it was taken for granted that at the death of one king the next succeeded immediately and his first regnal year began.

The student of the thirteenth century should note a peculiarity of the reckoning for the reign of King John, which has often led historians into error. John was crowned on Ascension Day 1199 and this movable feast became the date at which his regnal years began. They are thus of unequal length, and we are faced with the confusing fact (to take one example) that 12 May 1206 and 12 May 1207 both fall within the eighth year of the king.[2] But it must be observed that when the regnal year runs, as it usually does, from a fixed point in the year, there is sometimes confusion of a contrary sort: the movable feasts of the Church, not the days of the month, are

---

1. It is found in Final Concords made in the King's Court in the reign of Henry II, but hardly ever appears in products of his chancery.
2. The same phenomenon appears in the reckoning of regnal years of the Emperor Charles IV, who was crowned on Easter Day 1355.

doubled in one regnal year. Thus, Easter Day occurs twice in 11 Henry VIII, and in 2 and 13 Charles I; there was no Easter in 10 or 37 Henry VIII or in 3 and 14 Charles I.

One particular class of record introduces a complication into the reckoning of English regnal years. The exchequer period of account, which closed at Michaelmas, cut across the regnal year. Therefore, to date their annual account-roll, the Great Roll of the Pipe, the exchequer clerks reckoned according to the regnal year in which the accounts were either opened or closed. At different periods different practices prevailed. It follows that the student who refers to a Pipe Roll must take note of the system of dating which prevailed at the time. A table for this purpose is provided below (p. 45). But it cannot be emphasized too strongly that no evidence exists for the use of an 'Exchequer Year' dating for any other purpose than that of labelling records of the exchequer and the wardrobe.[3] The year from Michaelmas to Michaelmas was not treated in the exchequer as the regnal year by which external events were dated. Nor was it used for labelling all exchequer records; the Issue and Receipt Rolls, while they necessarily take Michaelmas (as also Easter) for a terminal point, refer to the regnal year as it was reckoned in the chancery. When, as often happened, a new regnal year opened in the middle of an exchequer term, the Issue and Receipt Rolls for that term either named both the regnal years involved or else named only the regnal year which was beginning.[4]

1 Rulers of England from the English settlement to AD 1154[5]

Kings of Kent

Hengest	*c.* 455; *d.* ?488
Oeric (Oisc)	488; *d.* ?512
Eormenric	?512; *d. c.* 560
Æthelberht I	560 or *c.* 585; *d.* 24 Feb. 616

3. E.g. the Memoranda Rolls of the remembrancers and certain of the Wardrobe Account Rolls are assigned to regnal years computed in this way.

4. The whole matter of the so-called 'Exchequer Year' is fully discussed by H. G. Richardson in the Society's *Transactions* of 1925 (see below, p. 46). Cf. also p. 105.

5. For more detailed bibliography and discussion of the dates presented here, see *Handbook of British Chronology*, 3rd edn, ed. E. B. Fryde, D. E. Greenway, S. Porter and I. Roy (London, 1986), pp. 1–49; and *The Blackwell Encyclopedia of Anglo-Saxon England*, ed. M. Lapidge, J. Blair, S. Keynes and D. Scragg (Oxford, 1999), pp. 494–510, Appendix, Rulers of the English, *c.* 450–1066, compiled by Dr Simon Keynes, to whom thanks are due for further help and clarification.

Eadbald	616; *d.* 20 Jan. 640
Earconberht	640; *d.* 14 July 664
Ecgberht I	664; *d.* 4 July 673
Hlothhere	673; *d.* 6 Feb. 685
Eadric	685; *d.* ?Aug. 686
['various usurpers or foreign kings' 686–690][6]	
Wihtred	690; *d.* 23 April 725
[Swæfheard	690–2][7]

On the death of Wihtred, the kingdom of Kent appears to have been divided in two

Kings of West Kent		*Kings of East Kent*	
Eadberht I	725; *d.* 748	Æthelberht II	725; *d.* 762
Eardwulf	?748; *d.* ? x 762		
Sigered	? x 762; *d. c.* 764	Eadberht II	762; *d. c.* 764
Ecgberht II	*c.* 764	Eanmund	*c.* 764; *d.* ?
		Heahberht	?*c.* 765; *d.* ?

In the eighth century Kent fell under the control of Æthelbald, king of the Mercians (716–57) and Offa (757–96) until the men of Kent broke free following the battle of Otford (776):

Ecgberht II	*d.* 779 x ?[8]
Ealhmund	by 784[9]

Offa reasserted his control in 784 or 785 and held it until his death in 796.

Eadberht Præn	796; captured 798; *d.* ?
Cuthred	798; *d.* 807[10]
Baldred	821; deposed *c.* 825[11]

---

6. Cf. Bede, *HE*, iv, 26n, and Susan Kelly, *Charters of St Augustine's, Canterbury* (Anglo-Saxon Charters IV), 1995, p. 203.
7. Reigned jointly with Wihtred who reigned alone from *c.* 692.
8. King of (?the whole of) Kent in late 770s.
9. King of (?the whole of) Kent; father of Ecgberht, king of the West Saxons (802–39).
10. Inserted by his brother Coenwulf, king of the Mercians (796–821). On his death, Coenwulf directly controlled Kent.
11. By Ecgberht, king of the West Saxons, from which point Kent was ruled by this dynasty.

Kings of the Northumbrians

At first divided between Deira (from the Humber to the Tyne, centring on York) and Bernicia (from the Tyne to the Tweed and beyond, centring on Bamburgh), the kingdom of the Northumbrians was formed when they were united in the mid seventh century, first under Oswald of Bernicia.

Kings of Deira

Ælle	560; *d.* 588 or 590
Æthelric	588; *d.* 593
Edwin	616; *d.* 12 Oct. 633
Osric	633; *d.* 634
Oswald[12]	634; *d.* 5 Aug. 642
Oswine	642/3; *d.* 20 Aug. 651
Oswiu[13]	651; *d.* 15 Feb. 670

Kings of Bernicia

Ida	547; *d.* 559 or 560
Glappa	559; *d.* 560
Adda	560; *d.* 568
Æthelric	568; *d.* 572
Theodric	572; *d.* 579
Frithuwald	579; *d.* 585
Hussa	585; *d.* 592
Æthelfrith	592; *d.* 616[14]
Eanfrith	633/4; *d.* 634
Oswald	634; *d.* 5 Aug. 642
Oswiu	642; *d.* 15 Feb. 670

Kings of the Northumbrians

Ecgfrith	670; *d.* 20 May 685[15]
Aldfrith	686; *d.* 14 Dec. 705
Eadwulf	705/6[16]
Osred I	706; *d.* 716

12. King of Bernicia (see below).
13. King of Bernicia (see below); sub-kings were installed by him in Deira (Oethelwald, *c.* 651–5; Alhfrith, *c.* 655–64; Ecgfrith, *c.* 664–70).
14. Oswald and Oswiu, sons of Æthelfrith, went into exile among the Irish or Picts during the reign of Edwin of Deira.
15. Ælfwine, son of Oswiu, probably ruled as sub-king of Deira *c.* 670–9.
16. Ruled for two months.

Coenred	716; *d.* 718
Osric	718; *d.* 9 May 729
Ceolwulf	729; resigned 737; *d. c.* 764[17]
Eadberht	737; resigned 758; *d.* 19/20 Aug. 768
Oswulf	758; *d.* 24/25 July 759
Æthelwald Moll	5 Aug. 759; deposed 30 Oct. 765; *d.* ?
Alhred	765; exiled 774; *d.* ?
Æthelred I	774; expelled 778 or 779; *d.* ?
Ælfwald I	778 or 779; *d.* 23 Sept. 788
Osred II	778; expelled 790; *d.* 14 Sept. 792
Æthelred I (again)	790; *d.* 18 April 796
Osbald	796; expelled 796;[18] *d.* 799
Eardwulf	796; expelled ? 806
Ælfwald II	?806; *d.* ?808
Eardwulf (again)	?808; *d.* ?810
Eanred	?810; *d.* 840 or 841
Æthelred II	840 or 841; expelled 844
Rædwulf	844; *d.* ?
Æthelred II (again)	844; *d.* ?848
Osberht	848 or 849; expelled 862 or 863
Ælle	862 or 863; *d.* 21 or 23 March 867
Osberht (again)	867; *d.* 21 or 23 March 867
Ecgberht I	867; expelled 872; *d.* 873[19]
Ricsige	873; *d.* 876
Ecgberht II	876; *d.* ?878
Eadwulf of Bamburgh	?878; *d.* 913
Aldred	913; *d.* 927 x ?[20]

Rulers of the Scandinavian Kingdom of York[21]

Halfdan I	875/6; driven out 877
Guthfrith	883; *d.* 24 Aug. ?895
Sigfrith (Sievert, Sigfred)	895–
Cnut	*fl.* 895

17. Deposed and restored, 731; retired to Lindisfarne, 737.
18. After a reign of 27 days.
19. Appointed by the Danes following their victory at York.
20. Aldred, son of Eadwulf, submitted to Edward the Elder in 920 and to Æthelstan in 927.
21. This section has also been revised in the light of David Rollason, with Derek Gore and Gillian Fellows-Jensen, *Sources for York history to AD 1100*, Yorkshire Archaeological Trust 1998, pp. 63–9.

Rulers of the Scandinavian Kingdom of York (cont.)

Æthelwold	899; *d.* ?902
Cnut (Knutr)	?901–
Halfdan II[22]	*d.* 910
Eowils (Ecwils)	*d.* 910
Ragnald I	914 or earlier; *d.* 920[23]
Sihtric II Caech (Sigtryggr Caech)	920/1; *d.* 927[24]
Olaf I Cuaran	?927
Guthfrith II	927; driven out 927; *d.* 934
Athelstan, k. of English	927–39
Olaf II Guthfrithson	939; *d.* 941
Olaf I Cuaran (again)	941; driven out 944[25]
Ragnald II Guthfrithson	943; driven out 944
Edmund, k. of English	944–6
Eadred, k. of English	946–7
Eric Bloodaxe	947; deserted by supporters 948
Eadred	948–950
Olaf I Cuaran (again)	949/50; driven out 952
Eric Bloodaxe (second reign)	952; driven out 954; *d.* 954

Thereafter Northumbria was ruled by the kings of England.

Kings of Mercia

Cearl	Reigning *c.* 600
Penda	626 or 632; *d.* 15 Nov. 655[26]
Wulfhere	658; *d.* 675
Æthelred	675; resigned 704; *d.* ?716
Coenred	704; resigned *c.* 709; *d. c.* 709
Ceolred	709; *d.* 716
Æthelbald	716; *d.* 757
Beornred	757; driven out 757;[27] *d.* 769
Offa	757; *d.* 29 July 796

22. Ruled jointly with Eowils.
23. Submitted to Edward the Elder in 920.
24. Sihtric 'the One-Eyed', king in Dublin, married a sister of King Æthelstan.
25. Olaf 'of the Sandal', son of Sihtric II, baptized 943, became king in Dublin.
26. Born around 605; his brother Eowa also acted as king in 642 according to the *Annales Cambriae* and was killed at the battle of Maserfelth, 642; following the death of Penda at the battle of Winwæd, Oswiu of Bernicia ruled Mercia for three years, during which Peada may have reigned with his permission for a year.
27. By Offa of Mercia.

Ecgfrith	796[28]; *d.* 17 Dec. 796
Coenwulf	796; *d.* 821
Ceolwulf I	821; deprived 823; *d.* ?
Beornwulf	823; *d.* 825
Ludeca	825; *d.* 827
Wiglaf	827; *d.* 840[29]
Berhtwulf	840; *d.* ?852
Burgred	?852; driven out by the Danes 873/4
Ceolwulf II	874[30]; *d.* ?879

From *c.* 880–911 the Mercians were ruled by Ealdorman Æthelred and from 911–18 by his widow, Æthelflæd, daughter of King Alfred, within the wider polity of the Anglo-Saxons; in 918 Ælfwyn, their daughter, was deprived of her authority and taken to Wessex.

Rulers of the Hwicce

Roughly co-terminus with the medieval diocese of Worcester; for further discussion see H. P. R. Finberg, 'Princes of the Hwicce', in his *Early charters of the West Midlands*, 2nd edn (1972), pp. 167–80, and P. Sims-Williams, *Religion and literature* (1990), pp. 16–53.

Eanhere	*fl.* 660s[31]
Eanfrith	*fl.* 660s
Osric	*fl.* 670s x 680s
Oshere	*fl.* 690s; *d.* by 716[32]
Æthelheard	*fl.* after 709
Æthelweard	*fl.* after 706; *d.* 716 x ?
Æthelric	? x 736; *d.* 736 x ?33
Eanberht	? x 755; not known after 759
Uhtred	? x 755; still *fl.* 777 x 779
Ealdred	? x 755; still *fl.* 778[34]

28. Consecrated king of the Mercians 787 during the reign of his father, Offa.
29. In 829 Ecgberht, king of the West Saxons, conquered Mercia and held the kingship for a year, but in 830 Wiglaf was restored.
30. Appointed by the Danes and said to have ruled for five years; Mercia was divided in 877 with the Danes.
31. Ruling jointly with his brother Eanfrith.
32. Succeeded by his sons Æthelheard and Æthelweard, and then by another son Æthelric, under the control of Coenred and Æthelbald, kings of the Mercians.
33. Under Offa of Mercia, the brothers Eanberht, Uhtred and Ealdred *fl.* 750s x 770s.
34. When Offa of Mercia called him 'my *subregulus*'.

Kings of Lindsey

Aldfrith, son of Eata	Reigning, *c.* 786 x 796[35]

Kings of the East Angles

Rædwald	? x 616; *d.* 616 x 627
Earpwald	616 x 627; *d.* 627 or 628
Richberht	627 or 628[36]
Sigeberht	630 or 631; *d.* ?[37]
Ecgric[38]	*c.* 630
Anna	?; *d.* 654
Æthelhere	654; *d.* ?[39]
Æthelwald	?; *d.* ?664
Aldwulf	663 or 664; *d.* 713
Ælfwald	713; *d.* 749
Hun, Beonna and Æthelberht I	Reigning jointly 749[40]
Æthelberht II	?; *d.* 794[41]
Eadwald	*c.* 800[42]
Æthelstan	*c.* 830 x 845[43]
Æthelweard	*c.* 845 x 855
Edmund	855; *d.* 20 Nov. 869
Æthelred	*c.* 875[44]
Oswald	*c.* 875

Scandinavian kings of East Anglia

Guthrum (Æthelstan)	*c.* 879 x 880; *d.* 890
Eohric	?; *d.* 902

Kings of the South Saxons

Ælle	*c.* 477; *d.* after 491[45]

35. Judged to have been king on the basis of a royal genealogy in the 'Anglian collection', and a charter in which a scribal error is probable (Sawyer 1183); normally Lindsey was subject to Mercia or Northumberland.
36. There is uncertainty over his recognition as king.
37. Ruled jointly with Ecgric, but resigned and retired to a monastery, before being killed in battle against Penda of Mercia.
38. Ruled jointly with Sigeberht and killed fighting Penda.
39. Fought on Penda's side at the battle of Winwæd, 15 Nov. 655, but it is not known whether he was killed there.
40. The kingdom was later controlled by Offa of Mercia.
41. Executed on the order of Offa.
42. Known only from coins; the kingdom then fell under Mercian control to 827.
43. Æthelstan and his successor are only known from coins.
44. Æthelred and Oswald are only known from coins.
45. Ælle landed in Sussex in 477 and was still reigning in 491; the first *Bretwalda* according to the *Anglo-Saxon Chronicle*. Nothing is known of his successors until the mid seventh century.

Æthelwalh	? x 674; *d. c.* 682
Nothhelm (Nunna)	? x 692; *d.* 714 x ?
Watt	? x 692; *d. c.* 700 x ?[46]
Æthelstan	? x 714; *d.* 714 x ?[47]
Æthelberht	714 x 733; *d.* 747 x 770[48]
Oswald	?before 772; *d.* 772 x ?[49]
Osmund	*c.* 760; *d.* 770 x 772[50]
Oslac	?760s; *d.* 780 x ?[51]
Ealdwulf	?760s; *d. c.* 790 x ?798[52]
Ælfwald	?760s; *d.* 772 x ?[53]

Kings of the East Saxons

Sæberht (Saba)	? x 604; *d.* 616 or 617[54]
Seaxred	616 or 617; *d. c.* 617
Sæweard	616 or 617; *d. c.* 617
[Their brother	616 or 617; *d. c.* 617]
Sigeberht I ('parvus')	*c.* 617 x ?; *d.* ?
Sigeberht II ('sanctus')	? x 653; *d.* 653 x 664
Swithelm	653 x 664; *d. c.* 664
Swithfrith	?; *d.* ?[55]
Sigehere	*c.* 664; *d. c.* 690[56]
Sebbi	*c.* 664; resigned *c.* 694; *d. c.* 694[57]
Sigeheard	*c.* 694; *d. c.* 705 x ?
Swæfred	*c.* 694; *d.* 704 x ?
Offa	*c.* 694 x 709; *d.* 709 x ?[58]

46. Attests charters of Nothhelm and is styled 'dux Suthsaxonum'.
47. Attests charters of Notthelm.
48. Cf. Susan Kelly, *Charters of Selsey* (1998), p. 38.
49. Possibly reigned before 772, and styled 'dux Suthsaxonum' in 772.
50. Styled 'dux' in 772.
51. Contemporary of Ealdwulf and Ælfwald; styled 'dux Suthsaxonum' in 780.
52. Contemporary of Oslac and Ælfwald, styled 'dux' after 772 and 'duc Suthsaxonum' in mid ?780s and ?791.
53. Styled 'dux' in 772. Offa of Mercia gained control of the kingdom of South Sussex in early 770s, reducing the former kings to the status of ealdormen (*dux*).
54. Probably ruling under the control of Æthelberht, king of Kent; died leaving three sons as heirs, who were all killed in battle against the *Gewisse*.
55. Brother of Swithelm.
56. Succeeded Swithelm in part of Essex, but subject to Wulhere of Mercia, later apostatized.
57. Succeeded Swithelm in part of Essex, but subject to Wulhere of Mercia, remained Christian and resigned to become a monk after ruling for thirty years. Swæfheard, son of Sebbi, was among the 'foreign' kings active in Kent *c.* 690.
58. Son of Sigehere, perhaps not a full king, accompanied Coenred of Mercia to Rome in 709, dying there as a monk.

Kings of the East Saxons (cont.)

Swæfberht	?c. 709; d. 738
Selered	?c. 738; d. 746
Swithred	?c. 746; d. ?
Sigeric I	?; resigned, ?798[59]
Sigered	?798; d. 823 x ?
Sigeric II	c. 825[60]

Kings of the West Saxons[61]

Cerdic	519; d. 534
Cynric	534; d. 560
Ceawlin	560; d. 593
Ceol	591; d. ?597
Ceolwulf	597; d. ?611
Cynegils	611; d. ?642
Cenwealh	642; d. 672[62]
Seaxburh (queen)	672; d. ?674
Æscwine	674; d. 676
Centwine	676; d. ?685
Cædwalla	685; resigned 688; d. 20 April 689
Ine	688; abdicated 726; d. ? 726
Æthelheard	726; d. ?740
Cuthred	740; d. 756
Sigeberht	756; deprived 757; d. 757 x ?
Cynewulf	757; d. 786
Beorhtric	786; d. 802
Ecgberht	802; d. 839
Æthelwulf	839; d. 858[63]
Æthelberht	858;[64] d. 865

59. In which year he went to Rome.
60. Styled 'king of the East Saxons' and *minister* of Wiglaf of Mercia c. 825, after which the kingdom became a dependency of the West Saxon kingdom.
61. From c. 825–80 the kings of the West Saxons also ruled other peoples, and from c. 880 may be termed 'Kings of the Anglo-Saxons'.
62. According to Bede (HE, iv, 12), on the death of Cenwealh *subreguli* divided the kingdom and ruled it for about ten years.
63. His son, Æthelstan, ruled as sub-king of Kent in 840s, dying 851 x 855. When Æthelwulf went to Rome (with his son, Alfred) in 855–6, he assigned the western part of his kingdom to another son Æthelbald, who continued to hold it after Æthelwulf's return, dying in 860. The eastern part was assigned to his son Æthelberht, who released it on Æthelwulf's return from Rome.
64. From 860 Æthelberht held both the eastern and western parts of the kingdom.

Æthelred I	865; *d.* 871
Alfred	After 15 April 871; *d.* 26 Oct. 899
Edward the Elder	After 26 Oct. 899; *d.* 17 July 924
[Ælfweard, k. of Wessex	17 July 924; *d.* 2 Aug. 924][65]
Æthelstan	After 17 July 924; *d.* 27 Oct. 939[66]

Kings of the English, 927–1154

Æthelstan	927; *d.* 27 Oct. 939
Edmund	939; *d.* 26 May 946[67]
Eadred	946; *d.* 23 Nov. 955
Eadwig	955; *d.* 1 Oct. 959
Edgar	959; *d.* 8 July 975[68]
Edward the Martyr	975; *d.* 18 March 978
Æthelred II the Unready	978; exiled 1013
Swein Forkbeard	1013; *d.* 3 Feb. 1014[69]
Æthelred II (again)	1014; *d.* 23 April 1016
Edmund Ironside	1016; *d.* 30 Nov. 1016[70]
Cnut	1016; *d.* 12 Nov. 1035[71]
Harthacnut/Harold	1035; 1037[72]
Harold I Harefoot	1037; *d.* 17 March 1040
Harthacnut	1040; *d.* 8 June 1042
Edward II the Confessor	1042; *d.* 5 Jan. 1066[73]
Harold II Godwinesson	1066; *d.* 14 Oct. 1066
William I the Conqueror	25 Dec. 1066; *d.* 9 Sep. 1087

65. Recognized as king in Wessex on death of his father, Edward the Elder.
66. Recognized as king in Mercia on death of his father, Edward the Elder, he acceded as 'king of the Anglo-Saxons and of the Danes', 2 Aug. 924 x 925, and was consecrated on 4 Sept. 925, finally becoming 'king of the English' when he acquired Northumbria in 927.
67. On the death of Æthelstan, Olaf Guthfrithson of Dublin became king of the Northumbrians and extended his control over the Five Boroughs, coming to terms with Edmund, who ruled south of Watling Street from 940–2, before recovering the Five Boroughs in 942 and Northumbria in 944.
68. After 9 May 957 Eadwig divided his kingdom, taking the region south of the Thames, with his younger brother Edgar, king of the Mercians and Northumbrians, before reuniting the kingdom in 959.
69. Succeeded his father Harold Bluetooth as King of the Danes, *c.* 987; on his death, his son, Cnut, was acknowledged as king of the Danish fleet.
70. Defeated by Cnut at Ashingdon, 18 Oct. 1016, from when he was recognized as king of 'Wessex'.
71. Also king of Denmark from 1018, extending his rule over Norway and parts of Sweden; on his death the kingdom was again divided north and south of the Thames.
72. Harthacnut ruled jointly with Harold south of the Thames *in absentia*; deserted by his supporters in 1037.
73. Exiled in Normandy 1016–41, where he was regarded as 'king of the English', sworn in as king in 1041 under Harthacnut.

Kings of the English, 927–1154 (cont.)

William II Rufus	26 Sep. 1087; *d.* 2 Aug. 1100
Henry I	5 Aug. 1100; *d.* 1 Dec. 1135
Stephen	22 Dec. 1135; *d.* 25 Oct. 1154

II Regnal years of rulers from AD 1154

Henry II

Regnal year		Table 8[74]		Regnal year		Table 8	
1	19 Dec. 1154–18 Dec. 1155	14,	6	19	19 Dec. 1172–18 Dec. 1173	26,	18
2	19 Dec. 1155–18 Dec. 1156	6,	25	20	19 Dec. 1173–18 Dec. 1174	18,	3
3	19 Dec. 1156–18 Dec. 1157	25,	10	21	19 Dec. 1174–18 Dec. 1175	3,	23
4	19 Dec. 1157–18 Dec. 1158	10,	30	22	19 Dec. 1175–18 Dec. 1176	23,	14
5	19 Dec. 1158–18 Dec. 1159	30,	22	23	19 Dec. 1176–18 Dec. 1177	14,	34
6	19 Dec. 1159–18 Dec. 1160	22,	6	24	19 Dec. 1177–18 Dec. 1178	34,	19
7	19 Dec. 1160–18 Dec. 1161	6,	26	25	19 Dec. 1178–18 Dec. 1179	19,	11
8	19 Dec. 1161–18 Dec. 1162	26,	18	26	19 Dec. 1179–18 Dec. 1180	11,	30
9	19 Dec. 1162–18 Dec. 1163	18,	3	27	19 Dec. 1180–18 Dec. 1181	30,	15
10	19 Dec. 1163–18 Dec. 1164	3,	22	28	19 Dec. 1181–18 Dec. 1182	15,	7
11	19 Dec. 1164–18 Dec. 1165	22,	14	29	19 Dec. 1182–18 Dec. 1183	7,	27
12	19 Dec. 1165–18 Dec. 1166	14,	34	30	19 Dec. 1183–18 Dec. 1184	27,	11
13	19 Dec. 1166–18 Dec. 1167	34,	19	31	19 Dec. 1184–18 Dec. 1185	11,	31
14	19 Dec. 1167–18 Dec. 1168	19,	10	32	19 Dec. 1185–18 Dec. 1186	31,	23
15	19 Dec. 1168–18 Dec. 1169	10,	30	33	19 Dec. 1186–18 Dec. 1187	23,	8
16	19 Dec. 1169–18 Dec. 1170	30,	15	34	19 Dec. 1187–18 Dec. 1188	8,	27
17	19 Dec. 1170–18 Dec. 1171	15,	7	35	19 Dec. 1188–6 July 1189	27,	19
18	19 Dec. 1171–18 Dec. 1172	7,	26				

Richard I

1	3 Sep. 1189–2 Sept. 1190	19,	4	6	3 Sep. 1194–2 Sep. 1195	20,	12
2	3 Sep. 1190–2 Sept. 1191	4,	24	7	3 Sep. 1195–2 Sep. 1196	12,	31
3	3 Sep. 1191–2 Sept. 1192	24,	15	8	3 Sep. 1196–2 Sep. 1197	31,	16
4	3 Sep. 1192–2 Sept. 1193	15,	7	9	3 Sep. 1197–2 Sep. 1198	16,	8
5	3 Sep. 1193–2 Sept. 1194	7,	20	10	3 Sep. 1198–6 Apr. 1199	8,	28

John

1	27 May 1199–17 May 1200	28,	19	5	15 May 1203–2 June 1204	16,	35
2	18 May 1200–2 May 1201	19,	4	6	3 June 1204–18 May 1205	35,	20
3	3 May 1201–22 May 1202	4,	24	7	19 May 1205–10 May 1206	20,	12
4	23 May 1202–14 May 1203	24,	16	8	11 May 1206–30 May 1207	12,	32

74. The numbers under this heading refer to the tables on pp. 155–225 below, which provide calendars for each year. Thus, of Henry II's first regnal year the period 19–31 Dec. will be found in Table **8/14**, the period 1 Jan.–18 Dec. in Table **8/6**.

Regnal year		Table 8		Regnal year		Table 8	
9	31 May 1207–14 May 1208	32,	16	14	3 May 1212–22 May 1213	4,	24
10	15 May 1208–6 May 1209	16,	8	15	23 May 1213–7 May 1214	24,	9
11	7 May 1209–26 May 1210	8,	28	16	8 May 1214–27 May 1215	9,	29
12	27 May 1210–11 May 1211	28,	13	17	28 May 1215–18 May 1216	29,	20
13	12 May 1211–2 May 1212	13,	4	18	19 May 1216–19 Oct. 1217		20

Henry III

1	28 Oct. 1216–27 Oct. 1217	20,	5	30	28 Oct. 1245–27 Oct. 1246	26,	18
2	28 Oct. 1217–27 Oct. 1218	5,	25	31	28 Oct. 1246–27 Oct. 1247	18,	10
3	28 Oct. 1218–27 Oct. 1219	25,	17	32	28 Oct. 1247–27 Oct. 1248	10,	29
4	28 Oct. 1219–27 Oct. 1220	17,	8	33	28 Oct. 1248–27 Oct. 1249	29,	14
5	28 Oct. 1220–27 Oct. 1221	8,	21	34	28 Oct. 1249–27 Oct. 1250	14,	6
6	28 Oct. 1221–27 Oct. 1222	21,	13	35	28 Oct. 1250–27 Oct. 1251	6,	26
7	28 Oct. 1222–27 Oct. 1223	13,	33	36	28 Oct. 1251–27 Oct. 1252	26,	10
8	28 Oct. 1223–27 Oct. 1224	33,	24	37	28 Oct. 1252–27 Oct. 1253	10,	30
9	28 Oct. 1224–27 Oct. 1225	24,	9	38	28 Oct. 1253–27 Oct. 1254	30,	22
10	28 Oct. 1225–27 Oct. 1226	9,	29	39	28 Oct. 1254–27 Oct. 1255	22,	7
11	28 Oct. 1226–27 Oct. 1227	29,	21	40	28 Oct. 1255–27 Oct. 1256	7,	26
12	28 Oct. 1227–27 Oct. 1228	21,	5	41	28 Oct. 1256–27 Oct. 1257	26,	18
13	28 Oct. 1228–27 Oct. 1229	5,	25	42	28 Oct. 1257–27 Oct. 1258	18,	3
14	28 Oct. 1229–27 Oct. 1230	25,	17	43	28 Oct. 1258–27 Oct. 1259	3,	23
15	28 Oct. 1230–27 Oct. 1231	17,	2	44	28 Oct. 1259–27 Oct. 1260	23,	14
16	28 Oct. 1231–27 Oct. 1232	2,	21	45	28 Oct. 1260–27 Oct. 1261	14,	34
17	28 Oct. 1232–27 Oct. 1233	21,	13	46	28 Oct. 1261–27 Oct. 1262	34,	19
18	28 Oct. 1233–27 Oct. 1234	13,	33	47	28 Oct. 1262–27 Oct. 1263	19,	11
19	28 Oct. 1234–27 Oct. 1235	33,	18	48	28 Oct. 1263–27 Oct. 1264	11,	30
20	28 Oct. 1235–27 Oct. 1236	18,	9	49	28 Oct. 1264–27 Oct. 1265	30,	15
21	28 Oct. 1236–27 Oct. 1237	9,	29	50	28 Oct. 1265–27 Oct. 1266	15,	7
22	28 Oct. 1237–27 Oct. 1238	29,	14	51	28 Oct. 1266–27 Oct. 1267	7,	27
23	28 Oct. 1238–27 Oct. 1239	14,	6	52	28 Oct. 1267–27 Oct. 1268	27,	18
24	28 Oct. 1239–27 Oct. 1240	6,	25	53	28 Oct. 1268–27 Oct. 1269	18,	3
25	28 Oct. 1240–27 Oct. 1241	25,	10	54	28 Oct. 1269–27 Oct. 1270	3,	23
26	28 Oct. 1241–27 Oct. 1242	10,	30	55	28 Oct. 1270–27 Oct. 1271	23,	15
27	28 Oct. 1242–27 Oct. 1243	30,	22	56	28 Oct. 1271–27 Oct. 1272	15,	34
28	28 Oct. 1243–27 Oct. 1244	22,	13	57	28 Oct. 1272–16 Nov. 1272		34
29	28 Oct. 1244–27 Oct. 1245	13,	26				

Edward I

1	20 Nov. 1272–19 Nov. 1273	34,	19	5	20 Nov. 1276–19 Nov. 1277	15,	7
2	20 Nov. 1273–19 Nov. 1274	19,	11	6	20 Nov. 1277–19 Nov. 1278	7,	27
3	20 Nov. 1274–19 Nov. 1275	11,	24	7	20 Nov. 1278–19 Nov. 1279	27,	12
4	20 Nov. 1275–19 Nov. 1276	24,	15	8	20 Nov. 1279–19 Nov. 1280	12,	31

Edward I (cont.)

Regnal year			Table 8	Regnal year			Table 8
9	20 Nov. 1280–19 Nov. 1281	31,	23	23	20 Nov. 1294–19 Nov. 1295	28,	13
10	20 Nov. 1281–19 Nov. 1282	23,	8	24	20 Nov. 1295–19 Nov. 1296	13,	4
11	20 Nov. 1282–19 Nov. 1283	8,	28	25	20 Nov. 1296–19 Nov. 1297	4,	24
12	20 Nov. 1283–19 Nov. 1284	28,	19	26	20 Nov. 1297–19 Nov. 1298	24,	16
13	20 Nov. 1284–19 Nov. 1285	19,	4	27	20 Nov. 1298–19 Nov. 1299	16,	29
14	20 Nov. 1285–19 Nov. 1286	4,	24	28	20 Nov. 1299–19 Nov. 1300	29,	20
15	20 Nov. 1286–19 Nov. 1287	24,	16	29	20 Nov. 1300–19 Nov. 1301	20	12
16	20 Nov. 1287–19 Nov. 1288	16,	7	30	20 Nov. 1301–19 Nov. 1302	12,	32
17	20 Nov. 1288–19 Nov. 1289	7,	20	31	20 Nov. 1302–19 Nov. 1303	32,	17
18	20 Nov. 1289–19 Nov. 1290	20,	12	32	20 Nov. 1303–19 Nov. 1304	17,	8
19	20 Nov. 1290–19 Nov. 1291	12,	32	33	20 Nov. 1304–19 Nov. 1305	8,	28
20	20 Nov. 1291–19 Nov. 1292	32,	16	34	20 Nov. 1305–19 Nov. 1306	28,	13
21	20 Nov. 1292–19 Nov. 1293	16,	8	35	20 Nov. 1306–7 July 1307	13,	5
22	20 Nov. 1293–19 Nov. 1294	8,	28				

Edward II

Regnal year			Table 8	Regnal year			Table 8
1	8 July 1307–7 July 1308	5,	24	11	8 July 1317–7 July 1318	13,	33
2	8 July 1308–7 July 1309	24,	9	12	8 July 1318–7 July 1319	33,	18
3	8 July 1309–7 July 1310	9,	29	13	8 July 1319–7 July 1320	18,	9
4	8 July 1310–7 July 1311	29,	21	14	8 July 1320–7 July 1321	9,	29
5	8 July 1311–7 July 1312	21,	5	15	8 July 1321–7 July 1322	29,	21
6	8 July 1312–7 July 1313	5,	25	16	8 July 1322–7 July 1323	21,	6
7	8 July 1313–7 July 1314	25,	17	17	8 July 1323–7 July 1324	6,	25
8	8 July 1314–7 July 1315	17,	2	18	8 July 1324–7 July 1325	25,	17
9	8 July 1315–7 July 1316	2,	21	19	8 July 1325–7 July 1326	17,	2
10	8 July 1316–7 July 1317	21,	13	20	8 July 1326–20 Jan. 1327	2,	22

Edward III

Regnal year			Table 8	Regnal year			Table 8
1	25 Jan. 1327–24 Jan. 1328	22,	13	13	25 Jan. 1339–24 Jan. 1340	7,	26
2	25 Jan. 1328–24 Jan. 1329	13,	33	14(F.1)[75]	25 Jan. 1340–24 Jan. 1341	26,	18
3	25 Jan. 1329–24 Jan. 1330	33,	18	15(F.2)	25 Jan. 1341–24 Jan. 1342	18,	10
4	25 Jan. 1330–24 Jan. 1331	18,	10	16(F.3)	25 Jan. 1342–24 Jan. 1343	10,	23
5	25 Jan. 1331–24 Jan. 1332	10,	29	17(F.4)	25 Jan. 1343–24 Jan. 1344	23,	14
6	25 Jan. 1332–24 Jan. 1333	29,	14	18(F.5)	25 Jan. 1344–24 Jan. 1345	14,	6
7	25 Jan. 1333–24 Jan. 1334	14,	6	19(F.6)	25 Jan. 1345–24 Jan. 1346	6,	26
8	25 Jan. 1334–24 Jan. 1335	6,	26	20(F.7)	25 Jan. 1346–24 Jan. 1347	26,	11
9	25 Jan. 1335–24 Jan. 1336	26,	10	21(F.8)	25 Jan. 1347–24 Jan. 1348	11,	30
10	25 Jan. 1336–24 Jan. 1337	10,	30	22(F.9)	25 Jan. 1348–24 Jan. 1349	30,	22
11	25 Jan. 1337–24 Jan. 1338	30,	22	23(F.10)	25 Jan. 1349–24 Jan. 1350	22,	7
12	25 Jan. 1338–24 Jan. 1339	22,	7	24(F.11)	25 Jan. 1350–24 Jan. 1351	7,	27

75. I.e. Edward's fourteenth year as king of England, his first year as king of France.

Regnal year		Table 8		Regnal year		Table 8	
25(F.12)	25 Jan. 1351–24 Jan. 1352	27,	18	39	25 Jan. 1365–24 Jan. 1366	23,	15
26(F.13)	25 Jan. 1352–24 Jan. 1353	18,	3	40	25 Jan. 1366–24 Jan. 1367	15,	28
27(F.14)	25 Jan. 1353–24 Jan. 1354	3,	23	41	25 Jan. 1367–24 Jan. 1368	28,	19
28(F.15)	25 Jan. 1354–24 Jan. 1355	23,	15	42	25 Jan. 1368–24 Jan. 1369	19,	11
29(F.16)	25 Jan. 1355–24 Jan. 1356	15,	34	43(F.30)	25 Jan. 1369–24 Jan. 1370	11,	24
30(F.17)	25 Jan. 1356–24 Jan. 1357	34,	19	44(F.31)	25 Jan. 1370–24 Jan. 1371	24,	16
31(F.18)	25 Jan. 1357–24 Jan. 1358	19,	11	45(F.32)	25 Jan. 1371–24 Jan. 1372	16,	7
32(F.19)	25 Jan. 1358–24 Jan. 1359	11,	31	46(F.33)	25 Jan. 1372–24 Jan. 1373	7,	27
33(F.20)	25 Jan. 1359–24 Jan. 1360	31,	15	47(F.34)	25 Jan. 1373–24 Jan. 1374	27,	12
34(F.21)[76]	25 Jan. 1360–24 Jan. 1361	15,	7	48(F.35)	25 Jan. 1374–24 Jan. 1375	12,	32
35	25 Jan. 1361–24 Jan. 1362	7,	27	49(F.36)	25 Jan. 1375–24 Jan. 1376	32,	23
36	25 Jan. 1362–24 Jan. 1363	27,	12	50(F.37)	25 Jan. 1376–24 Jan. 1377	23,	8
37	25 Jan. 1363–24 Jan. 1364	12,	3	51(F.38)	25 Jan. 1377–21 June 1377		8
38	25 Jan. 1364–24 Jan. 1365	3,	23				

Richard II

1	22 June 1377–21 June 1378	8,	28	13	22 June 1389–21 June 1390	28,	13
2	22 June 1378–21 June 1379	28,	20	14	22 June 1390–21 June 1391	13,	5
3	22 June 1379–21 June 1380	20,	4	15	22 June 1391–21 June 1392	5,	24
4	22 June 1380–21 June 1381	4,	24	16	22 June 1392–21 June 1393	24,	16
5	22 June 1381–21 June 1382	24,	16	17	22 June 1393–21 June 1394	16,	29
6	22 June 1382–21 June 1383	16,	1	18	22 June 1394–21 June 1395	29,	21
7	22 June 1383–21 June 1384	1,	20	19	22 June 1395–21 June 1396	21,	12
8	22 June 1384–21 June 1385	20,	12	20	22 June 1396–21 June 1397	12,	32
9	22 June 1385–21 June 1386	12,	32	21	22 June 1397–21 June 1398	32,	17
10	22 June 1386–21 June 1387	32,	17	22	22 June 1398–21 June 1399	17,	9
11	22 June 1387–21 June 1388	17,	8	23	22 June 1399–29 Sep. 1399		9
12	22 June 1388–21 June 1389	8,	28				

Henry IV

1	30 Sep. 1399–29 Sep. 1400	9,	28	8	30 Sep. 1406–29 Sep. 1407	21,	6
2	30 Sep. 1400–29 Sep. 1401	28,	13	9	30 Sep. 1407–29 Sep. 1408	6,	25
3	30 Sep. 1401–29 Sep. 1402	13,	5	10	30 Sep. 1408–29 Sep. 1409	25,	17
4	30 Sep. 1402–29 Sep. 1403	5,	25	11	30 Sep. 1409–29 Sep. 1410	17,	2
5	30 Sep. 1403–29 Sep. 1404	25,	9	12	30 Sep. 1410–29 Sep. 1411	2,	22
6	30 Sep. 1404–29 Sep. 1405	9,	29	13	30 Sep. 1411–29 Sep. 1412	22,	13
7	30 Sep. 1405–29 Sep. 1406	29,	21	14	30 Sep. 1412–20 March 1413	13,	33

76. Edward III undertook at Brétigny on 8 May 1360 to renounce the throne of France, but he continued to use the double form of dating (cf. *Fœdera*, III, i. 500). He repeated his undertaking at Calais on 24 Oct. 1360 and seems then to have dropped the double dating. His new seal omitted the French title. Formal renunciation was timed to take place at Bruges on 30 Nov. 1361, but this never occurred, and in June 1369 Edward III resumed his claim to the French throne, his former seal, and his system of double dating.

Rulers of England

Henry V

Regnal year		Table 8		Regnal year		Table 8	
1	21 March 1413–20 March 1414	33,	18	6	21 March 1418–20 March 1419	6,	26
2	21 March 1414–20 March 1415	18,	10	7	21 March 1419–20 March 1420	26,	17
3	21 March 1415–20 March 1416	10,	29	8	21 March 1420–20 March 1421	17,	2
4	21 March 1416–20 March 1417	29,	21	9	21 March 1421–20 March 1422	2,	22
5	21 March 1417–20 March 1418	21,	6	10	21 March 1422–31 Aug. 1422		22

Henry VI

Regnal year		Table 8		Regnal year		Table 8	
1	1 Sep. 1422–31 Aug. 1423	22,	14	22	1 Sep. 1443–31 Aug. 1444	31,	22
2	1 Sep. 1423–31 Aug. 1424	14,	33	23	1 Sep. 1444–31 Aug. 1445	22,	7
3	1 Sep. 1424–31 Aug. 1425	33,	18	24	1 Sep. 1445–31 Aug. 1446	7,	27
4	1 Sep. 1425–31 Aug. 1426	18,	10	25	1 Sep. 1446–31 Aug. 1447	27,	19
5	1 Sep. 1426–31 Aug. 1427	10,	30	26	1 Sep. 1447–31 Aug. 1448	19,	3
6	1 Sep. 1427–31 Aug. 1428	30,	14	27	1 Sep. 1448–31 Aug. 1449	3,	23
7	1 Sep. 1428–31 Aug. 1429	14,	6	28	1 Sep. 1449–31 Aug. 1450	23,	15
8	1 Sep. 1429–31 Aug. 1430	6,	26	29	1 Sep. 1450–31 Aug. 1451	15,	35
9	1 Sep. 1430–31 Aug. 1431	26,	11	30	1 Sep. 1451–31 Aug. 1452	35,	19
10	1 Sep. 1431–31 Aug. 1432	11,	30	31	1 Sep. 1452–31 Aug. 1453	19,	11
11	1 Sep. 1432–31 Aug. 1433	30,	22	32	1 Sep. 1453–31 Aug. 1454	11,	31
12	1 Sep. 1433–31 Aug. 1434	22,	7	33	1 Sep. 1454–31 Aug. 1455	31,	16
13	1 Sep. 1434–31 Aug. 1435	7,	27	34	1 Sep. 1455–31 Aug. 1456	16,	7
14	1 Sep. 1435–31 Aug. 1436	27,	18	35	1 Sep. 1456–31 Aug. 1457	7,	27
15	1 Sep. 1436–31 Aug. 1437	18,	10	36	1 Sep. 1457–31 Aug. 1458	27,	12
16	1 Sep. 1437–31 Aug. 1438	10,	23	37	1 Sep. 1458–31 Aug. 1459	12,	4
17	1 Sep. 1438–31 Aug. 1439	23,	15	38	1 Sep. 1459–31 Aug. 1460	4,	23
18	1 Sep. 1439–31 Aug. 1440	15,	6	39	1 Sep. 1460–4 Mar. 1461	23,	15
19	1 Sep. 1440–31 Aug. 1441	6,	26		*and*		
20	1 Sep. 1441–31 Aug. 1442	26,	11	49[77]	Sep.–Oct. 1470–11 Apr. 1471	32,	24
21	1 Sep. 1442–31 Aug. 1443	11,	31				

Edward IV

Regnal year		Table 8		Regnal year		Table 8	
1	4 March 1461–3 March 1462	15,	28	8	4 March 1468–3 March 1469	27,	12
2	4 March 1462–3 March 1463	28,	20	9	4 March 1469–3 March 1470	12,	32
3	4 March 1463–3 March 1464	20,	11	10	4 March 1470–3 March 1471[78]	32,	24
4	4 March 1464–3 March 1465	11,	24	11	4 March 1471–3 March 1472	24,	8
5	4 March 1465–3 March 1466	24,	16	12	4 March 1472–3 March 1473	8,	28
6	4 March 1466–3 March 1467	16,	8	13	4 March 1473–3 March 1474	28,	20
7	4 March 1467–3 March 1468	8,	27	14	4 March 1474–3 March 1475	20,	5

77. Edward IV fled the country on 29 Sep. 1470; Henry VI was released on 3 Oct. and re-crowned on 13 Oct.; letters patent and close in Henry VI's name are known from 9 Oct. onwards, dated in his 49th year 'et readeptionis nostre regie potestatis anno primo'. His restoration ended with his capture by Edward IV on 11 Apr. 1471.
78. See note 77 above.

Regnal year		Table 8		Regnal year		Table 8	
15	4 March 1475–3 March 1476	5,	24	20	4 March 1480–3 March 1481	12,	32
16	4 March 1476–3 March 1477	24,	16	21	4 March 1481–3 March 1482	32,	17
17	4 March 1477–3 March 1478	16,	1	22	4 March 1482–3 March 1483	17,	9
18	4 March 1478–3 March 1479	1,	21	23	4 March 1483–9 April 1483		9
19	4 March 1479–3 March 1480	21,	12				

Edward V

1	9 April 1483–25 June 1483	9

Richard III

1	26 June 1483–25 June 1484	9,	28	3	26 June 1485–22 Aug. 1485	13
2	26 June 1484–25 June 1485	28,	13			

Henry VII

1	22 Aug. 1485–21 Aug. 1486	13,	5	13	22 Aug. 1497–21 Aug. 1498	5,	25
2	22 Aug. 1486–21 Aug. 1487	5,	25	14	22 Aug. 1498–21 Aug. 1499	25,	10
3	22 Aug. 1487–21 Aug. 1488	25,	16	15	22 Aug. 1499–21 Aug. 1500	10,	29
4	22 Aug. 1488–21 Aug. 1489	16,	29	16	22 Aug. 1500–21 Aug. 1501	29,	21
5	22 Aug. 1489–21 Aug. 1490	29,	21	17	22 Aug. 1501–21 Aug. 1502	21,	6
6	22 Aug. 1490–21 Aug. 1491	21,	13	18	22 Aug. 1502–21 Aug. 1503	6,	26
7	22 Aug. 1491–21 Aug. 1492	13,	32	19	22 Aug. 1503–21 Aug. 1504	26,	17
8	22 Aug. 1492–21 Aug. 1493	32,	17	20	22 Aug. 1504–21 Aug. 1505	17,	2
9	22 Aug. 1493–21 Aug. 1494	17,	9	21	22 Aug. 1505–21 Aug. 1506	2,	22
10	22 Aug. 1494–21 Aug. 1495	9,	29	22	22 Aug. 1506–21 Aug. 1507	22,	14
11	22 Aug. 1495–21 Aug. 1496	29,	13	23	22 Aug. 1507–21 Aug. 1508	14,	33
12	22 Aug. 1496–21 Aug. 1497	13,	5	24	22 Aug. 1508–21 Apr. 1509	33,	18

Henry VIII

1	22 Apr. 1509–21 Apr. 1510	18,	10	15	22 Apr. 1523–21 Apr. 1524	15,	6
2	22 Apr. 1510–21 Apr. 1511	10,	30	16	22 Apr. 1524–21 Apr. 1525	6,	26
3	22 Apr. 1511–21 Apr. 1512	30,	21	17	22 Apr. 1525–21 Apr. 1526	26,	11
4	22 Apr. 1512–21 Apr. 1513	21,	6	18	22 Apr. 1526–21 Apr. 1527	11,	31
5	22 Apr. 1513–21 Apr. 1514	6,	26	19	22 Apr. 1527–21 Apr. 1528	31,	22
6	22 Apr. 1514–21 Apr. 1515	26,	18	20	22 Apr. 1528–21 Apr. 1529	22,	7
7	22 Apr. 1515–21 Apr. 1516	18,	2	21	22 Apr. 1529–21 Apr. 1530	7,	27
8	22 Apr. 1516–21 Apr. 1517	2,	22	22	22 Apr. 1530–21 Apr. 1531	27,	19
9	22 Apr. 1517–21 Apr. 1518	22,	14	23	22 Apr. 1531–21 Apr. 1532	19,	10
10	22 Apr. 1518–21 Apr. 1519	14,	34	24	22 Apr. 1532–21 Apr. 1533	10,	23
11	22 Apr. 1519–21 Apr. 1520	34,	18	25	22 Apr. 1533–21 Apr. 1534	23,	15
12	22 Apr. 1520–21 Apr. 1521	18,	10	26	22 Apr. 1534–21 Apr. 1535	15,	7
13	22 Apr. 1521–21 Apr. 1522	10,	30	27	22 Apr. 1535–21 Apr. 1536	7,	26
14	22 Apr. 1522–21 Apr. 1523	30,	15	28	22 Apr. 1536–21 Apr. 1537	26,	11

Henry VIII (cont.)

Regnal year		Table 8		Regnal year		Table 8	
29	22 Apr. 1537–21 Apr. 1538	11,	31	34	22 Apr. 1542–21 Apr. 1543	19,	4
30	22 Apr. 1538–21 Apr. 1539	31,	16	35	22 Apr. 1543–21 Apr. 1544	4,	23
31	22 Apr. 1539–21 Apr. 1540	16,	7	36	22 Apr. 1544–21 Apr. 1545	23,	15
32	22 Apr. 1540–21 Apr. 1541	7,	27	37	22 Apr. 1545–21 Apr. 1546	15,	35
33	22 Apr. 1541–21 Apr. 1542	27,	19	38	22 Apr. 1546–28 Jan. 1547	35,	20

Edward VI

1	28 Jan. 1547–27 Jan. 1548	20,	11	5	28 Jan. 1551–27 Jan. 1552	8,	27
2	28 Jan. 1548–27 Jan. 1549	11,	31	6	28 Jan. 1552–27 Jan. 1553	27,	12
3	28 Jan. 1549–27 Jan. 1550	31,	16	7	28 Jan. 1553–6 July 1553		12
4	28 Jan. 1550–27 Jan. 1551	16,	8				

Jane

1	6 July 1553–19 July 1553	12	

Mary

1	19 July 1553–5 July 1554	12,	4	2	6 July 1554[79]–24 July 1554		4

Philip and Mary

1 & 2	25 July 1554–5 July 1555	4,	24	3 & 5	6 July 1557–24 July 1557		28
1 & 3	6 July 1555–24 July 1555		24	4 & 5	25 July 1557–5 July 1558	28,	20
2 & 3	25 July 1555–5 July 1556	24,	15	4 & 6	6 July 1558–24 July 1558		20
2 & 4	6 July 1556–24 July 1556		15	5 & 6	25 July 1558–17 Nov. 1558		20
3 & 4	25 July 1556–5 July 1557	15,	28				

Elizabeth I

1	17 Nov. 1558–16 Nov. 1559	20,	5	14	17 Nov. 1571–16 Nov. 1572	25,	16
2	17 Nov. 1559–16 Nov. 1560	5,	24	15	17 Nov. 1572–16 Nov. 1573	16,	1
3	17 Nov. 1560–16 Nov. 1561	24,	16	16	17 Nov. 1573–16 Nov. 1574	1,	21
4	17 Nov. 1561–16 Nov. 1562	16,	8	17	17 Nov. 1574–16 Nov. 1575	21,	13
5	17 Nov. 1562–16 Nov. 1563	8,	21	18	17 Nov. 1575–16 Nov. 1576	13,	32
6	17 Nov. 1563–16 Nov. 1564	21,	12	19	17 Nov. 1576–16 Nov. 1577	32,	17
7	17 Nov. 1564–16 Nov. 1565	12,	32	20	17 Nov. 1577–16 Nov. 1578	17,	9
8	17 Nov. 1565–16 Nov. 1566	32,	24	21	17 Nov. 1578–16 Nov. 1579	9,	29
9	17 Nov. 1566–16 Nov. 1567	24,	9	22	17 Nov. 1579–16 Nov. 1580	29,	13
10	17 Nov. 1567–16 Nov. 1568	9,	28	23	17 Nov. 1580–16 Nov. 1581	13,	5
11	17 Nov. 1568–16 Nov. 1569	28,	20	24	17 Nov. 1581–16 Nov. 1582	5,	25
12	17 Nov. 1569–16 Nov. 1570	20,	5	25	17 Nov. 1582–16 Nov. 1583	25,	10
13	17 Nov. 1570–16 Nov. 1571	5,	25	26	17 Nov. 1583–16 Nov. 1584	10,	29

79. Mary dated her second year from 6 July, ignoring Jane's intrusion.

Regnal year		Table 8		Regnal year		Table 8	
27	17 Nov. 1584–16 Nov. 1585	29,	21	37	17 Nov. 1594–16 Nov. 1595	10,	30
28	17 Nov. 1585–16 Nov. 1586	21,	13	38	17 Nov. 1595–16 Nov. 1596	30,	21
29	17 Nov. 1586–16 Nov. 1587	13,	26	39	17 Nov. 1596–16 Nov. 1597	21,	6
30	17 Nov. 1587–16 Nov. 1588	26,	17	40	17 Nov. 1597–16 Nov. 1598	6,	26
31	17 Nov. 1588–16 Nov. 1589	17,	9	41	17 Nov. 1598–16 Nov. 1599	26,	18
32	17 Nov. 1589–16 Nov. 1590	9,	29	42	17 Nov. 1599–16 Nov. 1600	18,	2
33	17 Nov. 1590–16 Nov. 1591	29,	14	43	17 Nov. 1600–16 Nov. 1601	2,	22
34	17 Nov. 1591–16 Nov. 1592	14,	5	44	17 Nov. 1601–16 Nov. 1602	22,	14
35	17 Nov. 1592–16 Nov. 1593	5,	25	45	17 Nov. 1602–24 March 1603	14,	34
36	17 Nov. 1593–16 Nov. 1594	25,	10				

James I[80]

	Regnal year	Table 8			Regnal year	Table 8	
1	24 March 1603–23 March 1604	34,	18	13	24 March 1615–23 March 1616	19,	10
2	24 March 1604–23 March 1605	18,	10	14	24 March 1616–23 March 1617	10,	30
3	24 March 1605–23 March 1606	10,	30	15	24 March 1617–23 March 1618	30,	15
4	24 March 1606–23 March 1607	30,	15	16	24 March 1618–23 March 1619	15,	7
5	24 March 1607–23 March 1608	15,	6	17	24 March 1619–23 March 1620	7,	26
6	24 March 1608–23 March 1609	6,	26	18	24 March 1620–23 March 1621	26,	11
7	24 March 1609–23 March 1610	26,	18	19	24 March 1621–23 March 1622	11,	31
8	24 March 1610–23 March 1611	18,	3	20	24 March 1622–23 March 1623	31,	23
9	24 March 1611–23 March 1612	3,	22	21	24 March 1623–23 March 1624	23,	7
10	24 March 1612–23 March 1613	22,	14	22	24 March 1624–23 March 1625	7,	27
11	24 March 1613–23 March 1614	14,	34	23	24 March 1625–27 March 1625		27
12	24 March 1614–23 March 1615	34,	19				

Charles I

	Regnal year	Table 8			Regnal year	Table 8	
1	27 March 1625–26 March 1626	27,	19	13	27 March 1637–26 March 1638	19,	4
2	27 March 1626–26 March 1627	19,	4	14	27 March 1638–26 March 1639	4,	24
3	27 March 1627–26 March 1628	4,	23	15	27 March 1639–26 March 1640	24,	15
4	27 March 1628–26 March 1629	23,	15	16	27 March 1640–26 March 1641	15,	35
5	27 March 1629–26 March 1630	15,	7	17	27 March 1641–26 March 1642	35,	20
6	27 March 1630–26 March 1631	7,	20	18	27 March 1642–26 March 1643	20,	12
7	27 March 1631–26 March 1632	20,	11	19	27 March 1643–26 March 1644	12,	31
8	27 March 1632–26 March 1633	11,	31	20	27 March 1644–26 March 1645	31,	16
9	27 March 1633–26 March 1634	31,	16	21	27 March 1645–26 March 1646	16,	8
10	27 March 1634–26 March 1635	16,	8	22	27 March 1646–26 March 1647	8,	28
11	27 March 1635–26 March 1636	8,	27	23	27 March 1647–26 March 1648	28,	12
12	27 March 1636–26 March 1637	27,	19	24	27 March 1648–30 Jan. 1649	12,	4

80. When James VI of Scotland became James I of England, he was in the thirty-sixth year of his reign in Scotland. He used the regnal years of England and Scotland in subsequent dating. As the 36th year of Scotland did not end till 23 July 1603, one may ascertain the year of Scotland by adding to the regnal year of England 35 for dates up to 23 July and 36 for dates after 23 July.

The Commonwealth

After the execution of King Charles I on 30 January 1649, the kingship was abolished (17 March 1649) and government by a Council of State was set up on 14 February 1649. The council was dissolved on 20 April 1653 and replaced by another Council of State on 29 April 1653. Oliver Cromwell took the office of Lord Protector on 16 December 1653 and held it till his death on 3 September 1658. His son, Richard Cromwell, succeeded to the same office on the day of his father's death and abdicated on 24 May 1659. After a year of parliamentary government Charles II was proclaimed king on 5 May 1660 and arrived in London on 29 May 1660. During the whole of the period 1649–60 English official documents were dated by the year of grace. In proclaiming Charles II to be king, parliament declared that he had been *de jure* king since his father's death. Therefore Charles's establishment on the throne came in his twelfth regnal year, deemed to have begun on 30 January 1660. Before parliament proclaimed him, the king had already dated his declaration at Breda 'this 14th day of April 1660 in the twelfth year of our reign'.

Charles II[81]

Regnal year		Table 8		Regnal year		Table 8	
12	29 May 1660–29 Jan. 1661	32,	24	25	30 Jan. 1673–29 Jan. 1674	9,	29
13	30 Jan. 1661–29 Jan. 1662	24,	9	26	30 Jan. 1674–29 Jan. 1675	29,	14
14	30 Jan. 1662–29 Jan. 1663	9,	29	27	30 Jan. 1675–29 Jan. 1676	14,	5
15	30 Jan. 1663–29 Jan. 1664	29,	20	28	30 Jan. 1676–29 Jan. 1677	5,	25
16	30 Jan. 1664–29 Jan. 1665	20,	5	29	30 Jan. 1677–29 Jan. 1678	25,	10
17	30 Jan. 1665–29 Jan. 1666	5,	25	30	30 Jan. 1678–29 Jan. 1679	10,	30
18	30 Jan. 1666–29 Jan. 1667	25,	17	31	30 Jan. 1679–29 Jan. 1680	30,	21
19	30 Jan. 1667–29 Jan. 1668	17,	1	32	30 Jan. 1680–29 Jan. 1681	21,	13
20	30 Jan. 1668–29 Jan. 1669	1,	21	33	30 Jan. 1681–29 Jan. 1682	13,	26
21	30 Jan. 1669–29 Jan. 1670	21,	13	34	30 Jan. 1682–29 Jan. 1683	26,	18
22	30 Jan. 1670–29 Jan. 1671	13,	33	35	30 Jan. 1683–29 Jan. 1684	18,	9
23	30 Jan. 1671–29 Jan. 1672	33,	17	36	30 Jan. 1684–29 Jan. 1685	9,	29
24	30 Jan. 1672–29 Jan. 1673	17,	9	37	30 Jan. 1685–6 Feb. 1685		29

James II

		Table 8				Table 8	
1	6 Feb. 1685–5 Feb. 1686	29,	14	3	6 Feb. 1687–5 Feb. 1688	6,	25
2	6 Feb. 1686–5 Feb. 1687	14,	6	4	6 Feb. 1688–11 Dec. 1688		25

Interregnum 12 Dec. 1688–12 Feb. 1689 (Table **8**/25, 10)

---

81. Dating by Charles II's regnal year occurs very seldom until the Declaration of Breda. For an example, see *Eng. His. Rev.*, 5 (1890), 117–18: 'Given at our Court at Worcester this six & twentieth days of Aug[t] in the third yeere of our reigne.' It should be remembered that Charles was proclaimed in Edinburgh in proper form within a week of his father's execution.

William and Mary

Regnal year		Table 8		Regnal year		Table 8	
1	13 Feb. 1689–12 Feb. 1690	10,	30	4	13 Feb. 1692–12 Feb. 1693	6,	26
2	13 Feb. 1690–12 Feb. 1691	30,	22	5	13 Feb. 1693–12 Feb. 1694	26,	18
3	13 Feb. 1691–12 Feb. 1692	22,	6	6	13 Feb. 1694–27 Dec. 1694		18

William III

6	28 Dec. 1694–12 Feb. 1695	18,	3	11	28 Dec. 1699–12 Feb. 1700	19,	10
7	28 Dec. 1695–12 Feb. 1696	3,	22	12	28 Dec. 1700–12 Feb. 1701	10,	30
8	28 Dec. 1696–12 Feb. 1697	22,	14	13	28 Dec. 1701–12 Feb. 1702	30,	15
9	28 Dec. 1697–12 Feb. 1698	14,	34	14	28 Dec. 1702–8 March 1702		15
10	28 Dec. 1698–12 Feb. 1699	34,	19				

Anne

1	8 March 1702–7 March 1703	15,	7	8	8 March 1709–7 March 1710	34,	19
2	8 March 1703–7 March 1704	7,	26	9	8 March 1710–7 March 1711	19,	11
3	8 March 1704–7 March 1705	26,	18	10	8 March 1711–7 March 1712	11,	30
4	8 March 1705–7 March 1706	18,	3	11	8 March 1712–7 March 1713	30,	15
5	8 March 1706–7 March 1707	3,	23	12	8 March 1713–7 March 1714	15,	7
6	8 March 1707–7 March 1708	23,	14	13	8 March 1714–1 August 1714		7
7	8 March 1708–7 March 1709	14,	34				

George I

1	1 Aug. 1714–31 July 1715	7,	27	8	1 Aug. 1721–31 July 1722	19,	4
2	1 Aug. 1715–31 July 1716	27,	11	9	1 Aug. 1722–31 July 1723	4,	24
3	1 Aug. 1716–31 July 1717	11,	31	10	1 Aug. 1723–31 July 1724	24,	15
4	1 Aug. 1717–31 July 1718	31,	23	11	1 Aug. 1724–31 July 1725	15,	7
5	1 Aug. 1718–31 July 1719	23,	8	12	1 Aug. 1725–31 July 1726	7,	20
6	1 Aug. 1719–31 July 1720	8,	27	13	1 Aug. 1726–11 June 1727	20,	12
7	1 Aug. 1720–31 July 1721	27,	19				

George II

1	11 June 1727–10 June 1728	12,	31	12	11 June 1738–10 June 1739	12,	32
2	11 June 1728–10 June 1729	31,	16	13	11 June 1739–10 June 1740	32,	16
3	11 June 1729–10 June 1730	16,	8	14	11 June 1740–10 June 1741	16,	8
4	11 June 1730–10 June 1731	8,	28	15	11 June 1741–10 June 1742	8,	28
5	11 June 1731–10 June 1732	28,	19	16	11 June 1742–10 June 1743	28,	13
6	11 June 1732–10 June 1733	19,	4	17	11 June 1743–10 June 1744	13,	4
7	11 June 1733–10 June 1734	4,	24	18	11 June 1744–10 June 1745	4,	24
8	11 June 1734–10 June 1735	24,	16	19	11 June 1745–10 June 1746	24,	9
9	11 June 1735–10 June 1736	16,	35	20	11 June 1746–10 June 1747	9,	29
10	11 June 1736–10 June 1737	35,	20	21	11 June 1747–10 June 1748	29,	20
11	11 June 1737–10 June 1738	20,	12	22	11 June 1748–10 June 1749	20,	5

George II (cont.)

Regnal year		Table 8		Regnal year		Table 8	
23	11 June 1749–10 June 1750	5,	25	**29**	22 June 1755–21 June 1756	9,	28
24	11 June 1750–10 June 1751	25,	17	**30**	22 June 1756–21 June 1757	28,	20
25	11 June 1751–10 June 1752	17,	36	**31**	22 June 1757–21 June 1758	20,	5
26[82]	11 June 1752–21 June 1753	36,	32	**32**	22 June 1758–21 June 1759	5,	25
27	22 June 1753–21 June 1754	32,	24	**33**	22 June 1759–21 June 1760	25,	16
28	22 June 1754–21 June 1755	24,	9	**34**	22 June 1760–25 Oct. 1760		16

George III

Regnal year		Table 8		Regnal year		Table 8	
1	25 Oct. 1760–24 Oct. 1761	16,	1	**31**	25 Oct. 1790–24 Oct. 1791	14,	34
2	25 Oct. 1761–24 Oct. 1762	1,	21	**32**	25 Oct. 1791–24 Oct. 1792	34,	18
3	25 Oct. 1762–24 Oct. 1763	21,	13	**33**	25 Oct. 1792–24 Oct. 1793	18,	10
4	25 Oct. 1763–24 Oct. 1764	13,	32	**34**	25 Oct. 1793–24 Oct. 1794	10,	30
5	25 Oct. 1764–24 Oct. 1765	32,	17	**35**	25 Oct. 1794–24 Oct. 1795	30,	15
6	25 Oct. 1765–24 Oct. 1766	17,	9	**36**	25 Oct. 1795–24 Oct. 1796	15,	6
7	25 Oct. 1766–24 Oct. 1767	9,	29	**37**	25 Oct. 1796–24 Oct. 1797	6,	26
8	25 Oct. 1767–24 Oct. 1768	29,	13	**38**	25 Oct. 1797–24 Oct. 1798	26,	18
9	25 Oct. 1768–24 Oct. 1769	13,	5	**39**	25 Oct. 1798–24 Oct. 1799	18,	3
10	25 Oct. 1769–24 Oct. 1770	5,	25	**40**	25 Oct. 1799–24 Oct. 1800	3,	23
11	25 Oct. 1770–24 Oct. 1771	25,	10	**41**	25 Oct. 1800–24 Oct. 1801	23,	15
12	25 Oct. 1771–24 Oct. 1772	10,	29	**42**	25 Oct. 1801–24 Oct. 1802	15,	28
13	25 Oct. 1772–24 Oct. 1773	29,	21	**43**	25 Oct. 1802–24 Oct. 1803	28,	20
14	25 Oct. 1773–24 Oct. 1774	21,	13	**44**	25 Oct. 1803–24 Oct. 1804	20,	11
15	25 Oct. 1774–24 Oct. 1775	13,	26	**45**	25 Oct. 1804–24 Oct. 1805	11,	24
16	25 Oct. 1775–24 Oct. 1776	26,	17	**46**	25 Oct. 1805–24 Oct. 1806	24,	16
17	25 Oct. 1776–24 Oct. 1777	17,	9	**47**	25 Oct. 1806–24 Oct. 1807	16,	8
18	25 Oct. 1777–24 Oct. 1778	9,	29	**48**	25 Oct. 1807–24 Oct. 1808	8,	27
19	25 Oct. 1778–24 Oct. 1779	29,	14	**49**	25 Oct. 1808–24 Oct. 1809	27,	12
20	25 Oct. 1779–24 Oct. 1780	14,	5	**50**	25 Oct. 1809–24 Oct. 1810	12,	32
21	25 Oct. 1780–24 Oct. 1781	5,	25	**51**	25 Oct. 1810–24 Oct. 1811	32,	24
22	25 Oct. 1781–24 Oct. 1782	25,	10	**52**	25 Oct. 1811–24 Oct. 1812	24,	8
23	25 Oct. 1782–24 Oct. 1783	10,	30	**53**	25 Oct. 1812–24 Oct. 1813	8,	28
24	25 Oct. 1783–24 Oct. 1784	30,	21	**54**	25 Oct. 1813–24 Oct. 1814	28,	20
25	25 Oct. 1784–24 Oct. 1785	21,	6	**55**	25 Oct. 1814–24 Oct. 1815	20,	5
26	25 Oct. 1785–24 Oct. 1786	6,	26	**56**	25 Oct. 1815–24 Oct. 1816	5,	24
27	25 Oct. 1786–24 Oct. 1787	26,	18	**57**	25 Oct. 1816–24 Oct. 1817	24,	16
28	25 Oct. 1787–24 Oct. 1788	18,	2	**58**	25 Oct. 1817–24 Oct. 1818	16,	1
29	25 Oct. 1788–24 Oct. 1789	2,	22	**59**	25 Oct. 1818–24 Oct. 1819	1,	21
30	25 Oct. 1789–24 Oct. 1790	22,	14	**60**	25 Oct. 1819–29 Jan. 1820	21,	12

82. This regnal year was extended to 21 June 1753, so that it should consist of 365 days despite the omission of eleven days in Sep. 1752, when the New Style was adopted (above, p. 18).

George IV

Regnal year		Table 8		Regnal year		Table 8	
1	29 Jan. 1820–28 Jan. 1821	12,	32	7	29 Jan. 1826–28 Jan. 1827	5,	25
2	29 Jan. 1821–28 Jan. 1822	32,	17	8	29 Jan. 1827–28 Jan. 1828	25,	16
3	29 Jan. 1822–28 Jan. 1823	17,	9	9	29 Jan. 1828–28 Jan. 1829	16,	29
4	29 Jan. 1823–28 Jan. 1824	9,	28	10	29 Jan. 1829–28 Jan. 1830	29,	21
5	29 Jan. 1824–28 Jan. 1825	28,	13	11	29 Jan. 1830–26 June 1830		21
6	29 Jan. 1825–28 Jan. 1826	13,	5				

William IV

1	26 June 1830–25 June 1831	21,	13	5	26 June 1834–25 June 1835	9,	29
2	26 June 1831–25 June 1832	13,	32	6	26 June 1835–25 June 1836	29,	13
3	26 June 1832–25 June 1833	32,	17	7	26 June 1836–20 June 1837	13,	5
4	26 June 1833–25 June 1834	17,	9				

Victoria

1	20 June 1837–19 June 1838	5,	25	29	20 June 1865–19 June 1866	26,	11
2	20 June 1838–19 June 1839	25,	10	30	20 June 1866–19 June 1867	11,	31
3	20 June 1839–19 June 1840	10,	29	31	20 June 1867–19 June 1868	31,	22
4	20 June 1840–19 June 1841	29,	21	32	20 June 1868–19 June 1869	22,	7
5	20 June 1841–19 June 1842	21,	6	33	20 June 1869–19 June 1870	7,	27
6	20 June 1842–19 June 1843	6,	26	34	20 June 1870–19 June 1871	27,	19
7	20 June 1843–19 June 1844	26,	17	35	20 June 1871–19 June 1872	19,	10
8	20 June 1844–19 June 1845	17,	2	36	20 June 1872–19 June 1873	10,	23
9	20 June 1845–19 June 1846	2,	22	37	20 June 1873–19 June 1874	23,	15
10	20 June 1846–19 June 1847	22,	14	38	20 June 1874–19 June 1875	15,	7
11	20 June 1847–19 June 1848	14,	33	39	20 June 1875–19 June 1876	7,	26
12	20 June 1848–19 June 1849	33,	18	40	20 June 1876–19 June 1877	26,	11
13	20 June 1849–19 June 1850	18,	10	41	20 June 1877–19 June 1878	11,	31
14	20 June 1850–19 June 1851	10,	30	42	20 June 1878–19 June 1879	31,	23
15	20 June 1851–19 June 1852	30,	21	43	20 June 1879–19 June 1880	23,	7
16	20 June 1852–19 June 1853	21,	6	44	20 June 1880–19 June 1881	7,	27
17	20 June 1853–19 June 1854	6,	26	45	20 June 1881–19 June 1882	27,	19
18	20 June 1854–19 June 1855	26,	18	46	20 June 1882–19 June 1883	19,	4
19	20 June 1855–19 June 1856	18,	2	47	20 June 1883–19 June 1884	4,	23
20	20 June 1856–19 June 1857	2,	22	48	20 June 1884–19 June 1885	23,	15
21	20 June 1857–19 June 1858	22,	14	49	20 June 1885–19 June 1886	15,	35
22	20 June 1858–19 June 1859	14,	34	50	20 June 1886–19 June 1887	35,	20
23	20 June 1859–19 June 1860	34,	18	51	20 June 1887–19 June 1888	20,	11
24	20 June 1860–19 June 1861	18,	10	52	20 June 1888–19 June 1889	11,	31
25	20 June 1861–19 June 1862	10,	30	53	20 June 1889–19 June 1890	31,	16
26	20 June 1862–19 June 1863	30,	15	54	20 June 1890–19 June 1891	16,	8
27	20 June 1863–19 June 1864	15,	6	55	20 June 1891–19 June 1892	8,	27
28	20 June 1864–19 June 1865	6,	26	56	20 June 1892–19 June 1893	27,	12

Victoria (cont.)

Regnal year		Table 8		Regnal year		Table 8	
57	20 June 1893–19 June 1894	12,	4	61	20 June 1897–19 June 1898	28,	20
58	20 June 1894–19 June 1895	4,	24	62	20 June 1898–19 June 1899	20,	12
59	20 June 1895–19 June 1896	24,	15	63	20 June 1899–19 June 1900	12,	25
60	20 June 1896–19 June 1897	15,	28	64	20 June 1900–22 Jan. 1901	25,	17

Edward VII

1	22 Jan. 1901–21 Jan. 1902	17,	9	6	22 Jan. 1906–21 Jan. 1907	25,	10
2	22 Jan. 1902–21 Jan. 1903	9,	22	7	22 Jan. 1907–21 Jan. 1908	10,	29
3	22 Jan. 1903–21 Jan. 1904	22,	13	8	22 Jan. 1908–21 Jan. 1909	29,	21
4	22 Jan. 1904–21 Jan. 1905	13,	33	9	22 Jan. 1909–21 Jan. 1910	21,	6
5	22 Jan. 1905–21 Jan. 1906	33,	25	10	22 Jan. 1910–6 May 1910		6

George V

1	6 May 1910–5 May 1911	6,	26	14	6 May 1923–5 May 1924	11,	30
2	6 May 1911–5 May 1912	26,	17	15	6 May 1924–5 May 1925	30,	22
3	6 May 1912–5 May 1913	17,	2	16	6 May 1925–5 May 1926	22,	14
4	6 May 1913–5 May 1914	2,	22	17	6 May 1926–5 May 1927	14,	27
5	6 May 1914–5 May 1915	22,	14	18	6 May 1927–5 May 1928	27,	18
6	6 May 1915–5 May 1916	14,	33	19	6 May 1928–5 May 1929	18,	10
7	6 May 1916–5 May 1917	33,	18	20	6 May 1929–5 May 1930	10,	30
8	6 May 1917–5 May 1918	18,	10	21	6 May 1930–5 May 1931	30,	15
9	6 May 1918–5 May 1919	10,	30	22	6 May 1931–5 May 1932	15,	6
10	6 May 1919–5 May 1920	30,	14	23	6 May 1932–5 May 1933	6,	26
11	6 May 1920–5 May 1921	14,	6	24	6 May 1933–5 May 1934	26,	11
12	6 May 1921–5 May 1922	6,	26	25	6 May 1934–5 May 1935	11,	31
13	6 May 1922–5 May 1923	26,	11	26	6 May 1935–20 Jan. 1936	31,	22

Edward VIII

1	20 Jan. 1936–11 Dec. 1936	22	

George VI

1	11 Dec. 1936–10 Dec. 1937	22,	7	9	11 Dec. 1944–10 Dec. 1945	19,	11
2	11 Dec. 1937–10 Dec. 1938	7,	27	10	11 Dec. 1945–10 Dec. 1946	11,	31
3	11 Dec. 1938–10 Dec. 1939	27,	19	11	11 Dec. 1946–10 Dec. 1947	31,	16
4	11 Dec. 1939–10 Dec. 1940	19,	3	12	11 Dec. 1947–10 Dec. 1948	16,	7
5	11 Dec. 1940–10 Dec. 1941	3,	23	13	11 Dec. 1948–10 Dec. 1949	7,	27
6	11 Dec. 1941–10 Dec. 1942	23,	15	14	11 Dec. 1949–10 Dec. 1950	27,	19
7	11 Dec. 1942–10 Dec. 1943	15,	35	15	11 Dec. 1950–10 Dec. 1951	19,	4
8	11 Dec. 1943–10 Dec. 1944	35,	19	16	11 Dec. 1951–6 Feb. 1952	4,	23

Elizabeth II

Regnal year		Table 8		Regnal year		Table 8	
1	6 Feb. 1952–5 Feb. 1953	23,	15	25	6 Feb. 1976–5 Feb. 1977	28,	20
2	6 Feb. 1953–5 Feb. 1954	15,	28	26	6 Feb. 1977–5 Feb. 1978	20,	5
3	6 Feb. 1954–5 Feb. 1955	28,	20	27	6 Feb. 1978–5 Feb. 1979	5,	25
4	6 Feb. 1955–5 Feb. 1956	20,	11	28	6 Feb. 1979–5 Feb. 1980	25,	16
5	6 Feb. 1956–5 Feb. 1957	11,	31	29	6 Feb. 1980–5 Feb. 1981	16,	29
6	6 Feb. 1957–5 Feb. 1958	31,	16	30	6 Feb. 1981–5 Feb. 1982	29,	21
7	6 Feb. 1958–5 Feb. 1959	16,	8	31	6 Feb. 1982–5 Feb. 1983	21,	13
8	6 Feb. 1959–5 Feb. 1960	8,	27	32	6 Feb. 1983–5 Feb. 1984	13,	32
9	6 Feb. 1960–5 Feb. 1961	27,	12	33	6 Feb. 1984–5 Feb. 1985	32,	17
10	6 Feb. 1961–5 Feb. 1962	12,	32	34	6 Feb. 1985–5 Feb. 1986	17,	9
11	6 Feb. 1962–5 Feb. 1963	32,	24	35	6 Feb. 1986–5 Feb. 1987	9,	29
12	6 Feb. 1963–5 Feb. 1964	24,	8	36	6 Feb. 1987–5 Feb. 1988	29,	13
13	6 Feb. 1964–5 Feb. 1965	8,	28	37	6 Feb. 1988–5 Feb. 1989	13,	5
14	6 Feb. 1965–5 Feb. 1966	28,	20	38	6 Feb. 1989–5 Feb. 1990	5,	25
15	6 Feb. 1966–5 Feb. 1967	20,	5	39	6 Feb. 1990–5 Feb. 1991	25,	10
16	6 Feb. 1967–5 Feb. 1968	5,	24	40	6 Feb. 1991–5 Feb. 1992	10,	29
17	6 Feb. 1968–5 Feb. 1969	24,	16	41	6 Feb. 1992–5 Feb. 1993	29,	21
18	6 Feb. 1969–5 Feb. 1970	16,	8	42	6 Feb. 1993–5 Feb. 1994	21,	13
19	6 Feb. 1970–5 Feb. 1971	8,	21	43	6 Feb. 1994–5 Feb. 1995	13,	26
20	6 Feb. 1971–5 Feb. 1972	21,	12	44	6 Feb. 1995–5 Feb. 1996	26,	17
21	6 Feb. 1972–5 Feb. 1973	12,	32	45	6 Feb. 1996–5 Feb. 1997	17,	9
22	6 Feb. 1973–5 Feb. 1974	32,	24	46	6 Feb. 1997–5 Feb. 1998	9,	22
23	6 Feb. 1974–5 Feb. 1975	24,	9	47	6 Feb. 1998–5 Feb. 1999	22,	14
24	6 Feb. 1975–5 Feb. 1976	9,	28	48	6 Feb. 1999–	14,	

III Exchequer years of English rulers

Henry I	31st exchequer year ends 29 September 1130[83]
Henry II	2nd exchequer year ends 29 September 1156
Richard I	1st exchequer year ends 29 September 1189
John	1st exchequer year ends 29 September 1199
Henry III	2nd exchequer year ends 29 September 1218[84]
Edward I	1st exchequer year ends 29 September 1273
Edward II	1st exchequer year ends 29 September 1308
Edward III	1st exchequer year ends 29 September 1327
Richard II	1st exchequer year ends 29 September 1378
Henry IV	1st exchequer year ends 29 September 1400

83. This may be inferred from the one surviving Pipe Roll of Henry I's reign, after which the next complete record to show the practice of the Exchequer is the Pipe Roll of 2 Henry II.
84. The accounts for the *tempus guerræ*, including the first year of Henry III, do not appear on the Pipe Rolls.

Henry V	1st exchequer year ends 29 September 1413
Henry VI	1st exchequer year ends 29 September 1423
Edward IV	1st exchequer year ends 29 September 1461
Richard III[85]	1st exchequer year ends 29 September 1483
Henry VII	1st exchequer year ends 29 September 1486
Henry VIII	1st exchequer year ends 29 September 1510
Edward VI	1st exchequer year ends 29 September 1548
Mary	1st exchequer year ends 29 September 1554
Philip and Mary	1st exchequer year ends 29 September 1555
Elizabeth	1st exchequer year ends 29 September 1560
James I	1st exchequer year ends 29 September 1604
Charles I	1st exchequer year ends 29 September 1626
Charles II	11th exchequer year ends 29 September 1660[86]
James II	1st exchequer year ends 29 September 1686
William and Mary	1st exchequer year ends 29 September 1690
William III	1st exchequer year ends 29 September 1696
Anne	1st exchequer year ends 29 September 1703
George I	1st exchequer year ends 29 September 1715
George II	1st exchequer year ends 29 September 1728
George III	1st exchequer year ends 29 September 1762
George IV	1st exchequer year ends 29 September 1821
William IV	1st exchequer year ends 29 September 1831[87]

BIBLIOGRAPHY

The Blackwell Encyclopaedia of Anglo-Saxon England, ed. M. Lapidge, J. Blair, S. Keynes and D. Scragg (Oxford, 1999).

Hallam, E. M., *The itinerary of Edward II and his household* (London: List and Index Society, vol. 211, 1984).

Richardson, H. G., 'The exchequer year', *Trans. R. Hist. Soc.,* 4th series, 8 (1925), 171–90, 9 (1926), 175–6.

Rollason, D., with D. Gore and G. Fellows-Jensen, *Sources for York history to AD 1100* (Yorkshire Archaeological Trust, 1998).

Wallis, J. E. W., *English regnal years and titles, hand-lists, Easter dates, etc.* SPCK 'Helps for students of history', no. 40 (London, 1921).

Not always accurate, expecially in the matter of exchequer years.

The problems raised by the dating of documents of the chancery, privy seal office, etc., are discussed in

Maxwell-Lyte, Sir Henry C., *Historical notes on the use of the Great Seal of England* (London, 1926).

For detailed itineraries of English kings the student should consult the following:

Regesta regnum anglo-normannorum 1066–1154: vol. I, *1066–1100*, ed. H. W. C. Davis (Oxford, 1913); vol. II, *1100–1135*, ed. Charles Johnson and H. A. Cronne (Oxford, 1956); vol. III *1135–1154*, ed. H. A. Cronne and R. H. C. Davis (Oxford, 1968).

85. The accounts for the reign of Edward V are included in the Pipe Roll for 1 Richard III.
86. This is the year covered by the first Pipe Roll of Charles II.
87. The last complete Pipe Roll is for 2 William IV.

Regesta Regnum Anglo-Normannorum. The Acta of William I (1066–1087), ed. David Bates (Oxford, 1998).

Eyton, R. W., *Court, household, and itinerary of King Henry II* (London, 1878).

Gough, Henry, *The itinerary of King Edward I*. 2 vols. (Paisley, 1900).
   Should only be used after reference to Maxwell-Lyte's work.

Delisle, Léopold and Berger, Elie (ed.), *Recueil des actes de Henri II roi d' Angleterre et duc de Normandie concernant les provinces françaises et les affaires de France*. 4 vols. (Paris, 1909–27).
   The introductory volume by Delisle (of fundamental importance for the whole study of twelfth-century royal diplomatic) demonstrates the means of dating undated documents.

Landon, Lionel, *The itinerary of King Richard I*. Pipe Roll Soc. Publications, new series, vol. 13 (London, 1935).

Hardy, T. Duffus, *A description of the Patent Rolls* [and] *an itinerary of King John*. Record Commission (London, 1835). The itinerary is also printed in *Archaeologia*, 22 (1829), 124–60 and in *Rotuli litterarum patentium 1201–16*. Record Commission (London, 1835).

For lists of the rulers of Wales, Scotland, and the Isle of Man, see *Handbook of British Chronology* (3rd edn, cf. above, p. xiv), pp. 49–66, with a note on the Scottish regnal year, p. 56. For lists of continental rulers , see Mas Latrie (cited above p. xv).

3

List of Popes

The earliest surviving papal documents to bear dates (AD 384–9) make no use of the pontifical year. Instead, the system of dating by the consulate, taken over from the Roman imperial chancery, is employed. To this the regnal year of the emperor and the year of the indiction were later added, in accordance with the edict of the Emperor Justinian (*Novellæ*, XLVII. i, AD 537). But the political change which brought the papacy under the protection of the Frankish ruler Charlemagne is marked clearly by the disappearance of the Eastern imperial dating from papal letters. From AD 800 the papal chancery uses the imperial year of the emperor in the West at certain periods up to the twelfth century, and from the latter part of the tenth century usually adds the year of grace. Another dating element, however, is more constant and more significant: the pontifical year is generally placed alongside these other dates and often stands alone.

The year of pontificate came to be used as an element in the dating of papal documents late in the eighth century. The earliest known document to show this usage is dated on the Kalends of December in the tenth year of Pope Adrian I (1 December 781). Thereafter the pontifical year frequently appears, and from the eleventh century becomes a regular element, in the dating clause of solemn papal privileges. Its use was extended in February 1188 to other products of the papal chancery. Even outside the Curia, documents were sometimes dated by the pontifical year, but this practice was never common in England.

For purposes of dating official documents, the papal clerks of the twelfth century sometimes calculated the pontifical year from the day of the pope's election. Materials are not sufficiently abundant to prove that this had always been the case in earlier centuries or, indeed, that it was regular in the twelfth century. But from the time of Innocent III onwards, the day of the pope's coronation,[1] not his election, is the determining date.

---

1. Not, as Bresslau says, from his consecration (*Handbuch*, II, 422), for in the rare cases when coronation did not take place on the day of the consecration (as with Leo X), the later date marks the beginning of the pontifical year.

This conforms to the diplomatic practice of issuing only *dimidiæ bullæ* between election and coronation.[2] It is necessary to insist on this system of reckoning because, for the purpose of reckoning the *duration* of a pontificate, it has been usual since the eleventh century to reckon from the day of election,[3] and it is an established principle of canon law that the pope exercises full jurisdiction from that day.[4] At the same time, the reader must be warned that he may encounter dates in papal documents which are inconsistent with this rule. In the first place, the pope sometimes issued letters before coronation, using either the usual formula *pontificatus nostri anno primo* or a special one such as *suscepti a nobis apostolatus officii anno primo*; but the first anniversary of his coronation became the beginning of his second pontifical year, and thereafter the reckoning was normal. More serious divergences from the rule occur, but they may probably be accounted for on the supposition that the papal clerks of the fifteenth century and later sometimes lapsed into error; the inconsistency of letters dated 7 October 1647, *anno 4*, and 9 October 1647, *anno 3*, can hardly be otherwise explained.[5] In this period carelessness was perhaps the more likely to be condoned because the dating clause of all letters and briefs recorded the year of grace as well as the pontifical year.

In the following lists the letter *e* indicates the date of election. There is occasionally a difference of a day or two between this date and the date of publishing the election (e.g. of Leo X, Julius III, Paul V); but in these cases only the earlier date is recorded here. The letter *c* introduces the date of coronation, which is also usually that of consecration or benediction. If the pope-elect has not been chosen from the episcopate, consecration (= *ordinatio*) precedes his coronation. If the elect is already a bishop, the ceremony of benediction precedes the crowning. These ceremonies have usually been reserved for a Sunday or some important festival.

The lists have been compiled from the various souces cited in the bibliographical note, since none of the complete lists (in Gams, Grotefend, etc.) is entirely satisfactory. Even now, as the plentiful marks of interrogation show, many of the dates assigned to pontificates earlier that the twelfth century are conjectural. The indented, bracketed entries concern persons

---

2. These 'half seals' bore the effigies of St Peter and St Paul, but not the name of the new pope. See P. M. Baumgarten, *Aus Kanzlei und Kammer* (Freiburg, 1907), pp. 163–74 and G. Battelli, *Acta pontificum* (Exempla scripturarum, fasc. III, Vatican, 1933), nos. 13, 17, 28.

3. Poole, *Studies*, pp. 154–5.

4. P. Hinschius, *Systems des kath. Kirchenrechts*, I, 291.

5. *Bullarium romanum, sub anno.* Cf. the letter of Pope Paul III, dated 31 Oct. 1537 *anno 4* (*ibid.*, *s.a.*), with his letter dated 22 Oct. 1537 *anno 3* (Battelli, *Acta pontficum*, no. 29). For still earlier errors see *Calendar of papal letters*, ix, pp. xxix–xxx.

whose claim to be included in the list of popes is doubtful or who have definitely been stigmatized as anti-popes by the Roman Church. Some of these were included in the numeration of genuine popes, some were not. Their precise status in certain instances admits of doubt, but that is of no importance for the chronological purposes which this list serves.

1 St Peter and his successors to AD 590[6]

St Peter   *d. c.* 64
Linus   *c.* 66–*c.* 78
Anacletus   *c.* 79–*c.* 91
Clement I   *c.* 91–*c.* 101
Evaristus   *c.* 101–*c.* 109
Alexander I   *c.* 109–*c.* 116
Sixtus I   *c.* 116–*c.* 125
Telesphorus   *c.* 125–*c.* 136
Hyginus   *c.* 138–*c.* 142
Pius I   *c.* 142–*c.* 155
Anicetus   *c.* 155–*c.* 166
Soter   *c.* 166–*c.* 174
Eleutherius   *c.* 174–189
Victor I   189–198
Zephyrinus   198/9–217
Calixtus I   217–222
    [Hippolytus   217–235]
Urban I   222–30
Pontian   21 July 230–28 Sept. 235
Anterus   21 Nov. 235–3 Jan. 236
Fabian   10 Jan. 236–20 Jan. 250
Cornelius   Mar. 251–June 253
    [Novation   Mar. 251–258]
Lucius I   25 June 253–5 Mar. 254
Stephen I   12 May 254–2 Aug. 257
Sixtus II   Aug. 257–6 Aug. 258
Dionysius   22 July 260–26 Dec. 268
Felix I   3 Jan. 269–30 Dec. 274
Eutychian   4 Jan. 275–7 Dec. 283
Caius/Gaius   17 Dec. 283–22 Apr. 296
Marcellinus   30 June 296–?304
Marcellus I   Nov./Dec. 306–16 Jan. 308
Eusebius   18 Apr. 310–21 Oct. 310
Militiades/Melchiades   2 July 311–10 Jan. 314

6. Information principally derived from J. N. D. Kelly, *The Oxford Dictionary of Popes* (Oxford, 1986).

Silvester I   31 Jan. 314–31 Dec. 335
Mark   18 Jan. 336–7 Oct. 336
Julius I   6 Feb. 337–12 Apr. 352
Liberius   17 May 352–24 Sep. 366
    [Felix II   355–22 Nov. 365]
Damasus I   1 Oct. 366–11 Dec. 384
    [Ursinus   Sep. 366–Nov. 367]
Siricius   Dec. 384–26 Nov. 399
Anastasius I   27 Nov. 399–19 Dec. 401
Innocent I   21 Dec. 401–12 Mar. 417
Zosimus   18 Mar. 417–26 Dec. 418
    [Eulalius   27 Dec. 418–3 Apr. 419; *d.* 423]
Boniface I   28 Dec. 418–4 Sept. 422
Celestine I   10 Sep. 422–27 July 432
Sixtus III   31 July 432–19 Aug. 440
Leo I   Aug./Sep. 440–10 Nov. 461
Hilarus   19 Nov. 461–29 Feb. 468
Simplicius   3 Mar. 468–10 Mar. 483
Felix III   13 Mar. 483–1 Mar. 492
Gelasius I   1 Mar. 492–21 Nov. 496
Anastasius II   24 Nov. 496–19 Nov. 498
Symmachus   22 Nov. 498–19 July 514
    [Laurence   22 Nov. 498–Feb. 499; *d.* 507/8]
Hormisdas   20 July 514–6 Aug. 523
John I   13 Aug. 523–18 May 526
Felix IV (III)   12 July 526–22 Sep. 530
    [Dioscorus   22 Sep. 530–14 Oct. 530]
Boniface II   22 Sep. 530–17 Oct. 532
John II   2 Jan. 533–8 May 535
Agapitus I   13 May 535–22 Apr. 536
Silverus   8 June 536–*abdicated* 11 Nov. 537; *d.* 2 Dec. 537
Vigilius   29 March 537–7 June 555
Pelagius I   16 Apr. 556–3 Mar. 561
John III   17 July 561–13 July 574
Benedict I   2 June 575–30 July 579
Pelagius II   26 Nov. 579–7 Feb. 590

II   From Gregory the Great to John Paul II[7]

Gregory I   *e.* ? Feb. 590; *c.* 3 Sep. 590; *d.* 12 March 604
Sabinian   *c.* 13 Sep. 604; *d.* 22 Feb. 606
Boniface III   *c.* 19 Feb. 607; *d.* 12 Nov. 607
Boniface IV   *c.* 15 Sep. 608; *d.* 8 May 615

7. Amended principally from Kelly, *Dictionary of Popes*.

Deusdedit   *c.* 19 Oct. 615; *d.* 8 Nov. 618
Boniface V   *c.* 23 Dec. 619; *d.* 25 Oct. 625
Honorius I   *c.* ? 27 Oct. 625; *d.* 12 Oct. 638
Severinus   *e.* ? Oct. 638; *c.* 28 May 640; *d.* 2 Aug. 640
John IV   *c.* 24 Dec. 640; *d.* 12 Oct. 642
Theodore I   *c.* 24 Nov. 642; *d.* 14 May 649
Martin I   *c.* 5 July 649; *exiled* 17 June 653; *d.* 26 Sep. 655
Eugenius I   *c.* 10 Aug. 654; *d.* 2 June 657
Vitalian   *c.* 30 July 657; *d.* 27 Jan. 672
Adeodatus   *c.* 11 Apr. 672; *d.* 17 June 676
Donus   *e.* Aug. 676; *c.* 2 Nov. 676; *d.* 11 Apr. 678
Agatho   *c.* 27 June 678; *d.* 10 Jan. 681
Leo II   *e.* before Dec. 681; *c.* 17 Aug. 682; *d.* 3 July 683
Benedict II   *e.* Summer 683; *c.* 26 June 684; *d.* 8 May 685
John V   *c.* 23 July 685; *d.* 2 Aug. 686
Conon   *c.* 21 Oct. 686; *d.* 21 Sep. 687
    [Theodore   *e.* after 21 Sep. 687; *resigned* Oct.–Dec. 687]
    [Paschal   *e.* after 21 Sep. 687; *deposed* after 15 Dec. 687; *d.* ? 692]
Sergius I   *e.* Oct.–Dec. 687; *c.* 15 Dec. 687; *d.* 9 Sep. 701
John VI   *c.* 30 Oct. 701; *d.* 11 Jan. 705
John VII   *c.* 1 March 705; *d.* 18 Oct. 707
Sisinnius   *c.* 15 Jan. 708; *d.* 4 Feb. 708
Constantine I   *c.* 25 March 708; *d.* 9 Apr. 715
Gregory II   *c.* 19 May 715; *d.* 11 Feb. 731
Gregory III   *e.* 11 Feb. 731; *c.* 18 March 731; *d.* 28 Nov. 741
Zacharias   *c.* 3 Dec. 741; *d.* 15 March 752
Stephen (II)[8]   *e.* 22–3 March 752; *d.* 25–6 March 752
Stephen II (III)   *e.* 18–25 March 752; *c.* 26 March 752; *d.* ? 26 Apr. 757
Paul I   *e.* ? 26 Apr. 757; *c.* 29 May 757; *d.* 28 June 767
Constantine II   *e.* 28 June 767; *c.* 5 July 767; *deposed* 6 Aug. 768
    [Philip   *e.* 31 July 768; *deposed* 31 July 768]
Stephen III (IV)   *e.* 1 Aug. 768; *c.* 7 Aug. 768; *d.* 24 Jan. 772
Adrian I   *e.* 1 Feb. 772; *c.* 9 Feb. 772; *d.* 25 Dec. 795
Leo III   *e.* 26 Dec. 795; *c.* 27 Dec. 795; *d.* 12 June 816
Stephen IV (V)   *c.* 22 June 816; *d.* 24 Jan. 817
Paschal I   *c.* 24 Jan. 817; *d.* ? 11 Feb. 824
Eugenius II   *c.* before 6 June 824; *d.* ?27 Aug. 827
Valentine   *c.* ? Aug. 827; *d.* ? Sep. 827
Gregory IV   *e.* Dec. 827; *c.* 5 Jan. 828; *d.* 25 Jan. 844
    [John   ? Jan 844]
Sergius II   *c.* ? Jan. 844; *d. before* 27 Jan. 847
Leo IV   *c.* 10 Apr. 847; *d.* 17 July 855

8. This Stephen was not reckoned in the numeration of popes of this name in the Middle Ages. The more recent numbering of the later Stephens, which includes him, has no old authority and is not now regularly employed. Cf. R. L. Poole, *Studies*, pp. 168–70.

Benedict III   *e.* 17 July 855; *c.* ? 6 Oct. 855; *d.* ? 17 Apr. 858
    [Anastasius   *e.* Aug. 855; *expelled* 24 Sep. 855]
Nicholas I   *c.* 24 Apr. 858; *d.* 13 Nov. 867
Adrian II   *c.* 14 Dec. 867; *d.* ? 14 Dec. 872
John VIII   *c.* 14 Dec. 872; *d.* 16 Dec. 882
Marinus I (called Martin II)   *c.* 16 Dec. 882; *d.* 15 May 884
Adrian III   *c.* 17 May 884; *d.* Sep. 885
Stephen V (VI)   *c.* ? Sep. 885; *d.* 14 Sep. 891
Formosus   *e.* ? late Sep. 891; *c.* ? 6 Oct. 891; *d.* 4 Apr. 896
    [Boniface VI   *e.* Apr. 896; *d.* ? May 896]
Stephen VI (VII)   *e.* ? May 896; *expelled* ? Aug. 897
Romanus   *c.* ? early Aug. 897; *d.* ? Nov. 897
Theodore II   *c.* ? Nov. 897; *d.* ? Dec. 897
John IX   *e.* ? Jan. 898; *c.* June ? 898; *d.* Jan. 900
Benedict IV   *c.* 900; *d.* Aug. 903
Leo V   *e.* Aug. 903; *d.* early 904
    [Christopher   *c.* ? Sep. 903; *expelled* Jan. 904]
Sergius III   *c.* 29 Jan. 904; *d.* 14 Apr. 911
Anastasius III   *c.* ? June 911; *d.* Aug. 913
Lando   *c.* Aug. 913; *d.* Mar. 914
John X   *c.* March 914; *deposed* ? May 928; *d.* ? 929
Leo VI   *c.* ? May 928; *d.* ? Dec. 928
Stephen VII (VIII)   *c.* ? Dec. 928; *d.* ? Feb. 931
John XI   *c.* Feb.–Mar. 931; *d.* Dec. 935–Jan. 936
Leo VII   *c.* ? 3 Jan. 936; *d.* 13 July 939
Stephen VIII (IX)   *c.* ? 14 July 939; *d.* ? late Oct. 942
Marinus II (called Martin III)   *c.* ? 30 Oct. 942; *d.* early May 946
Agapitus II   *c.* 10 May 946; *d.* Dec. 955
John XII   *c.* ? 16 Dec. 955; *deposed* 4 Dec. 963; *d.* 14 May 964
Leo VIII   *e.* 4 Dec. 963; *c.* 6 Dec. 963; *d.* 1 March 965
Benedict V   *c.* ? 22 May 964; *deposed* 23 June 964; *d.* 4 July 966
John XIII   *c.* 1 Oct. 965; *d.* 6 Sep. 972
Benedict VI   *c.* 19 Jan. 973; *d.* July 974
    [Boniface VII   *e.* ? June 974; *expelled* ? July 974]
Benedict VII   *c.* Oct. 974; *d.* 10 July 983
John XIV[9]   *c.* ? Aug. or Dec. 983; *deposed* Apr. 984; *d.* 20 Aug. 984
    [Boniface VII   *returned* Aug. 984; *d.* July 985]
John XV   *c.* ? Aug. 985; *d.* Mar. 996
Gregory V   *c.* 3 May 996; *d.* 18 Feb. 999
    [John XVI   *c* .? Apr. 997; *deposed* May 998; *d.* 26 Aug. 1001]
Silvester II   *e.* ? early Apr. 999; *c.* ? 2 or 9 Apr. 999; *d.* 12 May 1003

9. Owing to a corrupt text, the period of this pontificate was in the thirteenth century
    assigned to two popes, John XIV and John XV; in consequence, the real John XV was
    reckoned as John XVI, and so on to John XIX, who was called John XX in some late lists.
    When in 1276 another pope took the name of John, he was called John XXI. Cf. R. L. Poole,
    Studies, pp. 166–7.

John XVII   *c.* 16 May 1003; *d.* 6 Nov. 1003
John XVIII   *c.* 25 Dec. 1003; *d.* ? July 1009
Sergius IV   *c.* ? 31 July 1009; *d.* 12 May 1012
Benedict VIII   *e.* ? 17 May 1012; *c.* 18 May 1012; *d.* 7 or 9 Apr. 1024
   [Gregory   *e.* ? May 1012; *expelled* late 1012]
John XIX   *c.* 19 April 1024; *d.* 20 Oct. 1032
Benedict IX   *e.* 21 Oct. 1032; *c.* ? 17 Dec. 1032; *resigned* Sept. 1044; 10 Mar.–1 May 1045;
          deposed 20 Dec. 1046
   [Silvester III   *e.* 10 Jan. 1045; *c.* 13 or 20 Jan. 1045; *deposed* 10 March 1045; *d.* 1063]
Gregory VI   *e.* 1 May 1045; *c.* ? 5 May 1045; *deposed* 20 Dec. 1046; *d.* 1047
Clement II   *e.* 24 Dec. 1046; *c.* 25 Dec. 1046; *d.* 9 Oct. 1047
Benedict IX   *returned* 8 Nov. 1047; *expelled* 16 July 1048; *d.* 1055/6
Damasus II   *e.* Dec. 1047; *c.* 17 July 1048; *d.* 9 Aug. 1048
Leo IX   *e.* Dec. 1048; *c.* 12 Feb. 1049; *d.* 19 Apr. 1054
Victor II   *e.* late 1054; *c.* 13 Apr. 1055; *d.* 28 July 1057
Stephen IX (X)   *e.* 2 Aug. 1057; *c.* 3 Aug. 1057; *d.* 29 March 1058
Benedict X   *e.* 4 or 5 Apr. 1058; *c.* 5 Apr. 1058; *deposed* 24 Jan. 1059
Nicholas II   *e.* 6 Dec. 1058; *c.* 24 Jan. 1059; *d.* 19 or 26 July 1061
Alexander II   *e.* 29 or 30 Sep. 1061; *c.* 30 Sep. 1061; 21 Apr. 1073
   [Honorius II   *c.* 28 Oct. 1061; *d.* late 1072]
Gregory VII   *e.* 22 Apr. 1073; *c.* 29 or 30 June 1073; *d.* 25 May 1085
   [Clement III   *e.* 25 June 1080; *c.* 24 March 1084; *d.* 8 Sep. 1100]
Victor III   *e.* 24 May 1086; *c.* 9 May 1087; *d.* 16 Sep. 1087
Urban II   *e.* and *c.* 12 March 1088; *d.* 29 July 1099
Paschal II   *e.* 13 Aug. 1099; *c.* 14 Aug. 1099; *d.* 21 Jan. 1118
   [Theodoric   *c.* Sep. 1100; *expelled* Jan. 1101; *d.* 1102]
   [Albert   *e.* and *deposed* Feb.–March 1101]
   [Silvester IV   *e.* 18 Nov. 1105; *deposed* 12 Apr. 1111]
Gelasius II   *e.* 24 Jan. 1118; *c.* 10 March 1118; *d.* 29 Jan. 1119
   [Gregory VIII   *e.* and *c.* 8 March 1118; *deposed* Apr. 1121; *d. c.* 1140]
Calixtus II   *e.* 2 Feb. 1119; *c.* 9 Feb. 1119; *d.* 14 Dec. 1124
Celestine (II)   *e.* 15/16 Dec. 1124; *d.* 1125/6
Honorius II   *e.* 16 Dec. 1124; *c.* 21 Dec. 1124; *d.* 13 or 14 Feb. 1130
Innocent II   *e.* 14 Feb. 1130; *c.* 23 Feb. 1130; *d.* 24 Sep. 1143
   [Anacletus II   *e.* 14 Feb. 1130; *c.* 23 Feb. 1130; *d.* 25 Jan. 1138]
   [Victor IV   *e.* ? 15 March 1138; *resigned* 29 May 1138]
Celestine II   *e.* and *c.* 26 Sep. 1143; 8 March 1144
Lucius II   *e.* 12 March 1144; *d.* 15 Feb. 1145
Eugenius III   *e.* 15 Feb. 1145; *c.* 18 Feb. 1145; *d.* 8 July 1153
Anastasius IV   *e.* or *c.* 8 July 1153; *d.* 3 Dec. 1154
Adrian IV   *e.* 4 Dec. 1154; *c.* 5 Dec. 1154; *d.* 1 Sep. 1159
Alexander III   *e.* 7 Sep. 1159; *c.* 20 Sep. 1159; *d.* 30 Aug. 1181
   [Victor IV   *e.* 7 Sep. 1159; *c.* 4 Oct. 1159; *d.* 20 Apr. 1164]
   [Paschal III   *e.* 22 Apr. 1164; *c.* 26 Apr. 1164; *d.* 20 Sep. 1168]
   [Calixtus III   *e.* ? Sep. 1168; *resigned* 29 Aug. 1178; *d. c.* 1183]
   [Innocent III   *e.* ? 29 Sep. 1179; *deposed* Jan. 1180]

Lucius III   *e.* 1 Sep. 1181; *c.* 6 Sep. 1181; *d.* 25 Nov. 1185
Urban III   *e.* 25 Nov. 1185; *c.* 1 Dec. 1185; *d.* 20 Oct. 1187
Gregory VIII   *e.* 21 Oct. 1187; *c.* 25 Oct. 1187; *d.* 17 Dec. 1187
Clement III   *e.* 19 Dec. 1187; *c.* 20 Dec. 1187; *d.* late March 1191
Celestine III   *e.* 30 March 1191; *c.* 14 Apr. 1191; *d.* 8 Jan. 1198
Innocent III   *e.* 8 Jan. 1198; *c.* 22 Feb. 1198; *d.* 16 July 1216
Honorius III   *e.* 18 July 1216; *c.* 24 July 1216; *d.* 18 March 1227
Gregory IX   *e.* 19 March 1227; *c.* 21 March 1227; *d.* 22 Aug. 1241
Celestine IV   *e.* 25 Oct. 1241; *c.* ? 27 Oct. 1241; *d.* 10 Nov. 1241
Innocent IV   *e.* 25 June 1243; *c.* 28 June 1243; *d.* 7 Dec. 1254
Alexander IV   *e.* 12 Dec. 1254; *c.* 20 Dec. 1254; *d.* 25 May 1261
Urban IV   *e.* 29 Aug. 1261; *c.* 4 Sep. 1261; *d.* 2 Oct. 1264
Clement IV   *e.* 5 Feb. 1265; *c.* 15 Feb. 1265; *d.* 29 Nov. 1268
Gregory X   *e.* 1 Sep. 1271; *c.* 27 March 1272; *d.* 10 Jan. 1276
Innocent V   *e.* 21 Jan. 1276; *c.* 22 Feb. 1276; *d.* 22 June 1276
Adrian V   *e.* 11 July 1276; *d.* 18 Aug. 1276
John XXI   *e.* ? 8 Sep. 1276; *c.* 20 Sep. 1276; *d.* 20 May 1277
Nicholas III   *e.* 25 Nov. 1277; *c.* 26 Dec. 1277; *d.* 22 Aug. 1280
Martin IV   *e.* 22 Feb. 1281; *c.* 23 March 1281; *d.* 28 March 1285
Honorius IV   *e.* 2 Apr. 1285; *c.* 20 May 1285; *d.* 3 Apr. 1287
Nicholas IV   *e.* 15–22 Feb. 1288; *c.* 22 Feb. 1288; *d.* 4 Apr. 1292
Celestine V   *e.* 5 July 1294; *c.* 29 Aug. 1294; *resigned* 13 Dec. 1294; *d.* 19 May 1296
Boniface VIII   *e.* 24 Dec. 1294; *c.* 23 Jan. 1295; *d.* 11 Oct. 1303
Benedict XI   *e.* 22 Oct. 1303; *c.* 27 Oct. 1303; *d.* 7 July 1304
Clement V   *e.* 5 June 1305; *c.* 14 Nov. 1305; *d.* 20 Apr. 1314
John XXII   *e.* 7 Aug. 1316; *c.* 5 Sep. 1316; *d.* 4 Dec. 1334
    [Nicholas V   *e.* 12 May 1328; *c.* 22 May 1328; *resigned* 25 July 1330; *d.* 16 Oct. 1333]
Benedict XII   *e.* 20 Dec. 1334; *c.* 8 Jan. 1335; *d.* 25 Apr. 1342
Clement VI   *e.* 7 May 1342; *c.* 19 May 1342; *d.* 6 Dec. 1352
Innocent VI   *e.* 18 Dec. 1352; *c.* 30 Dec. 1352; *d.* 12 Sep. 1362
Urban V   *e.* 28 Sep. 1362; *c.* 6 Nov. 1362; *d.* 19 Dec. 1370
Gregory XI   *e.* 30 Dec. 1370; *c.* 5 Jan. 1371; *d.* 27 March 1378
Urban VI   *e.* 8 Apr. 1378; *c.* 18 Apr. 1378; *d.* 15 Oct. 1389
    [Clement VII   *e.* 20 Sep. 1378; *c.* 31 Oct. 1378; *d.* 16 Sep. 1394]
Boniface IX   *e.* 2 Nov. 1389; *c.* 9 Nov. 1389; *d.* Oct. 1404
    [Benedict XIII   *e.* 28 Sep. 1394; *c.* 11 Oct. 1394; *deposed by Council of Pisa* 5 June 1409 *and
        by Council of Constance* 26 July 1417; *d.* 23 May 1423]
Innocent VII   *e.* 17 Oct. 1404; *c.* 11 Nov. 1404; *d.* 6 Nov. 1406
Gregory XII   *e.* 30 Nov. 1406; *c.* 19 Dec. 1406; *deposed by Council of Pisa* 5 June 1409;
        resigned 4 July 1415
Alexander V   *e.* 26 June 1409; *c.* 7 July 1409; *d.* 3 May 1410
John XXIII   *e.* 17 May 1410; *c.* 25 May 1410; *deposed by Council of Constance* 29 May 1415; *d.*
        22 Nov. 1419
Martin V   *e.* 11 Nov. 1417; *c.* 21 Nov. 1417; *d.* 20 Feb. 1431
    [Clement VIII   *e.* 10 June 1423; *resigned* 26 July 1429; *d.* 28 Dec. 1446]
    [Benedict XIV   *e.* 12 Nov. 1423; *d. c.*1430]

Eugenius IV   *e.* 3 March 1431; *c.* 11 March 1431; *suspended by Council of Basel* 24 Jan. 1438
   and deposed by the Council 25 June 1439; *d.* 23 Feb. 1447
[Felix V   *e.* 5 Nov. 1439; *c.* 24 July 1440; *resigned* 7 Apr. 1449; *d.* 7 Jan. 1451]
Nicholas V   *e.* 6 March 1447; *c.* 19 March 1447; *d.* 24 March 1455
Calixtus III   *e.* 8 Apr. 1455; *c.* 20 Apr. 1455; *d.* 6 Aug. 1458
Pius II   *e.* 19 Aug. 1458; *c.* 3 Sep. 1458; *d.* 15 Aug. 1464
Paul II   *e.* 30 Aug. 1464; *c.* 16 Sep. 1464; *d.* 26 July 1471
Sixtus IV   *e.* 9 Aug. 1471; *c.* 25 Aug. 1471; *d.* 12 Aug. 1484
Innocent VIII   *e.* 29 Aug. 1484; *c.* 12 Sep. 1484; *d.* 25 July 1492
Alexander VI   *e.* 11 Aug. 1492; *c.* 26 Aug. 1492; *d.* 18 Aug. 1503
Pius III   *e.* 22 Sep. 1503; *cons.* 1 Oct. 1503; *c.* 8 Oct. 1503; *d.* 18 Oct. 1503
Julius II   *e.* 1 Nov. 1503; *c.* 26 Nov. 1503; *d.* 20–21 Feb. 1513
Leo X   *e.* 11 March 1513; *cons.* 17 March 1513; *c.* 19 March 1513; *d.* 1 Dec. 1521
Adrian VI   *e.* 9 Jan. 1522; *c.* 31 Aug. 1522; *d.* 14 Sep. 1523
Clement VII   *e.* 19 Nov. 1523; *c.* 26 Nov. 1523; *d.* 25 Sep. 1534
Paul III   *e.* 13 Oct. 1534; *c.* 1 Nov. 1534; *d.* 10 Nov. 1549
Julius III   *e.* 8 Feb. 1550; *c.* 22 Feb. 1550; *d.* 23 March 1555
Marcellus II   *e.* 9 Apr. 1555; *c.* 10 Apr. 1555; *d.* 1 May 1555
Paul IV   *e.* 23 May 1555; *c.* 26 May 1555; *d.* 18 Aug. 1559
Pius IV   *e.* 25 Dec. 1559; *c.* 6 Jan. 1560; *d.* 9 Dec. 1565
Pius V   *e.* 7 Jan. 1566; *c.* 17 Jan. 1566; *d.* 1 May 1572
Gregory XIII   *e.* 14 May 1572; *c.* 25 May 1572; *d.* 10 Apr. 1585[10]
Sixtus V   *e.* 24 Apr. 1585; *c.* 1 May 1585; *d.* 27 Aug. 1590
Urban VII   *e.* 15 Sep. 1590; *d.* 27 Sep. 1590
Gregory XIV   *e.* 5 Dec. 1590; *c.* 8 Dec. 1590; *d.* 16 Oct. 1591
Innocent IX   *e.* 29 Oct. 1591; *c.* 3 Nov. 1591; *d.* 30 Dec. 1591
Clement VIII   *e.* 30 Jan. 1592; *c.* 9 Feb. 1592; *d.* 3 March 1605
Leo XI   *e.* 1 Apr. 1605; *c.* 10 Apr. 1605; *d.* 27 Apr. 1605
Paul V   *e.* 16 May 1605; *c.* 29 May 1605; *d.* 28 Jan. 1621
Gregory XV   *e.* 9 Feb. 1621; *c.* 14 Feb. 1621; *d.* 8 July 1623
Urban VIII   *e.* 6 Aug. 1623; *c.* 29 Sep. 1623; *d.* 29 July 1644
Innocent X   *e.* 15 Sep. 1644; *c.* 4 Oct. 1644; *d.* 1 Jan. 1655
Alexander VII   *e.* 7 Apr. 1655; *c.* 18 Apr. 1655; *d.* 22 May 1667
Clement IX   *e.* 20 June 1667; *c.* 26 June 1667; *d.* 9 Dec. 1669
Clement X   *e.* 29 Apr. 1670; *c.* 11 May 1670; *d.* 22 July 1676
Innocent XI   *e.* 21 Sep. 1676; *c.* 4 Oct. 1676; *d.* 12 Aug. 1689
Alexander VIII   *e.* 6 Oct. 1689; *c.* 16 Oct. 1689; *d.* 1 Feb. 1691
Innocent XII   *e.* 12 July 1691; *c.* 15 July 1691; *d.* 27 Sep. 1700
Clement XI   *e.* 23 Nov. 1700; *cons.* 30 Nov. 1700; *c.* 8 Dec. 1700; *d.* 19 Mar. 1721
Innocent XIII   *e.* 8 May 1721; *c.* 18 May 1721; *d.* 7 March 1724
Benedict XIII   *e.* 29 May 1724; *c.* 4 June 1724; *d.* 21 Feb. 1730
Clement XII   *e.* 12 July 1730; *c.* 16 July 1730; *d.* 6 Feb. 1740

10. This date, and all succeeding ones in this table, are given in the New Style introduced by
   Pope Gregory XIII's reformed calendar in 1582. For the adjustments necessary for turning
   these dates into the Old Style of reckoning, see p. 18.

Benedict XIV   *e.* 17 Aug. 1740; *c.* 22 Aug. 1740; *d.* 3 May 1758
Clement XIII   *e.* 6 July 1758; *c.* 16 July 1758; *d.* 2 Feb. 1769
Clement XIV   *e.* 19 May 1769; *cons.* 28 May 1769; *c.* 4 June 1769; *d.* 22 Sep. 1774
Pius VI   *e.* 15 Feb. 1775; *c.* 22 Feb. 1775; *d.* 29 Aug. 1799
Pius VII   *e.* 14 March 1800; *c.* 21 March 1800; *d.* 20 July 1823
Leo XII   *e.* 28 Sep. 1823; *c.* 5 Oct. 1823; *d.* 10 Feb. 1829
Pius VIII   *e.* 31 March 1829; *c.* 5 Apr. 1829; *d.* 30 Nov. 1830
Gregory XVI   *e.* 2 Feb. 1831; *c.* 6 Feb. 1631; *d.* 1 June 1846
Pius IX   *e.* 16 June 1846; *c.* 21 June 1846; *d.* 7 Feb. 1878
Leo XIII   *e.* 20 Feb. 1878; *c.* 3 March 1878; *d.* 20 July 1903
Pius X   *e.* 4 Aug. 1903; *c.* 9 Aug. 1903; *d.* 20 Aug. 1914
Benedict XV   *e.* 3 Sep. 1914; *c.* 6 Sep. 1914; *d.* 22 Jan. 1922
Pius XI   *e.* 6 Feb. 1922; *c.* 12 Feb. 1922; *d.* 10 Feb. 1939
Pius XII   *e.* 2 March 1939; *c.* 12 March 1939; *d.* 9 Oct. 1958
John XXIII   *e.* 28 Oct. 1958; *c.* 4 Nov. 1958; *d.* 3 June 1963
Paul VI   *e.* 21 June 1963; *c.* 30 June 1963; *d.* 6 Aug. 1978
John Paul I   *e.* 26 Aug. 1978; *c.* 3 Sept. 1978; *d.* 28 Sept. 1978
John Paul II   *e.* 16 Oct. 1978; *c.* 22 Oct. 1978

BIBLIOGRAPHY
Papal chronology

Annuario pontificio per l'anno 1980 (Vatican City, 1980).

> This official annual, replacing the earlier *La gerarchia cattolica*, contains a dated list of popes from St Peter to the present. The list has been taken into account (but not followed at all points) on pp. 50–7.

Buzzi, G., 'Per la cronologia d'alcuni pontefici dei dec. x e xi', *Archivio della Società romana di storia patria*, (1912), 611–22.

> Suggests some dates differing from the dating of Poole's studies (see below). Poole's dating is followed on pp. 53–4 above.

Cheney, C. R. and Mary G. (ed.), *The letters of Pope Innocent III (1198–1216) concerning England and Wales: a calendar with an appendix of texts* (Oxford, 1967).

*Duchesne, Louis (ed.), *Le Liber Pontificalis. Texte, introduction, et commentaire.* 2 vols. (Paris, 1886–92).

> Provides a list of popes to the thirteenth century which improves on Gams's list.

*Eubel, Conrad and Gauchat, Patricius, *Hierarchia catholica medii et recentioris aevi*. Vol. I, *1198–1431* (2nd edn, Münster, 1913); vol. II, *1431–1503* (2nd edn, 1914); vol. III, *1503–1600* (2nd edn, 1923); vol. IV, *1592–1667* (1935). Continued by R. Ritzler and R. Sefrin, vol. V, *1667–1730* (1952); vol. VI, *1730–1799* (1958); vol. VII, *1800–1846* (1968).

> More elaborate and accurate than Gams.

Gams, P. B., *Series episcoporum ecclesiae catholicae* (1873 and 1886, reprinted in one volume, Leipzig, 1931).

Kelly, J. N. D., *The Oxford Dictionary of Popes* (Oxford, 1986).

Menzer, A., 'Die Jahresmerkmale in den Datierung der Papsturkunden bis zum Ausgang des XI Jahrhunderts', *Römisches Quartalschrift*, 40 (1932), 27–99.

*Poole, R. L., 'Papal chronology in the eleventh century', *Eng. Hist. Rev.,* 32 (1917), 204–14, reprinted in Poole's *Studies*, pp. 144–55.

'The names and numbers of medieval popes', *Eng. Hist. Rev.,* 32 (1917), 465–78, reprinted
    in *Studies*, pp. 156–71.
'Imperial influences on the forms of papal documents', *Proceedings of the British Academy*, 8
    (1917), reprinted in *Studies*, pp. 172–84.

For detailed itineraries of medieval popes the student should consult the published calendars and collections of their acts, particularly:

*Bliss, W. H., et al., (ed.), *Calendar of entries in the papal registers relating to Great Britain and
    Ireland*, vols. I–XVIII. AD 1198–1503 (London, 1893–1960; Dublin: Irish Manuscripts
    Commission, 1978–94).

*Jaffe, P. (ed.), *Regesta pontificum romanorum ad annum 1198*. 2nd ed., by S. Loewenfeld, etc.
    2 vols. (Berlin, 1885–6).

*Potthast, August (ed.), *Regesta pontificum romanorum* A.D. *1198–1304* (Berlin, 1874–5).

Pressutti, P. (ed.), *Regesta Honorii papae tertii*, 2 vols. (Rome, 1888–95).

Registers published by the *Ecole française de Rome* during the past hundred years.

The *Bullarium romanum* provides material for the later period. The larger general histories
of the papacy also provide a starting-point for chronological enquiries: the works of
E. Caspar, H. K. Mann, and L. Pastor may be mentioned; also, F. Gregorovius' history of the
city of Rome (Eng. trans.), and C. J. Hefele's history of church councils in the French
edition by H. Leclercq.

4

Saints' days and festivals
used in dating

Reference has been made (above, p. 15) to the widespread practice of dating by the nearest festival of the Church. Sometimes this is additional to the dating by the Roman calendar, as when the Anglo-Saxon chronicler writes, *sub anno* 1122: 'Siððons on þaes daei vi Idus Sept. þet was on Sancte Marie messedaei'. At other times one observes in a single class of medieval records, or in a single chronicle, the use of either method indifferently. In the annals of Tewkesbury, for example, the abbot of Pershore and the Emperor Frederick II expire in adjacent sentences, the one on 'iii non. Martii' and the other 'in vigilia Sancti Lucæ'. A glance through any long series of letters of identical nature, such as the excuses sent by bishops, abbots, and others unable to attend parliament, preserved in the Public Record Office files of parliamentary proxies, illustrates the variety of methods in use. But in general it may be said that the method of dating by festivals was early in favour with chroniclers and only in the thirteenth century became usual in dating letters and other documents. It was also used very early for specifying the days of markets and fairs, or those on which rents or other payments were due: of some such we are reminded in modern times by the fact that our English quarter-days still correspond with four Church festivals (Christmas, the Annunciation, the Nativity of St John the Baptist, and Michaelmas), and other days were similarly used, such as the Conversion of St Paul and the feast of St James the Apostle.[1] Hocktide, the second Monday and Tuesday after Easter, was a movable feast often specified for the payment of rents.

A list of saints' days and festivals, in order to be of assistance in problems of dating, must be based on the material and the usage of the country concerned. The list given below is an attempt to help specially the student of English history indicating to him whence each entry is derived and

1. The Scottish quarter-days are the Purification, or Candlemas (2 February), Whit-Sunday (fixed at 15 May), Lammas (1 August), and Martinmas (11 November).

where he may expect to find a particular observance in use. The form of the list is dictated by the nature of its sources, and this must next be explained.

The medieval calendars, upon which such lists as this are naturally based, were themselves highly individual. It was not merely a question of what one might call geographical variation – between the use of Sarum, the use of York, and so on; between Scotland, Ireland, and Wales; between saints of giant ecclesiastical stature, universally honoured, and others who, though pigmies to the general vision, were in their own localities themselves giants. There was further variation due to emulation or tradition or prejudice of many kinds; between abbeys and churches in close geographical proximity; between (for a while) the Norman conqueror and the English he had conquered. The Abingdon chronicler tells us that the first Norman abbot forbade 'that any memorial or commemoration should be made of St Ethelwold or of St Edward, for he said they were English boors'. Eadmer tells us how doubtful Lanfranc was as to the claims of certain saints venerated by the English, and how Anselm convinced him that Alphege was indeed 'a great and glorious martyr'. All three saints, of course, retained their place in the affections of medieval England, despite these early dangers.[2] Similarly, whereas in the calendar prefixed to the psalter written by Eadwine, monk of Christ Church, Canterbury, about the middle of the twelfth century, 'very little notice is taken ... either of Augustine or his early successors',[3] because of the feud between the monastery and the adjacent abbey of St Augustine's, where the first ten archbishops lay buried, that too was a distinction which rightly disappeared in later Christ Church calendars.

It is not easy for the historian to bear always in mind the background which explains the dating peculiarities of the documents he is using. An example may illustrate the kind of problem which may arise. Two famous saints of the same name were St Thomas the Apostle and St Thomas of Canterbury. The feast of the former was observed on 21 December, his translation on 3 July; the feast of the latter was 29 December, his translation 7 July. In both cases, the dates are so near each other that the historian may be at a loss to know which is meant if no distinguishing epithet is given. Thus, when an exchequer ordinance of 1324 directed that the year of account for the royal wardrobe should end 'a la feste de la Translacion

---

2. Both incidents are cited by G. G. Coulton, *Five centuries of religion*, III, 4.

3. M. R. James, *The Canterbury psalter*, Introduction

Seynt Thomas', even so practised a medievalist as the late Professor Tout was caught napping. He commented: 'The regnal year of Edward II ended on 7 July. The wardrobe year, according to the ordinance, ended on 3 July. I do not understand why there was this difference of four days.'[4] The translation referred to however, was that of St Thomas of Canterbury, exactly coincident in date with the close of Edward II's regnal year. An exchequer clerk would take that for granted, for in calendars used for reference in his office, such as that prefixed to the thirteenth-century Black Book of the Exchequer,[5] he would see for St Thomas the Apostle merely his feast on 21 December, whereas there appeared for St Thomas of Canterbury his feast, its octave, and his translation.

It is of course impossible, in a mere hand-list for ready reference, to treat exhaustively problems of origin and variation.[6] It is hoped, however, that the appended list may at any rate draw attention to some important categories in which individuality of dating may be expected. Entries bear a superior letter showing the source from which they are derived. Thus a superior e (^{e}), indicating that the entry came from an exchequer source, marks the translation of St Thomas of Canterbury, but not that of his namesake, so that our list would give a hint towards the solution of the apparent discrepancy above. It must be clearly understood, however, that while the superior letter gives a guarantee that the feast so marked was in use in the category indicated, the inference must not be made that its use was exclusive to that category.

Three main groups of original sources were used in the compilation of the list:

(1) Its nucleus consists of 168 entries taken from the Black Book calendar mentioned above, which was probably first written between 1252 and 1260, with many additions inserted as time went on. This calendar was chosen as starting-point, partly because of its chronological position in the heart of the Middle Ages, partly because the ramifications of a financial department so old and so important produced innumerable records and influenced innumerable datings. The resultant list was then tested from an official source of a different kind and half a century later in date, namely, three rolls, covering the period from November 1299 to

4. T. F. Tout, *The place of Edward II in history* (2nd edn, 1936), p. 179, n. 1.
5. A Public Record Office MS (T. R. Misc. Books, no. 266); see Giuseppi, *Guide to the public records*, I, 210. It is not to be confused with the earlier 'liber niger parvus' (K. R. Misc. Books, series I, vol. 12), printed by Thomas Hearne (1728) under the title *Liber niger scaccarii*.
6. D. H. Farmer, *The Oxford Dictionary of Saints* (Oxford, 1978) provides more detailed discussion of variations in observance.

November 1302,[7] in which Edward I's almoner set down each day the number of poor fed at the king's expense as the court travelled about the country, and the name of the saint is thus honoured. Only seven fresh names were thus obtained, so that it is evident that the Black Book calendar might still serve at that date as a good guide to the saints most frequently quoted in court and official circles.

(2) It seemed desirable next to examine some source which presented a different range of interests and covered a wider period. This was found in the *Index et concordantia festorum*, compiled by Canon Christopher Wordsworth, from six calendars of the universities of Oxford, Cambridge, and Paris, varying in date from the fourteenth to late in the fifteenth century, together with the *Compotus manualis ad usum Oxoniensium* printed in 1519–20, from which he himself constructed a calendar.[8] The ninety entries added to our list from this source are of considerable interest. They bring in such saints as St Anne, whose commemoration was not introduced until late in the fourteenth century, scholastic philosophers or famous religious (St Thomas Aquinas, St Dominic, St Gilbert of Sempringham, St Anthony of Padua), and also names reflecting the varied origins of university students (St William of York, St Peter of Milan, St Patrick).

(3) The augmented list was next compared with calendars originating from Canterbury, Salisbury, Hereford, and York,[9] with the result that some ninety entries were added. Not many additions came from the Sarum, since that Use was the foundation of several calendars which had already been utilized. The Canterbury group, which ranged from the twelfth to the fifteenth century, included a secular specimen from the Black Book of the Archdeacon, as well as monastic examples from Christ Church and St Augustine's. The printed edition of the thirteenth-century Hereford breviary includes also a fifteenth-century Worcester small breviary; both sources provide additions. This section of the list was completed by a few entries of a miscellaneous kind (and therefore in most cases not marked in the list by any special indication), coming either from local uses (e.g., Glastonbury, Winchester, and Durham), or found in use in chronicles or other sources when a number of these were examined in order to

7. PRO, Exchequer Acts., KR, 357/29, 359/15, 361/21.
8. The *Index* occupies pp. 257–64 of Wordsworth's *Ancient Kalendar of the University of Oxford*; the other texts are printed in the same volume. Entries which appear in the Paris calendar only have not been included in the present list.
9. Examined in the texts listed in the bibliography, below, pp. 94–5.

test the usefulness of the list at the point now reached. Feasts of the dedication of churches have not been included.

The various Protestant Reformations of the sixteenth century introduced a series of new festal calendars, of which the Elizabethan one became standard. It cut the number of holy days down to those of the Apostles, Evangelists, and a few other major saints, but the number of days upon which bells were rung, services held, and popular celebrations organized was swelled from two political sources. One consisted of accession, coronation, and birth dates of reigning monarchs, of which Elizabeth's accession day (17 November) became the focus of an unofficial Protestant cult which lasted until the eighteenth century and Charles II's birthday was made the official annual thanksgiving for the Reformation, observed till the nineteenth. The other was the annual thanksgiving for the discovery of the Gunpowder Plot, which was officially maintained from 1606 to 1858, and still has much local commemoration at the present.[10]

Finally, the list includes selected appellations, local, liturgical, and traditional, given to certain days and seasons in medieval England. One liturgical dating element calls for note. Introits to the mass for Sundays after Pentecost are indicated here as they fitted into the normal English ecclesiastical calendars of the Middle Ages; but divergences of usage call for caution, as stressed by Grotefend, *Taschenbuch*, pp. 21–2.

I List of saints' days and other festivals[11]

Most of the abbreviations used below are obvious – *m.*, martyr, *reg.*, regina, etc. *Presbyter* is shortened to *pr.* and *papa* to *p.* The description used is not necessarily in every case that given in the calendar from which the entry was taken.

abb.	abbot/abbess
ap.	apostle
archiep.	archbishop
b.	blessed
doct.	doctor

10. Paragraph kindly contributed by Professor Ronald Hutton.
11. Readers searching for saints whose names do not appear in this list, are advised to consult D. H. Farmer, *The Oxford dictionary of saints*, 2nd edn (Oxford, 1987) and the *Bibliotheca sanctorum*, 13 vols. (Rome: Istituto Giovanni XXIII della Pontifica Universita Lateranense, 1961–70, and Supplement, 1987).

Saints' days and festivals

ep.	bishop
evan.	evangelist
m.	martyr
mm.	martyrs
pr.	priest
protom.	protomartyr
p.	pope
r.	king
reg.	queen
soc.	fellow (member of order)
v.	virgin

Sources are indicated by superior letters as follows

ᵃ = alms rolls
ᶜᵃ = Canterbury calendars
ᵉ = Black Book of the Exchequer
ʰ = Hereford breviary
ʰʷ = Hereford and Worcester breviaries
ˢᵃ = Sarum gradual
ᵘ = University calendars
ʷ = Worcester breviary
ʷⁱⁿ = Winchester calendar
ʸ = York breviary

A

Abdon et Sennes, *mm.*ᵉ	30 July
Absolution	*see Dies Absolutionis*
Achilleus	*see* Nereus et Achilleus
Ad te levavi	1st Sun. in Advent
Adam creatus est	23 March
Adauctus	*see* Felix et Adauctus
Adelburga	*see* Ethelburga
Adeldreda	*see* Etheldreda
Adorate dominum	3rd Sun. after Epiphany
Adrianus, *abb.*ᶜᵃ	9 Jan.
Adrianus, *m.*¹²	4 March
Adrianus, Hadrianus, *m.*ˢᵃ	8 Sep.
Advent Sunday	nearest Sun. to feast of St Andrew
Adventus domini	the 4 weeks preceding Christmas

12. Sometimes described as *miles*.

Aventus spiritus sancti super discipulos^{ca}	15 May
Aedburga	*see* Eadburga
Aelred, *abb.*	12 Jan.
Aeluric, *archiep. etc.*^{ca}	16 Nov.
Agapitus, *m.*	6 Aug.^u, 18 Aug.^e
Agatha, *v. et m.*^e	5 Feb.
Agnes, *v. et m.*^e	21 Jan.
secundo^e	28 Jan.[13]
Aidan, *ep. et c.*^y	31 Aug.
translatio	8 Oct.
Albanus, *m.*^e	20 June
translatio	2 Aug.
depositio	16 May
Albinus, *ep.*^u	1 March
Aldelmus, Aldhelmus, *ep. et c.*^e	25 May
Aldhelmus, translatio (986)	5 May
Alexander, *p.*^u	3 May
All Hallows, All Saints' Day	1 Nov.
All Souls' Day	2 Nov.
Alleluia	Septuagesima Sunday
Alphegus, *archiep. et m.*^e	19 April
translatio	8 June^{ca}
ordinatio	16 Nov.^{ca}
Amandus	*see* Vedastus et Amandus
Ambrosius, *ep. et c.*^e	4 April
Anastasius, *ep.*^u	27 April
Andreas, *ap.*^e	30 Nov.
translatio	9 May
Angarie	Ember Weeks
Angevine	8 Sep.
Anianus, *ep. et c.*^e	17 Nov.
Animarum commemoratio	*see Commemoratio fidelium*
Anna, mater b. Marie^u	26 July
Annunciato dominica^u	25 March
Anselmus, *archiep.*^{ca}	21 April
translatio	7 April
Antoninus, *m.*^{ca}	2 Sep.
Antonius, *m. et c.*^{sa}	17 Jan.
Antonius cordigerius^u[14]	13 June
Apollinaris, *m.*^e	23 July
Apollinaris et Timotheus	*see* Timotheus et Apollinaris
Apparitio domini	6 Jan.

13. Viz. her nativity. Sometimes entered in calendars as octave (e.g. in thirteenth-century calendar of St Augustine's, Canterbury; *see* Feltoe, pp. 8, 9).
14. I.e. Anthony of Padua, the Franciscan.

Apuleius et Marcellus	*see* Marcellus et Apuleius
Arnulfus, *ep. et m.*^e	18 July
Asaph, *ep. et conf.*	1 May
Ascensio, Ascensa, domini in celum	Thursday following Rogation Sunday
Ash Wednesday	1st day of Lent
Aspidiens a longe	1st Sun. in Advent
Assumptio domini, Christi	old name of Ascension Day
Audactus	*see* Felix et Adauctus
Audoenus, *ep. et c.*	24 Aug.^e, 25 Aug.^{ca}
Audrey	*see* Etheldreda
Augustinus, *Anglorum ap., archiep.*^e	26 May
translatio^{ca}	13 Sep.
Augustinus (magnus), *ep. et doct.*^e	28 Aug.
translatio	11 Oct.
Austreberta, Austroberta, *v.*	10 Feb.^{ca}, 20 Oct.^y
Aves incipiunt cantare[15]	12 Feb.

B

Babillus, Babylas, *ep., et soc.*^y	24 Jan.
Balthilides	*see* Batilda
Barbara, *v.*^{ca}	4 Dec.[16]
Barbara, *v.*^{ca}	15 Dec.[16]
Barnabas, *ap.*^e	11 June
Bartholemew, *ap.*^e	24 Aug.
Basilides, Curinus (Cirinus, Cyrinus), et Nabor, *mm.*	12 June
Basilius, *ep. et c.*^e	14 June
Batilda, Balthilides, Bathildis, *reg. et v.*^e	30 Jan.
Bavo	*see* Remigius, Germanus, Vedastus, et Bavo
Beatrix, *v. et m.*^e	29 July
Bede, the Ven.	27 May
translatio	10 May
Benedicta	Trinity Sunday
Benedictus, *abb.*^a	21 March
translatio^e	11 July
Benedictus, *abb.*^e (Benedictus Biscop)	12 Jan.
Berchtinus	*see* Bertinus
Bernardus, *abb.*^u	21 Aug.[17]
Bertelinus Staffordie^u	9 Sep.

---

15. This occurs in three Durham calendars (twelfth and fourteenth century).
16. 4 Dec. in archdeacon of Canterbury's Black Book (early fifteenth century); 15 Dec. in a Christchurch calendar, *c.* 1286. There are two different saints of the same name, and it is odd that the calendars should differ as to which was to be commemorated at Christchurch. The commemoration is on 16 Dec. in Whytford's *Martiloge* (H. Bradshaw Soc. Publ., III, 1893).
17. 20 Aug. in fourteenth-century calendar of university of Paris (*Chart. univ. paris.*, ii. 709–16).

Bertinus, Berchtinus, *abb.*[e]	5 Sep.
Birgitta (d. 1373)	8 Oct. (now 23 July)
Birinus, *ep. et c.*	3 Dec.
translatio	4 Sept.
Black Monday	Easter Monday[18]
Blasius, *ep. et m.*[e]	3 Feb.[19]
Bonefacius *et soc., mm.*[e]	5 June
Borae	*see Brandones*
Botulfus, *abb. et c.*[e]	17 June
Brancheria	Palm Sunday
Brandones, Borae, Burae, Bules	1st Sun. in Lent and week
	following
Bregwinus, *archiep.*[ca]	26 Aug.
Bricius, Briccius, *ep. et c.*	13 Nov.[e], 14 Nov.[sa]
Brigida, *abb. et v.*[e]	1 Feb.
Bules, Burae	*see Brandones*
Byrnstanus, *ep.*[win]	4 Nov.

C

Cadoc, *ep. et m.*	25 Sep.
Caesarius, *m.*[sa]	1 Nov.
Calixtus, Calestus, Kalixtus, *p. et m.*[e]	14 Oct.
Candelaria, candelatio, Candlemas	2 Feb.
Canite tuba or *Canite*	4th Sun. in Advent
Cantate domino	4th Sun. after Easter
Canutus, Cnutus, *r.*[20]	19 Jan.
Capitiluvium	Palm Sunday
Caput jejunii	Ash Wednesday
Cara cognatio	22 Feb.
Caradoc	13 April
Caramentranum, Caremprenium	Shrove Tuesday
Caristia	22 Feb.
Caristas dei	Sat. in Ember Week of Pentecost
Carle *or* Carling Sunday	5th Sun. in Lent
Carnibrevium	Shrove Tuesday
Carniprivium, Carnisprivium,	*either* (*a*) first days of Lent *or*
Privicarnium[21]	(*b*) Septuagesima Sunday *or*
	(*c*) Sexagesima Sunday
Carniprivium novum	Quinquagesima Sunday
Carniprivium sacerdotum	Septuagesima Sunday

18. For various early examples of the use of the 'Black Monday' for Easter Monday, see *Oxford English Dictionary, s.v.* Monday.
19. 14 June, in fifteenth-century calendar of univeristy of Cambridge.
20. Celebrated at Evesham on 10 July (Bodl. Lib., ms. Barlow 41).
21. For an example of an important historical point turning upon the variant uses of this term see 'The Parliament of Lincoln of 1316' (*Eng. Hist. Rev.*, 36, 53–7, 480).

Carniprivium vetus	Quadragesima Sunday[22]
Carnivora	Shrove Tuesday
Cathedra sancti Petri	22 Feb.
Catherina	*see* Katherina
Ceci nati	Wed. of 4th week in Lent
Cecilia, *v. et m.*[e]	22 Nov.
Cedda, Chad, *ep. et c.*[u]	2 March, otherwise 26 Oct.
Cena domini ⎫	⎧
Chare Thursday ⎭	⎨ Maundy Thursday
Childermas Day	28 Dec.
Christina, Cristina, *v. et m.*[u]	24 July
Christoforus et Cucufas, *mm.*	25 July
Chrysogonus, Grisogonus, *m.*[e]	24 Nov.
Cinerum	*see* Ash Wednesday
Ciprianus	*see* Cyprianus
Circumcisio domini	1 Jan.
Circumdederunt	Septuagesima Sunday
Ciriacus, *m.*[e]	8 Aug.
Ciricus et Julitta, *mm.*[e]	16 June
Cirinus, Cyrinus	*see* Basildes, Curinus, et Nabor
Clara, *v.*	12 Aug. (now 11 Aug.)
Clausum Pasche	Sun. after Easter
Clausum Pentecostes	Trinity Sunday
Clean Lent	the days of Lent reckoned from Ash Wednesday[23]
Clemens, *p. et m.*[e]	23 Nov. (24 Nov. in East)
Cletus, *p. et m.*[hw]	12 July, otherwise 26 April
Cnutus, Chnutus	*see* Canutus
Collop Monday	Mon. before Shrove Tuesday
Commemoratio fidelium defunctorum, Animarum commemoratio	2 Nov.
Commovisti terram et conturbasti eam	Sexagesima Sunday
Conception	*see* Maria, conceptio
Cornelius et Cyprianus, *mm.*[u]	14 Sept. (now 16 Sep.)
Corpus Christi	Thurs. after Trinity Sunday
Cosmas et Damianus, *mm.*[e]	27 Sep. (now 26 Sept.)
Crastiano	*see* Morrow
Crescentius	*see* Vitus, Modestus, et Crescentius
Crisanthus et Daria, *mm.*[y]	1 Dec.
Crisogonus	*see* Chrysogonus
Crispinus et Crispinianus, *mm.*[e]	25 Oct.
Cristina	*see* Christina

22. Till the ninth century, in the Latin church. Lenten abstinence did not begin until this day. *Inter duo carnisprivia* is used for the days of Quinquagesima week.
23. So that the first Mon. in Clean Lent will be the Monday after Quadragesima Sunday.

Cross Week	Rogation Week
Crouchmas, Crowchemesse Day	14 Sep.
Cruces nigre	25 April
Crucis, Adoratio (or *dies sancte crucis adorate, dies crucis adorande, veneris dies adoratus*)	Good Friday
Crucis, Exaltatio sancte[e]	14 Sep.
Crucis, Inventio sancte[e]	3 May
Cucufas	*see* Christoforus et Cucufas
Curinus, Cyrinus	*see* Basilides, Curinus, et Nabor
Cuthberga, Cuthburga, *v.*[e]	31 Aug.
Cuthbertus, *ep. et c.*[e]	20 March
translatio	4 Sep.
Cuthlac	*see* Guthlac
Cyprianus et Cornelius, *mm.*[u]	14 Sep. (now 16 Sept.)
Cyprianus et Justina, *mm.*[e]	26 Sep.
Cyriacus	*see* Ciriacus

D

Da pacem	19th Sun. after Pentecost
Daemon mutus	3rd Sun. in Lent
Damasus, *p.*	11 Dec.
Damianis	*see* Cosmas et Damianus
David, *ep. et c.*[a]	1 March
Decollation	*see* Johannes Bapt.
Deductio Christi in Egyptum	9 Jan.
Denis	*see* Dionysius
Depositio	day of death of a saint who is not a martyr
Deus in adjutorium	13th Sun. after Pentecost
Deus in loco sancto	12th Sun. after Pentecost
Deus qui errantibus	3rd Sun. after Easter
Deusdedit, archiep.[24]	15 July
Diabolus recessit a domino	15 Feb.
Dicit dominus	24th and 25th Sun. after Pentecost
Dies absolutionis	Thurs. before Good Friday
Dies adoratus	Good Friday
Dies animarum	2 Nov.
Dies burarum	1st Sun. in Lent
Dies cinerum	Ash Wednesday
Dies crucis adorande, adorate	Good Friday
Dies dominica, dominicus	*either* (*a*) Sunday *or* (*b*) Easter Day
Dies felicissimus	Easter Day
Dies florum	Palm Sunday

24. Frithona of Wessex, the first archbishop of English birth (Feltoe, p. 21).

Dies focorum	1st Sun. in Lent
Dies jovis	Thursday
Dies jovis absoluti	*see Dies absolutionis*
Dies lune	Monday
Dies lune periurata[25]	? Hock Monday
Dies mandati	Maundy Thursday
Dies martis	Tuesday
Dies mercurii, mercurinus, mercoris	Wednesday
Dies neophytorum	the six days between Easter Day and Quasimodo Sunday
Dies osanne *Dies palmarum* *Dies ramorum*	Palm Sunday
Dies sabbati	Saturday
Dies veneris	Friday
Dies veneris adoratus	Good Friday
Dies viginti	the twenty days between Christmas and the octave of Epiphany
Dionysius (Denis) *et soc., mm.*ᵉ	9 Oct.
Distaff Day	7 Jan.
Divisio apostolorum	15 July
Domine, in tua misericordia	2nd Sun. after Pentecost
Domine, ne longe	Palm Sunday
Dominica in albis, in albis depositis, post albas	1st Sun. after Easter
Dominica ante litanias	5th Sun. after Easter
Dominica Cananee	2nd Sun. in Lent
Dominica ad carnes levandas	Quinquagesima Sunday
Dominica duplex	Trinity Sunday
Dominica indulgentie	Palm Sunday
Dominica mapparum albarum	2nd Sun. after Easter
Dominica mediana	Passion Sunday (5th in Lent)
Dominica olivarum *Dominica osanna* *Dominica ad palmas, in ramis palmarum*	Palm Sunday
Dominica in passione domini	Passion Sunday
Dominica post focos, post ignes	2nd Sun. in Lent
Dominica post strenas	Sun. next after 1 Jan.
Dominica quintana	1st Sun. in Lent
Dominica refectionis	Mid-Lent Sunday
Dominica rogationum	5th Sun. after Easter

25. On day thus described, in a rental of 1185, a ward-penny was due from Rivenhall, Essex; a later rental speaks of payment due from Rivenhall *die ropemoneday* and from Cressing *ad hokeday*. The three expressions probably indicate the same day, Hocktide being a favourite time for Spring payments. *See* B. A. Lees, *Records of the Templars in England*, p. lxxviii and n.

Dominica de rosa, de rosis	Sun. in octave of Ascension
Dominica rose, rosata	4th Sun. in Lent
Dominica samaritani	4th Sun. after Easter
Dominica sancta	Easter Sunday
Dominica sancte trinitatis	Trinity Sunday
Dominica de transfiguratione	2nd Sun. in Lent
Dominica trium septimanarum Pasche	3rd Sun. after Easter
Dominicus, *c.*[u]	4 Aug.[26] (now 8 Aug.)
translatio[u]	24 May
Dominus fortitudo	7th Sun. after Pentecost
Dominus illuminatio mea	5th Sun. after Pentecost
Donatianus, *ep. et c.*[ca]	15 Oct.[27]
Donatus, *ep. et m.*[e]	7 Aug. or 22 Oct.
Dormitio sancte Marie	15 Aug.[28]
Dum clamarem	11th Sun. after Pentecost
Dum medium silentium	*either* (*a*) Sun. in octave of Christmas *or* (*b*) Sun. after 1 Jan., if this Sun. falls on the eve of Epiphany
Dunstanus, *archiep. et c.*[e]	19 May
ordinatio[29]	21 Oct.[ca]
translatio	7 Sep.[ca]

E

Eadburga, Edburga, Aedburga, *v. et abb.*[ca30]	12 *or* 13 Dec.
Eadburga, *v.*[win]	15 June
translatio	18 July
Eanswitha, *v.*[ca]	31 Aug.[31]
Easter	*see Pascha*
Ebdomada	*see Hebdomada*
Ecce Deus adjuvat	10th Sun. after Pentecost
Edburga	*see* Eadburga
Editha, *v.*[e]	16 Sep.
translatio	3 Nov.
Edmundus, *archiep. et c.*[e]	16 Nov.[32]
translatio[e]	9 June
Edmundus, *r. et. m.*[e]	20 Nov.
translatio[u]	29 April

26. 5 Aug. at Paris.
27. 24 May in France.
28. 18 Jan. in some ancient calendars.
29. Translation and ordination occur in Christchurch calendars only; when the saint's feast is found elsewhere the deposition is intended.
30. Abbess of Thanet.
31. In thirteenth-century calendar of St Augustine's, Canterbury, and in Jesus Coll., Cambridge, MS, Q 6 (twelfth-century psalter).
32. 30 May at Abingdon (his birthplace).

Edwardus, *r. et c.,* depositio[e] — 5 Jan.
    translatio[e] — 13 Oct.
Edwardus, *r. et m.*[e] — 18 March
Edwardus, *r. et m.,* translatio prima[e] — 18 Feb.
    translatio secunda[e] — 20 June
Egg Saturday — Sat. before Shrove Tuesday
Egidius, *abb.*[e] — 1 Sep.
Ego sum pastor bonus — 2nd Sun. after Easter
Egressus, Egressio, Noe de archa[u] — 29 April
Eligius, *ep. Noviomensis, c.*[u] — 1 Dec.
    translatio — 25 June
Ember Days — *see Quatuor tempora*
Emerentiana, *v. et m.*[ca] — 23 Jan.
Epimachus — *see* Gordianus et Epimachus
Epiphania domini, Theophania — Epiphany, 6 Jan.
Erconwaldus, Erkenwaldus, *ep.*
    London., *c.,* depositio[e] — 30 April
    translatio[e] — 1 Feb., 13 May and 14 Nov.
Ermenhilda, *v.*[win33] — 13 Feb.
Esto mihi — Quinquagesima Sunday
Ethelberht, *r. et m.* — 20 May
Ethelburga, *v. et abb.* — 11 Oct.
Etheldreda, Adeldreda, Audrey, *v.*[e] — 23 June
    translatio[u] — 17 Oct.
Ethelfleda, *v.* — 23 Oct.[34]
Ethelgarus, *archiep.*[ca] — 11 Feb.
Ethelred, *r. et c.* — 4 May
Ethelredus et Ethelbrictus, *mm.*[ca] — 17 Oct.
Ethelwoldus, *ep. et c.*[win] — 1 Aug.
    translatio — 10 Sep.
Eucharistia, Sancta — Corpus Christi
Eufemia, Lucianus, et Geminianus, *mm.*[e] — 16 Sep.
Eugenia, *v.*[ca] — 16 March
Eulalia, *v.*[ca] — 12 Feb.
Eusebius, *pr. et c.*[u] — 14 Aug.
Eustachius *et soc.*[e] — 2 Nov.
Eve — *see* Vigilia
Eventius, *m.*[u] — 3 May
Everilda, *v.*[y] — 9 July
Evurcius, *ep. et c.*[y35] — 7 Sep.
Exaudi domine — *either* (*a*) Sun. in the octave of Ascension
    or (*b*) 6th Sun. after Pentecost

---

33. She is really an Ely saint.
34. 27 Jan. at Winchester.
35. In James I's prayer-book of 1604, this saint appears, owing to a misreading, as 'Enurchus'; both are corruptions of Heortius.

Expectatio beate Marie	16 Dec. *or* 18 Dec.
Exsurge domine	Sexagesima Sunday

F

Fabianus et Sebastianus, *mm.*[e]	20 Jan.
Factus est dominus	3rd Sun. after Pentecost
Faith	*see* fides
Fastmas, Fastren's Eve	Shrove Tuesday
Fastyngong	Shrovetide
Faustinus, Faustus	*see* Felix et Faustinus
Felicianus	*see* Primus et Felicianus
Felicissimus et Agapitus, *mm.*[e]	6 Aug.
Felicitas, *v.*[e]	23 Nov.
Felicitas et Perpetua, *vv. et mm.*[e]	7 March
Felix, *ep. et c.*[36]	8 March
Felix, *ep.* (Nantes)	7 July
Felix (*in pincis*), *c.*[e]	14 Jan.
Felix et Adauctus (Audactus), *mm.*[e]	30 Aug.
Felix et Faustinus, Faustus, *mm.*[e]	29 July
Feria ad angelum	Wed. in Ember Week of Advent
Feria magni scrutinii	Wed. in 4th week in Lent
Feria prima	Sunday
Feria secunda major or *magna*[37]	Mon. of Passion Week
Festum animarum	*see Commemoratio fidelium*
Festum apostolorum	1 May
Festum architriclini	2nd Sun. after Epiphany
Festum axymorum	Easter Day
Festum candelarum	*see Candelaria*
Festum Christi	Christmas
Festum luminum	*see Candelaria*
Festum ovorum	*see* Egg Saturday
Festum primitiarum	1 Aug.
Festum stelle	6 Jan.
Festum stultorum	1 Jan.
Fides, *v. et m.*[e]	6 Oct.
translatio	14 Jan.
Firminus, *ep. et m.*[e]	25 Sep.
Firminus, *ep. et c.*	1 Sep.
Franciscus, *c.*[a]	4 Oct.
translatio[u]	25 May
Frideswida, Fredeswida, *v. et reg.*[e]	19 Oct.
inventio[u]	15 May
translatio[u]	12 Feb.
Furseus, *c.*[ca]	16 Jan.

36. The apostle of East Anglia.
37. And similarly *tertia major, quarta major,* etc., for the remaining days of this week.

G

Gacien, *ep.*	18 Dec.
Gamaliel[ca]	4 Aug.
Gang Days	Rogation Days
Gaudete in domino	3rd Sun. in Advent
Geminianus	*see* Lucianus et Geminianus
Georgius, *m.*[e]	23 April[38]
Gereon, Ieron, *et soc., mm.*[u]	10 Oct.
Germanicus, *m.*[y]	19 Jan.
Germanus, *c.*	*see* Remigius, Germanus, Vedastus, et Bavo
Germanus, *ep. et c.* [Auxerre][e]	31 July
translatio	1 Oct.
Germanus, *ep. et c.* [Capua][y]	30 Oct.
Germanus, *ep. et c.* [Paris][e]	28 May; 21 May[u]
Gervasius et Prothasius, *mm.*[e]	19 June
Gilbertus [de Sempringham], *c.*[u]	4 Feb.
translatio	13 Oct.
Gildardus	*see* Medardus et Gildardus
Giles	*see* Egidius
Good Friday	Friday next before Easter
Gordianus et Epimachus, *mm.*[e]	10 May
Gorgonius, *m.*[e]	9 Sep.
Gorgonius, *m.*[u]	24 Nov.
Grass Week	Rogation Week
Great Week	week before Easter Day
Gregorius I, *p.*[e]	12 March
ordinatio	3 Sep.
Gregorius VII, *p.*	25 May
Grimbaldus, Grumbaldus, Grimbambus, *c.*[ca39]	8 July
Grisogonus	*see* Chrysogonus
Gula Augusti	1 Aug.
Gunpowder Plot	5 Nov.
Guthlac, Cuthlac, *c.*[u]	11 April
translatio	30 Aug.

H

Hadrianus	*see* Adrianus
Hallowmas	1 Nov.
Hebdomada, ebdomada	a week

---

38. Entered both on 21 April and 23 April in thirteenth-century calendar of St Augustine's, Canterbury (Feltoe, p. 14).
39. Described in one Christchurch calendar as *c. et anchorita*.

Hebdomada authentica *Hebdomada crucis*	Holy Week
Hebdomada duplex or *trinitatis*	Week after Trinity Sunday
Hebdomada expectationis	Week after Ascension
Hebdomada indulgentie	Holy Week
Hebdomada magna	*either* (*a*) Holy Week *or* (*b*) week before Pentecost
Hebdomada mediana quadragesime	4th week in Lent
Hebdomada muta	Holy Week
Hebdomada penalis, penosa	Holy Week
Hebdomada sacra	(*a*) week before Easter, (*b*) week before Pentecost
Hermes, *m.*ca	28 Aug.
Heortius	*see* Evurcius
Hieronymus	*see* Jeronimus
Hilarion, *c.*	21 Oct.
Hilarius, Hillarius, *ep.*a	13 Jan.
Hilda, *v. et ab.*y	25 Aug., elsewhere 17 Nov.
translatio	15 Dec.
Hipolitus	*see* Hypolitus
Hock Day, Hoke Day	2nd Tues. after Easter
Hocktide, Hoketide	2nd Mon. and Tues. after Easter
Hogmanay	31 Dec.
Holy Friday	Good Friday
Holymas Day	1 Nov.
Holy Monday[40]	Mon. in Holy Week
Holy Rood Day	*see Crucis, Exaltatio sancte*
Holy Thursday	Ascension Day
Holy Week	the week before Easter
Honorina, *v.*ca	27 Feb.
Honorius, *archiep.*ca	30 Sep.
Hugo, *ep. Linc. et c.*e	17 Nov.
translatio	6 Oct.u, 7 Oct.a
Hyacinthus, Iacinctus	*see* Prothus et Hyacinthus
Hypapante, Hypapanti, Hypante	2 Feb.
Hypolitus, Ypolitus, *m. et soc.*e	13 Aug.
Hyreneus	*see* Irenus

I

Iacinctus	*see* Prothus et Hyacinthus
Ieron	*see* Gereon
In excelso throno	1st Sun. after Epiphany
In voluntate tua	22nd Sun. after Pentecost

40. And similarly Holy Tuesday, Wednesday, and Saturday

Incarnatio domini	25 Dec.
Inclina aurem tuam	16th Sun. after Pentecost
Innocentes, *mm.*^e	28 Dec.
Introitus Noe in archam^u	17 March
Invocavit me	1st Sun. in Lent
Ireneus, Hyreneus *et soc.*^{ca}	5 July, elsewhere in West 28 June
Isidorus, *ep.*^{ca}	2 Jan., elsewhere 4 April
Isti sunt dies	Passion Sunday
Ivo, *ep. et c.*	24 April

J

Jacobus, *ap.*^e	25 July
translatio	30 Dec.
Jambertus, *archiep.*^{ca}	12 Aug.
Jejunia temporalia	*see Quatuor tempora*
Jejunium autumnale or *septimi mensis*	Ember Days of Sep.
Jejunium estivale or *quarti mensis*	Ember Days of Pentecost
Jejunium hiemale or *decimi mensis*	Ember Days of Advent
Jejunium vernale or *primi mensis*	Ember Days of Lent
Jeronimus, Hieronymus, *pr. et doc.*^e	30 Sep.
Jesu nomen dulcissimum^u	7 Aug.
Johannes, *ap. et evan.*^e	27 Dec.
Johannes albus	24 June
Johannes ante portam latinam^e	6 May
Johannes Bapt., decollatio or natalis^e	29 Aug.
Nativitas^e	24 June
Johannes de Beverlaco^u	7 May
translatio^a	25 Oct.
Johannes de Bridlington	21 Oct.
translatio	11 May
Johannes et Paulus, *mm.*^e	26 June
Jubilate omnis terra	3rd Sun. after Easter
Judas	*see Simon et Judas*
Judica me	Passion Sunday
Judocus, *c.*^{ca}	13 Dec.
translatio^{win}	9 Jan.
Juliana, *v. et m.*^e	16 Feb.
Juliana, *v.*^u	23 Feb.
Julianus, *ep. et c.*^e	27 Jan.
Julitta	*see Ciricus et Julitta*
Justin^{sa}	28 Aug.[41]
Justina	*see Cyprianus et Justina*
Justus, *archiep.*^{ca}	10 Nov.

41. Displacing Hermes.

Justus[sa]	18 Oct.
Justus es Domine	18th Sun. after Pentecost

K

Kalixtus	*see* Calixtus
Katerina, Catherina, *v. et m.*[e]	25 Nov.
Kenelmus, Kynelmus, *r. et m.*[e]	17 July
Kentigern, *ab. et c.*	13 Jan.

L

Lady Day	25 March
Laetare Domine	Mid-Lent Sunday (4th Sunday in Lent)
Lambertus, Lanbertus, Landberhtus, *ep. et m.*[e]	17 Sep.
Lamfrancus, Lanfrancus, *archiep.*[ca]	28 May
Lammas Day	1 Aug.
Laurentius, *m.*[e]	10 Aug.
Laurentius, *archiep.*[ca]	3 Feb.
Lent	*see Quadragesima*
Leo II, *p.*[e]	28 June, now 10 Dec. in West.
Leodegarius, *ep. et m.*[e]	2 Oct.
Leonardus, *abb.*	6 Nov.
Letardus, *ep.*[ca42]	7 May
Letare Hierusalem	4th Sun. in Lent
Leufredus, Leothfredus, *abb.*[ca]	21 June
Lex Moysi data est	15 May
Linus, *p. et m.*[e]	26 Nov., elsewhere 23 Sep.
Litania major	25 April
Little Easter	Pentecost
Livinus, *ep. et m.*[ca]	12 Nov.
Long Friday	Friday next before Easter Day
Low Sunday	Sunday next after Easter Day
Lucas, *ev.*[e]	18 Oct.
Lucia, *v. et m.*[e]	13 Dec.
Lucianus, *pr. et m.*[u]	8 Jan.
Lucianus et Geminianus, *mm.*[e]	16 Sep.

M

Maccabaei, *mm.*[ca]	1 Aug.
Machutus, *ep. et c.*[e]	15 Nov.
Maglorius, *ep. et c.*[u]	24 Oct.
Magnus, *m.*[e]	19 Aug., elsewhere 16 April
Malo	11 July

42. Local. Liudhard, bishop of Senlis, who came to England with Queen Bertha (Feltoe, p. 17).

in hieme	15 Nov.
Mamertus, *ep. et c.*	11 May
Marcellianus	*see* Marcus et Marcellianus
Marcellinus et Petrus, *mm.*[e]	2 June
Marcellus, *p. et m.*[e]	16 Jan.
Marcellus, *m.*[u]	4 Sep.
Marcellus et Apuleius, *mm.*[e][43]	7 Oct.
Marcus, *ev.*[e]	25 April
Marcus et Marcellianus, *mm.*[e]	18 June
Margerata, *reg.*[44]	16 Nov.
Margareta, *v. et m.*[e]	20 July
Maria, *B. V.*, annunciato,[e]	25 March
Maria in Marcio[45]	
ascensio, assumptio[e]	15 Aug.[46]
conceptio[e]	8 Dec.
nativitas[e]	8 Sep.
oblatio[ca]	21 Nov.
pausatio	15 Aug.
presentatio[u]	21 Nov.
purificatio[e]	2 Feb.
salutatio	25 June
visitatio[sa]	2 July
Maria Egyptiaca[u]	2 April
Maria Magdalena[e]	22 July
Maria ad nives	5 Aug.
Maria Salome[u]	22 Oct.
Martha, *v.*[y]	27 July
Martinianus	*see* Processus et Martinianus
Martinus, *ep. et c.* (in hyeme)[e]	11 Nov.
ordinatio et translatio[e]	4 July
(Martinus calidus)	
Martinus, *p. et c.*[y]	10 Nov.[47]
Mass-day	*see* Missa
Mathias, *ap.*[e]	24 Feb.[48]
Mattheus, *ap. et ev.*	21 Sep.
Maundy Thursday	Thurs. before Good Friday
Mauricius *et soc.*, *mm.*[e]	22 Sep.
Maurilius, *ep. et c.*[y]	13 Sep.
Maurus, *abb.*[e]	15 Jan., now 5 Oct.

43. Entered as Marcus, Marcellus, et Apuleius in calendar of Black Book of the Exchequer.
44. Margaret, queen of Scotland.
45. Cf. *Reg. antiquissimum Linc.*, II, 643, line 18.
46. 'Betwixt the two St. Mary's masses' (*Anglo-Saxon Chron.*, RS, I, 343) is between the Assumption and the Nativity.
47. 12 Nov. is given as the date in most works of reference.
48. For the observance of this festival in leap years see above, p. 8.

Medardus et Gildardus, *epp. et cc.*[e]	8 June
Media Quadragesima	Mid-Lent Sunday (4th Sunday in Lent)
Meliorus, *m.*[a]	1 Oct.
Mellitus, *archiep.*[ca]	24 April
Memento mei[49]	4th Sun. in Advent
Menna, *m.*[e]	11 Nov.
Mensis fenalis	July
Mensis imbrium	April
Mensis magnus	June
Mensis messionum	August
Mensis novarum	April
Mensis Pasche	Month or *quindena* of Easter
Mensis purgatorius	2 Feb.
Michael, *archang.*[e]	29 Sep.
in Monte Gargano	8 May
in Monte Tumba[e]	16 Oct.
Mid-Lent Sunday	4th Sun. in Lent
Midummer Day	24 June
Midwinter Day	25 Dec.
Milburga, Mulburga, *v.*[ca]	23 Feb.
Mildreda, Mildritha, *v.*[u]	13 July
translatio[ca]	18 May
Mille martyres apud Lichefeld	2 Jan.
Miserere mei domine	17th Sun. after Pentecost
Misericordia domini	2nd Sun. after Easter
Missa, Mass-day	Feast-day of a Saint
Misse domini Alleluia	*Quasimodo* Sunday
Modestus	*see* Vitus et Modestus
Modwenna, *v.*	5(6) July
translatio	9 Nov.
Morrow	the day after any feast
Mothering Sunday	4th Sun. in Lent
Mulburga	*see* Milburga

N

Nabor	*see* Basilides, Curinus, et Nabor
Natilis Calicis	Holy Thursday
Natalis S. Johannis Baptiste	*see* Joh. Bapt. decollatio
Nativitas, natale, domini	25 Dec.
Neot, *abb.*[ca]	31 July
Nereus et Achilleus, *mm.*[e]	12 May
Nicasius	*see* Nigasius
Nichodemus, Nicodemus[ca]	4 Aug.

---

49. Former introit. Now *Rorate celi*.

Nicholas, *ep. et c.*[e]	6 Dec.
translatio[u]	9 May
Nichodemes, Nicodemes, *m.*	1 June,[e] 15 Sep.[ca]50
Nigasius *et soc., mm.*[e]	11 Oct.
Ninian, *ep.*	26 Aug.
Nothelmus, *archiep.*[ca]	17 Oct.
Nouvel Caresme	Quinquagesima Sunday

O

O sapientia	16 Dec.[51]
Octava infantium	Sun. in octave of Easter
Octave	the 8th day after any feast, the feast-day itself being counted
Oculi	3rd Sun. in Lent
Odo, *archiep.*[ca]	2 June, later 29 May or 4 July
Olavus, *r. et m.*	29 July
Omnes gentes	8th Sun. after Pentecost
Omnia que fecisti	21st Sun. after Pentecost
Omnis terra	2nd Sun. after Epiphany
Omnium sanctorum festivitas[e]	1 Nov.
Osanna	Palm Sunday
Ositha[ca] *reg. et m.*	7 Oct.
Osmundus, *ep. et c.*[u]	4 Dec.
translatio[u]	16 July
Oswaldus, *ep. et c.*[ca]	28 Feb.
Oswaldus, *r. et m.*[e]	5 Aug.
Oswinus, Oswynus, *r. et. m.*	20 Aug.
translatio	11 March
Owen	*see* Audoenus

P

Palm Sunday	6th Sun. in Lent
Pancake Tuesday	Shrove Tuesday
Pancratius, *m.*	12 May
Pantaleon, *m.*[e]	27 or 28 July
Parasceve	Good Friday
Pardon Sunday	Palm Sunday
Pascha	*either* (*a*) Easter Day, i.e. Sun. after full moon on or next after 21 March *or* (*b*) Easter week
Pascha competentium } *floridum, florum* }	Palm Sunday

50. 1 June is the dedication of his church, 15 Sep. the day of his death.
51. On this day and each of the octave the anthem sung at vespers begins with O. Cf. in French *les oleries, la feste Os.*

primum	22 March[52]
rosarum	Pentecost
Passionis dies	Good Friday
Passio sanctorum XL militum[ca]	9 March
Passion Sunday	5th Sun. in Lent
Passion Week	week before Easter
Paternus, *ep.*	16 April
Patricius, *ep.*[u]	17 March
Paulinus, *ep. et c.*[ca]	10 Oct.
Paulus, *ap.*, conversio[a]	25 Jan.
decollatio[ca]	30 June
translatio[53]	25 Jan.
Paulus, *er.*[ca]	10 Jan.
Paulus Aurelianus, *ep.*	12 March
Paulus et Johannes, *mm.*[e]	26 June
Paulus et Petrus, *app.*[e]	21 June
commemoratio	30 June
Pelagia[y]	8 Oct.
Pentecost (Whit-Sunday)	7th Sun. after Easter Day
Perdon Sunday	*see* Pardon Sunday
Pernella	*see* Petronilla
Perpetua et Felicitas, *vv. et mm.*[e]	7 March
Petrocus, *c.*[y]	4 June
translatio	1 Oct.
Petronilla, Pernella, *v.*[e]	31 May
Petrus ad vincula[e]	1 Aug.
Petrus in cathedra in Antiochia[e]	22 Feb.
Petrus Mediolanus, *predic. et m.*[e]	29 April
Petrus et Marcellinus	*see* Marcellinus et Petrus
Petrus et Paulus, *app.*[e]	29 June
Phillipus et Jacobus, *app.*[e]	1 May
Piranus, *ep.*[hw]	5 March
Plough Monday	Mon. after 6 Jan.
Policarpus, *ep. et m.*[y]	26 Jan., now 23 Feb.
Populus Sion	2nd Sun. in Advent
Potentiana, Pudentiana, *v. et m.*[u]	19 May
Powder Plot	5 Nov.
Praxedes, Praxedis, *v.*[e]	21 July
Prejectus, *m.*[e]	25 Jan.
Presentatio domini	2 Feb.
Preteriens Jesus	Wed. after *Letare Hierusalem*
Primus et Felicianus, *mm.*[e]	9 June
Prisca, *v.*[e]	18 Jan.

52. Because this is the earliest date upon which Easter can fall.
53. Rare. But cf. *Reg. palat. dunelmense*, III, 426, and *Acta sanctorum*, vii, 428, 431–2.

Priscus, *m.*ʷ	26 May
Priscus, *m.*ᵉ	1 Sep.
Privicarnium	*see Carniprivium*
Procession Week	Rogation Week
Processus et Martinianus, *mm.*ᵉ	2 July
Protector noster	15th Sun. after Pentecost
Prothasius	*see* Gervasius et Prothasius
Prothus et Hyacinthus (Iacinctus), *mm.*ᵉ	11 Sep.
Pudentiana	*see* Potentiana
Purification	*see* Maria, purificatio

Q

Quadragesima, Quadringisima	Lent, the 40 week-days preceding Easter[54]
Quadragesima intrans	*either* (*a*) opening of Lent *or* (*b*) 1st Sun. in Lent
Quadragesima major	the Lent of Easter
Quadragesima pura	*see* Clean Lent
Quadragesima Sunday	1st Sun. in Lent
Quadraginta	Quinquagesima Sunday[55]
Quasimodo	1st Sun. after Easter
Quatuor coronati martyresᵉ	8 Nov.
Quatuor tempora, jejunia temporalia	Ember days at the four seasons, viz. the Wed., Fri. and Sat. after (*a*) 1st Sun. in Lent, (*b*) Pentecost, (*c*) Holy Rood Day, (*d*) St Lucy's Day. If (*c*) and (*d*) fall on a Wed., the Ember Days begin on the Wed. following
Queen's Day	17 Nov.[56]
Quindena, quinzaine	quindene, 15th day after any feast, the date of the feast itself being included in the reckoning[57]
Quinquagesima	Usually Quinquagesima Sunday. Also used for (*a*) the 50 days from Easter to Pentecost, (*b*) the day of Pentecost
Quinquagesima Sunday	Sun. before Ash Wednesday
Quintana	1st Sun. in Lent
Quintinus, *m.*ᵉ	31 Oct.
Quinzaine, quindisme, quinsime	*see Quindena*

54. But formerly the Latin church also observed the Lent of Pentecost (40 days succeeding Pentecost) and the Lent of Christmas (40 days preceding Christmas).
55. Because the first response at Matins is 'Quadraginta dies et noctes', etc.
56. Date of accession of Queen Elizabeth I.
57. On some occasions 'infra quindanae Paschae' seems to mean 'in Easter Week', Holy Week and Easter Week being counted together (*ex inf.* Leofranc Holford-Strevens).

R

Radegonda, *reg.*[ca]	13 Aug.
Ramispalma	Palm Sunday
Reddite que sunt Caesaris Caesari	24th Sun. after Pentecost
Regressio de exilio	*see* Thomas, *archiep. et m.*
Relatio pueri Jesu de Egypto	7 Jan.
Relic Sunday[58]	1st Sun. after 7 July
Remigius, *ep. et c.*[y]	13 Jan.
Remigius,[59] Germanus, Vedastus, et Bavo, *epp.*[e]	1 Oct.
Reminiscere	2nd Sun. in Lent
Respice domine	14th Sun. after Pentecost
Respice in me	4th Sun. after Pentecost
Resurrectio domini[e]	27 March
Ricardus, *ep. et c.*[a] (Chichester)	3 April
translatio[u]	16 June
Rochus, *c.*[u]	16 Aug.
Rock Day	7 Jan.
Rogation Days	Mon., Tues., Wed., before Ascension Day
Rogation Sunday	5th Sun. after Easter Day
Roi des Dimanches	Trinity Sunday
Romanus, *m.*[e]	9 Aug.
Romanus, *archiep. et c.*[e]	23 Oct.
Ronanus, *ep. et c.*[ca]	19 Nov.
Rope Monday	2nd Mon. after Easter Day
Rorate celi[60]	4th Sun. in Advent.
Rosary, feast of the	1 Oct.
Royal Oak Day	29 May
Rufus, *m.*[e]	27 Aug.
Rushbearing	Often *either* (*a*) St Bartholemew's day, viz. 24 Aug. *or* (*b*) feast of the dedication of a particular church.[61]

58. This name almost certainly relates to the feast of Sarum relics. At Salisbury in the twelfth century the appointed day was 17 Sep., but it was changed in 1319 to the first Sun. after the feast of St Thomas of Canterbury. Thereafter it was widely used in dioceses where the Sarum Use was followed. It is also found at Hereford. Some churches had their own days, e.g. St Albans, 27 Jan.; Exeter, 23 May, later (mid xiv cent.), Mon. after Ascension; Lincoln, 10 July; Westminster, 16 July; Durham, 31 Aug.; Norwich, 16 Sep.; Glastonbury, 8 Oct.; Chichester, 13 Oct.; Wells, 14 Oct.; Worcester, 15 Oct.; Ely, 16 Oct.; York, 19 Oct.
59. 'Remedius' in *Bosworth psalter.*
60. Introit. Formerly *Memento mei.*
61. Thus at Warton, Lancs., dedicated to St Oswald, rushbearing was 5 Aug.; on the other hand at Altcar, Lancs., dedicated to St Michael, rushbearing was in July (Hampson, *Kalendarium*, i. 341).

S

Sabbata duodecim lectionum	the 4 Sats. of Ember Weeks
Sabbatum	Usually Sat.; sometimes used of the whole week.[62]
Sabbatum in albis	Sat. before 1st Sun. after Easter
Sabbatum Alleluia	
Sabbatum luminum	
Sabbatum magnum	Sat. before Easter Day
Sabbatum Pasche	
Sabbatum sanctum	
Sabina[sa]	29 Aug.
Salus populi	20th Sun. after Pentecost
Salvator[sa]	24 May
Salvius, *ep.*[ca]	26 June
Salvius, *ep. et m.*[ca]	11 Jan.
Sampson, Samson, *ep.*[e]	28 July
Saturninus, *m.*[e]	29 Nov.
Saturninus et Sisinnius, *mm.*[u]	29 Nov.
Scholastica, *v.*[e]	10 Feb.
Sebastianus	*see* Fabianus et Sebastianus
Sennes	*see* Abdon et Sennes
Septem dormientes[e]	27 July
Septem fratres martyres[e]	10 July
Septimana	a week; *see also Hebdomada*
Septimana communis	week beginning Sun. after Michaelmas Day
Septimana media jejuniorum paschalium[63]	3rd week in Lent
Septimana penosa	*see Hebdomada penosa*
Septuagesima Sunday	3rd. Sun. before Ash Wednesday
Sergius et Bacchus, *mm.*	7 Oct.
Sexagesima Sunday	2nd Sun. before Ash Wednesday
Sexburga, *v.*[ca]	6 July
Sexburga, *v.*[u]	8 April
Shere or Shrive Thursday	Thurs. in Holy Week
Shrove Monday	Mon. before Shrove Tuesday
Shrove Sunday	Sun. before Shrove Tuesday
Shrove Thursday	Thurs. after Shrove Tuesday
Shrove Tuesday	Tues. next after Quinquagesima Sunday
Si iniquitates	23rd Sun. after Pentecost
Sicut oculi servorum	Mon. after 1st Sun. in Lent
Silvester, *p. et c.*[e]	31 Dec.
Simon et Judas, *app.*[e]	28 Oct.

62. Thus *una* or *prima Sabbati* would be Sunday; *dua Sabbati* Monday; and so on.
63. Not to be confused with *Hebdomada mediana Quadragesime (q.v.)*.

Simplicius[e]	29 July
Sisinnius	*see* Saturninus et Sisinnius
Sitientes	Sat. before Passion Sunday
Sixtus, Xystus, *ep.*[u]	6 April
Sixtus I, *p. et m.*[e]	6 Aug.
Solemnitas solemnitatum	Easter Day
Sowlemas Day	2 Nov.
Stephanus, *p. et m.*[a]	2 Aug.
Stephanus, *protom.*[e]	26 Dec. in West, 27 Dec. in East
inventio[e]	3 Aug.; 4 Aug.[ca]
Sulpicius, *ep, et c.*[e]	17 Jan.
Suscepimus deus	9th Sun. after Pentecost
Swithinus, *ep. et c.*[e]	2 July
translatio[e]	15 July
Symphorianus	*see* Timotheus et Symphorianus
Sytha (Zita of Lucca), *v.*[ca]	27 April

T

Tathwinus, Tatwyn, *archiep. et c.*[ca]	31 July
Taurinus, *c.*[hw]	11 Aug.
Tecla, Thecla, *v. et m.*[e]	23 Sep.
Theodorus, *archiep.*[ca]	19 Sep.
ordinacio[ca]	26 March
Theodorus, *m.*[e]	9 Nov.
Theophania	Epiphany
Theophilus[ca]	28 Feb.
Thomas, *ap.*[e]	21 Dec.
translatio	3 July
Thomas de Aquino[u]	7 March, now 28 Jan.
Thomas, *archiep. Cantuar. et m.*[e]	29 Dec.
translatio[e]	7 July
regressio de exilio[ca]	1 Dec.
Thomas Herefordensis, *ep. et c.*[u]	2 Oct.
Thousand martyrs at Lichfield	*see* Mille martyres
Tiburtius, *m.*[e]	11 Aug.
Tiburtius et Valerianus, *mm.*[e]	14 April
Timotheus et Appolinaris, *mm.*[e]	23 Aug.
Timotheus et Symphorianus, *mm.*[e]	22 Aug.
Transfiguratio domini[u]	6 Aug.
Tres septimane	The three weeks beginning with Easter Day, Pentecost, Christmas, and St John Bapt., distinguished as Paschales, Pentecostes, Nativitatis, et Sancti Johannis Baptiste[64]

64. In many places these great festivals had three consecutive octaves, in others only two.

Trinitas estivalis	Trinity Sunday
Trinity Sunday	Sunday next after Pentecost
Trium magorum (regrum) dies	Epiphany
Twelfth Day	Epiphany
Typhayne	Epiphany

U

Undecim millia virgines[e]	21 Oct.[e]; 22 Aug.[u]
Urbanus, *p. et m.*[sa]	25 May
Ursula, *m.*	21 Oct.
Utas	The octave of any feast

V

Valentinus, *ep. et m.*[e]	14 Feb.
Valerianus, *ep. et m.*[u]	15 Dec.
Valerianus, *m.*	*see* Tiburtius et Valerianus
Vandregisilus, Wandregisilus, *abb.*[ca]	22 July
Vedastus et Amandus, *app.*[e]	6 Feb.
Vedastus, *ep.*	*see* Remigius, Germanus, Vedastus, et Bavo
Vigilia	the day before any feast
Vincentius, *m.*[e]	22 Jan.
Viri Galilei	Ascension Day
Vitalis, *m.*[e]	28 April
Vitus, Modestus, et Crescentius, *mm.*[e]	15 June
Vocem jucunditatis	5th Sun. after Easter
Vuilfridus	*see* Wilfridus
Vulganius, *c.*[ca]	3 Nov.
Vulmarus, *c.*[ca]	20 July

W

Waldef (Waltheof)	3 Aug.
Wandregisilus	*see* Vandregisilus
Wenceslas, *m.*	28 Sep.
Wenefrida, Winifreda, *v. et m.*[u]	3 Nov.
Werburga, *v.*[ca]	3 Feb.
translatio	21 June
Whit-Monday	Mon. following Whit-Sunday
Whit-Sunday (Pentecost)	7th Sun. after Easter Day
Whitsuntide	Whit-Sunday, -Monday, -Tuesday
Whit-Tuesday	Tues. following Whit-Sunday
Wilfridus, Vuilfridus, *archiep. et c.*[ca]	12 Oct.
translatio[y] [65]	24 April

65. 24 April was the day of Wilfred's death, and the primitive feast recorded in the Old English Martyrology. In the south it was displaced by the feast of St Mellitus of Canterbury, but survived at York, where, however, it was kept as a *translatio* (Gasquet and Bishop, *Bosworth psalter*, p. 159).

Willebrordus, *ep. et c.*[y]	7 Nov.
Willelmus, *archiep. Ebor.*[e]	8 June
translatio[u]	Sun. after Epiphany
Winifreda	*see* Wenefrida
Winwalocus, Wynewaldus	3 March
Withburga, *v.*[u]	17 March
translatio	8 July
Wives' Feast Day	2 Feb.
Wulfranus, *ep.*[e]	15 Oct.
Wulfstanus, Wolstanus, Waulstanus, *ep. et c.*[e]	19 Jan.
translatio[e]	7 June
Wulganus, *c.*[ca]	3 Nov.
Wynewaldus[u]	*see* Winwalocus

X

Xystus	*see* Sixtus

Y

Ypolitus	*see* Hypolitus
Yvo, *c.*	22 May

Z

Zeno, *ep.*	12 April
Zita of Lucca	*see* Sytha

II Saints' days in annual chronological order

2 Jan.	Isidorus
5 Jan.	Edwardus, *r. et c.*
8 Jan.	Lucianus
9 Jan.	Adrianus, *abb.*
10 Jan.	Paulus, *evan.*
11 Jan.	Salvius, *ep. et m.*
12 Jan.	Aelred, *abb.*, Benedict Biscop
13 Jan.	Hilarius, Kentigern, Remigius
14 Jan.	Felix (*in pincis*), *c.*
15 Jan.	Maurus, *abb.*
16 Jan.	Furseus, Marcellus, *p.*
17 Jan.	Antonius, Sulpicius
18 Jan.	Prisca
19 Jan.	Canutus, Germanicus, Wulfstanus, *ep.*
20 Jan.	Fabianus et Sebastianus
21 Jan.	Agnes
22 Jan.	Vincentius
23 Jan.	Emerentiana

24 Jan.	Babillus, *ep.*
25 Jan.	Paulus, *ap.*, *conversio et translatio*, Prejectus
26 Jan.	Policarpus
27 Jan.	Julianus
28 Jan.	Thomas de Aquino
30 Jan.	Batilda
1 Feb.	Brigida
2 Feb.	Hypapante, Maria, B.V., *purificatio*
3 Feb.	Blasius, Laurentius. *archiep.*, Werberga
4 Feb.	Gilbertus de Sempringham
5 Feb.	Agatha
6 Feb.	Vedastus et Amandus, *app.*
10 Feb.	Austreberta, Scholastica
11 Feb.	Ethelgarus
12 Feb.	Eulalia
13 Feb.	Ermenhilda
14 Feb.	Valentinus
16 Feb.	Juliana, *v. et m.*
22 Feb.	Petrus in cathedra in Antochia
23 Feb.	Juliana, *v.*, Milburga, Policarpus
24 Feb.	Mathias, *ap.*
27 Feb.	Honorina
28 Feb.	Oswaldus, *ep.*, Theophilus
1 March	Albinus, David
2 March	Chad
3 March	Winwalocus
4 March	Adrianus, *m.*
5 March	Piranus
7 March	Felicitus et Perpetua, Thomas de Aquino
8 March	Felix, *ep.*
12 March	Gregorius I, *p.*, Paulus Aurelianus, *ep.*
16 March	Eugenia
17 March	Patricius, Withburga
18 March	Edwardus, *r. et m.*
20 March	Cuthbertus
21 March	Benedictus, *abb.*
25 March	Maria, B.V., *annunciatio*
2 April	Maria Egyptiaca
3 April	Ricardus, *ep.* (Chichester)
4 April	Ambrosius, Isidorus
6 April	Sixtus, *ep.*
11 April	Guthlac
12 April	Zeno, *ep.*

13 April	Caradoc
14 April	Tiburtius et Valerianus
16 April	Magnus, Paternus, *ep.* (Vannes)
19 April	Alphegus
21 April	Anselm
23 April	Georgius
24 April	Ivo, *ep.* (Chartres), Mellitus, *archiep.*
25 April	Marcus, *ev.*
26 April	Cletus
27 April	Anastasius, Sytha (Zita of Lucca)
28 April	Vitalis
29 April	Petrus Mediolanus
30 April	Erconwaldus
1 May	Asaph, Philippus et Jacobus, *app.*
3 May	Alexander, Eventius
4 May	Ethelred, *r. et c.*
6 May	Johannes ante portam latinam
7 May	Johannes de Beverlaco, Letardus
8 May	Michael in Monte Gargano
10 May	Epimachus, Gordianus
11 May	Mamertus
12 May	Nereus et Achilleus, Pancratius
19 May	Dunstanus, Potentiana/Pudentiana
20 May	Ethelberht, *r. et m.*
21 May	Germanus, *ep. et c.* (Paris)
22 May	Yvo, *c.*
24 May	Salvator
25 May	Aldhelm, Gregorius VII, *p.*, Urbanus, *p. et m.*
26 May	Augustinus, *archiep.*, Priscus
27 May	Bede the Venerable
28 May	Germanus, *ep. et c.* (Paris), Lanfrancus
29 May	Odo, *archiep.*
31 May	Petronilla
1 June	Nicomedes
2 June	Marcellinus et Petrus, Odo, *archiep.*
4 June	Petrocus
5 June	Bonifacius
8 June	Medardus et Gildardus, Willelmus, *archiep. Ebor.*
9 June	Primus et Felicianus
11 June	Barnabas
12 June	Basilides, Curinus, Nabor
14 June	Basilius
15 June	Eadburga, *v.*
15 June	Vitus, Modestus et Crescentius

16 June	Ciricus, Julitta
17 June	Botulfus
18 June	Marcus et Marcellianus, *mm.*
19 June	Gervasius et Prothasius
20 June	Albanus
21 June	Leufredus
23 June	Etheldreda
24 June	Johannes albus, Johannes Bapt., Nativitas
25 June	Maria, B.V., *salutatio*
26 June	Johannes et Paulus, *mm.*, Salvius, *ep.*
28 June	Ireneus, Leo II, *p.*
29 June	Paulus et Petrus, *app.*
30 June	Paulus, *ap. decollatio*
2 July	Maria, B.V., visitatio, Processus et Martinianus, Swithinus, *ep.*
4 July	Odo, *archiep.*
5 July	Ireneus, Modwena, *v.*
6 July	Modwena, *v.*, Sexburga
7 July	Felix, *ep.* (Nantes)
8 July	Grimbaldus
9 July	Everilda
10 July	Martinus, *p. et c.*
11 July	Malo
12 July	Cletus
13 July	Mildreda
15 July	Deusdedit, Swithinus, *ep.*
17 July	Kenelmus
18 July	Arnulfus
20 July	Margareta, *v. et m.*, Vulmarus
21 July	Praxedes
22 July	Maria Magdalena, Vandregisilus
23 July	Apollinaris, Birgitta
24 July	Christina
25 July	Christopherus et Cucufus, Jacobus
26 July	Anna
27 July	Martha, Pantaleon
28 July	Pantaleon, Sampson, *ep.* (Dol)
29 July	Beatrix, Faustinus et Felix, Olavus, *r.* Simplicius
30 July	Abdon, Sens
31 July	Germanus, *e.* (Auxerre), Neot, Tathwinus, *archiep.*
1 Aug.	Ethelwoldus, *Petrus ad vincula*
2 Aug.	Stephanus, *p. et m.*
3 Aug.	Waldef
4 Aug.	Dominicus, Gamaliel, Nicodemus
5 Aug.	Maria ad nives, Oswaldus, *r. et m.*

6 Aug.	Agapitus et Felicissimus, Sixtus I, *p.*
7 Aug.	Donatus
8 Aug.	Ciriacus, Dominicus
9 Aug.	Romanus, *m.*
10 Aug.	Laurentius, *m.*
11 Aug.	Clara, Taurinus, Tiburtius
12 Aug.	Clara, Jambertus
13 Aug.	Hypolitus, Radegonda
14 Aug.	Eusebius
15 Aug.	Maria, B.V., *ascensio, assumptio et pausatio*
16 Aug.	Rochus
18 Aug.	Agapitus
19 Aug.	Magnus
20 Aug.	Oswinus, *r. et m.*
21 Aug.	Bernard, *abb.*
22 Aug.	Timotheus et Symphorianus
23 Aug.	Timotheus et Apollinaris
24 Aug.	Audoenus, Bartholemew
25 Aug.	Audoenus, Hilda
26 Aug.	Bregwinus, Ninnian
27 Aug.	Rufus
28 Aug.	Augustinus de Hippo, Hermes, Justin
29 Aug.	Johannes Bapt., *decollatio or natalis*, Sabina
30 Aug.	Felix, Audactus
31 Aug.	Aidan, Cuthberga, Eanswitha
1 Sep.	Egidius, Firminus, *ep. et c.*, Priscus
2 Sep.	Antonius
4 Sep.	Marcellus, *m.*
5 Sep.	Berinus
7 Sep.	Evurcius
8 Sep.	Adrianus (Hadrianus), *m.*, Maria, B.V., Nativitas
9 Sep.	Bertelinus, Gorgonius
11 Sep.	Prothus *et* Hyacinthus
13 Sep.	Maurillus, *ep.*
14 Sep.	Cornelius et Cyprianus
15 Sep.	Nicomedes
16 Sep.	Cornelius et Cyprianus, Editha, Eufemia, Lucianus et Germinianus
17 Sep.	Lambertus
19 Sep.	Theodorus, *archiep.*
21 Sep.	Matthaeus, *ap.*
22 Sep.	Mauricius
23 Sep.	Linus, Tecla
25 Sep.	Cadoc, Firminus, *ep. et m.*
26 Sep.	Cosmas et Damianus, Cyprianus et Justina, *mm.*
27 Sep.	Cosmas et Damianus

29 Sep.	Michael, archangel
30 Sep.	Honorius, Jeronimus

1 Oct.	Meliorus, Remigius, Germanus, Vedastus et Bavo
2 Oct.	Leodigarius, Thomas, *ep.* (Hereford)
4 Oct.	Franciscus
5 Oct.	Maurus, *ab.*
6 Oct.	Fides
7 Oct.	Marcellus et Apulleius, *mm.*, Ositha, *reg.*, Sergius et Bacchus
8 Oct.	Birgitta, Pelagia
9 Oct.	Denis/Dionysius
10 Oct.	Gereon, Paulinus
11 Oct.	Ethelburga, Nicasius
12 Oct.	Wilfridus, *archiep.*
14 Oct.	Calixtus
15 Oct.	Donatianus, Wulfranus
16 Oct.	Michael *in monte tumba*
17 Oct.	Ethelredus, Ethelbrictus, Nothelmus
18 Oct.	Justus, Lucas, *ev.*
19 Oct.	Frideswida
20 Oct.	Austreberta
21 Oct.	Hilarion, Johannes de Bridlington, Ursula
22 Oct.	Donatus, Maria Salome
23 Oct.	Ethelfleda, Romanus, *archiep.*
24 Oct.	Maglorius
25 Oct.	Crispinus et Crispinianus
26 Oct.	Chad
28 Oct.	Simon et Judas
30 Oct.	Germanus, *ep. et c.* (Capua)
31 Oct.	Quintinus

1 Nov.	Caesarius
2 Nov.	Eustachius
3 Nov.	Vulganius, Winifreda, Wulganus
4 Nov.	Byrstanus
6 Nov.	Leonardus
7 Nov.	Willibrordus, *ep.*
9 Nov.	Theodorus, *m.*
10 Nov.	Justus, *archiep.*
11 Nov.	Martinus, *ep. et c.*, Menna
12 Nov.	Livinus
13 Nov.	Briccius
14 Nov.	Briccius
15 Nov.	Machutus, Malo in hieme
16 Nov.	Aeluric, Edmundus, *archiep.*, Margareta, *reg.*
17 Nov.	Anianus, Hilda, Hugo, *ep.* (Lincoln)

19 Nov.	Ronanus, *ep.*
20 Nov.	Edmundus, *r.*
21 Nov.	Maria, B.V., *oblatio, presentatio*
22 Nov.	Cecilia
23 Nov.	Clemens, Felicitas
24 Nov.	Chrysogonus, Gorgonius
25 Nov.	Katerina
26 Nov.	Linus
29 Nov.	Saturninus et Sisinnius, *mm.*
30 Nov.	Andrew
1 Dec.	Crisanthus, Daria, Eligius
3 Dec.	Birinus
4 Dec.	Barbara, Osmundus, *ep.*
6 Dec.	Nicholas
8 Dec.	Maria, B.V., *conceptio*
10 Dec.	Leo II, *p.*
11 Dec.	Damasus
12 Dec.	Eadburga, *abb.*
13 Dec.	Eadburga, *abb.*, Judocus, Lucia
15 Dec.	Barbara, Valerianus
18 Dec.	Gacien, *e.*
21 Dec.	Thomas, *ap.*
26 Dec.	Stephanus, *protom.*
27 Dec.	Johannes, *ap. et evan.*
29 Dec.	Thomas, *archiep.* (Cantuar.)
31 Dec.	Silvester

III Days of the week

Dies dominica, dominicus (prima feria)	Sunday[66]
Dies lune (ii feria)	Monday
Dies martis (iii feria)	Tuesday
Dies mercurii, mercurinus, mercoris (iv feria)	Wednesday
Dies jovis (v feria)	Thursday
Dies veneris (vi feria)	Friday
Dies sabbati (sabbatum)	Saturday

IV The dating of episcopal *acta*[67]

Relatively few bishops' *acta* were dated before 1200, although there are some dated *acta* from almost every see. By the 1190s the *acta* of Godfrey de

66. *Dies dominicus* can also be used specifically for Easter Day.
67. Kindly contributed by Professor C. N. L. Brooke.

Lucy of Winchester and Henry Marshal of Exeter were commonly dated, and the practice spread rapidly in the thirteenth century. Some are dated by the year of the Incarnation; a few by extraneous events – some of Hugh de Nonant of Coventry by Richard I's departure on crusade, or the year of a pope; but most, from Godfrey de Lucy on, by the year of the pontificate of the bishop concerned.[68] 'So far as I can see', wrote Christopher Cheney in 1950, 'the pontifical years date from consecration, and the years of grace from the Annunciation'.[69] As a general rule, this may well be correct; but one needs to be cautious. The use of 25 March was certainly not universal in the late twelfth and early thirteenth centuries; the practice needs to be proved for every individual pontificate. Similarly with the pontifical year. Consecration was the natural and logical base; but it can be very hard to prove in individual cases, especially where election, return of the temporalities and consecration followed one another closely.

A special problem attaches to bishops and archbishops who had been translated. Here, in early days, Cheney said 'the system of reckoning is not evident'. The papal bull authorizing translation was definitive in the spiritual sphere, and appears to have been used; but return of temporalities or enthronement are theoretically possible alternatives. Professor David Smith has studied a number of late medieval archbishops of York and shown that in part at least of the fourteenth and early fifteenth centuries the papal bull was regarded as the base; but from the time of George Neville (translated 1465) onwards a variety of dates of no clear significance occur.

Throughout the Middle Ages it is thus wise to be cautious; it is evident that no precise rules were universally followed.

BIBLIOGRAPHY

Saints' days and festivals.

Attwater, Donald, *The Penguin dictionary of saints* (Harmondsworth, 1965).

Bedae opera de temporibus, ed. C. W. Jones (Cambridge, Mass., 1943).

Bibliotheca sanctorum, 13 vols. (Rome, Istituto Giovanni XXIII della Pontificia Università Lateranense, 1961–70, and supplement, 1987).

Bishop, Edmund, *Liturgica historica* (Oxford, 1918).
> Extremely important essays on the origins of the Feast of the Conception, on various Holy Week rites, etc.

The book of saints, compiled by the Benedictine monks of St Augustine's Abbey, Ramsgate (London, 1921).
> An unpretentious little dictionary of saints, which includes many of post-medieval times.

68. Cf. *English Episcopal Acta*, vols. 8, 11–12, 16.
69. *English Bishops' Chanceries*, p. 90 n. 3.

Farmer, D. H., *The Oxford dictionary of saints,* 2nd edn (Oxford, 1987).

Hampson, R. T., *Medii ævi kalendarium, or dates, charters, and customs of the Middle Ages,* 2 vols. (London, 1841).
A valuable collection of information, particularly useful for facts about festivals, and for the texts of calendars.

Holweck, F. *Calendarium liturgicum festorum Dei et Dei matris Mariae* (Philadelphia, 1925).

Jones, C. W., 'The Victorian and Dionysiac paschal tables', *Speculum,* 9 (1934), 408–21.

McCarthy, D. and Dáibhí Ó Cróinín, 'The "lost" Irish 84-year Easter table rediscovered', *Peritia* 6–7 (1987–88), 227–42.

Nicolas, Sir Nicholas Harris, *The chronology of history* (London, 1838), pp. 132–77, provides a substantial early list of saints' days and other festivals.

Pfaff, R. W., *Liturgical calendars, saints and services in medieval England* (Aldershot, 1998).

Wormald, Francis, *English kalendars before A.D. 1100,* vol. I (Henry Bradshaw Soc. Publications, 72, 1934).
English Benedictine kalendars after A.D. 1100, vol. I (Henry Bradshaw Soc. Publications, 77, 1939).

The following printed calendars from particular places have been used in the construction of the list of saints' days and festivals.

Canterbury
Feltoe, C. L., *Three Canterbury kalendars* (London, 1922).
Gasquet, F. A., and Bishop, E., *The Bosworth psalter* (London, 1908).
James, M. R., *The Canterbury psalter* (London, 1935).

Hereford
Frere, W. H., and Brown, L. E. G., *The Hereford breviary,* 3 vols. (Henry Bradshaw Soc. Publications, 26, 40, 46, 1904–15).

Oxford
Wordsworth, C., *The ancient kalendar of the University of Oxford* (Oxford Hist. Soc. Publications, 45, Oxford, 1904).

Salisbury
Frere, W. H., *Graduale sarisburiense* (Plainsong and Medieval Music Soc. Publications, 1894).

York
Lawley, Stephen, *The York breviary,* 2 vols. (Surtees Soc. Publications, 71, 75, 1880–3).

5

Legal chronology*

I The limit of legal memory

For certain very limited legal purposes 3 September 1189, the date of the coronation of Richard I, still retains its significance as the limit of legal memory.[1] Its original significance was solely that assigned to it by c. 39 of the statute of Westminster I (of 1275):[2] plaintiffs after 1276 were barred from bringing actions based on the seisin of any ancestor or predecessor at any period prior to that date. Initially this did not apply to actions brought by the king but Edward I accepted it even in respect of actions brought in his name as from 12 July 1293.[3] In the Statute of Quo Warranto of 1290 the king had also conceded that continuous exercise of a franchise ever since 1189 was in future to be an acceptable title to the continued exercise of that franchise.[4] It was, however, only gradually that it came to be held by the courts that this same limitation date also applied more widely in legal proceedings: that litigants could not rely on deeds made prior to 1189 or allege facts which had occurred prior to that date and that when they were trying to establish customary entitlements based on continuous possession or exercise of a right 'since time out of mind' all they needed to do was to prove continuous possession or exercise since 1189.[5]

II Limitation of actions

Although there was legislation early in the reign of Henry II that barred *anglici* from bringing claims to land based on the seisin of any ancestor at a date prior to the death of Henry I (1135), this may not have become a

*Chiefly revised by Dr Paul Brand.
  1. *Halsbury's laws of England* (4th edn, 1975), 12, paras 407–8, 421.
  2. *Statutes of the realm*, I, 36.
  3. *Placita de quo warranto*, pp. 203, 352.
  4. The statute itself envisages the need for a royal confirmation of this title but in practice these were not required: see Donald W. Sutherland, *Quo warranto proceedings in the reign of Edward I, 1278–1294* (Oxford, 1963), pp. 91–110, 203–5.
  5. Paul Brand, '"Time out of mind": the knowledge and use of the eleventh- and twelfth-century past in thirteenth-century litigation', *Anglo-Norman Studies* 16 (1994), 37–54.

general limitation date in actions of right for land and other forms of real property until shortly before 1200. Prior to that date litigants seem to have been able to bring actions based on the ancestor or predecessor at any time during Henry I's reign.[6] A separate rule had long barred litigants from basing their claim on a seisin during Stephen's reign. In 1237 the limitation date for actions of right was advanced by legislation to 1154 (the coronation of Henry II) to take effect in cases initiated after Whitsun 1238;[7] but there continued to be a trickle of cases based on pre-1154 seisins down to 1275 brought by litigants who could justify their claims on the basis that they were renewing claims first made prior to 1237. Further legislation of 1275 (Westminster I, c. 39) advanced the date once more to the coronation of Richard I (3 September 1189) to take effect in cases initiated after 8 July (two weeks after the Nativity of St John the Baptist) 1276;[8] cases brought by writs acquired prior to that date or renewing such suits were still being brought as late as 1291.[9] There were no further changes in the limitation dates until 1540. The reason for these changes in limitation dates was probably related to the logic of proof. A champion offering battle in the action of right was formally offering proof of what he had himself seen or of what his father had seen during his lifetime: the changing limitation dates reflect the most generous estimates of how far back two lifetimes might span. The failure to change the limitation date after 1275 may reflect the fact that the grand assize had come to be much more common than trial by battle as a means of proof in such actions and the fact that grand assize jurors for seisins after 1189 could often rely on written evidence to supplement their otherwise fallible collective memory.

Other forms of action had much shorter limitation periods. The earliest known limitation date in the assize of mort d'ancestor (included in the writ itself) required the ancestor on whose seisin at death the plaintiff was claiming to have died since Henry II's first coronation (19 December 1154).[10] This was advanced c. 1218–20 to Richard I's first coronation (3 September 1189); in 1238 (under legislation of 1237) to King John's last return from Ireland (24/26 August 1210) and in 1276 (under Westminster I, c. 39) to Henry III's first coronation (17 May 1220).[11] The same limitation

---

6. Brand, 'Time out of mind', 39–40.
7. *Close rolls, 1234–1237*, pp. 520–1: the legislation was later included in the generally accepted and circulated text of the statute of Merton of 1236 as c. 8 (*Statutes of the realm*, I. 3).
8. *Stat. Realm*, I. 36.
9. Brand, 'Time out of mind', 39–40.
10. *Glanvill*, XIII, 3 (ed. Hall, p. 150).
11. G. D. G. Hall, *Early registers of writs* (Selden Society, vol. 87 (1970)), pp. xxxvi–xxvii; *Statutes of the realm*, I. 36.

dates also applied in the action of naifty (by 1229 at latest), in almost all writs of entry (by 1238 at latest) and in the actions of aiel and cosinage. The earliest known limitation date in the assize of novel disseisin (also incorporated in the writ) is the king's (Henry II's) last voyage to Normandy, the limitation date included in the writ given in *Glanvill*.[12] In 1202 this became King John's coronation at Canterbury (at Easter 1201); in 1218 King John's last return from Ireland (24/26 August 1210); in 1229 King Henry III's first coronation at Westminster (17 May 1220); in 1237 King Henry III's first voyage to Brittany (1 May 1230) and in 1276 (under Westminster I, c. 39) King Henry III's first voyage to Gascony (8/9 May 1242).[13] There were no further changes to any of these limitation dates during the later Middle Ages despite some attempts to alter them.

The next major reform in limitation dates did not take place until 1540 when statute 32 Hen. VIII, c. 2 substituted fixed (but moving) limitation periods of sixty years in the writ of right and fifty years in other real actions for the late thirteenth-century limitation dates: by then the real actions were largely obsolete.[14]

iii The law terms

The Common Bench at Westminster, from the time of its separation from the Exchequer in the mid-1190s, seems to have heard and dealt with business on an almost continuous, day-by-day basis during four distinct periods of the year, the law terms, and separate plea rolls were compiled to record the business heard during each of these terms. The terms were so constituted as to avoid the major ecclesiastical festivals (Christmas and Easter, though not Whitsun) and the periods immediately preceding and succeeding them and so as to ensure that the court did not sit during Lent or harvest-time. The longest of the terms, *Michaelmas*, began one week after Michaelmas, at the end of the first week of October, a week later than the Exchequer. Prior to 1230, Michaelmas term commonly continued past Advent Sunday to end as late as 7 December (in 1200 and 1223) or even 9 December (in 1195) but thereafter it normally finished on about 1 December. After a break for Christmas and the feast of the Epiphany, *Hilary* term began one week after the feast of St Hilary (20 January) and always continued for at least two weeks, usually continued for at least

---

12. *Glanvill*, XIII, 33 (ed. Hall, p. 167).
13. Hall, *Early registers of writs*, pp. xxxv–xxxvi; *Statutes of the realm*, I, 36.
14. Holdsworth, *History of English law*, IV, 484.

three weeks and occasionally lasted for as many as four or five weeks (as in 1200, 1224, 1229, 1243 and 1278). The term regularly ran on past Septuagesima but ended before the beginning of Lent, perhaps because of the ecclesiastical prohibition on the taking of oaths during Lent: the differing lengths of the term were determined by the different dates for the beginning of Lent. *Easter* term always began two weeks (and a day) after Easter Sunday, again a week later than the Exchequer, and regularly continued past the feast of the Ascension to end one week after Ascensiontide. *Trinity* term was also of variable length. It always began a week and a day after Trinity Sunday and normally ended three weeks after the feast of the Nativity of St John the Baptist (14 July): its length depended on when Trinity Sunday fell in the year concerned. When the court of King's Bench was reconstituted on a permanent basis *c.* 1234 it too adopted a similar pattern of hearing business in termly sessions and its terms were of similar length to those of the Common Bench.

Between 1195 and 1200 final concords made in the Common Bench give the actual dates on which they were made[15] and these show that the court then commonly dealt with business on a Sunday. There is also some evidence from the reign of Henry III that shows the court dealing with business on a Sunday but by the reign of Edward I, Sunday had become a day on which business was not normally heard by the Common Bench.[16] In the early seventeenth century the Common Bench also did not sit on certain major feast days that fell within the four terms:[17] these were All Saints (1 November) and All Souls Days (2 November) in Michaelmas term; the feast of the Purification (2 February) in Hilary term; Ascensiontide in Easter term; and the Nativity of St John the Baptist (24 June) in Trinity term. This was probably also the case in the Middle Ages, and there seems to be no evidence to prove that the list of excluded days was then significantly longer than this.

The plea rolls of the Common Bench and King's Bench record business done in these courts under headings which allocate individual items not to the specific days on which they occurred, but to one of a number of 'return days' within the term concerned, each of which covered a period of up to six calendar days. After 1200, the final concords made in the

15. These are tabulated in *Pleas before the King and his justices, 1198–1212*, vol. III, ed. D. M. Stenton (Selden Society, vol. 83 (1966)), at pp. cii–clxv.
16. *Fleta*, book II, *c.* 35 (ed. Richardson and Sayles, p. 137) and for cases in which it is assumed that Sunday is not a normal day for business, see PRO CP 40/83, *m.* 85d; CP 40/141, *m.* 97. But for land being replevied before the justices on a Sunday in 1277 see CP 40/19, *m.* 75d.
17. Coke, *Institutes*, II, 135a.

Common Bench likewise record these agreements as made not on a specific actual day but on one of these same 'return days'. Each 'return day' was denominated by the day with which the period commenced (or sometimes the day *preceding* that day as with return days denominated in terms of the number of days or weeks after Easter or Trinity). The standard return days used in the Common Bench and King's Bench from the second quarter of the thirteenth century onwards (with the probable calendar duration of each being given, where possible) were:

Michaelmas
octaves of Michaelmas [6–12 October]
quindene of Michaelmas [13–19 October]
three weeks after Michaelmas [20–6 October]
one month after Michaelmas [27 October–3 November]
morrow of All Souls [2–8 November]
morrow of Martinmas [12–17 November]
octave of Martinmas [18–24 November]
quindene of Martinmas [25 November–1 December]

Hilary
octaves of Hilary [20–6 January]
quindene of Hilary [27 January–2 February]
three weeks after Hilary *or* morrow of the Purification [3–8 February]
*octaves of the Purification [9–15 February]
**quindene of the Purification [16–22 February]

Easter
quindene of Easter [beginning two weeks and a day after Easter Sunday]
three weeks afer Easter [beginning three weeks and a day after Easter
    Sunday]
one month after Easter [beginning four weeks and a day after Easter
    Sunday]
five weeks after Easter [beginning five weeks and a day after Easter
    Sunday]
morrow of the Ascension

Trinity
octaves of Trinity [beginning one week and one day after Trinity Sunday]
*quindene of Trinity [beginning two weeks and one day after Trinity
    Sunday]
**three weeks after Trinity [beginning three weeks and one day after
    Trinity Sunday]
**one month after Trinity [beginning four weeks and one day after Trinity
    Sunday]

morrow of St John the Baptist [25–30 June]
octaves of St John the Baptist [1–7 July]
quindene of St John the Baptist [8–14 July]

*sometimes omitted
** often omitted

'Return days' were not just a matter of the court's record-keeping. When litigants were summoned to appear in the court or adjourned for future appearance there the day they were given was not an actual calendar day but one of these 'return days'. From quite early in the thirteenth century there were complex rules about when within the 'return day' period certain procedural steps had to be taken. The essoin of bed-sickness (*de malo lecti*), available in actions of right, had to be presented by the essoiner three days *before* the first day of the 'return day', while other essoins had to be presented on the first day of the 'return day'; but in neither case was judgment given on the essoin until the fourth day of the 'return day'. A plaintiff suing mesne process against the defendant or seeking a judg-ment against them by default had to appear on each of the first three days of the 'return day' (excluding Sundays) before being able to secure judg-ment for the next stage of process or by default on the fourth day (hence the standard 'X. offered himself on the fourth day against Y'. of so many plea roll entries). If the defendant turned up on the first day of the 'return day' but the plaintiff did not he also would be required to make an appear-ance on the second and third days as well before being able to secure a judgment on the non-suit of the plaintiff (generally, dismissing the case), on the fourth day: the plaintiff could only save his initial default on the first day by producing a special excuse for his absence or persuading the defendant to waive the default. Cases where both parties appeared in court on the first day of the return day might be heard on any of the days of the 'return day' and by 1275 (according to Westminster I, c. 46) were also being heard during later 'return days';[18] when cases were adjourned for hearing later in the same term, this was not noted on the plea rolls of the courts.

By the middle of the thirteenth century, it had come to be the normal practice of the Common Bench when adjourning cases for a future hearing in the court (either because of the defendant's absence or for the appear-ance of a jury etc.) to fix the eighth 'return day' following for the next appearance in the case. This is the scheme of adjournments given in the

18. *Statutes of the realm*, I, 38.

pseudo-statutory *Dies communes de Banco* that is found in so many private statute books of the later thirteenth and fourteenth centuries and of which one version is printed in *Statutes of the realm*, I. 208. *Dies communes de banco* is, however, an idealized version which takes no adequate account of the differing lengths of Hilary and Trinity terms in any particular year: thus the adjournments recorded on the plea-rolls do not always match those given in this work. The justices of the court also seem long to have retained some flexibility to make shorter that standard adjournments in cases where they thought it desirable and also longer ones, though generally only when this was specifically requested by the plaintiff. Clause 6 of the Provisions of Westminster of 1259 required shorter adjournments to be given as a matter of course in all actions of dower *unde nichil habet* so as to allow such cases to come up for hearing before the court four times in a year.[19] When the legislation was reissued in 1263 this was amended to a minimum of five with six hearings in a year as a desirable target and this in turn was reissued in 1267 as part of c. 12 of the statute of Marlborough.[20] The pseudo-statutory *Dies communes de dote* reflects this legislation, with adjournments in such pleas being to a return day four return days distant: again this represents an idealised version of the actual practice of the court, rather than a useful practical guide to clerks and justices when making adjournments.[21]

The first attempt to fix specific periods of the year for the holding of sessions by the justices of assize was that made in 1285 by the statute of Westminster II, c. 30.[22] Since it was part of a wider rearrangement of the assize system which envisaged the justices of the central courts playing a significant role in the assize circuits the dates chosen for the most part fell within the vacations of those courts; between the quindene of St John the Baptist (8 July) and the Gules of August (1 August), immediately after the end of Trinity; between the feast of the Exaltation of the Cross (14 September) and the octaves of Michaelmas (6 October), immediately preceding Michaelmas term; and between the feast of the Epiphany (6 January) and the feast of the Purification (2 February), overlapping with the start of Hilary term. When the system was recast in 1293 with permanent full-time justices these term limitations were removed[23] but a further reorganization in 1303 brought back the previous assize terms.[24] From the

19. *Close rolls, 1259–1261*, p. 148.
20. *Statutes of the realm*, I, 9, 23.
21. *Statutes of the realm*, I, 208.
22. *Statutes of the realm*, I, 85–6.
23. *Rotuli parliamentorum*, I, 99.
24. *Cal. Close rolls, 1302–1307*, pp. 89–90.

fourteenth century onwards it came to be the norm for assize sessions (whose justices also acted as justices of gaol delivery and *nisi prius*) to be held in most counties only twice each year. By the sixteenth century these sessions had come to take place during the Lent vacation (after, rather than before, Hilary term) and in the Summer vacation (in July and early August).

To the scanty medieval legislation already mentioned we may add a statute defining the effect of leap year in 1256.[25] Later statutes dealt with the terms as follows:

32 Henry VIII, c. 21.   Trinity term in 1541 and for the future shall begin the morrow of Trinity for formal matters, and full term on the following Friday. The return days shall be Crastino trinitatis, octave, quindene and three weeks (tres septimanas); the act abolished the returns of the morrow, octave and quindene of St John the Baptist. (The result was to begin term a week earlier and to fix its duration, hitherto variable, at three weeks.)

16 Charles I, c. 6.   Michaelmas term (which conflicts with quarter sessions, causing great inconvenience) shall begin in and after 1641 three weeks from Michaelmas (full term four days later). The first two (octave and quindene of Michaelmas) of its eight traditional returns were abolished, the other six retained. (The result was to cut off two weeks at the commencement of term.)

24 George II, c. 48.   The early part of Michaelmas term being much interrupted by saints' days, term shall begin in 1752 and thenceforward on the morrow of All Souls, thus leaving only the last four of the traditional eight returns. The dates of naming sheriffs and swearing the Lord Mayor of London no longer falling within the shortened term, new dates were ordained (and further amended by 25 Geo. II, c. 30).

11 George IV and 1 William IV, c. 70.   In and after 1831 the dates of terms were fixed as follows: Hilary, 11–31 Jan.; Easter, 15 April–8 May; Trinity, 22 May–12 June; Michaelmas, 2–25 November. If this meant that Easter term would continue into the period between the Thursday before and the Wednesday after Easter Day, then the term would be suspended between those days. The days lost would be made up after Easter and in order to do so the start and end of the Trinity term would be adjusted accordingly. The Act also altered return days: those which were to fall on the fourth day before the commencement of the term, and then on the fifth, fifteenth and nineteenth days of term. If this meant that the return day fell on a Sunday, it was to be moved to the following Monday.

---

25. *Statutes of the realm*, I, 7; Maitland, *Bracton's note book*, I, 43.

2 and 3 William IV, c. 39. By s. 11 of this Uniformity of Process Act (1832), return days were abolished together with the procedures of which they formed a part.

36 and 37 Victoria, c. 66. By s. 26 of this Judicature Act (1873) terms were abolished. The sittings were now governed by the Rules of the Supreme Court, and have no procedural significance.

The above material should be sufficient to date legal proceedings with sufficient accuracy for most purposes. Minor points of difficulty abound, however. It has not been possible to get access to the early almanacks; those of the seventeenth century cited above contain some discrepancies in detail. Thus the four days which constitute a return are sometimes included in the term, and sometimes not.[26] Nor was it unusual for the dates to be altered by proclamation, especially in time of plague.[27] There was also a certain element of fiction, as when judgments were deemed to take effect from the first day of term; that rule was abolished in 1677 by the Statute of Frauds (29 Charles II, c. 3).

In using the Plea Rolls, Year Books, and early reports it will be observed that in certain reigns the regnal year changes in the course of a term; in strict practice that term ought to be ascribed to both years, and that is done in the Plea Rolls. Thus Michaelmas, 18 & 19 Edw. I would be described as *anno xviii finiente*, or *anno xviii, incipiente xix*.[28] The Year Books frequently omit the precaution, and thus leave it to be conjectured whether the term which they report is the one at the beginning or the end of the regnal year. The double year is often needed for John's Easter term, and always for the following:

Henry III: Michaelmas.

Edward I: Michaelmas (Year Books treat it as the last term of the year, neglecting the five days days which technically belong to the beginning of the next year).

Edward II: Trinity (the year changed on 8 July which as the quindene of St John and the last return day; the Year Books treat it as the last term of the year).

Richard II: Trinity (as far as has been ascertained, the Year Books always

26. In *Lord Sandes's Case* (1571), it was held that Full Term began on the *quartus dies post*, this 'related back' to the essoin-day; therefore, when the essoin-day fell in one regnal year and the *quartus dies* in the next term, the term was deemed to fall in both years. Thus Easter Term 1545, when the essoin-day was 20 April, had to be written Pas. 36 and 37 Hen. VIII (cf. *Selden Society* 109 (1994), 212 and 110 (1994), 222, a note owed to Professor J. H. Baker).
27. Leadam, *Court of requests* (Selden Society), 36, no. 7.
28. Cf. *List of Plea Rolls*.

regard the regnal year as beginning with Trinity term irrespective of the actual incidence of the term).

Richard III: Trinity (there is no printed Year Book for Trinity in any year of this king).

The position next occurs in Edward VI (Hilary) and Elizabeth (Michaelmas); by this time the reporters and their editors generally take care to use the double regnal year.

Finally, it should be remembered that in legal records (as elsewhere) the phrase 'in the morrow of' means 'the day following' rather than 'on the morning of'. On 3 February 1653/4, for example, Christopher Milton (brother of the poet) sold land to William Hobson. The foot of fines entry is dated 'in the morrow of the Purification of the blessed Mary in the yeare of our Lorde One thousand six hundred and ffifty three' (PRO, CP 25/2 462/572). Students should also be aware that the date of Michaelmas might vary by local custom.[29]

IV The exchequer of pleas

The reckoning of the exchequer's fiscal year is explained elsewhere. It seems to have influenced the dating of exchequer Plea Rolls although they do not actually use the fiscal dates. The medieval rolls are annual, not terminal; each roll contains a year's business, but divided according to the four terms and ascribed to the sessions within the term. Under Henry III the annual rolls begin with Michaelmas and generally bear a double year since the regnal year changes at mid-term. Thus the first extant roll contains a year's business beginning *in crastino sancti Michaelis anno xx incipiente xxi* – a period corresponding with the twenty-first exchequer year. Under Edward I the situation was similar, save that the year turned almost at the end of term; the exchequer of pleas continued, however, to begin its annual roll with Michaelmas under the double date (the Year Books would treat that same term as the last of the preceding year). The accident of the accession date in these two reigns was thus utilized in keeping the Plea Rolls in step with the fiscal year. The same chance allowed the Plea Rolls of Edward II's exchequer to begin with Michaelmas. But Edward III's accession in January made a double date again necessary; thus the roll 1 and 2 Edw. III contains the Michaelmas of the first year and Hilary, Easter, and Trinity of the second.

29. See e.g., *Doe d. Spicer v. Lea* (1809), 11 East 312 'old Michaelmas' (ex inf. Professor J. H. Baker).

The terms had less procedural significance than in the common pleas. Within the term certain days became habitual as sitting days rather than as return days. Thus in 1236–7 the sessions were:

the morrow, octave and three weeks of Michaelmas; octave of All Saints; quindene of St Martin; morrow and octave of St Andrew;

the morrow and octave of Hilary; the octave and quindene of the Purification; morrow of Ash Wednesday;

the morrow of the close of Easter; the quindene and the month; morrow of the Ascension;

the morrow and octave of Trinity; three weeks of St John.

In 52 Henry III a rule of the court attempted to check its growing encroachment upon common pleas jurisdiction by shortening this list, thus leaving more time for revenue cases, but apparently without success. It will be observed from these dates that the court sat within the first week of Advent and Lent. The exchequer of account sat as late as mid-Lent, and not infrequently on Sundays.

The material in this section is based largely upon *Select cases in the exchequer of pleas*, which ends at 1307. There is little subsequent material in print from which to reconstruct the court's chronology. One feature which may have remained characteristic for centuries is the fact that the court's terms began on the morrow of Trinity, Michaelmas, Hilary and the close of Easter, while the common pleas began on the octaves and quindene (and thus a week later). We still find in 1612 that 'the exchequer always opens eight days before any term, only excepting Trinity and then it openeth but four days before'.[30]

v Chancery and Star Chamber

The old tradition that 'the chancery is always open'[31] means that the court's procedure was not fettered by the common law system of terms and return days. Both chancery and Star Chamber, however, held their sessions, and to some extent organized their work, according to the common law terms.

vi Parliament and statutes

The chronological and procedural unit of parliamentary business is the session, and it has long been the rule that work (not being judicial or

30. Arthur Hopton, *Concordancy of yeeres* (1612), p. 245.
31. William Tothill, *Transactions of the high court of chancery* (1649), p. 9.

quasi-judicial) left incomplete in one session cannot be finished in the next, but must be re-commenced *de novo*, if at all.[32] The normal mode of terminating a session and beginning a new one is by prorogation. The matter is confused, however, by the fact that in former times some prorogations (especially those occasioned by Christmas or Easter) were regarded by contemporaries as merely adjournments and consequently as not 'discontinuing' business; it will further be observed that Hale (writing between 1674 and 1676) uses the words 'prorogation' and 'adjournment' interchangeably. In the sixteenth century, moreover, there was an opinion (*Commons' Journal*, 21 Nov. 1554) that a session was automatically determined by the royal assent to a bill (which for centuries past had normally taken place on the last day of the parliament). We find in consequence that even after the Restoration it was sometimes felt necessary to include a clause saying that the royal assent to this act shall not be held to have determined the session.

The construction of a chronological list of sessions, meaning thereby sittings whose uncompleted work was held by contemporary officials to have been 'discontinued', is therefore rendered difficult since the meaning of the words 'prorogation' and 'adjournment' is known to have varied, and the detailed history of the idea of a 'session' still awaits investigation.[33] The list in the *Interim report of the committee on House of Commons personnel*, 1932 (Cmd. 4130) is of great utility, but it does not fulfil these requirements since it seems to be based upon the assumption that a prorogation always ended a session. The list thus introduces some discrepancies: it discerns eight sessions in the Reformation Parliament, where the older books (based on the parliament roll) found only seven; on the other hand it enumerates sixteen sessions of the Cavalier Parliament, although the parliament roll as printed in the *Statutes of the realm* tells of seventeen. Other instances will be mentioned shortly. For historical reference, therefore, we need a list of the periods over which parliament actually sat, accompanied by an indication of how those periods were grouped into sessions for the purpose of parliamentary procedure. The dates in such a list should be in regnal as well as calendar years, since the resulting statutes are cited by the regnal years.

The dating and citing of statutes presents a number of problems, which are in no way simplified by the fact that the citation consists partly of a date.

32. M. Hale, *Jurisdiction of the Lords' House*, p. 167; Blackstone, *Commentaries*, i. 186; *Report of the joint committee on the suspension of bills*, 1929, HC 105.
33. Cf. A. F. Pollard in *The Times* newspaper of 11 Jan. 1940.

In one sense the date of a statute is the date when it comes into force. There is no difficulty when there is an 'appointed day' in the body of the act, but, failing that, recourse was made to the fiction that the whole of a parliamentary session was one day, and that the first day (which was of course normally well known through the writs of summons and election). This proposition, or something like it, appears in *Pilkington's Case* in 1455 (YB 33 Hen. VI, Pasch. no. 8). In a well-known essay, Maitland[34] questioned whether this doctrine was still held in 1559; but he seems to have overlooked the case of *Partridge v. Strange*[35] which had just reiterated the principle in 1553. However, it was held that if Parliament was not dissolved after the royal assent was given, but prorogued, the new session was treated as a distinct parliament for chronological purposes. That rule, still controverisal in the 1550s, was always observed thereafter.[36] Thus an act which received the royal assent at the end of a long session was deemed to have been in force ever since the first day. This retrospective operation resulting from the fictitious date caused great injustice, especially when the statute imposed penalties, but the principle was rigorously applied in the seventeenth and eighteenth centuries until 1793,[37] when the act of 33 Geo. III, c. 13, required that the date of the royal assent be endorsed upon the act, and that the act come into force that day, unless otherwise provided. If the date of the making (as distinct from the commencement) of a statute is required, the only sure method is to trace the stages of its progress through the *Journals* down to the royal assent in the *Lords' Journal*. It must be remembered that the *Journals*, like *Rotuli parliamentorum* and the *Statutes of the realm* all begin the year of grace on 25 March, until 1752.

The citation of a statute consists of a date and a chapter number. The present system is the result of the practices of the parliamentary officials, the printers of the sessions laws, the editors of various collections of statutes, and the increasingly strict requirements of the law courts in the pleading of statutes. The lack of uniformity, especially for the older statutes, is due to the fact that as the system slowly took shape, older statutes were reprinted with citations conformable to the newer fashion. The regnal year in the citation is the year of the session (or at least of the sitting) in which the statute was passed. Every act of a session forms a

---

34. *Collected papers*, III, 195.
35. Edmund Plowden, *Les comentaires, ou les reportes* (1571), 77.
36. Cf. *Selden Society* 109 (1994), pp. lv–lvi for examples.
37. Cf. the cases collected in Kent, *Commentaries*, I, 454 *sqq.*

chapter, but their order is not strictly chronological (thus in 33 Geo. III, cc. 26 and 28 received the royal assent on 30 April, c. 27 on 7 May). By a useful but modern convention public acts have the chapter number in arabic numerals, private acts are numbered separately in roman numerals. The following situations may occur:

(*a*) If there was but one session in the regnal year, and if that session lay wholly within the year, there is generally little difficulty and the statute will be cited by that year. Thus 12 Charles II, c. 1 (the 'Convention' Parliament sat April–December 1660, wholly within the regnal year; the parliament roll as printed in the *Statutes of the realm* treats this period as one session, but the *Interim report* finds two sessions there).

(*b*) If there were two sessions both wholly within the same regnal year, their acts are usually distinguished as 'statute I' and 'statute II' (or 'session I' and 'session II'). Thus 13 Charles II, stat. I, c. 1, is the Treason Act of 1661, and 13 Charles II, stat. II, c. 1, is the Corporations Act, 1661 (the 'Cavalier' Parliament sat May–July and November–December 1661 and the thirteenth regnal year ran from 30 Jan. 1661; the parliament roll groups the two sets of statutes separately, but the *Interim report* regards both of these two periods as forming a single session with the one next following).

(*c*) If one session extends over two regnal years, its acts must be cited by both years. Thus 13 and 14 Charles II, c. 23, reorganized the Insurance Court (the Cavalier Parliament reassembled on 7 Jan. 1662, 13 Charles II, and sat until 19 May 1662, 14 Charles II; the double citation is used in Ruffhead's *Statutes at large* but not in the *Statutes of the realm*. As an example of the confusion possible see the general index to Holdsworth, who, having used different citations for this statute in different volumes, listed them separately as though they were two different statutes).

(*d*) Occasional oddities occur such as the Long Parliament, which seems never to have been prorogued or adjourned by the king, with the result that all its legitimate acts bear the date 16 Charles I.

The above examples illustrate the application to old statutes of the modern system whose present working is explained by Sir Cecil Carr, 'The citation of statutes', in *Cambridge legal essays*. In the interests of uniformity it is desirable that acts down to 1713 should be cited as in the *Statutes of the realm* (but *not* by volume and page only). Since that work is not easily accessible it is worth remembering that the *Chronological table and index of statutes* issued annually since 1870 by the Stationery Office reproduces its citations, and also contains a table of differences betweeen the *Statutes of the realm* and Ruffhead's *Statutes at large*.

VII County court days

These days are of more than local interest since they determine the dates of (*a*) outlawry proceedings, (*b*) parliamentary elections. Data from which they can be calculated will be found in J. J. Alexander's note on 'The dates of county days' (see below, p. 144).

VIII The terms of the Court of Arches

There is very little material accessible on the terms kept by English ecclesi-astical courts in the Middle Ages. There is, however, a *Kalendere commune cum diebus non sessionis in curia de arcubus et obitibus episcoporum Cicestr* in the Bodleian MS Ashmole 1146, fos. 1v–7r. It was written in 1369–70, and it would seem that at that time the court of arches kept three sessions, thus:

(*a*) Prima dies sessionis: 14 Jan.

Dies non sessionis: St Wulfstan (19 Jan., dedication of the church of St Mary de arcubus); St Vincent (22 Jan.); Conversion of St Paul (25 Jan.); Purification of the BVM (2 Feb.); St Blasius (3 Feb.); Cathedra Petri (22 Feb.); St Matthias (24 Feb.); Ash Wednesday and the two preceding days; St Gregory (12 March); Annunciation of the BVM (25 March); St Ambrose (4 April); St Mark (25 April);

ultima dies sessionis: vigilia passionis dominice

(*b*) Prima dies sessionis: dies lune proxima post dominicam qua can-tatur officium 'Misericordia domini' [i.e. Monday after the second Sunday after Easter; hence 6 April is the earliest possible date].

Dies non sessionis: Sts Philip and James (1 May); Holy Cross (3 May); St John ante portam latinam (6 May); St Dunstan (19 May); St Augustine (26 May); three rogation days and the vigil of Pentecost; Transl. St Edmund (9 June); St Barnabas (11 June); St Etheldreda (23 June); St John the Baptist (24 June); Sts Peter and Paul (29 June); Conversion of St Paul (30 June); Transl. St Thomas the Martyr (7 July); St Margaret (20 July); St Mary Magdalene (22 July); St James (25 July);

ultima dies sessionis: 31 July

(*c*) Prima dies sessionis: 7 Oct.

Dies non sessionis: Transl. St Edward the king (13 Oct.); St Luke (18 Oct.); Sts Simon and Jude (28 Oct.); All Saints (1 Nov.); All Souls (2 Nov.); St Martin (11 Nov.); St Edmund the abp. (16 Nov.); St Edmund the king (20 Nov.); St Clement the pope (23 Nov.); St Katherine (25 Nov.); St Andrew (30 Nov.); St Nicholas (6 Dec.); Conception of the BVM (8 Dec.);

ultima dies sessionis: 16 December.

This scheme of apparently three sessions easily breaks into four terms, and had done so before Arthur Hopton published *Concordancy of yeeres* (1612). In his day Hilary term began on the morrow of Hilary (14 Jan.), Easter term on the fifteenth day after Easter, Trinity term on Trinity Monday, and Michaelmas term on the morrow of St Faith (7 Oct.). This closely corresponds with the Chichester calendar summarized above, save for the new term at Trinitytide. His list of holy days is similar but shorter, and he says that the court may dispense with those later in the term if pressed for time. Substantially the same scheme with minor variants will be found in T. Powell, *Attorneys academy* (1630). Thomas Oughton, *Ordo judiciorum*, title III, gives the commencement of the terms as above with some notes on earlier practice. In his day the official of the court named all days of business according to need, the only fixed days being the first day of every term.

ix Other ecclesiastical and civilian courts

Practitioners in the court of arches were also generally concerned with many other ecclesiastical courts, and also with the court of admiralty. There was a curious working arrangement which enabled them to conduct their multifarious business, described by both Hopton and Oughton. When business began on the first day of term, or was resumed after a holy day, the morning of the first day was devoted to the arches, and the afternoon to the admiralty; the morning of the second day was for the audience court of Canterbury, and the afternoon for the prerogative court of Canterbury; the morning of the third day was for the bishop of London's consistory court and the afternoon for the high court of delegates and commissioners of appeals.

5/x Tables of law terms from AD 1066 to AD 1830[38]

Hilary term

Year	Began	Ended		Year	Began	Ended
1066	23 Jan.	13 Feb.		1106	23 Jan.	12 Feb.
1067	23 Jan.	12 Feb.		1107	23 Jan.	12 Feb.
1068	23 Jan.	12 Feb.		1108	23 Jan.	12 Feb.
1069	23 Jan.	12 Feb.		1109	23 Jan.	12 Feb.
1070	23 Jan.	12 Feb.		1110	24 Jan.	12 Feb.
1071	24 Jan.	12 Feb.		1111	23 Jan.	13 Feb.
1072	23 Jan.	13 Feb.		1112	23 Jan.	12 Feb.
1073	23 Jan.	12 Feb.		1113	23 Jan.	12 Feb.
1074	23 Jan.	12 Feb.		1114	23 Jan.	12 Feb.
1075	23 Jan.	12 Feb.		1115	23 Jan.	12 Feb.
1076	23 Jan.	12 Feb.		1116	24 Jan.	12 Feb.
1077	23 Jan.	13 Feb.		1117	23 Jan.	12 Feb.
1078	23 Jan.	12 Feb.		1118	23 Jan.	12 Feb.
1079	23 Jan.	12 Feb.		1119	23 Jan.	12 Feb.
1080	23 Jan.	12 Feb.		1120	23 Jan.	12 Feb.
1081	23 Jan.	12 Feb.		1121	24 Jan.	12 Feb.
1082	24 Jan.	12 Feb.		1122	23 Jan.	13 Feb.
1083	23 Jan.	13 Feb.		1123	23 Jan.	12 Feb.
1084	23 Jan.	12 Feb.		1124	23 Jan.	12 Feb.
1085	23 Jan.	12 Feb.		1125	23 Jan.	12 Feb.
1086	23 Jan.	12 Feb.		1126	23 Jan.	12 Feb.
1087	23 Jan.	12 Feb.		1127	24 Jan.	12 Feb.
1088	24 Jan.	12 Feb.		1128	23 Jan.	13 Feb.
1089	23 Jan.	12 Feb.		1129	23 Jan.	12 Feb.
1090	23 Jan.	12 Feb.		1130	23 Jan.	12 Feb.
1091	23 Jan.	12 Feb.		1131	23 Jan.	12 Feb.
1092	23 Jan.	12 Feb.		1132	23 Jan.	12 Feb.
1093	24 Jan.	12 Feb.		1133	23 Jan.	13 Feb.
1094	23 Jan.	13 Feb.		1134	23 Jan.	12 Feb.
1095	23 Jan.	12 Feb.		1135	23 Jan.	12 Feb.
1096	23 Jan.	12 Feb.		1136	23 Jan.	12 Feb.
1097	23 Jan.	12 Feb.		1137	23 Jan.	12 Feb.
1098	23 Jan.	12 Feb.		1138	24 Jan.	12 Feb.
1099	24 Jan.	12 Feb.		1139	23 Jan.	13 Feb.
1100	23 Jan.	13 Feb.		1140	23 Jan.	12 Feb.
1101	23 Jan.	12 Feb.		1141	23 Jan.	12 Feb.
1102	23 Jan.	12 Feb.		1142	23 Jan.	12 Feb.
1103	23 Jan.	12 Feb.		1143	23 Jan.	12 Feb.
1104	23 Jan.	12 Feb.		1144	24 Jan.	12 Feb.
1105	23 Jan.	13 Feb.		1145	23 Jan.	12 Feb.

38. Originally prepared by A. T. Watson and published as an Appendix to the *Twenty-Eighth Report of the Deputy Keeper of the Public Records* (1867), 114–38.

Year	Began	Ended		Year	Began	Ended
1146	23 Jan.	12 Feb.		1195	23 Jan.	13 Feb.
1147	23 Jan.	12 Feb.		1196	23 Jan.	12 Feb.
1148	23 Jan.	12 Feb.		1197	23 Jan.	12 Feb.
1149	24 Jan.	12 Feb.		1198	23 Jan.	12 Feb.
1150	23 Jan.	13 Feb.		1199	23 Jan.	12 Feb.
1151	23 Jan.	12 Feb.		1200	24 Jan.	12 Feb.
1152	23 Jan.	12 Feb.		1201	23 Jan.	12 Feb.
1153	23 Jan.	12 Feb.		1202	23 Jan.	12 Feb.
1154	23 Jan.	12 Feb.		1203	23 Jan.	12 Feb.
1155	24 Jan.	12 Feb.		1204	23 Jan.	12 Feb.
1156	23 Jan.	13 Feb.		1205	24 Jan.	12 Feb.
1157	23 Jan.	12 Feb.		1206	23 Jan.	13 Feb.
1158	23 Jan.	12 Feb.		1207	23 Jan.	12 Feb.
1159	23 Jan.	12 Feb.		1208	23 Jan.	12 Feb.
1160	23 Jan.	12 Feb.		1209	23 Jan.	12 Feb.
1161	23 Jan.	13 Feb.		1210	23 Jan.	12 Feb.
1162	23 Jan.	12 Feb.		1211	24 Jan.	12 Feb.
1163	23 Jan.	12 Feb.		1212	23 Jan.	13 Feb.
1164	23 Jan.	12 Feb.		1213	23 Jan.	12 Feb.
1165	23 Jan.	12 Feb.		1214	23 Jan.	12 Feb.
1166	24 Jan.	12 Feb.		1215	23 Jan.	12 Feb.
1167	23 Jan.	13 Feb.		1216	23 Jan.	12 Feb.
1168	23 Jan.	12 Feb.		1217	23 Jan.	13 Feb.
1169	23 Jan.	12 Feb.		1218	23 Jan.	12 Feb.
1170	23 Jan.	12 Feb.		1219	23 Jan.	12 Feb.
1171	23 Jan.	12 Feb.		1220	23 Jan.	12 Feb.
1172	24 Jan.	12 Feb.		1221	23 Jan.	12 Feb.
1173	23 Jan.	12 Feb.		1222	24 Jan.	12 Feb.
1174	23 Jan.	12 Feb.		1223	23 Jan.	13 Feb.
1175	23 Jan.	12 Feb.		1224	23 Jan.	12 Feb.
1176	23 Jan.	12 Feb.		1225	23 Jan.	12 Feb.
1177	24 Jan.	12 Feb.		1226	23 Jan.	12 Feb.
1178	23 Jan.	13 Feb.		1227	23 Jan.	12 Feb.
1179	23 Jan.	12 Feb.		1228	24 Jan.	12 Feb.
1180	23 Jan.	12 Feb.		1229	23 Jan.	12 Feb.
1181	23 Jan.	12 Feb.		1230	23 Jan.	12 Feb.
1182	23 Jan.	12 Feb.		1231	23 Jan.	12 Feb.
1183	24 Jan.	12 Feb.		1232	23 Jan.	12 Feb.
1184	23 Jan.	13 Feb.		1233	24 Jan.	12 Feb.
1185	23 Jan.	12 Feb.		1234	23 Jan.	13 Feb.
1186	23 Jan.	12 Feb.		1235	23 Jan.	12 Feb.
1187	23 Jan.	12 Feb.		1236	23 Jan.	12 Feb.
1188	23 Jan.	12 Feb.		1237	23 Jan.	12 Feb.
1189	23 Jan.	13 Feb.		1238	23 Jan.	12 Feb.
1190	23 Jan.	12 Feb.		1239	24 Jan.	12 Feb.
1191	23 Jan.	12 Feb.		1240	23 Jan.	13 Feb.
1192	23 Jan.	12 Feb.		1241	23 Jan.	12 Feb.
1193	23 Jan.	12 Feb.		1242	23 Jan.	12 Feb.
1194	24 Jan.	12 Feb.		1243	23 Jan.	12 Feb.

Legal chronology

Year	Began	Ended	Year	Began	Ended
1244	23 Jan.	12 Feb.	1294	23 Jan.	12 Feb.
1245	23 Jan.	13 Feb.	1295	24 Jan.	12 Feb.
1246	23 Jan.	12 Feb.	1296	23 Jan.	13 Feb.
1247	23 Jan.	12 Feb.	1297	23 Jan.	12 Feb.
1248	23 Jan.	12 Feb.	1298	23 Jan.	12 Feb.
1249	23 Jan.	12 Feb.	1299	23 Jan.	12 Feb.
1250	24 Jan.	12 Feb.	1300	23 Jan.	12 Feb.
1251	23 Jan.	13 Feb.	1301	23 Jan.	13 Feb.
1252	23 Jan.	12 Feb.	1302	23 Jan.	12 Feb.
1253	23 Jan.	12 Feb.	1303	23 Jan.	12 Feb.
1254	23 Jan.	12 Feb.	1304	23 Jan.	12 Feb.
1255	23 Jan.	12 Feb.	1305	23 Jan.	12 Feb.
1256	24 Jan.	12 Feb.	1306	24 Jan.	12 Feb.
1257	23 Jan.	12 Feb.	1307	23 Jan.	13 Feb.
1258	23 Jan.	12 Feb.	1308	23 Jan.	12 Feb.
1259	23 Jan.	12 Feb.	1309	23 Jan.	12 Feb.
1260	23 Jan.	12 Feb.	1310	23 Jan.	12 Feb.
1261	24 Jan.	12 Feb.	1311	23 Jan.	12 Feb.
1262	23 Jan.	13 Feb.	1312	24 Jan.	12 Feb.
1263	23 Jan.	12 Feb.	1313	23 Jan.	12 Feb.
1264	23 Jan.	12 Feb.	1314	23 Jan.	12 Feb.
1265	23 Jan.	12 Feb.	1315	23 Jan.	12 Feb.
1266	23 Jan.	12 Feb.	1316	23 Jan.	12 Feb.
1267	24 Jan.	12 Feb.	1317	24 Jan.	12 Feb.
1268	23 Jan.	13 Feb.	1318	23 Jan.	13 Feb.
1269	23 Jan.	12 Feb.	1319	23 Jan.	12 Feb.
1270	23 Jan.	12 Feb.	1320	23 Jan.	12 Feb.
1271	23 Jan.	12 Feb.	1321	23 Jan.	12 Feb.
1272	23 Jan.	12 Feb.	1322	23 Jan.	12 Feb.
1273	23 Jan.	13 Feb.	1323	24 Jan.	12 Feb.
1274	23 Jan.	12 Feb.	1324	23 Jan.	13 Feb.
1275	23 Jan.	12 Feb.	1325	23 Jan.	12 Feb.
1276	23 Jan.	12 Feb.	1326	23 Jan.	12 Feb.
1277	23 Jan.	12 Feb.	1327	23 Jan.	12 Feb.
1278	24 Jan.	12 Feb.	1328	23 Jan.	12 Feb.
1279	23 Jan.	13 Feb.	1329	23 Jan.	13 Feb.
1280	23 Jan.	12 Feb.	1330	23 Jan.	12 Feb.
1281	23 Jan.	12 Feb.	1331	23 Jan.	12 Feb.
1282	23 Jan.	12 Feb.	1332	23 Jan.	12 Feb.
1283	23 Jan.	12 Feb.	1333	23 Jan.	12 Feb.
1284	24 Jan.	12 Feb.	1334	24 Jan.	12 Feb.
1285	23 Jan.	12 Feb.	1335	23 Jan.	13 Feb.
1286	23 Jan.	12 Feb.	1336	23 Jan.	12 Feb.
1287	23 Jan.	12 Feb.	1337	23 Jan.	12 Feb.
1288	23 Jan.	12 Feb.	1338	23 Jan.	12 Feb.
1289	24 Jan.	12 Feb.	1339	23 Jan.	12 Feb.
1290	23 Jan.	13 Feb.	1340	24 Jan.	12 Feb.
1291	23 Jan.	12 Feb.	1341	23 Jan.	12 Feb.
1292	23 Jan.	12 Feb.	1342	23 Jan.	12 Feb.
1293	23 Jan.	12 Feb.	1343	23 Jan.	12 Feb.

Year	Began	Ended		Year	Began	Ended
1344	23 Jan.	12 Feb.		1394	23 Jan.	12 Feb.
1345	24 Jan.	12 Feb.		1395	23 Jan.	12 Feb.
1346	23 Jan.	13 Feb.		1396	24 Jan.	12 Feb.
1347	23 Jan.	12 Feb.		1397	23 Jan.	12 Feb.
1348	23 Jan.	12 Feb.		1398	23 Jan.	12 Feb.
1349	23 Jan.	12 Feb.		1399	23 Jan.	12 Feb.
1350	23 Jan.	12 Feb.		1400	23 Jan.	12 Feb.
1351	24 Jan.	12 Feb.		1401	24 Jan.	12 Feb.
1352	23 Jan.	13 Feb.		1402	23 Jan.	13 Feb.
1353	23 Jan.	12 Feb.		1403	23 Jan.	12 Feb.
1354	23 Jan.	12 Feb.		1404	23 Jan.	12 Feb.
1355	23 Jan.	12 Feb.		1405	23 Jan.	12 Feb.
1356	23 Jan.	12 Feb.		1406	23 Jan.	12 Feb.
1357	23 Jan.	13 Feb.		1407	24 Jan.	12 Feb.
1358	23 Jan.	12 Feb.		1408	23 Jan.	13 Feb.
1359	23 Jan.	12 Feb.		1409	23 Jan.	12 Feb.
1360	23 Jan.	12 Feb.		1410	23 Jan.	12 Feb.
1361	23 Jan.	12 Feb.		1411	23 Jan.	12 Feb.
1362	24 Jan.	12 Feb.		1412	23 Jan.	12 Feb.
1363	23 Jan.	13 Feb.		1413	23 Jan.	13 Feb.
1364	23 Jan.	12 Feb.		1414	23 Jan.	12 Feb.
1365	23 Jan.	12 Feb.		1415	23 Jan.	12 Feb.
1366	23 Jan.	12 Feb.		1416	23 Jan.	12 Feb.
1367	23 Jan.	12 Feb.		1417	23 Jan.	12 Feb.
1368	24 Jan.	12 Feb.		1418	24 Jan.	12 Feb.
1369	23 Jan.	12 Feb.		1419	23 Jan.	13 Feb.
1370	23 Jan.	12 Feb.		1420	23 Jan.	12 Feb.
1371	23 Jan.	12 Feb.		1421	23 Jan.	12 Feb.
1372	23 Jan.	12 Feb.		1422	23 Jan.	12 Feb.
1373	24 Jan.	12 Feb.		1423	23 Jan.	12 Feb.
1374	23 Jan.	13 Feb.		1424	24 Jan.	12 Feb.
1375	23 Jan.	12 Feb.		1425	23 Jan.	12 Feb.
1376	23 Jan.	12 Feb.		1426	23 Jan.	12 Feb.
1377	23 Jan.	12 Feb.		1427	23 Jan.	12 Feb.
1378	23 Jan.	12 Feb.		1428	23 Jan.	12 Feb.
1379	24 Jan.	12 Feb.		1429	24 Jan.	12 Feb.
1380	23 Jan.	13 Feb.		1430	23 Jan.	13 Feb.
1381	23 Jan.	12 Feb.		1431	23 Jan.	12 Feb.
1382	23 Jan.	12 Feb.		1432	23 Jan.	12 Feb.
1383	23 Jan.	12 Feb.		1433	23 Jan.	12 Feb.
1384	23 Jan.	12 Feb.		1434	23 Jan.	12 Feb.
1385	23 Jan.	13 Feb.		1435	24 Jan.	12 Feb.
1386	23 Jan.	12 Feb.		1436	23 Jan.	13 Feb.
1387	23 Jan.	12 Feb.		1437	23 Jan.	12 Feb.
1388	23 Jan.	12 Feb.		1438	23 Jan.	12 Feb.
1389	23 Jan.	12 Feb.		1439	23 Jan.	12 Feb.
1390	24 Jan.	12 Feb.		1440	23 Jan.	12 Feb.
1391	23 Jan.	13 Feb.		1441	23 Jan.	13 Feb.
1392	23 Jan.	12 Feb.		1442	23 Jan.	12 Feb.
1393	23 Jan.	12 Feb.		1443	23 Jan.	12 Feb.

Year	Began	Ended	Year	Began	Ended
1444	23 Jan.	12 Feb.	1494	23 Jan.	12 Feb.
1445	23 Jan.	12 Feb.	1495	23 Jan.	12 Feb.
1446	24 Jan.	12 Feb.	1496	23 Jan.	12 Feb.
1447	23 Jan.	13 Feb.	1497	23 Jan.	13 Feb.
1448	23 Jan.	12 Feb.	1498	23 Jan.	12 Feb.
1449	23 Jan.	12 Feb.	1499	23 Jan.	12 Feb.
1450	23 Jan.	12 Feb.	1500	23 Jan.	12 Feb.
1451	23 Jan.	12 Feb.	1501	23 Jan.	12 Feb.
1452	24 Jan.	12 Feb.	1502	24 Jan.	12 Feb.
1453	23 Jan.	12 Feb.	1503	23 Jan.	13 Feb.
1454	23 Jan.	12 Feb.	1504	23 Jan.	12 Feb.
1455	23 Jan.	12 Feb.	1505	23 Jan.	12 Feb.
1456	23 Jan.	12 Feb.	1506	23 Jan.	12 Feb.
1457	24 Jan.	12 Feb.	1507	23 Jan.	12 Feb.
1458	23 Jan.	13 Feb.	1508	24 Jan.	12 Feb.
1459	23 Jan.	12 Feb.	1509	23 Jan.	12 Feb.
1460	23 Jan.	12 Feb.	1510	23 Jan.	12 Feb.
1461	23 Jan.	12 Feb.	1511	23 Jan.	12 Feb.
1462	23 Jan.	12 Feb.	1512	23 Jan.	12 Feb.
1463	24 Jan.	12 Feb.	1513	24 Jan.	12 Feb.
1464	23 Jan.	13 Feb.	1514	23 Jan.	13 Feb.
1465	23 Jan.	12 Feb.	1515	23 Jan.	12 Feb.
1466	23 Jan.	12 Feb.	1516	23 Jan.	12 Feb.
1467	23 Jan.	12 Feb.	1517	23 Jan.	12 Feb.
1468	23 Jan.	12 Feb.	1518	23 Jan.	12 Feb.
1469	23 Jan.	13 Feb.	1519	24 Jan.	12 Feb.
1470	23 Jan.	12 Feb.	1520	23 Jan.	13 Feb.
1471	23 Jan.	12 Feb.	1521	23 Jan.	12 Feb.
1472	23 Jan.	12 Feb.	1522	23 Jan.	12 Feb.
1473	23 Jan.	12 Feb.	1523	23 Jan.	12 Feb.
1474	24 Jan.	12 Feb.	1524	23 Jan.	12 Feb.
1475	23 Jan.	13 Feb.	1525	23 Jan.	13 Feb.
1476	23 Jan.	12 Feb.	1526	23 Jan.	12 Feb.
1477	23 Jan.	12 Feb.	1527	23 Jan.	12 Feb.
1478	23 Jan.	12 Feb.	1528	23 Jan.	12 Feb.
1479	23 Jan.	12 Feb.	1529	23 Jan.	12 Feb.
1480	24 Jan.	12 Feb.	1530	24 Jan.	12 Feb.
1481	23 Jan.	12 Feb.	1531	23 Jan.	13 Feb.
1482	23 Jan.	12 Feb.	1532	23 Jan.	12 Feb.
1483	23 Jan.	12 Feb.	1533	23 Jan.	12 Feb.
1484	23 Jan.	12 Feb.	1534	23 Jan.	12 Feb.
1485	24 Jan.	12 Feb.	1535	23 Jan.	12 Feb.
1486	23 Jan.	13 Feb.	1536	24 Jan.	12 Feb.
1487	23 Jan.	12 Feb.	1537	23 Jan.	12 Feb.
1488	23 Jan.	12 Feb.	1538	23 Jan.	12 Feb.
1489	23 Jan.	12 Feb.	1539	23 Jan.	12 Feb.
1490	23 Jan.	12 Feb.	1540	23 Jan.	12 Feb.
1491	24 Jan.	12 Feb.	1541	24 Jan.	12 Feb.
1492	23 Jan.	13 Feb.	1542	23 Jan.	13 Feb.
1493	23 Jan.	12 Feb.	1543	23 Jan.	12 Feb.

Year	Began	Ended	Year	Began	Ended
1544	23 Jan.	12 Feb.	1594	23 Jan.	12 Feb.
1545	23 Jan.	12 Feb.	1595	23 Jan.	12 Feb.
1546	23 Jan.	12 Feb.	1596	23 Jan.	12 Feb.
1547	24 Jan.	12 Feb.	1597	24 Jan.	12 Feb.
1548	23 Jan.	13 Feb.	1598	23 Jan.	13 Feb.
1549	23 Jan.	12 Feb.	1599	23 Jan.	12 Feb.
1550	23 Jan.	12 Feb.	1600	23 Jan.	12 Feb.
1551	23 Jan.	12 Feb.	1601	23 Jan.	12 Feb.
1552	23 Jan.	12 Feb.	1602	23 Jan.	12 Feb.
1553	23 Jan.	13 Feb.	1603	24 Jan.	12 Feb.
1554	23 Jan.	12 Feb.	1604	23 Jan.	13 Feb.
1555	23 Jan.	12 Feb.	1605	23 Jan.	12 Feb.
1556	23 Jan.	12 Feb.	1606	23 Jan.	12 Feb.
1557	23 Jan.	12 Feb.	1607	23 Jan.	12 Feb.
1558	24 Jan.	12 Feb.	1608	23 Jan.	12 Feb.
1559	23 Jan.	13 Feb.	1609	23 Jan.	13 Feb.
1560	23 Jan.	12 Feb.	1610	23 Jan.	12 Feb.
1561	23 Jan.	12 Feb.	1611	23 Jan.	12 Feb.
1562	23 Jan.	12 Feb.	1612	23 Jan.	12 Feb.
1563	23 Jan.	12 Feb.	1613	23 Jan.	12 Feb.
1564	24 Jan.	12 Feb.	1614	24 Jan.	12 Feb.
1565	23 Jan.	12 Feb.	1615	23 Jan.	13 Feb.
1566	23 Jan.	12 Feb.	1616	23 Jan.	12 Feb.
1567	23 Jan.	12 Feb.	1617	23 Jan.	12 Feb.
1568	23 Jan.	12 Feb.	1618	23 Jan.	12 Feb.
1569	24 Jan.	12 Feb.	1619	23 Jan.	12 Feb.
1570	23 Jan.	13 Feb.	1620	24 Jan.	12 Feb.
1571	23 Jan.	12 Feb.	1621	23 Jan.	12 Feb.
1572	23 Jan.	12 Feb.	1622	23 Jan.	12 Feb.
1573	23 Jan.	12 Feb.	1623	23 Jan.	12 Feb.
1574	23 Jan.	12 Feb.	1624	23 Jan.	12 Feb.
1575	24 Jan.	12 Feb.	1625	24 Jan.	12 Feb.
1576	23 Jan.	13 Feb.	1626	23 Jan.	13 Feb.
1577	23 Jan.	12 Feb.	1627	23 Jan.	12 Feb.
1578	23 Jan.	12 Feb.	1628	23 Jan.	12 Feb.
1579	23 Jan.	12 Feb.	1629	23 Jan.	12 Feb.
1580	23 Jan.	12 Feb.	1630	23 Jan.	12 Feb.
1581	23 Jan.	13 Feb.	1631	24 Jan.	12 Feb.
1582	23 Jan.	12 Feb.	1632	23 Jan.	13 Feb.
1583	23 Jan.	12 Feb.	1633	23 Jan.	12 Feb.
1584	23 Jan.	12 Feb.	1634	23 Jan.	12 Feb.
1585	23 Jan.	12 Feb.	1635	23 Jan.	12 Feb.
1586	24 Jan.	12 Feb.	1636	23 Jan.	12 Feb.
1587	23 Jan.	13 Feb.	1637	23 Jan.	13 Feb.
1588	23 Jan.	12 Feb.	1638	23 Jan.	12 Feb.
1589	23 Jan.	12 Feb.	1639	23 Jan.	12 Feb.
1590	23 Jan.	12 Feb.	1640	23 Jan.	12 Feb.
1591	23 Jan.	12 Feb.	1641	23 Jan.	12 Feb.
1592	24 Jan.	12 Feb.	1642	24 Jan.	12 Feb.
1593	23 Jan.	12 Feb.	1643	23 Jan.	13 Feb.

Legal chronology

Year	Began	Ended	Year	Began	Ended
1644	23 Jan.	12 Feb.	1694	23 Jan.	12 Feb.
1645	23 Jan.	12 Feb.	1695	23 Jan.	12 Feb.
1646	23 Jan.	12 Feb.	1696	23 Jan.	12 Feb.
1647	23 Jan.	12 Feb.	1697	23 Jan.	12 Feb.
1648	24 Jan.	12 Feb.	1698	24 Jan.	12 Feb.
1649	23 Jan.	12 Feb.	1699	23 Jan.	13 Feb.
1650	23 Jan.	12 Feb.	1700	23 Jan.	12 Feb.
1651	23 Jan.	12 Feb.	1701	23 Jan.	12 Feb.
1652	23 Jan.	12 Feb.	1702	23 Jan.	12 Feb.
1653	24 Jan.	12 Feb.	1703	23 Jan.	12 Feb.
1654	23 Jan.	13 Feb.	1704	24 Jan.	12 Feb.
1655	23 Jan.	12 Feb.	1705	23 Jan.	12 Feb.
1656	23 Jan.	12 Feb.	1706	23 Jan.	12 Feb.
1657	23 Jan.	12 Feb.	1707	23 Jan.	12 Feb.
1658	23 Jan.	12 Feb.	1708	23 Jan.	12 Feb.
1659	24 Jan.	12 Feb.	1709	24 Jan.	12 Feb.
1660	23 Jan.	13 Feb.	1710	23 Jan.	13 Feb.
1661	23 Jan.	12 Feb.	1711	23 Jan.	12 Feb.
1662	23 Jan.	12 Feb.	1712	23 Jan.	12 Feb.
1663	23 Jan.	12 Feb.	1713	23 Jan.	12 Feb.
1664	23 Jan.	12 Feb.	1714	23 Jan.	12 Feb.
1665	23 Jan.	13 Feb.	1715	24 Jan.	12 Feb.
1666	23 Jan.	12 Feb.	1716	23 Jan.	13 Feb.
1667	23 Jan.	12 Feb.	1717	23 Jan.	12 Feb.
1668	23 Jan.	12 Feb.	1718	23 Jan.	12 Feb.
1669	23 Jan.	12 Feb.	1719	23 Jan.	12 Feb.
1670	24 Jan.	12 Feb.	1720	23 Jan.	12 Feb.
1671	23 Jan.	13 Feb.	1721	23 Jan.	13 Feb.
1672	23 Jan.	12 Feb.	1722	23 Jan.	12 Feb.
1673	23 Jan.	12 Feb.	1723	23 Jan.	12 Feb.
1674	23 Jan.	12 Feb.	1724	23 Jan.	12 Feb.
1675	23 Jan.	12 Feb.	1725	23 Jan.	12 Feb.
1676	24 Jan.	12 Feb.	1726	24 Jan.	12 Feb.
1677	23 Jan.	12 Feb.	1727	23 Jan.	13 Feb.
1678	23 Jan.	12 Feb.	1728	23 Jan.	12 Feb.
1679	23 Jan.	12 Feb.	1729	23 Jan.	12 Feb.
1680	23 Jan.	12 Feb.	1730	23 Jan.	12 Feb.
1681	24 Jan.	12 Feb.	1731	23 Jan.	12 Feb.
1682	23 Jan.	13 Feb.	1732	24 Jan.	12 Feb.
1683	23 Jan.	12 Feb.	1733	23 Jan.	12 Feb.
1684	23 Jan.	12 Feb.	1734	23 Jan.	12 Feb.
1685	23 Jan.	12 Feb.	1735	23 Jan.	12 Feb.
1686	23 Jan.	12 Feb.	1736	23 Jan.	12 Feb.
1687	24 Jan.	12 Feb.	1737	24 Jan.	12 Feb.
1688	23 Jan.	13 Feb.	1738	23 Jan.	13 Feb.
1689	23 Jan.	12 Feb.	1739	23 Jan.	12 Feb.
1690	23 Jan.	12 Feb.	1740	23 Jan.	12 Feb.
1691	23 Jan.	12 Feb.	1741	23 Jan.	12 Feb.
1692	23 Jan.	12 Feb.	1742	23 Jan.	12 Feb.
1693	23 Jan.	13 Feb.	1743	24 Jan.	12 Feb.

5/X Law terms from AD 1066 to AD 1830

Year	Began	Ended	Year	Began	Ended
1744	23 Jan.	13 Feb.	1788	23 Jan.	12 Feb.
1745	23 Jan.	12 Feb.	1789	23 Jan.	12 Feb.
1746	23 Jan.	12 Feb.	1790	23 Jan.	12 Feb.
1747	23 Jan.	12 Feb.	1791	24 Jan.	12 Feb.
1748	23 Jan.	12 Feb.	1792	23 Jan.	13 Feb.
1749	23 Jan.	13 Feb.	1793	23 Jan.	12 Feb.
1750	23 Jan.	12 Feb.	1794	23 Jan.	12 Feb.
1751[39]			1795	23 Jan.	12 Feb.
1752	23 Jan.	12 Feb.	1796	23 Jan.	12 Feb.
1753	23 Jan.	12 Feb.	1797	23 Jan.	13 Feb.
1754	23 Jan.	12 Feb.	1798	23 Jan.	12 Feb.
1755	23 Jan.	12 Feb.	1799	23 Jan.	12 Feb.
1756	23 Jan.	12 Feb.	1800	23 Jan.	12 Feb.
1757	24 Jan.	12 Feb.	1801	23 Jan.	12 Feb.
1758	23 Jan.	13 Feb.	1802	23 Jan.	12 Feb.
1759	23 Jan.	12 Feb.	1803	24 Jan.	12 Feb.
1760	23 Jan.	12 Feb.	1804	23 Jan.	13 Feb.
1761	23 Jan.	12 Feb.	1805	23 Jan.	12 Feb.
1762	23 Jan.	12 Feb.	1806	23 Jan.	12 Feb.
1763	24 Jan.	12 Feb.	1807	23 Jan.	12 Feb.
1764	23 Jan.	13 Feb.	1808	23 Jan.	12 Feb.
1765	23 Jan.	12 Feb.	1809	23 Jan.	13 Feb.
1766	23 Jan.	12 Feb.	1810	23 Jan.	12 Feb.
1767	23 Jan.	12 Feb.	1811	23 Jan.	12 Feb.
1768	23 Jan.	12 Feb.	1812	23 Jan.	12 Feb.
1769	23 Jan.	13 Feb.	1813	23 Jan.	12 Feb.
1770	23 Jan.	12 Feb.	1814	24 Jan.	12 Feb.
1771	23 Jan.	12 Feb.	1815	23 Jan.	13 Feb.
1772	23 Jan.	12 Feb.	1816	23 Jan.	12 Feb.
1773	23 Jan.	12 Feb.	1817	23 Jan.	12 Feb.
1774	24 Jan.	12 Feb.	1818	23 Jan.	12 Feb.
1775	23 Jan.	13 Feb.	1819	23 Jan.	12 Feb.
1776	23 Jan.	12 Feb.	1820	24 Jan.	12 Feb.
1777	23 Jan.	12 Feb.	1821	23 Jan.	12 Feb.
1778	23 Jan.	12 Feb.	1822	23 Jan.	12 Feb.
1779	23 Jan.	12 Feb.	1823	23 Jan.	12 Feb.
1780	24 Jan.	12 Feb.	1824	23 Jan.	12 Feb.
1781	23 Jan.	12 Feb.	1825	24 Jan.	12 Feb.
1782	23 Jan.	12 Feb.	1826	23 Jan.	13 Feb.
1783	23 Jan.	12 Feb.	1827	23 Jan.	12 Feb.
1784	23 Jan.	12 Feb.	1828	23 Jan.	12 Feb.
1785	24 Jan.	12 Feb.	1829	23 Jan.	12 Feb.
1786	23 Jan.	13 Feb.	1830	23 Jan.	12 Feb.
1787	23 Jan.	12 Feb.			

Hilary Term was fixed by Statute I Will. 4. cap. 70, (passed 22 July 1830), which provides that in the year 1831, and afterwards, Hilary Term shall begin on the 11th and end 31 January.

39. This year there was no term, in consequence of the alteration of the Julian or Old Style. The computation according to which the year began 25 March was not used after 31 December, and 1 January was reckoned as the first day of the year 1752.

Legal chronology

Easter term

Year	Began	Ended		Year	Began	Ended
1066	3 May	29 May		1113	23 April	19 May
1067	25 April	21 May		1114	15 April	11 May
1068	9 April	5 May		1115	5 May	31 May
1069	29 April	25 May		1116	19 April	15 May
1070	21 April	17 May		1117	11 April	7 May
1071	11 May	6 June		1118	1 May	27 May
1072	25 April	21 May		1119	16 April	12 May
1073	17 April	13 May		1120	5 May	31 May
1074	7 May	2 June		1121	27 April	23 May
1075	22 April	18 May		1122	12 April	8 May
1076	13 April	9 May		1123	2 May	28 May
1077	3 May	29 May		1124	23 April	19 May
1078	25 April	21 May		1125	15 April	11 May
1079	10 April	6 May		1126	28 April	24 May
1080	29 April	25 May		1127	20 April	16 May
1081	21 April	17 May		1128	9 May	4 June
1082	11 May	6 June		1129	1 May	27 May
1083	26 April	22 May		1130	16 April	12 May
1084	17 April	13 May		1131	6 May	1 June
1085	7 May	2 June		1132	27 April	23 May
1086	22 April	18 May		1133	12 April	8 May
1087	14 April	10 May		1134	2 May	28 May
1088	3 May	29 May		1135	24 April	20 May
1089	18 April	14 May		1136	8 April	4 May
1090	8 May	3 June		1137	28 April	24 May
1091	30 April	26 May		1138	20 April	16 May
1092	14 April	10 May		1139	10 May	5 June
1093	4 May	30 May		1140	24 April	20 May
1094	26 April	22 May		1141	16 April	12 May
1095	11 April	7 May		1142	6 May	1 June
1096	30 April	26 May		1143	21 April	17 May
1097	22 April	18 May		1144	12 April	8 May
1098	14 April	10 May		1145	2 May	28 May
1099	27 April	23 May		1146	17 April	13 May
1100	18 April	14 May		1147	7 May	2 June
1101	8 May	3 June		1148	28 April	24 May
1102	23 April	19 May		1149	20 April	16 May
1103	15 April	11 May		1150	3 May	29 May
1104	4 May	30 May		1151	25 April	21 May
1105	26 April	22 May		1152	16 April	12 May
1106	11 April	7 May		1153	6 May	1 June
1107	1 May	27 May		1154	21 April	17 May
1108	22 April	18 May		1155	13 April	9 May
1109	12 May	7 June		1156	2 May	28 May
1110	27 April	23 May		1157	17 April	13 May
1111	19 April	15 May		1158	7 May	2 June
1112	8 May	3 June		1159	29 April	25 May

Year	Began	Ended	Year	Began	Ended
1160	13 April	9 May	1209	15 April	11 May
1161	3 May	29 May	1210	5 May	31 May
1162	25 April	21 May	1211	20 April	16 May
1163	10 April	6 May	1212	11 April	7 May
1164	29 April	25 May	1213	1 May	27 May
1165	21 April	17 May	1214	16 April	12 May
1166	11 May	6 June	1215	6 May	1 June
1167	26 April	22 May	1216	27 April	23 May
1168	17 April	13 May	1217	12 April	8 May
1169	7 May	2 June	1218	2 May	28 May
1170	22 April	18 May	1219	24 April	20 May
1171	14 April	10 May	1220	15 April	11 May
1172	3 May	29 May	1221	28 April	24 May
1173	25 April	21 May	1222	20 April	16 May
1174	10 April	6 May	1223	10 May	5 June
1175	30 April	26 May	1224	1 May	27 May
1176	21 April	17 May	1225	16 April	12 May
1177	11 May	6 June	1226	6 May	1 June
1178	26 April	22 May	1227	28 April	24 May
1179	18 April	14 May	1228	12 April	8 May
1180	7 May	2 June	1229	2 May	28 May
1181	22 April	18 May	1230	24 April	20 May
1182	14 April	10 May	1231	9 April	5 May
1183	4 May	30 May	1232	28 April	24 May
1184	18 April	14 May	1233	20 April	16 May
1185	8 May	3 June	1234	10 May	5 June
1186	30 April	26 May	1235	25 April	21 May
1187	15 April	11 May	1236	16 April	12 May
1188	4 May	30 May	1237	6 May	1 June
1189	26 April	22 May	1238	21 April	17 May
1190	11 April	7 May	1239	13 April	9 May
1191	1 May	27 May	1240	2 May	28 May
1192	22 April	18 May	1241	17 April	13 May
1193	14 April	10 May	1242	7 May	2 June
1194	27 April	23 May	1243	29 April	25 May
1195	19 April	15 May	1244	20 April	16 May
1196	8 May	3 June	1245	3 May	29 May
1197	23 April	19 May	1246	25 April	21 May
1198	15 April	11 May	1247	17 April	13 May
1199	5 May	31 May	1248	6 May	1 June
1200	26 April	22 May	1249	21 April	17 May
1201	11 April	7 May	1250	13 April	9 May
1202	1 May	27 May	1251	3 May	29 May
1203	23 April	19 May	1252	17 April	13 May
1204	12 May	7 June	1253	7 May	2 June
1205	27 April	23 May	1254	29 April	25 May
1206	19 April	15 May	1255	14 April	10 May
1207	9 May	4 June	1256	3 May	29 May
1208	23 April	19 May	1257	25 April	21 May

Legal chronology

Year	Began	Ended		Year	Began	Ended
1258	10 April	6 May		1307	12 April	8 May
1259	30 April	26 May		1308	1 May	27 May
1260	21 April	17 May		1309	16 April	12 May
1261	11 May	6 June		1310	6 May	1 June
1262	26 April	22 May		1311	28 April	24 May
1263	18 April	14 May		1312	12 April	8 May
1264	7 May	2 May		1313	2 May	28 May
1265	22 April	18 May		1314	24 April	20 May
1266	14 April	10 May		1315	9 April	5 May
1267	4 May	30 May		1316	28 April	24 May
1268	25 April	21 May		1317	20 April	16 May
1269	10 April	6 May		1318	10 May	5 June
1270	30 April	26 May		1319	25 April	21 May
1271	22 April	18 May		1320	16 April	12 May
1272	11 May	6 June		1321	6 May	1 June
1273	26 April	22 May		1322	28 April	24 May
1274	18 April	14 May		1323	13 April	9 May
1275	1 May	27 May		1324	2 May	28 May
1276	22 April	18 May		1325	24 April	20 May
1277	14 April	10 May		1326	9 April	5 May
1278	4 May	30 May		1327	29 April	25 May
1279	19 April	15 May		1328	20 April	16 May
1280	8 May	3 June		1329	10 May	5 June
1281	30 April	26 May		1330	25 April	21 May
1282	15 April	11 May		1331	17 April	13 May
1283	5 May	31 May		1332	6 May	1 June
1284	26 April	22 May		1333	21 April	17 May
1285	11 April	7 May		1334	13 April	9 May
1286	1 May	27 May		1335	3 May	29 May
1287	23 April	19 May		1336	17 April	13 May
1288	14 April	10 May		1337	7 May	2 June
1289	27 April	23 May		1338	29 April	25 May
1290	19 April	15 May		1339	14 April	10 May
1291	9 May	4 June		1340	3 May	29 May
1292	23 April	19 May		1341	25 April	21 May
1293	15 April	11 May		1342	17 April	13 May
1294	5 May	31 May		1343	30 April	26 May
1295	20 April	16 May		1344	21 April	17 May
1296	11 April	7 May		1345	13 April	9 May
1297	1 May	27 May		1346	3 May	29 May
1298	23 April	19 May		1347	18 April	14 May
1299	6 May	1 June		1348	7 May	2 June
1300	27 April	23 May		1349	29 April	25 May
1301	19 April	15 May		1350	14 April	10 May
1302	9 May	4 June		1351	4 May	30 May
1303	24 April	20 May		1352	25 April	21 May
1304	15 April	11 May		1353	10 April	6 May
1305	5 May	31 May		1354	30 April	26 May
1306	20 April	16 May		1355	22 April	18 May

Year	Began	Ended	Year	Began	Ended
1356	11 May	6 June	1405	6 May	1 June
1357	26 April	22 May	1406	28 April	24 May
1358	18 April	14 May	1407	13 April	9 May
1359	8 May	3 June	1408	2 May	28 May
1360	22 April	18 May	1409	24 April	20 May
1361	14 April	10 May	1410	9 April	5 May
1362	4 May	30 May	1411	29 April	25 May
1363	19 April	15 May	1412	20 April	16 May
1364	10 April	6 May	1413	10 May	5 June
1365	30 April	26 May	1414	25 April	21 May
1366	22 April	18 May	1415	17 April	13 May
1367	5 May	31 May	1416	6 May	1 June
1368	26 April	22 May	1417	28 April	24 May
1369	18 April	14 May	1418	13 April	9 May
1370	1 May	27 May	1419	3 May	29 May
1371	23 April	19 May	1420	24 April	20 May
1372	14 April	10 May	1421	9 April	5 May
1373	4 May	30 May	1422	29 April	25 May
1374	19 April	15 May	1423	21 April	17 May
1375	9 May	4 June	1424	10 May	5 June
1376	30 April	26 May	1425	25 April	21 May
1377	15 April	11 May	1426	17 April	13 May
1378	5 May	31 May	1427	7 May	2 June
1379	27 April	23 May	1428	21 April	17 May
1380	11 April	7 May	1429	13 April	9 May
1381	1 May	27 May	1430	3 May	29 May
1382	23 April	19 May	1431	18 April	14 May
1383	8 April	4 May	1432	7 May	2 June
1384	27 April	23 May	1433	29 April	25 May
1385	19 April	15 May	1434	14 April	10 May
1386	9 May	4 June	1435	4 May	30 May
1387	24 April	20 May	1436	25 April	21 May
1388	15 April	11 May	1437	17 April	13 May
1389	5 May	31 May	1438	30 April	26 May
1390	20 April	16 May	1439	22 April	18 May
1391	12 April	8 May	1440	13 April	9 May
1392	1 May	27 May	1441	3 May	29 May
1393	23 April	19 May	1442	18 April	14 May
1394	6 May	1 June	1443	8 May	3 June
1395	28 April	24 May	1444	29 April	25 May
1396	19 April	15 May	1445	14 April	10 May
1397	9 May	4 June	1446	4 May	30 May
1398	24 April	20 May	1447	26 April	22 May
1399	16 April	12 May	1448	10 April	6 May
1400	5 May	31 May	1449	30 April	26 May
1401	20 April	16 May	1450	22 April	18 May
1402	12 April	8 May	1451	12 May	7 June
1403	2 May	28 May	1452	26 April	22 May
1404	16 April	12 May	1453	18 April	14 May

Legal chronology

Year	Began	Ended	Year	Began	Ended
1454	8 May	3 June	1503	3 May	29 May
1455	23 April	19 May	1504	24 April	20 May
1456	14 April	10 May	1505	9 April	5 May
1457	4 May	30 May	1506	29 April	25 May
1458	19 April	15 May	1507	21 April	17 May
1459	11 April	7 May	1508	10 May	5 June
1460	30 April	26 May	1509	25 April	21 May
1461	22 April	18 May	1510	17 April	13 May
1462	5 May	31 May	1511	7 May	2 June
1463	27 April	23 May	1512	28 April	24 May
1464	18 April	14 May	1513	13 April	9 May
1465	1 May	27 May	1514	3 May	29 May
1466	23 April	19 May	1515	25 April	21 May
1467	15 April	11 May	1516	9 April	5 May
1468	4 May	30 May	1517	29 April	25 May
1469	19 April	15 May	1518	21 April	17 May
1470	9 May	4 June	1519	11 May	6 June
1471	1 May	27 May	1520	25 April	21 May
1472	15 April	11 May	1521	17 April	13 May
1473	5 May	31 May	1522	7 May	2 June
1474	27 April	23 May	1523	22 April	18 May
1475	12 April	8 May	1524	13 April	9 May
1476	1 May	27 May	1525	3 May	29 May
1477	23 April	19 May	1526	18 April	14 May
1478	8 April	4 May	1527	8 May	3 June
1479	28 April	24 May	1528	29 April	25 May
1480	19 April	15 May	1529	14 April	10 May
1481	9 May	4 June	1530	4 May	30 May
1482	24 April	20 May	1531	26 April	22 May
1483	16 April	12 May	1532	17 April	13 May
1484	5 May	31 May	1533	30 April	26 May
1485	20 April	16 May	1534	22 April	18 May
1486	12 April	8 May	1535	14 April	10 May
1487	2 May	28 May	1536	3 May	29 May
1488	23 April	19 May	1537	18 April	14 May
1489	6 May	1 June	1538	8 May	3 June
1490	28 April	24 May	1539	23 April	19 May
1491	20 April	16 May	1540	14 April	10 May
1492	9 May	4 June	1541	4 May	30 May
1493	24 April	20 May	1542	26 April	22 May
1494	16 April	12 May	1543	11 April	7 May
1495	6 May	1 June	1544	30 April	26 May
1496	20 April	16 May	1545	22 April	18 May
1497	12 April	8 May	1546	12 May	7 June
1498	2 May	28 May	1547	27 April	23 May
1499	17 April	13 May	1548	18 April	14 May
1500	6 May	1 June	1549	8 May	3 June
1501	28 April	24 May	1550	23 April	19 May
1502	13 April	9 May	1551	15 April	11 May

Year	Began	Ended	Year	Began	Ended
1552	4 May	30 May	1601	29 April	25 May
1553	19 April	15 May	1602	21 April	17 May
1554	11 April	7 May	1603	11 May	6 June
1555	1 May	27 May	1604	25 April	21 May
1556	22 April	18 May	1605	17 April	13 May
1557	5 May	31 May	1606	7 May	2 June
1558	27 April	23 May	1607	22 April	18 May
1559	12 April	8 May	1608	13 April	9 May
1560	1 May	27 May	1609	3 May	29 May
1561	23 April	19 May	1610	25 April	21 May
1562	15 April	11 May	1611	10 April	6 May
1563	28 April	24 May	1612	29 April	25 May
1564	19 April	15 May	1613	21 April	17 May
1565	9 May	4 June	1614	11 May	6 June
1566	1 May	27 May	1615	26 April	22 May
1567	16 April	12 May	1616	17 April	13 May
1568	5 May	31 May	1617	7 May	2 June
1569	27 April	23 May	1618	22 April	18 May
1570	12 April	8 May	1619	14 April	10 May
1571	2 May	28 May	1620	3 May	29 May
1572	23 April	19 May	1621	18 April	14 May
1573	8 April	4 May	1622	8 May	3 June
1574	28 April	24 May	1623	30 April	26 May
1575	20 April	16 May	1624	14 April	10 May
1576	9 May	4 June	1625	4 May	30 May
1577	24 April	20 May	1626	26 April	22 May
1578	16 April	12 May	1627	11 April	7 May
1579	6 May	1 June	1628	30 April	26 May
1580	20 April	16 May	1629	22 April	18 May
1581	12 April	8 May	1630	14 April	10 May
1582	2 May	28 May	1631	27 April	23 May
1583	17 April	13 May	1632	18 April	14 May
1584	6 May	1 June	1633	8 May	3 June
1585	28 April	24 May	1634	23 April	19 May
1586	20 April	16 May	1635	15 April	11 May
1587	3 May	29 May	1636	4 May	30 May
1588	24 April	20 May	1637	26 April	22 May
1589	16 April	12 May	1638	11 April	7 May
1590	6 May	1 June	1639	1 May	27 May
1591	21 April	17 May	1640	22 April	18 May
1592	12 April	8 May	1641	12 May	7 June
1593	2 May	28 May	1642	27 April	23 May
1594	17 April	13 May	1643	19 April	15 May
1595	7 May	2 June	1644	8 May	3 June
1596	28 April	24 May	1645	23 April	19 May
1597	13 April	9 May	1646	15 April	11 May
1598	3 May	29 May	1647	5 May	31 May
1599	25 April	21 May	1648	19 April	15 May
1600	9 April	5 May	1649	11 April	7 May

Legal chronology

Year	Began	Ended		Year	Began	Ended
1650	1 May	27 May		1700	17 April	13 May
1651	16 April	12 May		1701	7 May	2 June
1652	5 May	31 May		1702	22 April	18 May
1653	27 April	23 May		1703	14 April	10 May
1654	12 April	8 May		1704	3 May	29 May
1655	2 May	28 May		1705	25 April	21 May
1656	23 April	19 May		1706	10 April	6 May
1657	15 April	11 May		1707	30 April	26 May
1658	28 April	24 May		1708	21 April	17 May
1659	20 April	16 May		1709	11 May	6 June
1660	9 May	4 June		1710	26 April	22 May
1661	1 May	27 May		1711	18 April	14 May
1662	16 April	12 May		1712	7 May	2 June
1663	6 May	1 June		1713	22 April	18 May
1664	27 April	23 May		1714	14 April	10 May
1665	12 April	8 May		1715	4 May	30 May
1666	2 May	28 May		1716	18 April	14 May
1667	24 April	20 May		1717	8 May	3 June
1668	8 April	4 May		1718	30 April	26 May
1669	28 April	24 May		1719	15 April	11 May
1670	20 April	16 May		1720	4 May	30 May
1671	10 May	5 June		1721	26 April	22 May
1672	24 April	20 May		1722	11 April	7 May
1673	16 April	12 May		1723	1 May	27 May
1674	6 May	1 June		1724	22 April	18 May
1675	21 April	17 May		1725	14 April	10 May
1676	12 April	8 May		1726	27 April	23 May
1677	2 May	28 May		1727	19 April	15 May
1678	17 April	13 May		1728	8 May	3 June
1679	7 May	2 June		1729	23 April	19 May
1680	28 April	24 May		1730	15 April	11 May
1681	20 April	16 May		1731	5 May	31 May
1682	3 May	29 May		1732	26 April	22 May
1683	25 April	21 May		1733	11 April	7 May
1684	16 April	12 May		1734	1 May	27 May
1685	6 May	1 June		1735	23 April	19 May
1686	21 April	17 May		1736	12 May	7 June
1687	13 April	9 May		1737	27 April	23 May
1688	2 May	28 May		1738	19 April	15 May
1689	17 April	13 May		1739	9 May	4 June
1690	7 May	2 June		1740	23 April	19 May
1691	29 April	25 May		1741	15 April	11 May
1692	13 April	9 May		1742	5 May	31 May
1693	3 May	29 May		1743	20 April	16 May
1694	25 April	21 May		1744	11 April	7 May
1695	10 April	6 May		1745	1 May	27 May
1696	29 April	25 May		1746	16 April	12 May
1697	21 April	17 May		1747	6 May	1 June
1698	11 May	6 June		1748	27 April	23 May
1699	26 April	22 May		1749	12 April	8 May

5/X Law terms from AD 1066 to AD 1830

Year	Began	Ended	Year	Began	Ended
1750	2 May	28 May	1791	11 May	6 June
1751	24 April	20 May	1792	25 April	21 May
1752	15 April	11 May	1793	17 April	13 May
1753	9 May	4 June	1794	7 May	2 June
1754	1 May	27 May	1795	22 April	18 May
1755	16 April	12 May	1796	13 April	9 May
1756	5 May	31 May	1797	3 May	29 May
1757	27 April	23 May	1798	25 April	21 May
1758	12 April	8 May	1799	10 April	6 May
1759	2 May	28 May	1800	30 April	26 May
1760	23 April	19 May	1801	22 April	18 May
1761	8 April	4 May	1802	5 May	31 May
1762	28 April	24 May	1803	27 April	23 May
1763	20 April	16 May	1804	18 April	14 May
1764	9 May	4 June	1805	1 May	27 May
1765	24 April	20 May	1806	23 April	19 May
1766	16 April	12 May	1807	15 April	11 May
1767	6 May	1 June	1808	4 May	30 May
1768	20 April	16 May	1809	19 April	15 May
1769	12 April	8 May	1810	9 May	4 June
1770	2 May	28 May	1811	1 May	27 May
1771	17 April	13 May	1812	15 April	11 May
1772	6 May	1 June	1813	5 May	31 May
1773	28 April	24 May	1814	27 April	23 May
1774	20 April	16 May	1815	12 April	8 May
1775	3 May	29 May	1816	1 May	27 May
1776	24 April	20 May	1817	23 April	19 May
1777	16 April	12 May	1818	8 April	4 May
1778	6 May	1 June	1819	28 April	24 May
1779	21 April	17 May	1820	19 April	15 May
1780	12 April	8 May	1821	9 May	4 June
1781	2 May	28 May	1822	24 April	20 May
1782	17 April	13 May	1823	16 April	12 May
1783	7 May	2 June	1824	5 May	31 May
1784	28 April	24 May	1825	20 April	16 May
1785	13 April	9 May	1826	12 April	8 May
1786	3 May	29 May	1827	2 May	28 May
1787	25 April	21 May	1828	23 April	19 May
1788	9 April	5 May	1829	6 May	1 June
1789	29 April	25 May	1830	28 April	24 May
1790	21 April	17 May			

Easter Term was fixed by Statute 1 Will. 4. cap. 70 (passed 22 July 1830), which provides that in the year 1831, and afterwards, Easter Term shall begin on 15 April, and end on 8 May; and by Stat. Will. 4. cap. 3. (passed 23 December 1830) it was further provided, 'that in the case the day of the month on which any Term, according to the Act of 1 Will. 4. cap. 70., is to end, shall fall to be on a Sunday, then the Monday next after such day shall be deemed and taken to be the last day of the Term; and that in case any of the days between the Thursday before and the Wednesday next after Easter shall fall within Easter Term, then such days shall be deemed and taken to be a part of such Term, although there shall be no sittings in banco on any of such intervening days'.

Trinity term

Year	Began	Ended	Year	Began	Ended
1066	21 June	12 July	1114	3 June	24 June
1067	13 June	4 July	1115	23 June	14 July
1068	28 May	18 June	1116	7 June	28 June
1069	17 June	8 July	1117	30 May	20 June
1070	9 June	30 June	1118	19 June	10 July
1071	29 June	20 July	1119	4 June	25 June
1072	13 June	4 July	1120	23 June	14 July
1073	5 June	26 June	1121	15 June	6 July
1074	25 June	16 July	1122	31 May	21 June
1075	10 June	1 July	1123	20 June	11 July
1076	1 June	22 June	1124	11 June	2 July
1077	21 June	12 July	1125	3 June	24 June
1078	13 June	4 July	1126	16 June	7 July
1079	29 May	19 June	1127	8 June	29 June
1080	17 June	8 July	1128	27 June	18 July
1081	9 June	30 June	1129	19 June	10 July
1082	29 June	20 July	1130	4 June	25 June
1083	14 June	5 July	1131	24 June	15 July
1084	5 June	26 June	1132	15 June	6 July
1085	25 June	16 July	1133	31 May	21 June
1086	10 June	1 July	1134	20 June	11 July
1087	2 June	23 June	1135	12 June	3 July
1088	21 June	12 July	1136	27 May	17 June
1089	6 June	27 June	1137	16 June	7 July
1090	26 June	17 July	1138	8 June	29 June
1091	18 June	9 July	1139	28 June	19 July
1092	2 June	23 June	1140	12 June	3 July
1093	22 June	13 July	1141	4 June	25 June
1094	14 June	5 July	1142	24 June	15 July
1095	30 May	20 June	1143	9 June	30 June
1096	18 June	9 July	1144	31 May	21 June
1097	10 June	1 July	1145	20 June	11 July
1098	2 June	23 June	1146	5 June	26 June
1099	15 June	6 July	1147	25 June	16 July
1100	6 June	27 June	1148	16 June	7 July
1101	26 June	17 July	1149	8 June	29 June
1102	11 June	2 July	1150	21 June	12 July
1103	3 June	24 June	1151	13 June	4 July
1104	22 June	13 July	1152	4 June	25 June
1105	14 June	5 July	1153	24 June	15 July
1106	30 May	20 June	1154	9 June	30 June
1107	19 June	10 July	1155	1 June	22 June
1108	10 June	1 July	1156	20 June	11 July
1109	30 June	21 July	1157	5 June	26 June
1110	15 June	6 July	1158	25 June	16 July
1111	7 June	28 June	1159	17 June	8 July
1112	26 June	17 July	1160	1 June	22 June
1113	11 June	2 July	1161	2 June	12 July

5/X Law terms from AD 1066 to AD 1830

Year	Began	Ended	Year	Began	Ended
1162	13 June	4 July	1212	30 May	20 June
1163	29 May	19 June	1213	19 June	10 July
1164	17 June	8 July	1214	4 June	25 June
1165	9 June	30 June	1215	24 June	15 July
1166	29 June	20 July	1216	15 June	6 July
1167	14 June	5 July	1217	31 May	21 June
1168	5 June	26 June	1218	20 June	11 July
1169	25 June	16 July	1219	12 June	3 July
1170	10 June	1 July	1220	3 June	24 June
1171	2 June	23 June	1221	16 June	7 July
1172	21 June	12 July	1222	8 June	29 June
1173	13 June	4 July	1223	28 June	19 July
1174	29 May	19 June	1224	19 June	10 July
1175	18 June	9 July	1225	4 June	25 June
1176	9 June	30 June	1226	24 June	15 July
1177	29 June	20 July	1227	16 June	7 July
1178	14 June	5 July	1228	31 May	21 June
1179	6 June	27 June	1229	20 June	11 July
1180	25 June	16 July	1230	12 June	3 July
1181	10 June	1 July	1231	28 May	18 June
1182	2 June	23 June	1232	16 June	7 July
1183	22 June	13 July	1233	8 June	29 June
1184	6 June	27 June	1234	28 June	19 July
1185	26 June	17 July	1235	13 June	4 July
1186	18 June	9 July	1236	4 June	25 June
1187	3 June	24 June	1237	24 June	15 July
1188	22 June	13 July	1238	9 June	30 June
1189	14 June	5 July	1239	1 June	22 June
1190	30 May	20 June	1240	20 June	11 July
1191	19 June	10 July	1241	5 June	26 June
1192	10 June	1 July	1242	25 June	16 July
1193	2 June	23 June	1243	17 June	8 July
1194	15 June	6 July	1244	8 June	29 June
1195	7 June	28 June	1245	21 June	12 July
1196	26 June	17 July	1246	13 June	4 July
1197	11 June	2 July	1247	5 June	26 June
1198	3 June	24 June	1248	24 June	15 July
1199	23 June	14 July	1249	9 June	30 June
1200	14 June	5 July	1250	1 June	22 June
1201	30 May	20 June	1251	21 June	12 July
1202	19 June	10 July	1252	5 June	26 June
1203	11 June	2 July	1253	25 June	16 July
1204	30 June	21 July	1254	17 June	8 July
1205	15 June	6 July	1255	2 June	23 June
1206	7 June	28 June	1256	21 June	12 July
1207	27 June	18 July	1257	13 June	4 July
1208	11 June	2 July	1258	29 May	19 June
1209	3 June	24 June	1259	18 June	9 July
1210	23 June	14 July	1260	9 June	30 June
1211	8 June	29 June	1261	29 June	20 July

Legal chronology

Year	Began	Ended	Year	Began	Ended
1262	14 June	5 July	1312	31 May	21 June
1263	6 June	27 June	1313	20 June	11 July
1264	25 June	16 July	1314	12 June	3 July
1265	10 June	1 July	1315	28 May	18 June
1266	2 June	23 June	1316	16 June	7 July
1267	22 June	13 July	1317	8 June	29 June
1268	13 June	4 July	1318	28 June	19 July
1269	29 May	19 June	1319	13 June	4 July
1270	18 June	9 July	1320	4 June	25 June
1271	10 June	1 July	1321	24 June	15 July
1272	29 June	20 July	1322	16 June	7 July
1273	14 June	5 July	1323	1 June	22 June
1274	6 June	27 June	1324	20 June	11 July
1275	19 June	10 July	1325	12 June	3 July
1276	10 June	1 July	1326	28 May	18 June
1277	2 June	23 June	1327	17 June	8 July
1278	22 June	13 July	1328	8 June	29 June
1279	7 June	28 June	1329	28 June	19 July
1280	26 June	17 July	1330	13 June	4 July
1281	18 June	9 July	1331	5 June	26 June
1282	3 June	24 June	1332	24 June	15 July
1283	23 June	14 July	1333	9 June	30 June
1284	14 June	5 July	1334	1 June	22 June
1285	30 May	20 June	1335	21 June	12 July
1286	19 June	10 July	1336	5 June	26 June
1287	11 June	2 July	1337	25 June	16 July
1288	2 June	23 June	1338	17 June	8 July
1289	15 June	6 July	1339	2 June	23 June
1290	7 June	28 June	1340	21 June	12 July
1291	27 June	18 July	1341	13 June	4 July
1292	11 June	2 July	1342	5 June	26 June
1293	3 June	24 June	1343	18 June	9 July
1294	23 June	14 July	1344	9 June	30 June
1295	8 June	29 June	1345	1 June	22 June
1296	30 May	20 June	1346	21 June	12 July
1297	19 June	10 July	1347	6 June	27 June
1298	11 June	2 July	1348	25 June	16 July
1299	24 June	15 July	1349	17 June	8 July
1300	15 June	6 July	1350	2 June	23 June
1301	7 June	28 June	1351	22 June	13 July
1302	27 June	18 July	1352	13 June	4 July
1303	12 June	3 July	1353	29 May	19 June
1304	3 June	24 June	1354	18 June	9 July
1305	23 June	14 July	1355	10 June	1 July
1306	8 June	29 June	1356	29 June	20 July
1307	31 May	21 June	1357	14 June	5 July
1308	19 June	10 July	1358	6 June	27 June
1309	4 June	25 June	1359	26 June	17 July
1310	24 June	15 July	1360	10 June	1 July
1311	16 June	7 July	1361	2 June	23 June

Year	Began	Ended	Year	Began	Ended
1362	22 June	13 July	1412	8 June	29 June
1363	7 June	28 June	1413	28 June	19 July
1364	29 May	19 June	1414	13 June	4 July
1365	18 June	9 July	1415	5 June	26 June
1366	10 June	1 July	1416	24 June	15 July
1367	23 June	14 July	1417	16 June	7 July
1368	14 June	5 July	1418	1 June	22 June
1369	6 June	27 June	1419	21 June	12 July
1370	19 June	10 July	1420	12 June	3 July
1371	11 June	2 July	1421	28 May	18 June
1372	2 June	23 June	1422	17 June	8 July
1373	22 June	13 July	1423	9 June	30 June
1374	7 June	28 June	1424	28 June	19 July
1375	27 June	18 July	1425	13 June	4 July
1376	18 June	9 July	1426	5 June	26 June
1377	3 June	24 June	1427	25 June	16 July
1378	23 June	14 July	1428	9 June	30 June
1379	15 June	6 July	1429	1 June	22 June
1380	30 May	20 June	1430	21 June	12 July
1381	19 June	10 July	1431	6 June	27 June
1382	11 June	2 July	1432	25 June	16 July
1383	27 May	17 June	1433	17 June	8 July
1384	15 June	6 July	1434	2 June	23 June
1385	7 June	28 June	1435	22 June	13 July
1386	27 June	18 July	1436	13 June	4 July
1387	12 June	3 July	1437	5 June	26 June
1388	3 June	24 June	1438	18 June	9 July
1389	23 June	14 July	1439	10 June	1 July
1390	8 June	29 June	1440	1 June	22 June
1391	31 May	21 June	1441	21 June	12 July
1392	19 June	10 July	1442	6 June	27 June
1393	11 June	2 July	1443	26 June	17 July
1394	24 June	15 July	1444	17 June	8 July
1395	16 June	7 July	1445	2 June	23 June
1396	7 June	28 June	1446	22 June	13 July
1397	27 June	18 July	1447	14 June	5 July
1398	12 June	3 July	1448	29 May	19 June
1399	4 June	25 June	1449	18 June	9 July
1400	23 June	14 July	1450	10 June	1 July
1401	8 June	29 June	1451	30 June	21 July
1402	31 May	21 June	1452	14 June	5 July
1403	20 June	11 July	1453	6 June	27 June
1404	4 June	25 June	1454	26 June	17 July
1405	24 June	15 July	1455	11 June	2 July
1406	16 June	7 July	1456	2 June	23 June
1407	1 June	22 June	1457	22 June	13 July
1408	20 June	11 July	1458	7 June	28 June
1409	12 June	3 July	1459	30 May	20 June
1410	28 May	18 June	1460	18 June	9 July
1411	17 June	8 July	1461	10 June	1 July

Legal chronology

Year	Began	Ended	Year	Began	Ended
1462	23 June	14 July	1512	16 June	7 July
1463	15 June	6 July	1513	1 June	22 June
1464	6 June	27 June	1514	21 June	12 July
1465	19 June	10 July	1515	13 June	4 July
1466	11 June	2 July	1516	28 May	18 June
1467	3 June	24 June	1517	17 June	8 July
1468	22 June	13 July	1518	9 June	30 June
1469	7 June	28 June	1519	29 June	20 July
1470	27 June	18 July	1520	13 June	4 July
1471	19 June	10 July	1521	5 June	26 June
1472	3 June	24 June	1522	25 June	16 July
1473	23 June	14 July	1523	10 June	1 July
1474	15 June	6 July	1524	1 June	22 June
1475	31 May	21 June	1525	21 June	12 July
1476	19 June	10 July	1526	6 June	27 June
1477	11 June	2 July	1527	26 June	17 July
1478	27 May	17 June	1528	17 June	8 July
1479	16 June	7 July	1529	2 June	23 June
1480	7 June	28 June	1530	22 June	13 July
1481	27 June	18 July	1531	14 June	5 July
1482	12 June	3 July	1532	5 June	26 June
1483	4 June	25 June	1533	18 June	9 July
1484	23 June	14 July	1534	10 June	1 July
1485	8 June	29 June	1535	2 June	23 June
1486	31 May	21 June	1536	21 June	12 July
1487	20 June	11 July	1537	6 June	27 June
1488	11 June	2 July	1538	26 June	17 July
1489	24 June	15 July	1539	11 June	2 July
1490	16 June	7 July	1540	2 June	23 June
1491	8 June	29 June	1541	17 June	6 July
1492	27 June	18 July	1542	9 June	28 June
1493	12 June	3 July	1543	25 May	13 June
1494	4 June	25 June	1544	13 June	2 July
1495	24 June	15 July	1545	5 June	24 June
1496	8 June	29 June	1546	25 June	14 July
1497	31 May	21 June	1547	10 June	29 June
1498	20 June	11 July	1548	1 June	20 June
1499	5 June	26 June	1549	21 June	10 July
1500	24 June	15 July	1550	6 June	25 June
1501	16 June	7 July	1551	29 May	17 June
1502	1 June	22 June	1552	17 June	6 July
1503	21 June	12 July	1553	2 June	21 June
1504	12 June	3 July	1554	25 May	13 June
1505	28 May	18 June	1555	14 June	3 July
1506	17 June	8 July	1556	5 June	24 June
1507	9 June	30 June	1557	18 June	7 July
1508	28 June	19 July	1558	10 June	29 June
1509	13 June	4 July	1559	26 May	14 June
1510	5 June	26 June	1560	14 June	3 July
1511	25 June	16 July	1561	6 June	25 June

Year	Began	Ended	Year	Began	Ended
1562	29 May	17 June	1612	12 June	1 July
1563	11 June	30 June	1613	4 June	23 June
1564	2 June	21 June	1614	24 June	13 July
1565	22 June	11 July	1615	9 June	28 June
1566	14 June	3 July	1616	31 May	19 June
1567	30 May	18 June	1617	20 June	9 July
1568	18 June	7 July	1618	5 June	24 June
1569	10 June	29 June	1619	28 May	16 June
1570	26 May	14 June	1620	16 June	5 July
1571	15 June	4 July	1621	1 June	20 June
1572	6 June	25 June	1622	21 June	10 July
1573	22 May	10 June	1623	13 June	2 July
1574	11 June	30 June	1624	28 May	16 June
1575	3 June	22 June	1625	17 June	6 July
1576	22 June	11 July	1626	9 June	28 June
1577	7 June	26 June	1627	25 May	13 June
1578	30 May	18 June	1628	13 June	2 July
1579	19 June	8 July	1629	5 June	24 June
1580	3 June	22 June	1630	28 May	16 June
1581	26 May	14 June	1631	10 June	29 June
1582	15 June	4 July	1632	1 June	20 June
1583	31 May	19 June	1633	21 June	10 July
1584	19 June	8 July	1634	6 June	25 June
1585	11 June	30 June	1635	29 May	17 June
1586	3 June	22 June	1636	17 June	6 July
1587	16 June	5 July	1637	9 June	28 June
1588	7 June	26 June	1638	25 May	13 June
1589	30 May	18 June	1639	14 June	3 July
1590	19 June	8 July	1640	5 June	24 June
1591	4 June	23 June	1641	25 June	14 July
1592	26 May	14 June	1642	10 June	29 June
1593	15 June	4 July	1643	2 June	21 June
1594	31 May	19 June	1644	21 June	10 July
1595	20 June	9 July	1645	6 June	25 June
1596	11 June	30 June	1646	29 May	17 June
1597	27 May	15 June	1647	18 June	7 July
1598	16 June	5 July	1648	2 June	21 June
1599	8 June	27 June	1649	25 May	13 June
1600	23 May	11 June	1650	14 June	3 July
1601	12 June	1 July	1651	30 May	18 June
1602	4 June	23 June	1652	18 June	7 July
1603	24 June	13 July	1653	10 June	29 June
1604	8 June	27 June	1654	26 May	14 June
1605	31 May	19 June	1655	15 June	4 July
1606	20 June	9 July	1656	6 June	25 June
1607	5 June	24 June	1657	29 May	17 June
1608	27 May	15 June	1658	11 June	30 June
1609	16 June	5 July	1659	3 June	22 June
1610	8 June	27 June	1660	22 June	11 July
1611	24 May	12 June	1661	14 June	3 July

Legal chronology

Year	Began	Ended	Year	Began	Ended
1662	30 May	18 June	1712	20 June	9 July
1663	19 June	8 July	1713	5 June	24 June
1664	10 June	29 June	1714	28 May	16 June
1665	26 May	14 June	1715	17 June	6 July
1666	15 June	4 July	1716	1 June	20 June
1667	7 June	26 June	1717	21 June	10 July
1668	22 May	10 June	1718	13 June	2 July
1669	11 June	30 June	1719	29 May	17 June
1670	3 June	22 June	1720	17 June	6 July
1671	23 June	12 July	1721	9 June	28 June
1672	7 June	26 June	1722	25 May	13 June
1673	30 May	18 June	1723	14 June	3 July
1674	19 June	8 July	1724	5 June	24 June
1675	4 June	23 June	1725	28 May	16 June
1676	26 May	14 June	1726	10 June	29 June
1677	15 June	4 July	1727	2 June	21 June
1678	31 May	19 June	1728	21 June	10 July
1679	20 June	9 July	1729	6 June	25 June
1680	11 June	30 June	1730	29 May	17 June
1681	3 June	22 June	1731	18 June	7 July
1682	16 June	5 July	1732	9 June	28 June
1683	8 June	27 June	1733	25 May	13 June
1684	30 May	18 June	1734	14 June	3 July
1685	19 June	8 July	1735	6 June	25 June
1686	4 June	23 June	1736	25 June	14 July
1687	27 May	15 June	1737	10 June	29 June
1688	15 June	4 July	1738	2 June	21 June
1689	31 May	19 June	1739	22 June	11 July
1690	20 June	9 July	1740	6 June	25 June
1691	12 June	1 July	1741	29 May	17 June
1692	27 May	15 June	1742	18 June	7 July
1693	16 June	5 July	1743	3 June	22 June
1694	8 June	27 June	1744	25 May	13 June
1695	24 May	12 June	1745	14 June	3 July
1696	12 June	1 July	1746	30 May	18 June
1697	4 June	23 June	1747	19 June	8 July
1698	24 June	13 July	1748	10 June	29 June
1699	9 June	28 June	1749	26 May	14 June
1700	31 May	19 June	1750	15 June	4 July
1701	20 June	9 July	1751	7 June	26 June
1702	5 June	24 June	1752	29 May	17 June
1703	28 May	16 June	1753	22 June	11 July
1704	16 June	5 July	1754	14 June	3 July
1705	8 June	27 June	1755	30 May	18 June
1706	24 May	12 June	1756	18 June	7 July
1707	13 June	2 July	1757	10 June	29 June
1708	4 June	23 June	1758	26 May	14 June
1709	24 June	13 July	1759	15 June	4 July
1710	9 June	28 June	1760	6 June	25 June
1711	1 June	20 June	1761	22 May	10 June

5/X Law terms from AD 1066 to AD 1830

Year	Began	Ended	Year	Began	Ended
1762	11 June	30 June	1797	16 June	5 July
1763	3 June	22 June	1798	8 June	27 June
1764	22 June	11 July	1799	24 May	12 June
1765	7 June	26 June	1800	13 June	2 July
1766	30 May	18 June	1801	5 June	24 June
1767	19 June	8 July	1802	18 June	7 July
1768	3 June	22 June	1803	10 June	29 June
1769	26 May	14 June	1804	1 June	20 June
1770	15 June	4 July	1805	14 June	3 July
1771	31 May	19 June	1806	6 June	25 June
1772	19 June	8 July	1807	29 May	17 June
1773	11 June	30 June	1808	17 June	6 July
1774	3 June	22 June	1809	2 June	21 June
1775	16 June	5 July	1810	22 June	11 July
1776	7 June	26 June	1811	14 June	3 July
1777	30 May	18 June	1812	29 May	17 June
1778	19 June	8 July	1813	18 June	7 July
1779	4 June	23 June	1814	10 June	29 June
1780	26 May	14 June	1815	26 May	14 June
1781	15 June	4 July	1816	14 June	3 July
1782	31 May	19 June	1817	6 June	25 June
1783	20 June	9 July	1818	22 May	10 June
1784	11 June	30 June	1819	11 June	30 June
1785	27 May	15 June	1820	2 June	21 June
1786	16 June	5 July	1821	22 June	11 July
1787	8 June	27 June	1822	7 June	26 June
1788	23 May	11 June	1823	30 May	18 June
1789	12 June	1 July	1824	18 June	7 July
1790	4 June	23 June	1825	3 June	22 June
1791	24 June	13 July	1826	26 May	14 June
1792	8 June	27 June	1827	15 June	4 July
1793	31 May	19 June	1828	6 June	25 June
1794	20 June	9 July	1829	19 June	8 July
1795	5 June	24 June	1830	11 June	30 June
1796	27 May	15 June			

Prior to the passing of Statute 32 Hen. 8. c. 21. (1540) Trinity Term commenced on the octaves of the Holy Trinity; but the full Term did not commence until the Wednesday after Corpus Christi Day.

In 1541, and after, Trinity Term commenced on the Monday next after Trinity Sunday, for keeping of the profers, essoins, returns, &c., instead, as previously, on the octaves of the Holy Trinity, and the full Term of Trinity Term commenced on the Friday next after Corpus Christi Day, instead of on the Wednesday next after that festival.

This Table has been calculated as commencing with the full Term.

Trinity Term was fixed by Statute 1 Will. 4. cap. 70. (passed 22 July 1830), which provides that in the year 1831, and afterwards, Trinity Term shall begin on 22 May, and end on 12 June.

Michaelmas term

Year	Began	Ended	Year	Began	Ended
1066	9 Oct.	28 Nov.	1114	9 Oct.	28 Nov.
1067	9 Oct.	28 Nov.	1115	9 Oct.	29 Nov.
1068	9 Oct.	28 Nov.	1116	9 Oct.	28 Nov.
1069	9 Oct.	28 Nov.	1117	9 Oct.	28 Nov.
1070	9 Oct.	29 Nov.	1118	9 Oct.	28 Nov.
1071	10 Oct.	28 Nov.	1119	9 Oct.	28 Nov.
1072	9 Oct.	28 Nov.	1120	9 Oct.	29 Nov.
1073	9 Oct.	28 Nov.	1121	10 Oct.	28 Nov.
1074	9 Oct.	28 Nov.	1122	9 Oct.	28 Nov.
1075	9 Oct.	28 Nov.	1123	9 Oct.	28 Nov.
1076	10 Oct.	28 Nov.	1124	9 Oct.	28 Nov.
1077	9 Oct.	28 Nov.	1125	9 Oct.	28 Nov.
1078	9 Oct.	28 Nov.	1126	9 Oct.	29 Nov.
1079	9 Oct.	28 Nov.	1127	10 Oct.	28 Nov.
1080	9 Oct.	28 Nov.	1128	9 Oct.	28 Nov.
1081	9 Oct.	29 Nov.	1129	9 Oct.	28 Nov.
1082	10 Oct.	28 Nov.	1130	9 Oct.	28 Nov.
1083	9 Oct.	28 Nov.	1131	9 Oct.	28 Nov.
1084	9 Oct.	28 Nov.	1132	10 Oct.	28 Nov.
1085	9 Oct.	28 Nov.	1133	9 Oct.	28 Nov.
1086	9 Oct.	28 Nov.	1134	9 Oct.	28 Nov.
1087	9 Oct.	29 Nov.	1135	9 Oct.	28 Nov.
1088	9 Oct.	28 Nov.	1136	9 Oct.	28 Nov.
1089	9 Oct.	28 Nov.	1137	9 Oct.	29 Nov.
1090	9 Oct.	28 Nov.	1138	10 Oct.	28 Nov.
1091	9 Oct.	28 Nov.	1139	9 Oct.	28 Nov.
1092	9 Oct.	29 Nov.	1140	9 Oct.	28 Nov.
1093	10 Oct.	28 Nov.	1141	9 Oct.	28 Nov.
1094	9 Oct.	28 Nov.	1142	9 Oct.	28 Nov.
1095	9 Oct.	28 Nov.	1143	9 Oct.	29 Nov.
1096	9 Oct.	28 Nov.	1144	9 Oct.	28 Nov.
1097	9 Oct.	28 Nov.	1145	9 Oct.	28 Nov.
1098	9 Oct.	29 Nov.	1146	9 Oct.	28 Nov.
1099	10 Oct.	28 Nov.	1147	9 Oct.	28 Nov.
1100	9 Oct.	28 Nov.	1148	9 Oct.	29 Nov.
1101	9 Oct.	28 Nov.	1149	10 Oct.	28 Nov.
1102	9 Oct.	28 Nov.	1150	9 Oct.	28 Nov.
1103	9 Oct.	28 Nov.	1151	9 Oct.	28 Nov.
1104	10 Oct.	28 Nov.	1152	9 Oct.	28 Nov.
1105	9 Oct.	28 Nov.	1153	9 Oct.	28 Nov.
1106	9 Oct.	28 Nov.	1154	9 Oct.	29 Nov.
1107	9 Oct.	28 Nov.	1155	10 Oct.	28 Nov.
1108	9 Oct.	28 Nov.	1156	9 Oct.	28 Nov.
1109	9 Oct.	29 Nov.	1157	9 Oct.	28 Nov.
1110	10 Oct.	28 Nov.	1158	9 Oct.	28 Nov.
1111	9 Oct.	28 Nov.	1159	9 Oct.	28 Nov.
1112	9 Oct.	28 Nov.	1160	10 Oct.	28 Nov.
1113	9 Oct.	28 Nov.	1161	9 Oct.	28 Nov.

Year	Began	Ended	Year	Began	Ended
1162	9 Oct.	28 Nov.	1212	9 Oct.	28 Nov.
1163	9 Oct.	28 Nov.	1213	9 Oct.	28 Nov.
1164	9 Oct.	28 Nov.	1214	9 Oct.	28 Nov.
1165	9 Oct.	29 Nov.	1215	9 Oct.	28 Nov.
1166	10 Oct.	28 Nov.	1216	10 Oct.	28 Nov.
1167	9 Oct.	28 Nov.	1217	9 Oct.	28 Nov.
1168	9 Oct.	28 Nov.	1218	9 Oct.	28 Nov.
1169	9 Oct.	28 Nov.	1219	9 Oct.	28 Nov.
1170	9 Oct.	28 Nov.	1220	9 Oct.	28 Nov.
1171	9 Oct.	29 Nov.	1221	9 Oct.	29 Nov.
1172	9 Oct.	28 Nov.	1222	10 Oct.	28 Nov.
1173	9 Oct.	28 Nov.	1223	9 Oct.	28 Nov.
1174	9 Oct.	28 Nov.	1224	9 Oct.	28 Nov.
1175	9 Oct.	28 Nov.	1225	9 Oct.	28 Nov.
1176	9 Oct.	29 Nov.	1226	9 Oct.	28 Nov.
1177	10 Oct.	28 Nov.	1227	9 Oct.	29 Nov.
1178	9 Oct.	28 Nov.	1228	9 Oct.	28 Nov.
1179	9 Oct.	28 Nov.	1229	9 Oct.	28 Nov.
1180	9 Oct.	28 Nov.	1230	9 Oct.	28 Nov.
1181	9 Oct.	28 Nov.	1231	9 Oct.	28 Nov.
1182	9 Oct.	29 Nov.	1232	9 Oct.	29 Nov.
1183	10 Oct.	28 Nov.	1233	10 Oct.	28 Nov.
1184	9 Oct.	28 Nov.	1234	9 Oct.	28 Nov.
1185	9 Oct.	28 Nov.	1235	9 Oct.	28 Nov.
1186	9 Oct.	28 Nov.	1236	9 Oct.	28 Nov.
1187	9 Oct.	28 Nov.	1237	9 Oct.	28 Nov.
1188	10 Oct.	28 Nov.	1238	9 Oct.	29 Nov.
1189	9 Oct.	28 Nov.	1239	10 Oct.	28 Nov.
1190	9 Oct.	28 Nov.	1240	9 Oct.	28 Nov.
1191	9 Oct.	28 Nov.	1241	9 Oct.	28 Nov.
1192	9 Oct.	28 Nov.	1242	9 Oct.	28 Nov.
1193	9 Oct.	29 Nov.	1243	9 Oct.	28 Nov.
1194	10 Oct.	28 Nov.	1244	10 Oct.	28 Nov.
1195	9 Oct.	28 Nov.	1245	9 Oct.	28 Nov.
1196	9 Oct.	28 Nov.	1246	9 Oct.	28 Nov.
1197	9 Oct.	28 Nov.	1247	9 Oct.	28 Nov.
1198	9 Oct.	28 Nov.	1248	9 Oct.	28 Nov.
1199	9 Oct.	29 Nov.	1249	9 Oct.	29 Nov.
1200	9 Oct.	28 Nov.	1250	10 Oct.	28 Nov.
1201	9 Oct.	28 Nov.	1251	9 Oct.	28 Nov.
1202	9 Oct.	28 Nov.	1252	9 Oct.	28 Nov.
1203	9 Oct.	28 Nov.	1253	9 Oct.	28 Nov.
1204	9 Oct.	29 Nov.	1254	9 Oct.	28 Nov.
1205	10 Oct.	28 Nov.	1255	9 Oct.	29 Nov.
1206	9 Oct.	28 Nov.	1256	9 Oct.	28 Nov.
1207	9 Oct.	28 Nov.	1257	9 Oct.	28 Nov.
1208	9 Oct.	28 Nov.	1258	9 Oct.	28 Nov.
1209	9 Oct.	28 Nov.	1259	9 Oct.	28 Nov.
1210	9 Oct.	29 Nov.	1260	9 Oct.	29 Nov.
1211	10 Oct.	28 Nov.	1261	10 Oct.	28 Nov.

Legal chronology

Year	Began	Ended	Year	Began	Ended
1262	9 Oct.	28 Nov.	1312	9 Oct.	28 Nov.
1263	9 Oct.	28 Nov.	1313	9 Oct.	28 Nov.
1264	9 Oct.	28 Nov.	1314	9 Oct.	28 Nov.
1265	9 Oct.	28 Nov.	1315	9 Oct.	28 Nov.
1266	9 Oct.	29 Nov.	1316	9 Oct.	29 Nov.
1267	10 Oct.	28 Nov.	1317	10 Oct.	28 Nov.
1268	9 Oct.	28 Nov.	1318	9 Oct.	28 Nov.
1269	9 Oct.	28 Nov.	1319	9 Oct.	28 Nov.
1270	9 Oct.	28 Nov.	1320	9 Oct.	28 Nov.
1271	9 Oct.	28 Nov.	1321	9 Oct.	28 Nov.
1272	10 Oct.	28 Nov.	1322	9 Oct.	29 Nov.
1273	9 Oct.	28 Nov.	1323	10 Oct.	28 Nov.
1274	9 Oct.	28 Nov.	1324	9 Oct.	28 Nov.
1275	9 Oct.	28 Nov.	1325	9 Oct.	28 Nov.
1276	9 Oct.	28 Nov.	1326	9 Oct.	28 Nov.
1277	9 Oct.	29 Nov.	1327	9 Oct.	28 Nov.
1278	10 Oct.	28 Nov.	1328	10 Oct.	28 Nov.
1279	9 Oct.	28 Nov.	1329	9 Oct.	28 Nov.
1280	9 Oct.	28 Nov.	1330	9 Oct.	28 Nov.
1281	9 Oct.	28 Nov.	1331	9 Oct.	28 Nov.
1282	9 Oct.	28 Nov.	1332	9 Oct.	28 Nov.
1283	9 Oct.	29 Nov.	1333	9 Oct.	29 Nov.
1284	9 Oct.	28 Nov.	1334	10 Oct.	28 Nov.
1285	9 Oct.	28 Nov.	1335	9 Oct.	28 Nov.
1286	9 Oct.	28 Nov.	1336	9 Oct.	28 Nov.
1287	9 Oct.	28 Nov.	1337	9 Oct.	28 Nov.
1288	9 Oct.	29 Nov.	1338	9 Oct.	28 Nov.
1289	10 Oct.	28 Nov.	1339	9 Oct.	29 Nov.
1290	9 Oct.	28 Nov.	1340	9 Oct.	28 Nov.
1291	9 Oct.	28 Nov.	1341	9 Oct.	28 Nov.
1292	9 Oct.	28 Nov.	1342	9 Oct.	28 Nov.
1293	9 Oct.	28 Nov.	1343	9 Oct.	28 Nov.
1294	9 Oct.	29 Nov.	1344	9 Oct.	29 Nov.
1295	10 Oct.	28 Nov.	1345	10 Oct.	28 Nov.
1296	9 Oct.	28 Nov.	1346	9 Oct.	28 Nov.
1297	9 Oct.	28 Nov.	1347	9 Oct.	28 Nov.
1298	9 Oct.	28 Nov.	1348	9 Oct.	28 Nov.
1299	9 Oct.	28 Nov.	1349	9 Oct.	28 Nov.
1300	10 Oct.	28 Nov.	1350	9 Oct.	29 Nov.
1301	9 Oct.	28 Nov.	1351	10 Oct.	28 Nov.
1302	9 Oct.	28 Nov.	1352	9 Oct.	28 Nov.
1303	9 Oct.	28 Nov.	1353	9 Oct.	28 Nov.
1304	9 Oct.	28 Nov.	1354	9 Oct.	28 Nov.
1305	9 Oct.	29 Nov.	1355	9 Oct.	28 Nov.
1306	10 Oct.	28 Nov.	1356	10 Oct.	28 Nov.
1307	9 Oct.	28 Nov.	1357	9 Oct.	28 Nov.
1308	9 Oct.	28 Nov.	1358	9 Oct.	28 Nov.
1309	9 Oct.	28 Nov.	1359	9 Oct.	28 Nov.
1310	9 Oct.	28 Nov.	1360	9 Oct.	28 Nov.
1311	9 Oct.	29 Nov.	1361	9 Oct.	29 Nov.

Year	Began	Ended	Year	Began	Ended
1362	10 Oct.	28 Nov.	1412	10 Oct.	28 Nov.
1363	9 Oct.	28 Nov.	1413	9 Oct.	28 Nov.
1364	9 Oct.	28 Nov.	1414	9 Oct.	28 Nov.
1365	9 Oct.	28 Nov.	1415	9 Oct.	28 Nov.
1366	9 Oct.	28 Nov.	1416	9 Oct.	28 Nov.
1367	9 Oct.	29 Nov.	1417	9 Oct.	29 Nov.
1368	9 Oct.	28 Nov.	1418	10 Oct.	28 Nov.
1369	9 Oct.	28 Nov.	1419	9 Oct.	28 Nov.
1370	9 Oct.	28 Nov.	1420	9 Oct.	28 Nov.
1371	9 Oct.	28 Nov.	1421	9 Oct.	28 Nov.
1372	9 Oct.	29 Nov.	1422	9 Oct.	28 Nov.
1373	10 Oct.	28 Nov.	1423	9 Oct.	29 Nov.
1374	9 Oct.	28 Nov.	1424	9 Oct.	28 Nov.
1375	9 Oct.	28 Nov.	1425	9 Oct.	28 Nov.
1376	9 Oct.	28 Nov.	1426	9 Oct.	28 Nov.
1377	9 Oct.	28 Nov.	1427	9 Oct.	28 Nov.
1378	9 Oct.	29 Nov.	1428	9 Oct.	29 Nov.
1379	10 Oct.	28 Nov.	1429	10 Oct.	28 Nov.
1380	9 Oct.	28 Nov.	1430	9 Oct.	28 Nov.
1381	9 Oct.	28 Nov.	1431	9 Oct.	28 Nov.
1382	9 Oct.	28 Nov.	1432	9 Oct.	28 Nov.
1383	9 Oct.	28 Nov.	1433	9 Oct.	28 Nov.
1384	10 Oct.	28 Nov.	1434	9 Oct.	29 Nov.
1385	9 Oct.	28 Nov.	1435	10 Oct.	28 Nov.
1386	9 Oct.	28 Nov.	1436	9 Oct.	28 Nov.
1387	9 Oct.	28 Nov.	1437	9 Oct.	28 Nov.
1388	9 Oct.	28 Nov.	1438	9 Oct.	28 Nov.
1389	9 Oct.	29 Nov.	1439	9 Oct.	28 Nov.
1390	10 Oct.	28 Nov.	1440	10 Oct.	28 Nov.
1391	9 Oct.	28 Nov.	1441	9 Oct.	28 Nov.
1392	9 Oct.	28 Nov.	1442	9 Oct.	28 Nov.
1393	9 Oct.	28 Nov.	1443	9 Oct.	28 Nov.
1394	9 Oct.	28 Nov.	1444	9 Oct.	28 Nov.
1395	9 Oct.	29 Nov.	1445	9 Oct.	29 Nov.
1396	9 Oct.	28 Nov.	1446	10 Oct.	28 Nov.
1397	9 Oct.	28 Nov.	1447	9 Oct.	28 Nov.
1398	9 Oct.	28 Nov.	1448	9 Oct.	28 Nov.
1399	9 Oct.	28 Nov.	1449	9 Oct.	28 Nov.
1400	9 Oct.	29 Nov.	1450	9 Oct.	28 Nov.
1401	10 Oct.	28 Nov.	1451	9 Oct.	29 Nov.
1402	9 Oct.	28 Nov.	1452	9 Oct.	28 Nov.
1403	9 Oct.	28 Nov.	1453	9 Oct.	28 Nov.
1404	9 Oct.	28 Nov.	1454	9 Oct.	28 Nov.
1405	9 Oct.	28 Nov.	1455	9 Oct.	28 Nov.
1406	9 Oct.	29 Nov.	1456	9 Oct.	28 Nov.
1407	10 Oct.	28 Nov.	1457	10 Oct.	28 Nov.
1408	9 Oct.	28 Nov.	1458	9 Oct.	29 Nov.
1409	9 Oct.	28 Nov.	1459	9 Oct.	28 Nov.
1410	9 Oct.	28 Nov.	1460	9 Oct.	28 Nov.
1411	9 Oct.	28 Nov.	1461	9 Oct.	28 Nov.

Legal chronology

Year	Began	Ended		Year	Began	Ended
1462	9 Oct.	29 Nov.		1512	9 Oct.	29 Nov.
1463	10 Oct.	28 Nov.		1513	10 Oct.	28 Nov.
1464	9 Oct.	28 Nov.		1514	9 Oct.	28 Nov.
1465	9 Oct.	28 Nov.		1515	9 Oct.	28 Nov.
1466	9 Oct.	28 Nov.		1516	9 Oct.	28 Nov.
1467	9 Oct.	28 Nov.		1517	9 Oct.	28 Nov.
1468	10 Oct.	28 Nov.		1518	9 Oct.	29 Nov.
1469	9 Oct.	28 Nov.		1519	10 Oct.	28 Nov.
1470	9 Oct.	28 Nov.		1520	9 Oct.	28 Nov.
1471	9 Oct.	28 Nov.		1521	9 Oct.	28 Nov.
1472	9 Oct.	28 Nov.		1522	9 Oct.	28 Nov.
1473	9 Oct.	29 Nov.		1523	9 Oct.	28 Nov.
1474	10 Oct.	28 Nov.		1524	10 Oct.	28 Nov.
1475	9 Oct.	28 Nov.		1525	9 Oct.	28 Nov.
1476	9 Oct.	28 Nov.		1526	9 Oct.	28 Nov.
1477	9 Oct.	28 Nov.		1527	9 Oct.	28 Nov.
1478	9 Oct.	28 Nov.		1528	9 Oct.	28 Nov.
1479	9 Oct.	29 Nov.		1529	9 Oct.	29 Nov.
1480	9 Oct.	28 Nov.		1530	10 Oct.	28 Nov.
1481	9 Oct.	28 Nov.		1531	9 Oct.	28 Nov.
1482	9 Oct.	28 Nov.		1532	9 Oct.	28 Nov.
1483	9 Oct.	28 Nov.		1533	9 Oct.	28 Nov.
1484	9 Oct.	29 Nov.		1534	9 Oct.	28 Nov.
1485	10 Oct.	28 Nov.		1535	9 Oct.	29 Nov.
1486	9 Oct.	28 Nov.		1536	9 Oct.	28 Nov.
1487	9 Oct.	28 Nov.		1537	9 Oct.	28 Nov.
1488	9 Oct.	28 Nov.		1538	9 Oct.	28 Nov.
1489	9 Oct.	28 Nov.		1539	9 Oct.	28 Nov.
1490	9 Oct.	29 Nov.		1540	9 Oct.	29 Nov.
1491	10 Oct.	28 Nov.		1541	10 Oct.	28 Nov.
1492	9 Oct.	28 Nov.		1542	9 Oct.	28 Nov.
1493	9 Oct.	28 Nov.		1543	9 Oct.	28 Nov.
1494	9 Oct.	28 Nov.		1544	9 Oct.	28 Nov.
1495	9 Oct.	28 Nov.		1545	9 Oct.	28 Nov.
1496	10 Oct.	28 Nov.		1546	9 Oct.	29 Nov.
1497	9 Oct.	28 Nov.		1547	10 Oct.	28 Nov.
1498	9 Oct.	28 Nov.		1548	9 Oct.	28 Nov.
1499	9 Oct.	28 Nov.		1549	9 Oct.	28 Nov.
1500	9 Oct.	28 Nov.		1550	9 Oct.	28 Nov.
1501	9 Oct.	29 Nov.		1551	9 Oct.	28 Nov.
1502	10 Oct.	28 Nov.		1552	10 Oct.	28 Nov.
1503	9 Oct.	28 Nov.		1553	9 Oct.	28 Nov.
1504	9 Oct.	28 Nov.		1554	9 Oct.	28 Nov.
1505	9 Oct.	28 Nov.		1555	9 Oct.	28 Nov.
1506	9 Oct.	28 Nov.		1556	9 Oct.	28 Nov.
1507	9 Oct.	29 Nov.		1557	9 Oct.	29 Nov.
1508	9 Oct.	28 Nov.		1558	10 Oct.	28 Nov.
1509	9 Oct.	28 Nov.		1559	9 Oct.	28 Nov.
1510	9 Oct.	28 Nov.		1560	9 Oct.	28 Nov.
1511	9 Oct.	28 Nov.		1561	9 Oct.	28 Nov.

Year	Began	Ended	Year	Began	Ended
1562	9 Oct.	28 Nov.	1612	9 Oct.	28 Nov.
1563	9 Oct.	29 Nov.	1613	9 Oct.	29 Nov.
1564	9 Oct.	28 Nov.	1614	10 Oct.	28 Nov.
1565	9 Oct.	28 Nov.	1615	9 Oct.	28 Nov.
1566	9 Oct.	28 Nov.	1616	9 Oct.	28 Nov.
1567	9 Oct.	28 Nov.	1617	9 Oct.	28 Nov.
1568	9 Oct.	29 Nov.	1618	9 Oct.	28 Nov.
1569	10 Oct.	28 Nov.	1619	9 Oct.	29 Nov.
1570	9 Oct.	28 Nov.	1620	9 Oct.	28 Nov.
1571	9 Oct.	28 Nov.	1621	9 Oct.	28 Nov.
1572	9 Oct.	28 Nov.	1622	9 Oct.	28 Nov.
1573	9 Oct.	28 Nov.	1623	9 Oct.	28 Nov.
1574	9 Oct.	29 Nov.	1624	9 Oct.	29 Nov.
1575	10 Oct.	28 Nov.	1625	10 Oct.	28 Nov.
1576	9 Oct.	28 Nov.	1626	9 Oct.	28 Nov.
1577	9 Oct.	28 Nov.	1627	9 Oct.	28 Nov.
1578	9 Oct.	28 Nov.	1628	9 Oct.	28 Nov.
1579	9 Oct.	28 Nov.	1629	9 Oct.	28 Nov.
1580	10 Oct.	28 Nov.	1630	9 Oct.	29 Nov.
1581	9 Oct.	28 Nov.	1631	10 Oct.	28 Nov.
1582	9 Oct.	28 Nov.	1632	9 Oct.	28 Nov.
1583	9 Oct.	28 Nov.	1633	9 Oct.	28 Nov.
1584	9 Oct.	28 Nov.	1634	9 Oct.	28 Nov.
1585	9 Oct.	29 Nov.	1635	9 Oct.	28 Nov.
1586	10 Oct.	28 Nov.	1636	10 Oct.	28 Nov.
1587	9 Oct.	28 Nov.	1637	9 Oct.	28 Nov.
1588	9 Oct.	28 Nov.	1638	9 Oct.	28 Nov.
1589	9 Oct.	28 Nov.	1639	9 Oct.	28 Nov.
1590	9 Oct.	28 Nov.	1640	9 Oct.	28 Nov.
1591	9 Oct.	29 Nov.	1641	23 Oct.	29 Nov.
1592	9 Oct.	28 Nov.	1642	24 Oct.	28 Nov.
1593	9 Oct.	28 Nov.	1643	23 Oct.	28 Nov.
1594	9 Oct.	28 Nov.	1644	23 Oct.	28 Nov.
1595	9 Oct.	28 Nov.	1645	23 Oct.	28 Nov.
1596	9 Oct.	29 Nov.	1646	23 Oct.	28 Nov.
1597	10 Oct.	28 Nov.	1647	23 Oct.	29 Nov.
1598	9 Oct.	28 Nov.	1648	23 Oct.	28 Nov.
1599	9 Oct.	28 Nov.	1649	23 Oct.	28 Nov.
1600	9 Oct.	28 Nov.	1650	23 Oct.	28 Nov.
1601	9 Oct.	28 Nov.	1651	23 Oct.	28 Nov.
1602	9 Oct.	29 Nov.	1652	23 Oct.	29 Nov.
1603	10 Oct.	28 Nov.	1653	24 Oct.	28 Nov.
1604	9 Oct.	28 Nov.	1654	23 Oct.	28 Nov.
1605	9 Oct.	28 Nov.	1655	23 Oct.	28 Nov.
1606	9 Oct.	28 Nov.	1656	23 Oct.	28 Nov.
1607	9 Oct.	28 Nov.	1657	23 Oct.	28 Nov.
1608	10 Oct.	28 Nov.	1658	23 Oct.	29 Nov.
1609	9 Oct.	28 Nov.	1659	24 Oct.	28 Nov.
1610	9 Oct.	28 Nov.	1660	23 Oct.	28 Nov.
1611	9 Oct.	28 Nov.	1661	23 Oct.	28 Nov.

Legal chronology

Year	Began	Ended	Year	Began	Ended
1662	23 Oct.	28 Nov.	1712	23 Oct.	28 Nov.
1663	23 Oct.	28 Nov.	1713	23 Oct.	28 Nov.
1664	24 Oct.	28 Nov.	1714	23 Oct.	29 Nov.
1665	23 Oct.	28 Nov.	1715	24 Oct.	28 Nov.
1666	23 Oct.	28 Nov.	1716	23 Oct.	28 Nov.
1667	23 Oct.	28 Nov.	1717	23 Oct.	28 Nov.
1668	23 Oct.	28 Nov.	1718	23 Oct.	28 Nov.
1669	23 Oct.	29 Nov.	1719	23 Oct.	28 Nov.
1670	24 Oct.	28 Nov.	1720	24 Oct.	28 Nov.
1671	23 Oct.	28 Nov.	1721	23 Oct.	28 Nov.
1672	23 Oct.	28 Nov.	1722	23 Oct.	28 Nov.
1673	23 Oct.	28 Nov.	1723	23 Oct.	28 Nov.
1674	23 Oct.	28 Nov.	1724	23 Oct.	28 Nov.
1675	23 Oct.	29 Nov.	1725	23 Oct.	29 Nov.
1676	23 Oct.	28 Nov.	1726	24 Oct.	28 Nov.
1677	23 Oct.	28 Nov.	1727	23 Oct.	28 Nov.
1678	23 Oct.	28 Nov.	1728	23 Oct.	28 Nov.
1679	23 Oct.	28 Nov.	1729	23 Oct.	28 Nov.
1680	23 Oct.	29 Nov.	1730	23 Oct.	28 Nov.
1681	24 Oct.	28 Nov.	1731	23 Oct.	29 Nov.
1682	23 Oct.	28 Nov.	1732	23 Oct.	28 Nov.
1683	23 Oct.	28 Nov.	1733	23 Oct.	28 Nov.
1684	23 Oct.	28 Nov.	1734	23 Oct.	28 Nov.
1685	23 Oct.	28 Nov.	1735	23 Oct.	28 Nov.
1686	23 Oct.	29 Nov.	1736	23 Oct.	29 Nov.
1687	24 Oct.	28 Nov.	1737	24 Oct.	28 Nov.
1688	23 Oct.	28 Nov.	1738	23 Oct.	28 Nov.
1689	23 Oct.	28 Nov.	1739	23 Oct.	28 Nov.
1690	23 Oct.	28 Nov.	1740	23 Oct.	28 Nov.
1691	23 Oct.	28 Nov.	1741	23 Oct.	28 Nov.
1692	24 Oct.	28 Nov.	1742	23 Oct.	29 Nov.
1693	23 Oct.	28 Nov.	1743	24 Oct.	28 Nov.
1694	23 Oct.	28 Nov.	1744	23 Oct.	28 Nov.
1695	23 Oct.	28 Nov.	1745	23 Oct.	28 Nov.
1696	23 Oct.	28 Nov.	1746	23 Oct.	28 Nov.
1697	23 Oct.	29 Nov.	1747	23 Oct.	28 Nov.
1698	24 Oct.	28 Nov.	1748	24 Oct.	28 Nov.
1699	23 Oct.	28 Nov.	1749	23 Oct.	28 Nov.
1700	23 Oct.	28 Nov.	1750	23 Oct.	28 Nov.
1701	23 Oct.	28 Nov.	1751	23 Oct.	28 Nov.
1702	23 Oct.	28 Nov.	1752	6 Nov.	28 Nov.
1703	23 Oct.	29 Nov.	1753	6 Nov.	28 Nov.
1704	23 Oct.	28 Nov.	1754	6 Nov.	28 Nov.
1705	23 Oct.	28 Nov.	1755	6 Nov.	28 Nov.
1706	23 Oct.	28 Nov.	1756	6 Nov.	29 Nov.
1707	23 Oct.	28 Nov.	1757	7 Nov.	28 Nov.
1708	23 Oct.	29 Nov.	1758	6 Nov.	28 Nov.
1709	24 Oct.	28 Nov.	1759	6 Nov.	28 Nov.
1710	23 Oct.	28 Nov.	1760	6 Nov.	28 Nov.
1711	23 Oct.	28 Nov.	1761	6 Nov.	28 Nov.

5/X Law terms from AD 1066 to AD 1830

Year	Began	Ended	Year	Began	Ended
1762	6 Nov.	29 Nov.	1797	6 Nov.	28 Nov.
1763	7 Nov.	28 Nov.	1798	6 Nov.	28 Nov.
1764	6 Nov.	28 Nov.	1799	6 Nov.	28 Nov.
1765	6 Nov.	28 Nov.	1800	6 Nov.	28 Nov.
1766	6 Nov.	28 Nov.	1801	6 Nov.	28 Nov.
1767	6 Nov.	28 Nov.	1802	6 Nov.	29 Nov.
1768	7 Nov.	28 Nov.	1803	7 Nov.	28 Nov.
1769	6 Nov.	28 Nov.	1804	6 Nov.	28 Nov.
1770	6 Nov.	28 Nov.	1805	6 Nov.	28 Nov.
1771	6 Nov.	28 Nov.	1806	6 Nov.	28 Nov.
1772	6 Nov.	28 Nov.	1807	6 Nov.	28 Nov.
1773	6 Nov.	29 Nov.	1808	7 Nov.	28 Nov.
1774	7 Nov.	28 Nov.	1809	6 Nov.	28 Nov.
1775	6 Nov.	28 Nov.	1810	6 Nov.	28 Nov.
1776	6 Nov.	28 Nov.	1811	6 Nov.	28 Nov.
1777	6 Nov.	28 Nov.	1812	6 Nov.	28 Nov.
1778	6 Nov.	28 Nov.	1813	6 Nov.	29 Nov.
1779	6 Nov.	29 Nov.	1814	7 Nov.	28 Nov.
1780	6 Nov.	28 Nov.	1815	6 Nov.	28 Nov.
1781	6 Nov.	28 Nov.	1816	6 Nov.	28 Nov.
1782	6 Nov.	28 Nov.	1817	6 Nov.	28 Nov.
1783	6 Nov.	28 Nov.	1818	6 Nov.	28 Nov.
1784	6 Nov.	29 Nov.	1819	6 Nov.	29 Nov.
1785	7 Nov.	28 Nov.	1820	6 Nov.	28 Nov.
1786	6 Nov.	28 Nov.	1821	6 Nov.	28 Nov.
1787	6 Nov.	28 Nov.	1822	6 Nov.	28 Nov.
1788	6 Nov.	28 Nov.	1823	6 Nov.	28 Nov.
1789	6 Nov.	28 Nov.	1824	6 Nov.	29 Nov.
1790	6 Nov.	29 Nov.	1825	7 Nov.	28 Nov.
1791	7 Nov.	28 Nov.	1826	6 Nov.	28 Nov.
1792	6 Nov.	28 Nov.	1827	6 Nov.	28 Nov.
1793	6 Nov.	28 Nov.	1828	6 Nov.	28 Nov.
1794	6 Nov.	28 Nov.	1829	6 Nov.	28 Nov.
1795	6 Nov.	28 Nov.	1830	6 Nov.	29 Nov.
1796	7 Nov.	28 Nov.			

Until 29 September 1641, Michaelmas Term began on the fourth day of the octaves of
St Michael, *i.e.*, on 9 October, unless that day fell on Sunday, then on the next day, and ended on
28 November, unless that day fell on Sunday, then on the next day; on and after 29 September
1641, Michaelmas Term began on the fourth day of the three weeks of St Michael, *i.e.*,
23 October, and ended on 28 November, unless those days fell on Sundays, then on the next day;
but in 1752 it was enacted that Michaelmas Term should commence on the morrow of All Souls,
i.e., on 3 November, unless that day fell on a Sunday, in which case it was to begin on the next
day, for the keeping of essoins, profers, &c.; and the full term of St Michael (by which this table
has been worked out) was ordered to begin on the fourth day of the said morrow of All Souls,
excepting the said fourth day fell on a Sunday, and then on the next day.

Michaelmas Term was fixed by Statute 1 Will. 4. cap. 70. (passed 22 July 1830), which provides
that in the year 1831, and afterwards, Michaelmas Term shall begin on 2 and end on
25 November.

Legal chronology

BIBLIOGRAPHY

Legal chronology

There is no satisfactory treatise devoted specifically to this subject, and to discover the practice of the various courts at different periods the student must often have recourse to the actual records of legal proceedings. Some parts of the subject have, however, received attention from scholars, and the works which are here listed have been of particular use in the preparation of this chapter.

Alexander, J. J., 'The dates of county days', *Bulletin of the Institute of Historical Research*, 3 (1925–6), 89–95.

Brand, P. A., '"Time out of mind": the knowledge and use of eleventh- and twelfth-century past in thirteenth-century litigation', *Anglo-Norman Studies*, 16 (1994), 37–54.

Carr, Cecil T., 'The citation of statutes', in *Cambridge legal essays in honour of H. Bond, W. W. Buckland, and C. S. Kenny* (Cambridge, 1926).

Chronological table of the statutes (1925–1968) (London, HMSO, 1969).

  A companion work is the *Index to the statutes in force*. 2 vols. (London, HMSO, 1968).

Finch, Henry, *Law, or a discourse thereof, in foure bookes* (London, 1627).

Hall, G. D. G., *Early registers of writs*, Selden Society, vol. 87 (1970).

Hopton, Arthur, *Concordancy of yeeres* (London, 1612).

  Also a new edition by John Penkethman, entitled *Hopton's concordancy enlarged* (London, 1635)

Jenkinson, Hilary and Formoy, Beryl E. R. (ed.), *Select cases in the exchequer of pleas* (Selden Soc. Publications, vol. 48, 1932).

List of Plea Rolls of various courts. Public Record Office, Lists and Indexes, no. 4, revised edition (London, HMSO, 1910).

Oughton, Thomas, *Ordo judiciorum*. 2 vols. (London, 1728–38).

Palmer, Robert C., *The county courts of medieval England, 1150–1350* (Princeton, N. J., 1982), esp. Chapter 1, 'Venue and scheduling' (pp. 3–27) and Appendix 1, 'The dates of county days' (pp. 307–12).

Sayles, G. O. (ed.), *Select cases in the court of king's bench, Edw. 1–Hen. V* (Selden Soc. Pub., nos. 55, 57, 58, 74, 76, 82, 88, 1936–71).

Spelman, Henry, 'The original of the four terms of the year', in *Reliquiæ spelmannianæ*, ed. Edmund Gibson (London, 1723), II, 69–104.

6

The Roman calendar

The Middle Ages inherited from the Roman world not only its system of reckoning the years (see above p. 1), but also its method of describing the months and days. The Romans divided the year into twelve months, and each month into the periods of Kalends, Nones, and Ides, reckoning the days after the Ides in relation to the Kalends of the ensuing month. The following table sets this out at large. In leap years the extra day, or *dies bissextus*, preceded *vi kal. Mar.* In these years, therefore, 24 February became *bis vi kal. Mar.* and 25 February became *vi kal. Mar.*, and the feast of St Matthias (with any other ceremonies commonly observed on the 24th) was held on 24 or 25 February.[1] While the Roman calendar of days was commonly used, particularly by ecclesiastical authorities, throughout the Middle Ages, and lingered on in the use of the papal curia until the nineteenth century, it was in competition, from the early Middle Ages onwards, with the modern system of reckoning the days of the month and with dating by reference to the feasts of the Church.[2]

The table reproduced below gives the Julian calendar as modified by Augustus. It is well to remember that the medieval clerk or chronicler, while using the Roman calendar, occasionally departed from its classical form. In the first place, he sometimes described *pridie kal.* as *ii kal.*

---

1. Classical authors are not clear about the position of the extra twenty-four hours, before or after *vi kal. Mar.,* in ancient times. See the discussion of sources in Pauly-Wissowa, *Real-Encyclopadie d. class. Altertumswissenschaft* (1893–), III. i, 503 (*s.v.* Bissextum). In the twelfth century, the reckoning prescribed for liturgical purposes was set out by Pope Alexander III: 'Ipsum autem festum [Sancti Mathie] sive fiat in precedenti die sive sequenti, qui duo quasi pro uno reputantur' (*Decretales Greg. IX*, 5.40.16). In English civil records dated by the days of the month in continuous sequence the chancery of the thirteenth century and after naturally dated its letters in bissextile years on every day from 24 to 29 February (e.g. *Rotuli lit. clausarum* (Record Commission, 1833–4), I, 249–50). It was declared in a royal writ to the justices of the bench, 9 May 1240, 'de modo surgendi de malo lecti' that when an essoin was given for a month or a year which included the *dies bissextus*, that day and the preceding day should count as one: 'computentur dies ille et dies proximus precedens pro unico die' (*Close Rolls 1254–56* (HMSO 1931), 414–15; *Statutes of the realm*, I. ii, 7).
2. It is worth remembering that other saints whose days were on 25–8 February in common years were also shifted to 26–9 February in leap years, since their days were governed by Roman days (a note owed to Leofranc Holford-Strevens).

Secondly, instead of reckoning the calends, etc., in retrograde order, he sometimes reckoned them in direct order and described the fourteenth day of January as *prima die kalendarum Feb.* (or *in capite kalendarum Feb.*) instead of *xix kal. Feb.*, and so on. Finally, he might exclude from his reckoning the actual day of the calends, nones, or ides, so that 14 January became *xviii kal. Feb.* instead of *xix kal. Feb.* But it is, in the nature of things, extremely unusual for the historian to be able to detect these peculiarities or to be sure that they are not simply errors of calculation or copying; the student should certainly not be in a hurry to assume aberrations of this kind without good evidence.

The Roman calendar

	Jan.	Feb.	Mar.	Apr.	May	Jun.	Jul.	Aug.	Sep.	Oct.	Nov.	Dec.
1	KAL.	KAL.	KAL.	KAL.	KAL.	KAL.	KAL.	KAL.	KAL.	KAL.	KAL.	KAL.
2	4 Non	4 Non	6 Non	4 Non	6 Non	4 Non	6 Non	4 Non	4 Non	6 Non	4 Non	4 Non
3	3 Non	3 Non	5 Non	3 Non	5 Non	3 Non	5 Non	3 Non	3 Non	5 Non	3 Non	3 Non
4	2 Non	2 Non	4 Non	2 Non	4 Non	2 Non	4 Non	2 Non	2 Non	4 Non	2 Non	2 Non
5	NONAE	NONAE	3 Non	NONAE	3 Non	NONAE	3 Non	NONAE	NONAE	3 Non	NONAE	NONAE
6	8 Id	8 Id	2 Non	8 Id	2 Non	8 Id	2 Non	8 Id	8 Id	2 Non	8 Id	8 Id
7	7 Id	7 Id	NONAE	7 Id	NONAE	7 Id	NONAE	7 Id	7 Id	NONAE	7 Id	7 Id
8	6 Id	6 Id	8 Id	6 Id	8 Id	6 Id	8 Id	6 Id	6 Id	8 Id	6 Id	6 Id
9	5 Id	5 Id	7 Id	5 Id	7 Id	5 Id	7 Id	5 Id	5 Id	7 Id	5 Id	5 Id
10	4 Id	4 Id	6 Id	4 Id	6 Id	4 Id	6 Id	4 Id	4 Id	6 Id	4 Id	4 Id
11	3 Id	3 Id	5 Id	3 Id	5 Id	3 Id	5 Id	3 Id	3 Id	5 Id	3 Id	3 Id
12	2 Id	2 Id	4 Id	2 Id	4 Id	2 Id	4 Id	2 Id	2 Id	4 Id	2 Id	2 Id
13	IDUS	IDUS	3 Id	IDUS	3 Id	IDUS	3 Id	IDUS	IDUS	3 Id	IDUS	IDUS
14	19 KF	16 KM	2 Id	18 KM	2 Id	18 KJ	2 Id	19 KS	18 KO	2 Id	18 KD	19 KJ
15	18 KF	15 KM	IDUS	17 KM	IDUS	17 KJ	IDUS	18 KS	17 KO	IDUS	17 KD	18 KJ
16	17 KF	14 KM	17 KA	16 KM	17 KJ	16 KJ	17 KA	17 KS	16 KO	17 KN	16 KD	17 KJ
17	16 KF	13 KM	16 KA	15 KM	16 KJ	15 KJ	16 KA	16 KS	15 KO	16 KN	15 KD	16 KJ
18	15 KF	12 KM	15 KA	14 KM	15 KJ	14 KJ	15 KA	15 KS	14 KO	15 KN	14 KD	15 KJ
19	14 KF	11 KM	14 KA	13 KM	14 KJ	13 KJ	14 KA	14 KS	13 KO	14 KN	13 KD	14 KJ
20	13 KF	10 KM	13 KA	12 KM	13 KJ	12 KJ	13 KA	13 KS	12 KO	13 KN	12 KD	13 KJ
21	12 KF	9 KM	12 KA	11 KM	12 KJ	11 KJ	12 KA	12 KS	11 KO	12 KN	11 KD	12 KJ
22	11 KF	8 KM	11 KA	10 KM	11 KJ	10 KJ	11 KA	11 KS	10 KO	11 KN	10 KD	11 KJ
23	10 KF	7 KM	10 KA	9 KM	10 KJ	9 KJ	10 KA	10 KS	9 KO	10 KN	9 KD	10 KJ
24	9 KF	6 KM	9 KA	8 KM	9 KJ	8 KJ	9 KA	9 KS	8 KO	9 KN	8 KD	9 KJ
25	8 KF	5 KM	8 KA	7 KM	8 KJ	7 KJ	8 KA	8 KS	7 KO	8 KN	7 KD	8 KJ
26	7 KF	4 KM	7 KA	6 KM	7 KJ	6 KJ	7 KA	7 KS	6 KO	7 KN	6 KD	7 KJ
27	6 KF	3 KM	6 KA	5 KM	6 KJ	5 KJ	6 KA	6 KS	5 KO	6 KN	5 KD	6 KJ
28	5 KF	2 KM	5 KA	4 KM	5 KJ	4 KJ	5 KA	5 KS	4 KO	5 KN	4 KD	5 KJ
29	4 KF		4 KA	3 KM	4 KJ	3 KJ	4 KA	4 KS	3 KO	4 KN	3 KD	4 KJ
30	3 KF		3 KA	2 KM	3 KJ	2 KJ	3 KA	3 KS	2 KO	3 KN	2 KD	3 KJ
31	2 KF		2 KA		2 KJ		2 KA	2 KS		2 KN		2 KJ

Leap-year: February

24 = 6 KM bis; 25 = 6 KM; 26 = 5 KM; 27 = 4 KM; 28 = 3 KM; 29 = 2 KM

7

Celtic and Roman (Alexandrian) Easter days, AD 400–768[1]

This table has been put together from Giry's Julian Calendar dates for Easter and the 84-year Celtic Easter Cycle, described by D. McCarthy and D. Ó Cróinín ('The "Lost" Irish 84-year Easter Table rediscovered', *Peritia*, 6–7 (1987–8), 227–42). It will be seen that where the dates differ, they do so by 7, 21 or 28 days. Users should note that the Celtic dates are 'authentic' but that the 'Roman' dates are simply calculated. It sometimes happens that neither Rome nor Gaul got the correct Alexandrian date. So before about 600–50 the date given for the Alexandrian Easter may be irrelevant to the medieval west. Giry provides a more detailed table of divergences, some of the information of which is contained here in the column 'Comment'. Leap years are printed in **bold** type.

AD	Celtic	Alexandrian	Comment
400	1 April	1 April	
401	14 April	14 April	21 April in some western churches
402	6 April	6 April	30 March in some western churches
403	29 March	29 March	
404	17 April	17 April	10 April in some western churches
405	2 April	2 April	
406	22 April	22 April	
407	14 April	14 April	
408	29 March	29 March	
409	18 April	18 April	
410	10 April	10 April	
411	26 March	26 March	
412	14 April	14 April	
413	6 April	6 April	
414	19 April	22 March	29 March in Egypt
415	11 April	11 April	
416	2 April	2 April	
417	22 April	22 April	25 March in some western churches
418	7 April	7 April	
419	30 March	30 April	

1. Compiled from information provided by Dr Richard Sharpe.

Celtic and Roman Easter days

AD	Celtic	Alexandrian	Comment
420	18 April	18 April	
421	3 April	3 April	
422	26 March	26 March	
423	15 April	15 April	
424	30 March	6 April	23 March in Africa
425	19 April	19 April	22 March in some western churches
426	1 April	11 April	
427	27 March	3 April	
428	15 April	22 April	
429	7 April	7 April	
430	30 March	30 March	
431	12 April	19 April	
432	3 April	3 April	
433	26 March	26 March	
434	15 April	15 April	
435	31 March	31 March	
436	19 April	19 April	
437	11 April	11 April	
438	27 March	27 March	
439	16 April	16 April	
440	7 April	7 April	
441	20 April	23 March	30 March in some western churches
442	12 April	12 April	
443	4 April	4 April	
444	23 April	23 April	26 March in some western churches
445	8 April	8 April	
446	31 March	31 March	
447	20 April	20 April	
448	4 April	11 April	
449	27 March	27 March	
450	16 April	16 April	
451	1 April	8 April	
452	20 April	23 March	
453	12 April	12 April	
454	28 March	4 April	17 April in some western churches
455	17 April	24 April	
456	8 April	8 April	
457	31 March	31 March	
458	13 April	20 April	
459	5 April	5 April	
460	27 March	27 March	
461	16 April	16 April	
462	1 April	1 April	
463	21 April	21 April	24 March in some western churches (first year of the Victorine cycle)
464	12 April	12 April	
465	28 March	28 March	
466	17 April	17 April	
467	9 April	9 April	
468	21 April	31 March	

AD 400–768

AD	Celtic	Alexandrian	Comment
469	13 April	13 April	
470	5 April	5 April	
471	18 April	28 March	
472	9 April	16 April	
473	1 April	1 April	
474	21 April	April	
475	6 April	6 April	13 April in Gaul
476	28 March	28 March	
477	17 April	17 April	
478	2 April	9 April	
479	22 April	25 March	
480	13 April	13 April	
481	29 March	5 April	
482	18 April	25 April	21 March in some western churches
483	10 April	10 April	
484	1 April	1 April	
485	14 April	21 April	
486	6 April	6 April	
487	29 March	29 March	
488	17 April	17 April	
489	2 April	2 April	
490	22 April	25 March	
491	14 April	14 April	
492	29 March	5 April	
493	18 April	18 April	
494	10 April	10 April	
495	26 March	26 March	2 April in Gaul
496	14 April	14 April	21 April in Gaul
497	6 April	6 April	
498	19 April	29 March	
499	11 April	11 April	18 April in Gaul
500	2 April	2 April	
501	22 April	22 April	25 March in some western churches
502	7 March	14 March	
503	30 March	30 March	
504	18 April	18 April	
505	3 April	10 April	
506	26 March	26 March	
507	15 April	15 April	
508	30 March	6 April	
509	19 April	22 March	
510	11 April	11 April	
511	27 March	3 April	
512	15 April	22 April	
513	7 April	7 April	
514	30 March	30 March	
515	12 April	19 April	
516	3 April	3 April	10 April in Gaul
517	26 March	26 March	
518	15 April	15 April	

Celtic and Roman Easter days

AD	Celtic	Alexandrian	Comment
519	31 March	31 March	
520	19 April	19 April	22 March in some western churches
521	11 April	11 April	
522	27 March	3 April	
523	16 April	16 April	
524	7 April	7 April	
525	20 April	30 March	
526	12 April	19 April	
527	4 April	4 April	
528	23 April	26 March	
529	8 April	15 April	
530	3 March	31 March	
531	20 April	20 April	
532	4 April	11 April	
533	27 March	27 March	
534	16 April	16 April	
535	1 April	8 April	
536	20 April	23 March	30 March in Gaul
537	12 April	12 April	
538	28 March	4 April	
539	17 April	24 April	
540	8 April	8 April	
541	31 March	31 March	
542	13 April	20 April	
543	5 April	5 April	
544	27 March	27 March	
545	16 April	16 April	
546	1 April	8 April	
547	21 April	24 March	
548	12 April	12 April	
549	28 March	4 April	
550	17 April	24 April	17 April in Gaul
551	9 April	9 April	
552	21 April	31 March	
553	13 April	20 April	
554	5 April	5 April	
555	18 April	28 March	
556	9 April	16 April	
557	1 April	1 April	
558	21 April	21 April	24 March in some western churches
559	6 April	13 April	
560	28 March	28 March	
561	17 April	17 April	
562	2 April	9 April	
563	22 April	25 March	
564	13 April	13 April	
565	29 March	5 April	
566	18 April	28 March	
567	10 April	10 April	
568	1 April	1 April	

AD	Celtic	Alexandrian	Comment
569	14 April	21 April	
570	6 April	6 April	13 April in Gaul
571	29 March	29 March	
572	17 April	17 April	
573	2 April	9 April	
574	22 April	25 March	
575	14 April	14 April	
576	29 March	5 April	
577	18 April	25 April	18 April in Gaul
578	10 April	10 April	
579	26 March	2 April	
580	14 April	21 April	
581	6 April	6 April	
582	19 April	29 March	
583	11 April	18 April	
584	23 April	2 April	
585	22 April	25 March	
586	7 April	14 April	
587	30 March	30 March	
588	18 April	18 April	
589	3 April	10 April	
590	26 March	26 March	2 April in some western churches
591	15 April	15 April	
592	30 March	6 April	
593	19 April	29 March	
594	11 April	11 April	18 April in Gaul
595	27 March	3 April	
596	15 April	22 April	25 March in some western churches
597	7 April	14 April	
598	30 March	30 March	
599	12 April	19 April	
600	3 April	10 April	
601	26 March	26 March	
602	15 April	15 April	
603	31 March	7 April	
604	19 April	22 March	
605	11 April	11 April	
606	27 March	3 April	
607	16 April	23 April	
608	7 April	7 April	
609	20 April	30 March	
610	12 April	19 April	
611	4 April	4 April	
612	23 April	26 March	
613	8 April	15 April	
614	31 March	31 March	
615	20 April	20 April	
616	4 April	11 April	
617	27 March	3 April	
618	16 April	16 April	

Celtic and Roman Easter days

AD	Celtic	Alexandrian	Comment
619	1 April	8 April	
620	20 April	30 March	
621	12 April	19 April	
622	28 March	4 April	
623	17 April	27 March	
624	8 April	15 April	
625	31 March	31 March	
626	13 April	20 April	
627	5 April	12 April	
628	27 March	27 March	
629	16 April	16 April	
630	1 April	8 April	
631	21 April	24 March	
632	12 April	12 April	
633	28 March	4 April	
634	17 April	24 April	
635	9 April	9 April	
636	21 April	31 March	
637	13 April	20 April	
638	5 April	5 April	
639	18 April	28 March	
640	9 April	16 April	
641	1 April	8 April	
642	21 April	24 March	
643	6 April	13 April	
644	28 March	4 April	
645	17 April	24 April	
646	2 April	9 April	
647	22 April	1 April	
648	13 April	20 April	
649	29 March	5 April	
650	18 April	28 March	
651	10 April	17 April	
652	1 April	1 April	
653	14 April	21 April	24 March in some western churches
654	6 April	13 April	
655	29 March	29 March	
656	17 April	17 April	
657	2 April	9 April	
658	22 April	25 March	
659	14 April	14 April	
660	29 March	5 April	
661	18 April	28 March	
662	10 April	10 April	
663	26 March	2 April	
664	14 April	21 April	
665	6 April	6 April	13 April in Gaul
666	19 April	29 March	
667	11 April	18 April	
668	2 April	9 April	

AD	Celtic	Alexandrian	Comment
669	22 April	25 March	
670	7 April	14 April	
671	30 March	6 April	
672	18 April	25 April	21 March in some western churches
673	3 April	10 April	
674	26 March	2 April	
675	15 April	22 April	
676	30 March	6 April	
677	19 April	29 March	
678	11 April	18 April	
679	27 March	3 April	
680	15 April	25 March	
681	7 April	14 April	
682	30 March	30 March	
683	12 April	19 April	
684	3 April	10 April	
685	26 March	26 March	
686	15 April	15 April	
687	31 March	7 April	
688	19 April	29 March	
689	11 April	11 April	18 April in Gaul
690	27 March	3 April	
691	16 April	23 April	
692	7 April	14 April	
693	20 April	30 March	
694	12 April	19 April	
695	4 April	11 April	
696	23 April	26 March	
697	8 April	15 April	
698	31 March	7 April	
699	20 April	23 March	
700	4 April	11 April	
701	27 March	3 April	
702	16 April	23 April	
703	1 April	8 April	
704	20 April	30 March	
705	12 April	19 April	
706	28 March	4 April	
707	17 April	27 March	
708	8 April	15 April	
709	31 March	31 March	
710	13 April	20 April	21 March in some western churches
711	5 April	12 April	
712	27 March	3 April	
713	16 April	16 April	
714	1 April	8 April	
715	21 April	31 March	
716	12 April	19 April	
717	28 March	4 April	
718	17 April	27 March	

Celtic and Roman Easter days

AD	Celtic	Alexandrian	Comment
719	9 April	16 April	
720	21 April	31 March	
721	13 April	20 April	
722	5 April	12 April	
723	18 April	28 March	
724	9 April	16 April	
725	1 April	8 April	
726	21 April	24 March	
727	6 April	13 April	
728	28 March	4 April	
729	17 April	24 April	
730	2 April	9 April	
731	22 April	1 April	
732	13 April	20 April	
733	29 March	5 April	
734	18 April	28 March	
735	10 April	17 April	
736	1 April	8 April	
737	14 April	24 March	
738	6 April	13 April	
739	29 March	5 April	
740	17 April	24 April	17 April in some western churches
741	2 April	9 April	
742	22 April	1 April	
743	14 April	14 April	
744	29 March	5 April	
745	18 April	28 March	
746	10 April	1 April	
747	26 March	2 April	
748	14 April	21 April	24 March in some western churches
749	6 April	13 April	
750	19 April	29 March	
751	11 April	18 April	
752	2 April	9 April	
753	22 April	25 March	
754	7 April	14 April	
755	30 March	6 April	
756	18 April	28 March	
757	3 April	10 April	
758	26 March	2 April	
759	15 April	22 April	
760	30 March	6 April	13 April in Gaul
761	19 April	29 March	
762	11 April	18 April	
763	27 March	3 April	
764	15 April	25 March	
765	7 April	14 April	
766	30 March	6 April	
767	12 April	19 April	
768	3 April	10 April	

8

Calendars for all possible dates of Easter, AD 400–2100

This table replaces those unnumbered from one to thirty-six in the original edition. It is based on those of Grotefend, Giry and Fry. The 'Old Style years' at the head of the left-hand pages include all years of the Julian calendar from AD 400 to 1752, when England celebrated Easter according to the Old Style of reckoning for the last time. The 'New Style years' on the right-hand pages give all years of the Gregorian calendar since its first introduction in Catholic countries abroad in 1582. The opportunity has been taken in Tables **9** and **10**, to eliminate a cause of some confusion in previous printings, by presenting as two separate lists the Chronological Table of Easter Days according to Old Style, AD 400–1752 and New Style, 1583–2100, rather than as one composite table. In addition, Table **12** provides a summary of the dates at which the Gregorian calendar was adopted in particular European states, territories and cities. This edition continues to display a special calendar for England for 1752 (**11**). It has not seemed necessary to include in the calendars all the fixed feasts, some capriciously chosen, which Grotefend and Fry included; following Cheney, we have retained only a few which are of special importance in the dating of events (e.g. the quarter days); on the other hand, the Ember days have been added to the series of movable feasts.

To find the complete calendar for any year from AD 400 to 2100, the student has simply to look up the year in the appropriate chronological Easter table (**9** and **10**, depending on whether Old or New Style dating is used) and then turn to the full calendar for the appropriate date of Easter in Table **8/1–35**.

When a student uses these calendars to check a date, he or she must first satisfy themselves that the year-date is that of the 'historical' year, that is, begins on 1 January; if it is not, it must be corrected to the historical year before turning to the table. Thus an English record dated Wednesday, 29 February 1351 belongs to the historical year AD 1352 (a leap year), and the Julian calendar for 1352 (below pp. 190–1) shows that 29 February fell on a Wednesday.

8/1 Easter Day 22 March

Dominical letter D for Common Years
Dominical letter ED for Leap Years (*in bold figures*)
Old style years   414, 509, **604**, 851, 946, 1041, **1136**, 1383, 1478, 1573, **1668**

Leap years

JANUARY	FEBRUARY
W1	S 1
T 2	
F 3	....
S 4	S 2 *Quinquag.*
....	M3
S 5	T 4 *Shrove Tu.*
M6 *Epiphany*	W5 *Ash Wed.*
T 7	T 6
W8	F 7
T 9	s 8
F 10	....
S 11	S 9 *Quadrag.*
....	M10
S 12 *Epiph. 1*	T 11
M13 *Hilary*	W12 *Ember*
T 14	T 13
W15	F 14 *Ember*
T 16	s 15 *Ember*
F 17	....
S 18	S 16 *Lent 2*
....	M17
S 19 *Septuag.*	T 18
M20	W19
T 21	T 20
W22	F 21
T 23	S 22
F 24	....
S 25	S 23 *Lent 3*
....	M24
s 26 *Sexages.*	T 25 *Matthias*
M27	W26
T 28	T 27
W29	F 28
T 30	S 29
F 31	

JANUARY	FEBRUARY	MARCH	APRIL	MAY
T 1	S 1 *Quinquag.*	S 1 *Lent 4*	W1	F 1
F 2	M2 *Purific. M.*	M2	T 2	S 2
S 3	T 3 *Shrove Tu.*	T 3	F 3	....
....	W4 *Ash Wed.*	W4	S 4	S 3 *Ascens. 1*
S 4	T 5	T 5	....	M4
M5	F 6	F 6	S 5 *Easter 2*	T 5
T 6 *Epiphany*	S 7	S 7	M6	W6
W7	....	....	T 7	T 7
T 8	S 8 *Quadrag.*	S 8 *Passion*	W8	F 8
F 9	M9	M9	T 9	S 9
S 10	T 10	T 10	F 10	....
....	W11 *Ember*	W11	S 11	S 10 *Whit Sun.*
S 11 *Epiph. 1*	T 12	T 12	....	M11
M12	F 13 *Ember*	F 13	S 12 *Easter 3*	T 12
T 13 *Hilary*	s 14 *Ember*	S 14	M13	W13 *Ember*
W14	....	....	T 14	T 14
T 15	S 15 *Lent 2*	S 15 *Palm*	W15	F 15 *Ember*
F 16	M16	M16	T 16	s 16 *Ember*
S 17	T 17	T 17	F 17	....
....	W18	W18	S 18	S 17 *Trinity*
S 18 *Septuag.*	T 19	T 19	....	M18
M19	F 20	F 20 *Good Fri.*	S 19 *Easter 4*	T 19
T 20	S 21	S 21	M20	W20
W21	....	....	T 21	T 21 *Corpus C.*
T 22	S 22 *Lent 3*	S 22 ***Easter Day***	W22	F 22
F 23	M23	M23	T 23	S 23
S 24	T 24 *Matthias*	T 24	F 24	....
....	W25	W25 *Annunc.*	S 25	S 24 *Trinity 1*
S 25 *Sexages.*	T 26	T 26	....	M25
M26	F 27	F 27	S 26 *Rogation*	T 26
T 27	S 28	S 28	M27	W27
W28			T 28	T 28
T 29		....	W29	F 29
F 30		S 29 *Quasimodo*	T 30 *Ascension*	S 30
S 31		M30		....
		T 31		S 31 *Trinity 2*

Easter Day 22 March 8/1

Dominical letter D for Common Years
Dominical letter ED for Leap Years (*in bold figures*)
New style years 1598, 1693, 1761, 1818

JUNE	JULY	AUGUST	SEPTEMBER	OCTOBER	NOVEMBER	DECEMBER
M1	W1	s 1 *Lammas*	T 1	T 1	S 1 *Trinity 24*	T 1
T 2	T 2		W2	F 2	M2	W2
W3	F 3	....	T 3	S 3	T 3	T 3
T 4	S 4	S 2 *Trinity 11*	F 4		W4	F 4
F 5		M3	S 5	....	T 5	S 5
s 6	....	T 4		S 4 *Trinity 20*	F 6	
	S 5 *Trinity 7*	W5		M5	S 7	....
	M6	T 6	S 6 *Trinity 16*	T 6		S 6 *Advent 2*
S 7 *Trinity 3*	T 7	F 7	M7	W7	....	M7
M8	W8	s 8	T 8	T 8	S 8 *Trinity 25*	T 8
T 9	T 9		W9	F 9	M9	W9
W10	F 10	....	T 10	S 10	T 10	T 10
T 11	S 11	S 9 *Trinity 12*	F 11		W11 *Martin*	F 11
F 12		M10	S 12	....	T 12	S 12
S 13	....	T 11		S 11 *Trinity 21*	F 13	
	S 12 *Trinity 8*	W12	....	M12	S 14	....
	M13	T 13	S 13 *Trinity 17*	T 13		S 13 *Advent 3*
S 14 *Trinity 4*	T 14	F 14	M14 *Exalt. C.*	W14	....	M14
M15	W15	s 15	T 15	T 15	S 15 *Trinity 26*	T 15
T 16	T 16		W16 *Ember*	F 16	M16	W16 *Ember*
W17	F 17	....	T 17	S 17	T 17	T 17
T 18	s 18	S 16 *Trinity 13*	F 18 *Ember*		W18	F 18 *Ember*
F 19		M17	s 19 *Ember*	....	T 19	s 19 *Ember*
S 20	....	T 18		S 18 *Trinity 22*	F 20	
	S 19 *Trinity 9*	W19	....	M19	S 21	....
....	M20	T 20	S 20 *Trinity 18*	T 20		S 20 *Advent 4*
S 21 *Trinity 5*	T 21	F 21	M21	W21	....	M21
M22	W22	s 22	T 22	T 22	S 22 *Trinity 27*	T 22
T 23	T 23		W23	F 23	M23	W23
W24 *Nat.J.Bap.*	F 24	....	T 24	S 24	T 24	T 24
T 25	S 25	S 23 *Trinity 14*	F 25		W25	F 25 *Christmas*
F 26		M24	S 26	....	T 26	s 26
S 27	....	T 25		S 25 *Trinity 23*	F 27	
	S 26 *Trinity 10*	W26	....	M26	S 28	....
....	M27	T 27	S 27 *Trinity 19*	T 27		S 27
S 28 *Trinity 6*	T 28	F 28	M28	W28	....	M28
M29	W29	s 29	T 29 *Michael A.*	T 29	S 29 *Advent 1*	T 29
T 30	T 30	....	W30	F 30	M30	W30
	F 31	S 30 *Trinity 15*		S 31		T 31
		M31				

8/2 Easter Day 23 March

Dominical letter E for Common Years
Dominical letter FE for Leap Years (*in bold figures*)
Old style years 441, **452, 536**, 699, 783, 794, 878, 889, 973, **984, 1068**, 1231, 1315, 1326, 1410, 1421, 1505, **1516, 1600**

Common years

JANUARY
T 1
W2
T 3
F 4
S 5
········
S 6 *Epiphany*
M7
T 8
W9
T 10
F 11
S 12
········
S 13 *Epiph. 1*
M14
T 15
W16
T 17
F 18
S 19
········
S 20 *Septuag.*
M21
T 22
W23
T 24
F 25
S 26
········
S 27 *Sexages.*
M28
T 29
W30
T 31

FEBRUARY
F 1
S 2 *Purific. M.*
········
S 3 *Quinquag.*
M4
T 5 *Shrove Tu.*
w6 *Ash Wed.*
T 7
F 8
S 9
········
S 10 *Quadrag.*
M11
T 12
W13 *Ember*
T 14
F 15 *Ember*
s 16 *Ember*
········
S 17 *Lent 2*
M18
T 19
W20
T 21
F 22
S 23
········
S 24 *Lent 3*
M25
T 26
W27
T 28
F 29

Leap years

JANUARY
W1
T 2
F 3
S 4
········
S 5
M6 *Epiphany*
T 7
W8
T 9
F 10
S 11
········
S 12 *Epiph. 1*
M13 *Hilary*
T 14
W15
T 16
F 17
S 18
········
S 19 *Septuag.*
M20
T 21
W22
T 23
F 24
S 25
········
S 26 *Sexages.*
M27
T 28
W29
T 30
F 31

FEBRUARY
S 1
········
S 2 *Quinquag.*
M3
T 4 *Shrove Tu.*
W5 *Ash Wed.*
T 6
F 7
s 8
········
S 9 *Quadrag.*
M10
T 11
W12 *Ember*
T 13
F 14 *Ember*
s 15 *Ember*
········
S 16 *Lent 2*
M17
T 18
W19
T 20
F 21
S 22
········
S 23 *Lent 3*
M24 *Matthias*
T 25
w26
T 27
F 28

MARCH
S 1
········
S 2 *Lent 4*
M3
T 4
W5
T 6
F 7
s 8
········
S 9 *Passion*
M10
T 11
W12
T 13
F 14
S 15
········
S 16 *Palm*
M17
T 18
W19
T 20
F 21 *Good Fri.*
S 22
········
S 23 ***Easter Day***
M24
T 25 *Annunc.*
w26
T 27
F 28
S 29
········
S 30 *Quasimodo*
M31

APRIL
T 1
W2
T 3
F 4
S 5
········
S 6 *Easter 2*
M7
T 8
W9
T 10
F 11
S 12
········
S 13 *Easter 3*
M14
T 15
W16
T 17
F 18
S 19
········
S 20 *Easter 4*
M21
T 22
W23
T 24
F 25
S 26
········
S 27 *Rogation*
M28
T 29
W30

MAY
T 1 *Ascension*
F 2
S 3
········
S 4 *Ascens. 1*
M5
T 6
W7
T 8
F 9
S 10
········
S 11 *Whit Sun.*
M12
T 13
W14 *Ember*
T 15
F 16 *Ember*
s 17 *Ember*
········
S 18 *Trinity*
M19
T 20
W21
T 22 *Corpus C.*
F 23
S 24
········
S 25 *Trinity 1*
M26
T 27
W28
T 29
F 30
S 31

Easter Day 23 March 8/2

Dominical letter E for Common Years
Dominical letter FE for Leap Years (*in bold figures*)
New style years **1636**, **1704**, 1788, 1845, **1856**, 1913, **2008**

JUNE	JULY	AUGUST	SEPTEMBER	OCTOBER	NOVEMBER	DECEMBER
S 1 *Trinity 2*	T 1	F 1 *Lammas*	M 1	W 1	s 1	M 1
M 2	W 2	s 2	T 2	T 2		T 2
T 3	T 3		W 3	F 3	S 2 *Trinity 24*	W 3
W 4	F 4	S 3 *Trinity 11*	T 4	s 4	M 3	T 4
T 5	s 5	M 4	F 5		T 4	F 5
F 6		T 5	s 6	S 5 *Trinity 20*	W 5	s 6
s 7	S 6 *Trinity 7*	W 6		M 6	T 6	
S 8 *Trinity 3*	M 7	T 7	S 7 *Trinity 16*	T 7	F 7	S 7 *Advent 2*
M 9	T 8	F 8	M 8	W 8	s 8	M 8
T 10	W 9	s 9	T 9	T 9		T 9
W 11	T 10		W 10	F 10	S 9 *Trinity 25*	W 10
T 12	F 11	S 10 *Trinity 12*	T 11	s 11	M 10	F 11
F 13	s 12	M 11	F 12		T 11 *Martin*	F 12
s 14		T 12	s 13	S 12 *Trinity 21*	W 12	s 13
S 15 *Trinity 4*	S 13 *Trinity 8*	W 13		M 13	T 13	
M 16	M 14	T 14	S 14 *Trinity 17*	T 14	F 14	S 14 *Advent 3*
T 17	T 15	F 15	M 15	W 15	s 15	M 15
W 18	W 16	s 16	T 16	T 16		T 16
F 19	T 17		W 17 *Ember*	F 17	S 16 *Trinity 26*	W 17 *Ember*
F 20	F 18	S 17 *Trinity 13*	T 18	s 18	M 17	T 18
s 21	s 19	M 18	F 19 *Ember*		T 18	F 19 *Ember*
S 22 *Trinity 5*		T 19	s 20 *Ember*	S 19 *Trinity 22*	W 19	s 20 *Ember*
M 23	S 20 *Trinity 9*	W 20		M 20	T 20	
T 24 *Nat.J.Bap.*	M 21	T 21	S 21 *Trinity 18*	T 21	F 21	S 21 *Advent 4*
W 25	T 22	F 22	M 22	W 22	s 22	M 22
F 26	W 23	s 23	T 23	T 23		T 23
s 27	T 24		W 24	F 24	S 23 *Trinity 27*	W 24
s 28	F 25	S 24 *Trinity 14*	T 25	s 25	M 24	T 25 *Christmas*
	s 26	M 25	F 26		T 25	F 26
S 29 *Trinity 6*		T 26	s 27	S 26 *Trinity 23*	W 26	s 27
M 30	S 27 *Trinity 10*	W 27		M 27	T 27	
	M 28	T 28	S 28 *Trinity 19*	T 28	F 28	S 28
	T 29	F 29	M 29 *Michael A.*	W 29	s 29	M 29
	W 30	s 30	T 30	T 30		T 30
	T 31			F 31	S 30 *Advent 1*	W 31
		S 31 *Trinity 15*				

8/3 Easter Day 24 March

Dominical letter F for Common Years
Dominical letter GF for Leap Years (*in bold figures*)
Old style years   547, 631, 642, 726, 737, 821, **832**, **916**, 1079, 1163, 1174, 1258, 1269, 1353, **1364**, **1448**, 1611, 1695, 1706

Leap years						
JANUARY	FEBRUARY	JANUARY	FEBRUARY	MARCH	APRIL	MAY
M 1	T 1	T 1	F 1	F 1	M 1	W 1
T 2	F 2 *Purific. M.*	W 2	S 2 *Purific. M.*	S 2	T 2	T 2 *Ascension*
W 3	S 3	T 3			W 3	F 3
T 4		F 4	....	....	T 4	S 4
F 5	....	S 5	S 3 *Quinquag.*	S 3 *Lent 4*	F 5	
s 6 *Epiphany*	S 4 *Quinquag.*		M 4	M 4	s 6	....
	M 5		T 5 *Shrove Tu.*	T 5		S 5 *Ascens. 1*
....	T 6 *Shrove Tu.*	S 6 *Epiphany*	w 6 *Ash Wed.*	W 6		M 6
S 7 *Epiph. 1*	w 7 *Ash Wed.*	M 7	T 7	T 7	S 7 *Easter 2*	T 7
M 8	T 8	T 8	F 8	F 8	M 8	W 8
T 9	F 9	W 9	S 9	S 9	T 9	T 9
W 10	S 10	T 10			W 10	F 10
T 11		F 11	....	....	T 11	S 11
F 12	....	S 12	S 10 *Quadrag.*	S 10 *Passion*	F 12	
s 13 *Hilary*	S 11 *Quadrag.*		M 11	M 11	s 13	....
	M 12	....	T 12	T 12		S 12 *Whit Sun.*
....	T 13	S 13 *Epiph. 1*	w 13 *Ember*	W 13	....	M 13
S 14 *Epiph. 2*	w 14 *Ember*	M 14	T 14	T 14	S 14 *Easter 3*	T 14
M 15	T 15	T 15	F 15 *Ember*	F 15	M 15	W 15 *Ember*
T 16	F 16 *Ember*	W 16	s 16 *Ember*	S 16	T 16	T 16
W 17	s 17 *Ember*	T 17			W 17	F 17 *Ember*
T 18		F 18	....	....	T 18	s 18 *Ember*
F 19	....	S 19	S 17 *Lent 2*	S 17 *Palm*	F 19	
S 20	S 18 *Lent 2*		M 18	M 18	S 20	....
	M 19	....	T 19	T 19		S 19 *Trinity*
....	T 20	S 20 *Septuag.*	W 20	W 20	....	M 20
S 21 *Septuag.*	W 21	M 21	T 21	T 21	S 21 *Easter 4*	T 21
M 22	T 22	T 22	F 22	F 22 *Good Fri.*	M 22	W 22
T 23	F 23	W 23	S 23	S 23	T 23	T 23 *Corpus C.*
W 24	S 24	T 24			W 24	F 24
T 25		F 25	....	....	T 25	S 25
F 26	....	S 26	S 24 *Lent 3*	S 24 ***Easter Day***	F 26	
S 27	S 25 *Lent 3*		M 25	M 25 *Annunc.*	S 27	....
	M 26	....	T 26	T 26		S 26 *Trinity 1*
....	T 27	S 27 *Sexages.*	W 27	W 27	....	M 27
S 28 *Sexages.*	W 28	M 28	T 28	T 28	S 28 *Rogation*	T 28
M 29	T 29	T 29		F 29	M 29	W 29
T 30		W 30		S 30	T 30	T 30
W 31		T 31				F 31
				....		
				S 31 *Quasimodo*		

Dominical letter F for Common Years
Dominical letter GF for Leap Years (*in bold figures*)
New style years 1799, **1940**

JUNE	JULY	AUGUST	SEPTEMBER	OCTOBER	NOVEMBER	DECEMBER
S 1	M 1	T 1 *Lammas*	S 1 *Trinity 15*	T 1	F 1	S 1 *Advent 1*
	T 2	F 2	M 2	W 2	S 2	M 2
S 2 *Trinity 2*	W 3	S 3	T 3	T 3		T 3
M 3	T 4		W 4	F 4	S 3 *Trinity 24*	W 4
T 4	F 5	S 4 *Trinity 11*	T 5	S 5	M 4	T 5
W 5	S 6	M 5	F 6		T 5	F 6
T 6		T 6	S 7	S 6 *Trinity 20*	W 6	S 7
F 7	S 7 *Trinity 7*	W 7		M 7	T 7	
S 8	M 8	T 8	S 8 *Trinity 16*	T 8	F 8	S 8 *Advent 2*
	T 9	F 9	M 9	W 9	S 9	M 9
S 9 *Trinity 3*	W 10	S 10	T 10	T 10		T 10
M 10	T 11		W 11	F 11	S 10 *Trinity 25*	W 11
T 11	F 12	S 11 *Trinity 12*	T 12	S 12	M 11 *Martin*	T 12
W 12	S 13	M 12	F 13		T 12	F 13
T 13		T 13	S 14 *Exalt. C.*	S 13 *Trinity 21*	W 13	S 14
F 14	S 14 *Trinity 8*	W 14		M 14	T 14	
S 15	M 15	T 15	S 15 *Trinity 17*	T 15	F 15	S 15 *Advent 3*
	T 16	F 16	M 16	W 16	S 16	M 16
S 16 *Trinity 4*	W 17	S 17	T 17	T 17		T 17
M 17	T 18		W 18 *Ember*	F 18	S 17 *Trinity 26*	W 18 *Ember*
T 18	F 19	S 18 *Trinity 13*	T 19	S 19	M 18	T 19
W 19	S 20	M 19	F 20 *Ember*		T 19	F 20 *Ember*
T 20		T 20	S 21 *Ember*	S 20 *Trinity 22*	W 20	S 21 *Ember*
F 21	S 21 *Trinity 9*	W 21		M 21	T 21	
S 22	M 22	T 22	S 22 *Trinity 18*	T 22	F 22	S 22 *Advent 4*
	T 23	F 23	M 23	W 23	S 23	M 23
S 23 *Trinity 5*	W 24	S 24	T 24	T 24		T 24
M 24 *Nat. J. Bap*	T 25		W 25	F 25	S 24 *Trinity 27*	W 25 *Christmas*
T 25	F 26	S 25 *Trinity 14*	T 26	S 26	M 25	T 26
W 26	S 27	M 26	F 27		T 26	F 27
T 27		T 27	S 28	S 27 *Trinity 23*	W 27	S 28
F 28	S 28 *Trinity 10*	W 28		M 28	T 28	
S 29	M 29	T 29	S 29 *Trinity 19*	T 29	F 29	S 29
	T 30	F 30	M 30	W 30	S 30	M 30
S 30 *Trinity 6*	W 31	S 31		T 31		T 31

8/4 Easter Day 25 March

Dominical letter G for Common Years
Dominical letter AG for Leap Years (*in bold figures*)
Old style years 479, 490, 563, 574, 585, 658, 669, **680**, 753, **764**, **848**, 927, 1011, 1022, 1095, 1106, 1117, 1190, 1201, **1212**, 1285, **1296**, **1380**, 1459, 1543, 1554, 1627, 1638, 1649, 1722, 1733, **1744**

Leap years						
JANUARY	FEBRUARY	JANUARY	FEBRUARY	MARCH	APRIL	MAY
S 1	W1	M1	T 1	T 1	S 1 *Quasimodo*	T 1
M2	T 2 *Purific. M.*	T 2	F 2 *Purific. M.*	F 2	M2	W2
T 3	F 3	W3	S 3	S 3	T 3	T 3 *Ascension*
W4	S 4	T 4			W4	F 4
T 5		F 5			T 5	S 5
F 6 *Epiphany*		s 6 *Epiphany*	S 4 *Quinquag.*	S 4 *Lent 4*	F 6	
S 7	S 5 *Quinquag.*		M5	M5	S 7	
	M6		T 6 *Shrove Tu.*	T 6		S 6 *Ascens. 1*
	T 7 *Shrove Tu.*	S 7 *Epiph. 1*	W7 *Ash Wed.*	W7		M7
S 8 *Eph. 1*	w8 *Ash Wed.*	M8	T 8	T 8	S 8 *Easter 2*	T 8
M9	T 9	T 9	F 9	F 9	M9	W9
T 10	F 10	W10	S 10	S 10	T 10	T 10
W11	S 11	T 11			W11	F 11
T 12		F 12			T 12	S 12
F 13 *Hilary*		s 13 *Hilary*	S 11 *Quadrag.*	S 11 *Passion*	F 13	
S 14	S 12 *Quadrag.*		M12	M12	S 14	
	M13		T 13	T 13		S 13 *Whit Sun.*
	T 14	S 14 *Epiph. 2*	W14 *Ember*	W14		M14
S 15 *Epiph. 2*	W15 *Ember*	M15	T 15	T 15	S 15 *Easter 3*	T 15
M16	T 16	T 16	F 16 *Ember*	F 16	M16	W16 *Ember*
T 17	F 17 *Ember*	W17	s 17 *Ember*	S 17	T 17	T 17
W18	s 18 *Ember*	T 18			W18	F 18 *Ember*
T 19		F 19			T 19	s 19 *Ember*
F 20		S 20	S 18 *Lent 2*	S 18 *Palm*	F 20	
S 21	S 19 *Lent 2*		M19	M19	S 21	
	M20		T 20	T 20		S 20 *Trinity*
	T 21	S 21 *Septuag.*	W21	W21		M21
S 22 *Septuag.*	W22	M22	T 22	T 22	S 22 *Easter 4*	T 22
M23	T 23	T 23	F 23	F 23 *Good Fri.*	M23	W23
T 24	F 24	W24	s 24 *Matthias*	S 24	T 24	T 24 *Corpus C.*
W25	s 25 *Matthias*	T 25			W25	F 25
T 26		F 26			T 26	s 26
F 27		S 27	S 25 *Lent 3*	S 25 ***Easter Day***	F 27	
S 28	S 26 *Lent 3*		M26	M26	S 28	
	M27		T 27	T 27		S 27 *Trinity 1*
	T 28	S 28 *Sexages.*	W28	W28		M28
S 29 *Sexages.*	W29	M29		T 29	S 29 *Rogation*	T 29
M30		T 30		F 30	M30	W30
T 31		W31		S 31		T 31

Easter Day 25 March 8/4

Dominical letter G for Common Years
Dominical letter AG for Leap Years (*in bold figures*)
New style years   1663, 1674, 1731, 1742, 1883, 1894, 1951, 2035, 2046

JUNE	JULY	AUGUST	SEPTEMBER	OCTOBER	NOVEMBER	DECEMBER
F 1	S 1 *Trinity 6*	W 1 *Lammas*	S 1	M 1	T 1	S 1
S 2	M 2	T 2		T 2	F 2	
	T 3	F 3	S 2 *Trinity 15*	W 3	S 3	
S 3 *Trinity 2*	W 4	S 4	M 3	T 4		S 2 *Advent 1*
M 4	T 5		T 4	F 5		M 3
T 5	F 6	S 5 *Trinity 11*	W 5	S 6	S 4 *Trinity 24*	T 4
W 6	S 7	M 6	T 6		M 5	W 5
T 7		T 7	F 7	S 7 *Trinity 20*	T 6	T 6
F 8	S 8 *Trinity 7*	W 8	S 8	M 8	W 7	F 7
S 9	M 9	T 9		T 9	T 8	S 8
	T 10	F 10	S 9 *Trinity 16*	W 10	F 9	
S 10 *Trinity 3*	W 11	S 11	M 10	T 11	S 10	S 9 *Advent 2*
M 11	T 12		T 11	F 12		M 10
T 12	F 13	S 12 *Trinity 12*	W 12	S 13	S 11 *Trinity 25*	T 11
W 13	S 14	M 13	T 13		M 12	W 12
T 14		T 14	F 14 *Exalt. C.*	S 14 *Trinity 21*	T 13	T 13
F 15	S 15 *Trinity 8*	W 15	S 15	M 15	W 14	F 14
S 16	M 16	T 16		T 16	T 15	S 15
	T 17	F 17	S 16 *Trinity 17*	W 17	F 16	
S 17 *Trinity 4*	W 18	S 18	M 17	T 18	S 17	S 16 *Advent 3*
M 18	T 19		T 18	F 19		M 17
T 19	F 20	S 19 *Trinity 13*	W 19 *Ember*	S 20	S 18 *Trinity 26*	T 18
W 20	S 21	M 20	T 20		M 19	W 19 *Ember*
T 21		T 21	F 21 *Ember*	S 21 *Trinity 22*	T 20	T 20
F 22	S 22 *Trinity 9*	W 22	S 22 *Ember*	M 22	W 21	F 21 *Ember*
S 23	M 23	T 23		T 23	T 22	S 22 *Ember*
	T 24	F 24	S 23 *Trinity 18*	W 24	F 23	
S 24 *Trinity 5*	W 25	S 25	M 24	T 25	S 24	S 23 *Advent 4*
M 25	T 26		T 25	F 26		M 24
T 26	F 27	S 26 *Trinity 14*	W 26	S 27	S 25 *Trinity 27*	T 25 *Christmas*
W 27	S 28	M 27	T 27		M 26	W 26
T 28		T 28	F 28	S 28 *Trinity 23*	T 27	T 27
F 29	S 29 *Trinity 10*	W 29	S 29 *Michael A.*	M 29	W 28	F 28
S 30	M 30	T 30		T 30	T 29	S 29
	T 31	F 31	S 30 *Trinity 19*	W 31	F 30	
						S 30
						M 31

8/5 Easter Day 26 March

Dominical letter A for Common Years
Dominical letter BA for Leap Years (*in bold figures*)
Old style years   411, 422, 433, 495, 506, 517, **528**, 590, 601, **612**, 685, **696**, 775, **780**, 859, 870, 943, 954, 965, 1027, 1038, 1049, **1060**, 1122, 1133, **1144**, 1217, **1228**, 1307, **1312**, 1391, 1402, 1475, 1486, 1497, 1559, 1570, 1581, **1592**, 1654, 1665, **1676**, 1749

		Leap years				
JANUARY	FEBRUARY	JANUARY	FEBRUARY	MARCH	APRIL	MAY
S 1	T 1	S 1	W1	W1	S 1	M1
	W2 *Purific. M.*	M2	T 2 *Purific. M.*	T 2		T 2
S 2	T 3	T 3	F 3	F 3	S 2 *Quasimodo*	W3
M3	F 4	W4	S 4	S 4	M3	T 4 *Ascension*
T 4	S 5	T 5			T 4	F 5
W5		F 6 *Epiphany*	S 5 *Quinquag.*	S 5 *Lent 4*	W5	S 6
T 6 *Epiphany*	S 6 *Quinquag.*	S 7	M6	M6	T 6	
F 7	M7		T 7 *Shrove Tu.*	T 7	F 7	S 7 *Ascens. 1*
S 8	T 8 *Shrove Tu.*	S 8 *Epiph. 1*	W8 *Ash Wed.*	W8	S 8	M8
	W9 *Ash Wed.*	M9	T 9	T 9		T 9
S 9 *Epiph. 1*	T 10	T 10	F 10	F 10	S 9 *Easter 2*	W10
M10	F 11	W11	S 11	S 11	M10	T 11
T 11	S 12	T 12			T 11	F 12
W12		F 13 *Hilary*	S 12 *Quadrag.*	S 12 *Passion*	W12	S 13
T 13 *Hilary*	S 13 *Quadrag.*	S 14	M13	M13	T 13	
F 14	M14		T 14	T 14	F 14	S 14 *Whit Sun.*
S 15	T 15	S 15 *Epiph. 2*	W15 *Ember*	W15	S 15	M15
	W16 *Ember*	M16	T 16	T 16		T 16
S 16 *Epiph. 2*	T 17	T 17	F 17 *Ember*	F 17	S 16 *Easter 3*	W17 *Ember*
M17	F 18 *Ember*	W18	S 18 *Ember*	S 18	M17	T 18
T 18	S 19 *Ember*	T 19			T 18	F 19 *Ember*
W19		F 20	S 19 *Lent 2*	S 19 *Palm*	W19	S 20 *Ember*
T 20	S 20 *Lent 2*	S 21	M20	M20	T 20	
F 21	M21		T 21	T 21	F 21	S 21 *Trinity*
S 22	T 22	S 22 *Septuag.*	W22	W22	S 22	M22
	W23	M23	T 23	T 23		T 23
S 23 *Septuag.*	T 24	T 24	F 24 *Matthias*	F 24 *Good Fri.*	S 23 *Easter 4*	W24
M24	F 25 *Matthias*	W25	S 25	S 25 *Annunc.*	M24	T 25 *Corpus C.*
T 25	S 26	T 26			T 25	F 26
W26		F 27	S 26 *Lent 3*	S 26 *Easter Day*	W26	S 27
T 27	S 27 *Lent 3*	S 28	M27	M27	T 27	
F 28	M28		T 28	T 28	F 28	S 28 *Trinity 1*
S 29	T 29	S 29 *Sexagues.*		W29	S 29	M29
		M30		T 30		T 30
S 30 *Sexages.*		T 31		F 31	S 30 *Rogation*	W31
M31						

164

Easter Day 26 March 8/5

Dominical letter A for Common Years
Dominical letter BA for Leap Years (*in bold figures*)
New style years 1595, 1606, 1617, 1690, 1758, 1769, **1780**, 1815, 1826, 1837, 1967, 1978, 1989, 2062, 2073, **2084**

JUNE	JULY	AUGUST	SEPTEMBER	OCTOBER	NOVEMBER	DECEMBER
T 1	S 1	T 1 *Lammas*	F 1	S 1 *Trinity 19*	W 1	F 1
F 2	W 2	W 2	S 2	M 2	T 2	S 2
S 3	....	T 3	....	T 3	F 3	....
....	S 2 *Trinity 6*	F 4	S 3 *Trinity 15*	W 4	S 4	S 3 *Advent 1*
S 4 *Trinity 2*	M 3	S 5	M 4	T 5	....	M 4
M 5	T 4	....	T 5	F 6	S 5 *Trinity 24*	T 5
T 6	W 5	S 6 *Trinity 11*	W 6	S 7	M 6	W 6
W 7	T 6	M 7	T 7	....	T 7	T 7
T 8	F 7	T 8	F 8	S 8 *Trinity 20*	W 8	F 8
F 9	S 8	W 9	S 9	M 9	T 9	S 9
S 10	....	T 10	....	T 10	F 10	....
....	S 9 *Trinity 7*	F 11	S 10 *Trinity 16*	W 11	S 11 *Martin*	S 10 *Advent 2*
S 11 *Trinity 3*	M 10	S 12	M 11	T 12	....	M 11
M 12	T 11	....	T 12	F 13	S 12 *Trinity 25*	T 12
T 13	W 12	S 13 *Trinity 12*	W 13	S 14	M 13	W 13
W 14	T 13	M 14	T 14 *Exalt. C.*	....	T 14	T 14
T 15	F 14	T 15	F 15	S 15 *Trinity 21*	W 15	F 15
F 16	S 15	W 16	S 16	M 16	T 16	S 16
S 17	....	T 17	....	T 17	F 17	....
....	S 16 *Trinity 8*	F 18	S 17 *Trinity 17*	W 18	S 18	S 17 *Advent 3*
S 18 *Trinity 4*	M 17	S 19	M 18	T 19	....	M 18
M 19	T 18	....	T 19	F 20	S 19 *Trinity 26*	T 19
T 20	W 19	S 20 *Trinity 13*	W 20 *Ember*	S 21	M 20	W 20 *Ember*
W 21	T 20	M 21	T 21	....	T 21	T 21
T 22	F 21	T 22	F 22 *Ember*	S 22 *Trinity 22*	W 22	F 22 *Ember*
F 23	S 22	W 23	S 23 *Ember*	M 23	T 23	S 23 *Ember*
S 24 *Nat. J. Bap*	....	T 24	....	T 24	F 24	....
....	S 23 *Trinity 9*	F 25	S 24 *Trinity 18*	W 25	S 25	S 24 *Advent 4*
S 25 *Trinity 5*	M 24	S 26	M 25	T 26	....	M 25 *Christmas*
M 26	T 25	....	T 26	F 27	S 26 *Trinity 27*	T 26
T 27	W 26	S 27 *Trinity 14*	W 27	S 28	M 27	W 27
W 28	F 27	M 28	T 28	....	T 28	T 28
T 29	S 28	T 29	F 29 *Michael A.*	S 29 *Trinity 23*	W 29	F 29
F 30	S 29	W 30	S 30	M 30	T 30	S 30
	....	T 31		T 31		....
	S 30 *Trinity 10*					S 31
	M 31					

8/6 Easter Day 27 March

Dominical letter B for Common Years
Dominical letter CB for Leap Years (*in bold figures*)
Old style years   438, 449, **460**, 533, **544**, 623, **628**, 707, 718, 791, 802, 813, 875, 886, 897, **908**, 970, 981, **992**, 1065, **1076**, 1155, **1160**, 1239, 1250, 1323, 1334, 1345, 1407, 1418, 1429, **1440**, 1502, 1513, **1524**, 1597, **1608**, 1687, **1692**

Leap years

JANUARY	FEBRUARY
F 1	M1
S 2	T 2 *Purific. M.*
	W3
S 3	T 4
M4	F 5
T 5	s 6
W6 *Epiphany*	
T 7	S 7 *Quinquag.*
F 8	M8
S 9	T 9 *Shrove Tu.*
	W10 *Ash Wed.*
S 10 *Epiph. 1*	T 11
M11	F 12
T 12	S 13
W13 *Hilary*	
T 14	S 14 *Quadrag.*
F 15	M15
S 16	T 16
	W17 *Ember*
S 17 *Epiph. 2*	T 18
M18	F 19 *Ember*
T 19	S 20 *Ember*
W20	
T 21	S 21 *Lent 2*
F 22	M22
S 23	T 23
	W24
S 24 *Septuag.*	T 25 *Matthias*
M25	F 26
T 26	S 27
W27	
T 28	S 28 *Lent3*
F 29	M29
S 30	
S 31 *Sexages.*	

JANUARY	FEBRUARY	MARCH	APRIL	MAY
S 1	T 1	T 1	F 1	S 1 *Rogation*
	W2 *Purific. M.*	W2	S 2	M2
S 2	T 3	T 3		T 3
M3	F 4	F 4	S 3 *Quasimodo*	W4
T 4	S 5	S 5	M4	T 5 *Ascension*
W5			T 5	F 6
T 6 *Epiphany*	S 6 *Quinquag.*	S 6 *Lent 4*	W6	S 7
F 7	M7	M7	T 7	
s 8	T 8 *Shrove Tu.*	T 8	F 8	S 8 *Ascens. 1*
	W9 *Ash Wed.*	W9	S 9	M9
S 9 *Epiph. 1*	T 10	T 10		T 10
M10	F 11	F 11	S 10 *Easter 2*	W11
T 11	S 12	S 12	M11	T 12
W12			T 12	F 13
T 13 *Hilary*	S 13 *Quadrag.*	S 13 *Passion*	W13	S 14
F 14	M14	M14	T 14	
S 15	T 15	T 15	F 15	S 15 *Whit Sun.*
	W16 *Ember*	W16	S 16	M16
S 16 *Epiph. 2*	T 17	T 17		T 17
M17	F 18 *Ember*	F 18	S 17 *Easter 3*	W18 *Ember*
T 18	S 19 *Ember*	S 19	M18	T 19
W19			T 19	F 20 *Ember*
T 20	S 20 *Lent 2*	S 20 *Palm*	W20	S 21 *Ember*
F 21	M21	M21	T 21	
S 22	T 22	T 22	F 22	S 22 *Trinity*
	W23	W23	S 23	M23
S 23 *Septuag.*	T 24	T 24		T 24
M24	F 25 *Matthias*	F 25 *Good Fri.*	S 24 *Easter 4*	W25
T 25	S 26	S 26	M25	T 26 *Corpus C.*
W26			T 26	F 27
T 27	S 27 *Lent 3*	S 27 ***Easter Day***	W27	s 28
F 28	M28	M28	T 28	
S 29	T 29	T 29	F 29	S 29 *Trinity 1*
		W30	S 30	M30
S 30 *Sexages.*		T 31		T 31
M31			S 31	

Easter Day 27 March 8/6

Dominical letter B for Common Years
Dominical letter CB for Leap Years (*in bold figures*)
New style years   1622, 1633, **1644**, 1701, **1712**, 1785, **1796**, 1842, 1853, **1864**, 1910, 1921, **1932**, 2005, **2016**

JUNE	JULY	AUGUST	SEPTEMBER	OCTOBER	NOVEMBER	DECEMBER
W 1	F 1	M 1 *Lammas*	T 1	S 1	T 1	T 1
T 2	S 2	T 2	F 2		W 2	F 2
F 3		W 3	S 3	S 2 *Trinity 19*	T 3	S 3
S 4	S 3 *Trinity 6*	T 4		M 3	F 4	
	M 4	F 5	S 4 *Trinity 15*	T 4	S 5	S 4 *Advent 2*
S 5 *Trinity 2*	T 5	S 6	M 5	W 5		M 5
M 6	W 6		T 6	T 6	S 6 *Trinity 24*	T 6
T 7	T 7	S 7 *Trinity 11*	W 7	F 7	M 7	W 7
W 8	F 8	M 8	T 8	S 8	T 8	T 8
T 9	S 9	T 9	F 9		W 9	F 9
F 10		W 10	S 10	S 9 *Trinity 20*	T 10	S 10
S 11	S 10 *Trinity 7*	T 11		M 10	F 11 *Martin*	
	M 11	F 12	S 11 *Trinity 16*	T 11	S 12	S 11 *Advent 3*
S 12 *Trinity 3*	T 12	S 13	M 12	W 12		M 12
M 13	W 13		T 13	T 13	S 13 *Trinity 25*	T 13
T 14	T 14	S 14 *Trinity 12*	W 14 *Exalt. C.*	F 14	M 14	W 14 *Ember*
W 15	F 15	M 15	T 15	S 15	T 15	T 15
T 16	S 16	T 16	F 16		W 16	F 16 *Ember*
F 17		W 17	S 17		T 17	S 17 *Ember*
S 18	S 17 *Trinity 8*	T 18		S 16 *Trinity 21*	F 18	
	M 18	F 19	S 18 *Trinity 17*	M 17	S 19	S 18 *Advent 4*
S 19 *Trinity 4*	T 19	S 20	M 19	T 18		M 19
M 20	W 20		T 20	W 19	S 20 *Trinity 26*	T 20
T 21	T 21	S 21 *Trinity 13*	W 21 *Ember*	T 20	M 21	W 21
W 22 *Nat. J. Bap.*	F 22	M 22	T 22	F 21	T 22	T 22
T 23	S 23	T 23	F 23 *Ember*	S 22	W 23	F 23
F 24		W 24	S 24 *Ember*		T 24	S 24
S 25	S 24 *Trinity 9*	T 25		S 23 *Trinity 22*	F 25	
	M 25	F 26	S 25 *Trinity 18*	M 24	S 26	S 25 *Christmas*
S 26 *Trinity 5*	T 26	S 27	M 26	T 25		M 26
M 27	W 27		T 27	W 26	S 27 *Advent 1*	T 27
T 28	T 28	S 28 *Trinity 14*	W 28	T 27	M 28	W 28
W 29	F 29	M 29	T 29 *Michael A.*	F 28	T 29	T 29
T 30	S 30	T 30	F 30	S 29	W 30	F 30
		W 31				S 31
	S 31 *Trinity 10*			S 30 *Trinity 23*		
				M 31		

8/7 Easter Day 28 March

Dominical letter C for Common Years
Dominical letter DC for Leap Years (*in bold figures*)
Old style years   465, 471, 555, **560**, 566, 639, 650, 661, 723, 734, 745, **756**, 807, 818, 829, **840**, 902, 913, **924**, 997, 1003, **1008**, 1087, **1092**, 1098, 1171, 1182, 1193, 1255, 1266, 1277, **1288**, 1339, 1350, 1361, **1372**, 1434, 1445, **1456**, 1529, 1535, **1540**, 1619, **1624** 1630, 1703, 1714, 1725

Leap years						
JANUARY	FEBRUARY	JANUARY	FEBRUARY	MARCH	APRIL	MAY
T 1	S 1 *Sexages.*	F 1	M1	M1	T 1	S 1
F 2	M2 *Purific. M.*	S 2	T 2 *Purific. M.*	T 2	F 2	
S 3	T 3		W3	W3	S 3	
	W4	S 3	T 4	T 4		S 2 *Rogation*
S 4	T 5	M4	F 5	F 5	S 4 *Quasimodo*	M3
M5	F 6	T 5	s 6	s 6	M5	T 4
T 6 *Epiphany*	S 7	w6 *Epiphany*			T 6	W5
W7		T 7	S 7 *Quinquag.*	S 7 *Lent 4*	W7	T 6 *Ascension*
T 8		F 8	M8	M8	T 8	F 7
F 9	S 8 *Quinquag.*	S 9	T 9 *Shrove Tu.*	T 9	F 9	s 8
S 10	M9		W10 *Ash Wed.*	W10	S 10	
	T 10 *Shrove Tu.*	S 10 *Epiph. 1*	T 11	T 11		S 9 *Ascens. 1*
S 11 *Epiph. 1*	W11 *Ash Wed.*	M11	F 12	F 12	S 11 *Easter 2*	M10
M12	T 12	T 12	S 13	S 13	M12	T 11
T 13 *Hilary*	F 13	W13 *Hilary*			T 13	W12
W14	S 14	T 14	S 14 *Quadrag.*	S 14 *Passion*	W14	T 13
T 15		F 15	M15	M15	T 15	F 14
F 16	S 15 *Quadrag.*	S 16	T 16	T 16	F 16	S 15
S 17	M16		W17 *Ember*	W17	S 17	
	T 17	S 17 *Epiph. 2*	T 18	T 18		S 16 *Whit Sun.*
S 18 *Epiph. 2*	W18 *Ember*	M18	F 19 *Ember*	F 19	S 18 *Easter 3*	M17
M19	T 19	T 19	s 20 *Ember*	s 20	M19	T 18
T 20	F 20 *Ember*	W20			T 20	W19 *Ember*
W21	S 21 *Ember*	T 21	S 21 *Lent 2*	S 21 *Palm*	W21	T 20
T 22		F 22	M22	M22	T 22	F 21 *Ember*
F 23	S 22 *Lent 2*	S 23	T 23	T 23	F 23	s 22 *Ember*
S 24	M23		W24 *Matthias*	W24	S 24	
	T 24	S 24 *Septuag.*	T 25	T 25 *Annunc.*		S 23 *Trinity*
S 25 *Septuag.*	W25 *Matthias*	M25	F 26	F 26 *Good Fri.*	S 25 *Easter 4*	M24
M26	T 26	T 26	S 27	S 27	M26	T 25
T 27	F 27	W27			T 27	W26
W28	S 28	T 28	S 28 *Lent 3*	S 28 *Easter Day*	W28	T 27 *Corpus C.*
T 29	S 29 *Lent 3*	F 29		M29	T 29	F 28
F 30		S 30		T 30	F 30	S 29
S 31				W31		
		S 31 *Sexages.*				S 30 *Trinity 1*
						M31

168

Dominical letter C for Common Years
Dominical letter DC for Leap Years (*in bold figures*)
New style years   1655, **1660**, 1717, 1723, **1728**, 1869, 1875, **1880**, 1937, **1948**, 2027, **2032**, 2100

JUNE	JULY	AUGUST	SEPTEMBER	OCTOBER	NOVEMBER	DECEMBER
T 1	T 1	S 1 *Trinity 10*	W1	F 1	M1	W1
W2	F 2	M2	T 2	S 2	T 2	T 2
T 3	S 3	T 3	F 3		W3	F 3
F 4		W4	S 4		T 4	S 4
S 5	S 4 *Trinity 6*	T 5		S 3 *Trinity 19*	F 5	
	M5	F 6		M4	S 6	S 5 *Advent 2*
S 6 *Trinity 2*	T 6	S 7	S 5 *Trinity 15*	T 5		M6
M7	W7		M6	W6		T 7
T 8	T 8	S 8 *Trinity 11*	T 7	T 7	S 7 *Trinity 24*	W8
W9	F 9	M9	W8	F 8	M8	T 9
T 10	S 10	T 10	T 9	S 9	T 9	F 10
F 11		W11	F 10		W10	S 11
S 12	S 11 *Trinity 7*	T 12	S 11	S 10 *Trinity 20*	T 11 *Martin*	
	M12	F 13		M11	F 12	S 12 *Advent 3*
S 13 *Trinity 3*	T 13	S 14	S 12 *Trinity 16*	T 12	S 13	M13
M14	W14		M13	W13		T 14
T 15	T 15	S 15 *Trinity 12*	T 14 *Exalt. C.*	T 14	S 14 *Trinity 25*	W15 *Ember*
W16	F 16	M16	W15 *Ember*	F 15	M15	T 16
T 17	S 17	T 17	T 16	S 16	T 16	F 17 *Ember*
F 18		W18	F 17 *Ember*		W17	s 18 *Ember*
S 19	S 18 *Trinity 8*	T 19	s 18 *Ember*	S 17 *Trinity 21*	T 18	
	M19	F 20		M18	F 19	S 19 *Advent 4*
S 20 *Trinity 4*	T 20	S 21	S 19 *Trinity 17*	T 19	S 20	M20
M21	W21		M20	W20		T 21
T 22	T 22	S 22 *Trinity 13*	T 21	T 21	S 21 *Trinity 26*	W22
W23	F 23	M23	W22	F 22	M22	T 23
T 24 *Nat. J. Bap.*	S 24	T 24	T 23	S 23	T 23	F 24
F 25		W25	F 24		W24	s 25 *Christmas*
s 26	S 25 *Trinity 9*	T 26	S 25	S 24 *Trinity 22*	T 25	
	M26	F 27		M25	F 26	S 26
S 27 *Trinity 5*	T 27	s 28	S 26 *Trinity 18*	T 26	S 27	M27
M28	W28		M27	W27		T 28
T 29	T 29	S 29 *Trinity 14*	T 28	T 28	S 28 *Advent 1*	W29
W30	F 30	M30	W29 *Michael A.*	F 29	M29	T 30
	S 31	T 31	T 30	S 30	T 30	F 31
				S 31 *Trinity 23*		

8/8 Easter Day 29 March

Dominical letter D for Common Years
Dominical letter ED for Leap Years (*in bold figures*)
Old style years 403, **408**, 487, 498, 571, 582, 593, 655, 666, 677, **688**, 750, 761, **772**, 845, **856**, 935, **940**, 1019, 1030, 1103, 1114, 1125, 1187, 1198, 1209, **1220**, 1282, 1293, **1304**, 1377, **1388**, 1467, **1472**, 1551, 1562, 1635, 1646, 1657, 1719, 1730, 1741
[for **1752** see table **11** below]

Leap years

JANUARY
- W1
- T2
- F3
- S4
- S5
- M6 *Epiphany*
- T7
- W8
- T9
- F10
- S11
- S12 *Epiph. 1*
- M13 *Hilary*
- T14
- W15
- T16
- F17
- S18
- S19 *Epiph. 2*
- M20
- T21
- W22
- T23
- F24
- S25
- S26 *Septuag.*
- M27
- T28
- W29
- T30
- F31

FEBRUARY
- S 1
- S 2 *Sexages.*
- M3
- T 4
- W5
- T 6
- F 7
- s 8
- S 9 *Quinquag.*
- M10
- T 11 *Shrove Tu.*
- W12 *Ash Wed.*
- T 13
- F 14
- S 15
- S 16 *Quadrag.*
- M17
- T 18
- W19 *Ember*
- T 20
- F 21 *Ember*
- s 22 *Ember*
- S 23 *Lent 2*
- M24
- T 25 *Matthias*
- W26
- T 27
- F 28
- S 29

JANUARY
- T 1
- F 2
- S 3
- S 4
- M5
- T 6 *Epiphany*
- W7
- T 8
- F 9
- S 10
- S 11 *Epiph. 1*
- M12
- T 13 *Hilary*
- W14
- T 15
- F 16
- S 17
- S 18 *Epiph. 2*
- M19
- T 20
- W21
- T 22
- F 23
- S 24
- S 25 *Septuag.*
- M26
- T 27
- W28
- T 29
- F 30
- S 31

FEBRUARY
- S 1 *Sexages.*
- M2 *Purific. M.*
- T 3
- W4
- T 5
- F 6
- s 7
- S 8 *Quinquag.*
- M9
- T 10 *Shrove Tu.*
- W11 *Ash Wed.*
- T 12
- F 13
- S 14
- S 15 *Quadrag.*
- M16
- T 17
- W18 *Ember*
- T 19
- F 20 *Ember*
- s 21 *Ember*
- S 22 *Lent 2*
- M23
- T 24
- W25 *Matthias*
- T 26
- F 27
- s 28

MARCH
- S 1 *Lent 3*
- M2
- T 3
- W4
- T 5
- F 6
- s 7
- S 8 *Lent 4*
- M9
- T 10
- W11
- T 12
- F 13
- S 14
- S 15 *Passion*
- M16
- T 17
- W18
- T 19
- F 20
- S 21
- S 22 *Palm*
- M23
- T 24
- W25 *Annunc.*
- T 26
- F 27 *Good Fri.*
- s 28
- S 29 ***Easter Day***
- M30
- T 31

APRIL
- W1
- T 2
- F 3
- S 4
- S 5 *Quasimodo*
- M6
- T 7
- W8
- T 9
- F 10
- S 11
- S 12 *Easter 2*
- M13
- T 14
- W15
- T 16
- F 17
- S 18
- S 19 *Easter 3*
- M20
- T 21
- W22
- T 23
- F 24
- S 25
- S 26 *Easter 4*
- M27
- T 28
- W29
- T 30

MAY
- F 1
- S 2
- S 3 *Rogation*
- M4
- T 5
- W6
- T 7 *Ascension*
- F 8
- S 9
- S 10 *Ascens. 1*
- M11
- T 12
- W13
- T 14
- F 15
- S 16
- S 17 *Whit Sun.*
- M18
- T 19
- W20 *Ember*
- T 21
- F 22 *Ember*
- s 23 *Ember*
- S 24 *Trinity*
- M25
- T 26
- W27
- T 28 *Corpus C.*
- F 29
- S 30
- S 31 *Trinity 1*

Easter Day 29 March 8/8
Dominical letter D for Common Years
Dominical letter ED for Leap Years (*in bold figures*)
New style years 1587, **1592**, 1671, 1682, 1739, **1744** (German Protestant Style), 1750, 1807, **1812**, 1891,
1959, **1964**, 1970, 2043, 2054, 2065

JUNE	JULY	AUGUST	SEPTEMBER	OCTOBER	NOVEMBER	DECEMBER
M1	W1	S 1 *Lammas*	T 1	T 1	S 1 *Trinity 23*	T 1
T 2	T 2		W2	F 2	M2	W2
W3	F 3	....	T 3	S 3	T 3	T 3
T 4	S 4	S 2 *Trinity 10*	F 4		W4	F 4
F 5		M3	S 5	....	T 5	S 5
s 6	....	T 4		S 4 *Trinity 19*	F 6	
	S 5 *Trinity 6*	W5	....	M5	S 7	....
....	M6	T 6	S 6 *Trinity 15*	T 6		S 6 *Advent 2*
S 7 *Trinity 2*	T 7	F 7	M7	W7	....	M7
M8	W8	s 8	T 8	T 8	S 8 *Trinity 24*	T 8
T 9	T 9		W9	F 9	M9	W9
W10	F 10	....	T 10	S 10	T 10	T 10
T 11	S 11	S 9 *Trinity 11*	F 11		W11 *Martin*	F 11
F 12		M10	S 12	....	T 12	S 12
S 13	....	T 11		S 11 *Trinity 20*	F 13	
	S 12 *Trinity 7*	W12	....	M12	S 14	....
....	M13	T 13	S 13 *Trinity 16*	T 13		S 13 *Advent 3*
S 14 *Trinity 3*	T 14	F 14	M14 *Exalt. C.*	W14	....	M14
M15	W15	S 15	T 15	T 15	S 15 *Trinity 25*	T 15
T 16	T 16		W16 *Ember*	F 16	M16	W16 *Ember*
W17	F 17	....	T 17	S 17	T 17	T 17
T 18	S 18	S 16 *Trinity 12*	F 18 *Ember*		W18	F 18 *Ember*
F 19		M17	s 19 *Ember*	....	T 19	s 19 *Ember*
S 20	....	T 18		S 18 *Trinity 21*	F 20	
	S 19 *Trinity 8*	W19	....	M19	S 21	....
....	M20	T 20	S 20 *Trinity 17*	T 20		S 20 *Advent 4*
S 21 *Trinity 4*	T 21	F 21	M21	W21	....	M21
M22	W22	S 22	T 22	T 22	S 22 *Trinity 26*	T 22
T 23	T 23		W23	F 23	M23	W23
W24 *Nat. J. Bap.*	F 24	....	T 24	S 24	T 24	T 24
T 25	S 25	S 23 *Trinity 13*	F 25		W25	F 25 *Christmas*
F 26		M24	s 26	....	T 26	s 26
S 27	....	T 25		S 25 *Trinity 22*	F 27	
	S 26 *Trinity 9*	W26	....	M26	s 28	....
....	M27	T 27	S 27 *Trinity 18*	T 27		S 27
S 28 *Trinity 5*	T 28	F 28	M28	W28	....	M28
M29	W29	S 29	T 29 *Michael A.*	T 29	S 29 *Advent 1*	T 29
T 30	T 30		W30	F 30	M30	W30
	F 31	....		S 31		T 31
		S 30 *Trinity 14*				
		M31				

8/9 Easter Day 30 March

Dominical letter E for Common Years
Dominical letter FE for Leap Years (*in bold figures*)
Old style years 419, 430, 503, 514, 525, 587, 598, 609, **620**, 682, 693, **704**, 777, **788**, 867, **872**, 951, 962, 1035, 1046, 1057, 1119, 1130, 1141, **1152**, 1214, 1225, **1236**, 1309, **1320**, 1399, **1404**, 1483, 1494, 1567, 1578, 1589, 1651, 1662, 1673, **1684**, 1746

Leap years						
JANUARY	FEBRUARY	JANUARY	FEBRUARY	MARCH	APRIL	MAY
T 1	F 1	W1	S 1	S 1	T 1	T 1
W2	S 2 *Purific. M.*	T 2			W2	F 2
T 3		F 3	S 2 *Sexages.*	S 2 *Lent 3*	T 3	S 3
F 4	S 3 *Sexages.*	S 4	M3	M3	F 4	
S 5	M4		T 4	T 4	S 5	S 4 *Rogation*
	T 5	S 5	W5	W5		M5
S 6 *Epiphany*	W6	M6 *Epiphany*	T 6	T 6	S 6 *Quasimodo*	T 6
M7	T 7	T 7	F 7	F 7	M7	W7
T 8	F 8	W8	S 8	S 8	T 8	T 8 *Ascension*
W9	S 9	T 9			W9	F 9
T 10		F 10	S 9 *Quinquag.*	S 9 *Lent 4*	T 10	S 10
F 11	S 10 *Quinquag.*	S 11	M10	M10	F 11	
S 12	M11		T 11 *Shrove Tu.*	T 11	S 12	S 11 *Ascens. 1*
	T 12 *Shrove Tu.*	S 12 *Epiph. 1*	W12 *Ash Wed.*	W12		M12
S 13 *Epiph. 1*	W13 *Ash Wed.*	M13 *Hilary*	T 13	T 13	S 13 *Easter 2*	T 13
M14	T 14	T 14	F 14	F 14	M14	W14
T 15	F 15	W15	S 15	S 15	T 15	T 15
W16	S 16	T 16			W16	F 16
T 17		F 17	S 16	S 16 *Passion*	T 17	S 17
F 18	S 17 *Quadrag.*	S 18	M17	M17	F 18	
S 19	M18		T 18	T 18	S 19	S 18 *Whit Sun.*
	T 19	S 19 *Epiph. 2*	W19 *Ember*	W19		M19
S 20 *Epiph. 2*	W20 *Ember*	M20	T 20	T 20	S 20 *Easter 3*	T 20
M21	T 21	T 21	F 21 *Ember*	F 21	M21	W21 *Ember*
T 22	F 22 *Ember*	W22	S 22 *Ember*	S 22	T 22	T 22
W23	S 23 *Ember*	T 23			W23	F 23 *Ember*
T 24		F 24	S 23 *Lent 2*	S 23 *Palm*	T 24	S 24 *Ember*
F 25	S 24 *Lent 2*	S 25	M24	M24	F 25	
S 26	M25 *Matthias*		T 25 *Matthias*	T 25 *Annunc.*	S 26	S 25 *Trinity*
	T 26	S 26 *Septuag.*	W26	W26		M26
S 27 *Septuag.*	W27	M27	T 27	T 27	S 27 *Easter 4*	T 27
M28	T 28	T 28	F 28	F 28 *Good Fri.*	M28	W28
T 29	F 29	W29		S 29	T 29	T 29 *Corpus C.*
W30		T 30		S 30 *Easter Day*	W30	F 30
T 31		F 31		M31		S 31

Dominical letter E for Common Years
Dominical letter FE for Leap Years (*in bold figures*)
New style years   1603, 1614, 1625, 1687, 1698, 1755, 1766, 1777, 1823, 1834, 1902, 1975, 1986, 1997, 2059, 2070, 2081, **2092**

JUNE	JULY	AUGUST	SEPTEMBER	OCTOBER	NOVEMBER	DECEMBER
S 1 *Trinity 1*	T 1	F 1 *Lammas*	M 1	W 1	S 1	M 1
M 2	W 2	S 2	T 2	T 2		T 2
T 3	T 3		W 3	F 3	....	W 3
W 4	F 4	....	T 4	S 4	S 2 *Trinity 23*	T 4
T 5	S 5	S 3 *Trinity 10*	F 5		M 3	F 5
F 6		M 4	S 6	....	T 4	S 6
S 7	....	T 5		S 5 *Trinity 19*	W 5	
	S 6 *Trinity 6*	W 6	....	M 6	T 6	....
....	M 7	T 7	S 7 *Trinity 15*	T 7	F 7	S 7 *Advent 2*
S 8 *Trinity 2*	T 8	F 8	M 8	W 8	S 8	M 8
M 9	W 9	S 9	T 9	T 9		T 9
T 10	T 10		W 10	F 10	....	W 10
W 11	F 11	....	T 11	S 11	S 9 *Trinity 24*	T 11
T 12	S 12	S 10 *Trinity 11*	F 12		M 10	F 12
F 13		M 11	S 13	....	T 11 *Martin*	S 13
S 14	....	T 12		S 12 *Trinity 20*	W 12	
	S 13 *Trinity 7*	W 13	....	M 13	T 13	....
....	M 14	T 14	S 14 *Trinity 16*	T 14	F 14	S 14 *Advent 3*
S 15 *Trinity 3*	T 15	F 15	M 15	W 15	S 15	M 15
M 16	W 16	S 16	T 16	T 16		T 16
T 17	T 17		W 17 *Ember*	F 17	....	W 17 *Ember*
W 18	F 18	....	T 18	S 18	S 16 *Trinity 25*	T 18
T 19	S 19	S 17 *Trinity 12*	F 19 *Ember*		M 17	F 19 *Ember*
F 20		M 18	S 20 *Ember*	....	T 18	S 20 *Ember*
S 21	....	T 19		S 19 *Trinity 21*	W 19	
	S 20 *Trinity 8*	W 20	....	M 20	T 20	....
....	M 21	T 21	S 21 *Trinity 17*	T 21	F 21	S 21 *Advent 4*
S 22 *Trinity 4*	T 22	F 22	M 22	W 22	S 22	M 22
M 23	W 23	S 23	T 23	T 23		T 23
T 24 *Nat. J. Bap.*	T 24		W 24	F 24	....	W 24
W 25	F 25	....	T 25	S 25	S 23 *Trinity 26*	T 25 *Christmas*
T 26	S 26	S 24 *Trinity 13*	F 26		M 24	F 26
F 27		M 25	S 27	....	T 25	S 27
S 28	....	T 26		S 26 *Trinity 22*	W 26	
	S 27 *Trinity 9*	W 27	....	M 27	T 27	....
....	M 28	T 28	S 28 *Trinity 18*	T 28	F 28	S 28
S 29 *Trinity 5*	T 29	F 29	M 29 *Michael A.*	W 29	S 29	M 29
M 30	W 30	S 30	T 30	T 30		T 30
	T 31			F 31	....	W 31
		....			S 30 *Advent 1*	
		S 31 *Trinity 14*				

8/10 Easter Day 31 March

Dominical letter F for Common Years
Dominical letter GF for Leap Years (*in bold figures*)
Old style years   435, 446, 457, **468**, 519, 530, 541, **552**, 614, 625, **636**, 709, 715, **720**, 799, **804**, 810, 883, 894, 905, 967, 978, 989, **1000**, 1051, 1062, 1073, **1084**, 1146, 1157, **1168**, 1241, 1247, **1252**, 1331, **1336**, 1342, 1415, 1426, 1437, 1499, 1510, 1521, **1532**, 1583, 1594, 1605, **1616**, 1678, 1689, **1700**

Leap years

JANUARY (Leap years)
M1
T 2
W3
T 4
F 5
s 6 *Epiphany*
S 7 *Epiph. 1*
M8
T 9
W10
T 11
F 12
s 13 *Hilary*
S 14 *Epiph. 2*
M15
T 16
W17
T 18
F 19
S 20
S 21 *Epiph. 3*
M22
T 23
W24
T 25
F 26
S 27
S 28 *Septuag.*
M29
T 30
W31

FEBRUARY (Leap years)
T 1
F 2 *Purific. M.*
S 3
S 4 *Sexages.*
M5
T 6
W7
T 8
F 9
S 10
S 11 *Quinquag.*
M12
T 13 *Shrove Tu.*
W14 *Ash Wed.*
T 15
F 16
S 17
S 18 *Quadrag.*
M19
T 20
W21 *Ember*
T 22
F 23 *Ember*
s 24 *Ember*
S 25 *Lent 2*
M26
T 27
W28
T 29

JANUARY
T 1
W2
T 3
F 4
S 5
S 6 *Epiphany*
M7
T 8
W9
T 10
F 11
S 12
S 13 *Epiph. 1*
M14
T 15
W16
T 17
F 18
S 19
S 20 *Epiph. 2*
M21
T 22
W23
T 24
F 25
S 26
S 27 *Septuag.*
M28
T 29
W30
T 31

FEBRUARY
F 1
S 2 *Purific. M.*
S 3 *Sexages.*
M4
T 5
w6
T 7
F 8
S 9
S 10 *Quinquag.*
M11
T 12 *Shrove Tu.*
W13 *Ash Wed.*
T 14
F 15
S 16
S 17 *Quadrag.*
M18
T 19
W20 *Ember*
T 21
F 22 *Ember*
s 23 *Ember*
S 24 *Lent 2*
M25
T 26
W27
T 28

MARCH
F 1
S 2
S 3 *Lent 3*
M4
T 5
w6
T 7
F 8
S 9
S 10 *Lent 4*
M11
T 12
W13
T 14
F 15
S 16
S 17 *Passion*
M18
T 19
W20
T 21
F 22
S 23
S 24 *Palm*
M25 *Annunc.*
T 26
W27
T 28
F 29 *Good Fri.*
S 30
S 31 ***Easter Day***

APRIL
M1
T 2
W3
T 4
F 5
s 6
S 7 *Quasimodo*
M8
T 9
W10
T 11
F 12
S 13
S 14 *Easter 2*
M15
T 16
W17
T 18
F 19
S 20
S 21 *Easter 3*
M22
T 23
W24
T 25
F 26
S 27
S 28 *Easter 4*
M29
T 30

MAY
W1
T 2
F 3
S 4
S 5 *Rogation*
M6
T 7
W8
T 9 *Ascension*
F 10
S 11
S 12 *Ascens. 1*
M13
T 14
W15
T 16
F 17
S 18
S 19 *Whit Sun.*
M20
T 21
W22 *Ember*
T 23
F 24 *Ember*
s 25 *Ember*
S 26 *Trinity*
M27
T 28
W29
T 30 *Corpus C.*
F 31

Easter Day 31 March 8/10
Dominical letter F for Common Years
Dominical letter GF for Leap Years (*in bold figures*)
New style years   1619, 1630, 1641, **1652**, 1709, **1720**, 1771, 1782, 1793, 1839, 1850, 1861, **1872**, 1907, 1918,
1929, 1991, 2002, 2013, **2024**, 2086, 2097

JUNE	JULY	AUGUST	SEPTEMBER	OCTOBER	NOVEMBER	DECEMBER
S 1	M1	T 1 *Lammas*	S 1 *Trinity 14*	T 1	F 1	S 1 *Advent 1*
	T 2	F 2	M2	W2	S 2	M2
S 2 *Trinity 1*	W3	S 3	T 3	T 3		T 3
M3	T 4		W4	F 4	S 3 *Trinity 23*	W4
T 4	F 5	S 4 *Trinity 10*	T 5	S 5	M4	T 5
W5	s 6	M5	F 6		T 5	F 6
T 6		T 6	S 7	S 6 *Trinity 19*	W6	S 7
F 7	S 7 *Trinity 6*	W7		M7	T 7	
s 8	M8	T 8	S 8 *Trinity 15*	T 8	F 8	S 8 *Advent 2*
	T 9	F 9	M9	W9	S 9	M9
S 9 *Trinity 2*	W10	S 10	T 10	T 10		T 10
M10	T 11		W11	F 11	S 10 *Trinity 24*	W11
T 11	F 12	S 11 *Trinity 11*	T 12	S 12	M11 *Martin*	T 12
W12	S 13	M12	F 13		T 12	F 13
T 13		T 13	s 14 *Exalt. C.*	S 13 *Trinity 20*	W13	S 14
F 14	S 14 *Trinity 7*	W14		M14	T 14	
S 15	M15	T 15	S 15 *Trinity 16*	T 15	F 15	S 15 *Advent 3*
	T 16	F 16	M16	W16	S 16	M16
S 16 *Trinity 3*	W17	S 17	T 17	T 17		T 17
M17	T 18		W18 *Ember*	F 18	S 17 *Trinity 25*	W18 *Ember*
T 18	F 19	S 18 *Trinity 12*	T 19	S 19	M18	T 19
W19	S 20	M19	F 20 *Ember*		T 19	F 20 *Ember*
T 20		T 20	s 21 *Ember*	S 20 *Trinity 21*	W20	s 21 *Ember*
F 21	S 21 *Trinity 8*	W21		M21	T 21	
S 22	M22	T 22	S 22 *Trinity 17*	T 22	F 22	S 22 *Advent 4*
	T 23	F 23	M23	W23	S 23	M23
S 23 *Trinity 4*	W24	S 24	T 24	T 24		T 24
M24 *Nat. J. Bap.*	T 25		W25	F 25	S 24 *Trinity 26*	W25 *Christmas*
T 25	F 26	S 25 *Trinity 13*	T 26	S 26	M25	T 26
W26	S 27	M26	F 27		T 26	F 27
T 27		T 27	s 28	S 27 *Trinity 22*	W27	S 28
F 28	S 28 *Trinity 9*	W28		M28	T 28	
S 29	M29	T 29	S 29 *Trinity 18*	T 29	F 29	S 29
	T 30	F 30	M30	W30	S 30	M30
S 30 *Trinity 5*	W31	S 31		T 31		T 31

8/11 Easter Day 1 April

Dominical letter G for Common Years
Dominical letter AG for Leap Years (*in bold figures*)
Old style years **400**, 462, 473, **484**, 557, **568**, 647, **652**, 731, 742, 815, 826, 837, 899, 910, 921, **932**, 994, 1005, **1016**, 1089, **1100**, 1179, **1184**, 1263, 1274, 1347, 1358, 1369, 1431, 1442, 1453, **1464**, 1526, 1537, **1548**, 1621, **1632**, 1711, **1716**

		Leap years				
JANUARY	FEBRUARY	JANUARY	FEBRUARY	MARCH	APRIL	MAY
S 1	W1	M1	T 1	T 1	S 1 *Easter Day*	T 1
M2	T 2 *Purific. M.*	T 2	F 2 *Purific. M.*	F 2	M2	W2
T 3	F 3	W3	S 3	S 3	T 3	T 3
W4	S 4	T 4			W4	F 4
T 5		F 5	S 4 *Sexages.*	S 4 *Lent 3*	T 5	S 5
F 6 *Epiphany*	S 5 *Sexages.*	s 6 *Epiphany*	M5	M5	F 6	
S 7	M6		T 6	T 6	S 7	S 6 *Rogation*
	T 7	S 7 *Epiph. 1*	W7	W7		M7
S 8 *Epiph. 1*	W8	M8	T 8	T 8	S 8 *Quasimodo*	T 8
M9	T 9	T 9	F 9	F 9	M9	W9
T 10	F 10	W10	S 10	S 10	T 10	T 10 *Ascension*
W11	S 11	T 11			W11	F 11
T 12		F 12			T 12	S 12
F 13 *Hilary*	S 12 *Quinquag.*	s 13 *Hilary*	S 11 *Quinquag.*	S 11 *Lent 4*	F 13	
S 14	M13		M12	M12	S 14	S 13 *Ascens. 1*
	T 14 *Shrove Tu.*	S 14 *Epiph. 2*	T 13 *Shrove Tu.*	T 13		M14
S 15 *Epiph. 2*	W15 *Ash Wed.*	M15	W14 *Ash Wed.*	W14	S 15 *Easter 2*	T 15
M16	T 16	T 16	T 15	T 15	M16	W16
T 17	F 17	W17	F 16	F 16	T 17	T 17
W18	S 18	T 18	S 17	S 17	W18	F 18
T 19		F 19			T 19	S 19
F 20	S 19 *Quadrag.*	S 20	S 18 *Quadrag.*	S 18 *Passion*	F 20	
S 21	M20		M19	M19	S 21	S 20 *Whit Sun.*
	T 21	S 21 *Epiph. 3*	T 20	T 20		M21
S 22 *Epiph. 3*	W22 *Ember*	M22	W21 *Ember*	W21	S 22 *Easter 3*	T 22
M23	T 23	T 23	T 22	T 22	M23	W23 *Ember*
T 24	F 24 *Ember*	W24	F 23 *Ember*	F 23	T 24	T 24
W25	s 25 *Ember*	T 25	s 24 *Ember*	S 24	W25	F 25 *Ember*
T 26		F 26			T 26	s 26 *Ember*
F 27	S 26 *Lent 2*	S 27	S 25 *Lent 2*	S 25 *Palm*	F 27	
S 28	M27		M26	M26	S 28	S 27 *Trinity*
	T 28	S 28 *Septuag.*	T 27	T 27		M28
S 29 *Septuag.*	W29	M29	W28	W28	S 29 *Easter 4*	T 29
M30		T 30		T 29	M30	W30
T 31		W31		F 30 *Good Fri.*		T 31 *Corpus C.*
				S 31		

Dominical letter G for Common Years
Dominical letter AG for Leap Years (*in bold figures*)
New style years **1584**, 1646, 1657, **1668**, 1714, 1725, **1736**, **1804**, 1866, 1877, **1888**, 1923, 1934, 1945, **1956**,
2018, 2029, **2046**

JUNE	JULY	AUGUST	SEPTEMBER	OCTOBER	NOVEMBER	DECEMBER
F 1	S 1 *Trinity 5*	W 1 *Lammas*	S 1	M 1	T 1	S 1
S 2	M 2	T 2		T 2	F 2	
	T 3	F 3	S 2 *Trinity 14*	W 3	S 3	S 2 *Advent 1*
S 3 *Trinity 1*	W 4	S 4	M 3	T 4		M 3
M 4	T 5		T 4	F 5	S 4 *Trinity 23*	T 4
T 5	F 6	S 5 *Trinity 10*	W 5	s 6	M 5	W 5
W 6	S 7	M 6	T 6		T 6	T 6
T 7		T 7	F 7	S 7 *Trinity 19*	W 7	F 7
F 8	S 8 *Trinity 6*	W 8	s 8	M 8	T 8	s 8
S 9	M 9	T 9		T 9	F 9	
	T 10	F 10	S 9 *Trinity 15*	W 10	S 10	S 9 *Advent 2*
S 10 *Trinity 2*	W 11	S 11	M 10	T 11		M 10
M 11	T 12		T 11	F 12	S 11 *Trinity 24*	T 11
T 12	F 13	S 12 *Trinity 11*	W 12	s 13	M 12	W 12
W 13	S 14	M 13	T 13		T 13	T 13
T 14		T 14	F 14 *Exalt. C.*	S 14 *Trinity 20*	W 14	F 14
F 15	S 15 *Trinity 7*	W 15	s 15	M 15	T 15	s 15
S 16	M 16	T 16		T 16	F 16	
	T 17	F 17	S 16 *Trinity 16*	W 17	S 17	S 16 *Advent 3*
S 17 *Trinity 3*	W 18	S 18	M 17	T 18		M 17
M 18	T 19		T 18	F 19	S 18 *Trinity 25*	T 18
T 19	F 20	S 19 *Trinity 12*	W 19 *Ember*	s 20	M 19	W 19 *Ember*
W 20	S 21	M 20	T 20		T 20	T 20
T 21		T 21	F 21 *Ember*	S 21 *Trinity 21*	W 21	F 21 *Ember*
F 22	S 22 *Trinity 8*	W 22	s 22 *Ember*	M 22	T 22	s 22 *Ember*
S 23	M 23	T 23		T 23	F 23	
	T 24	F 24	S 23 *Trinity 17*	W 24	S 24	S 23 *Advent 4*
S 24 *Trinity 4*	W 25	S 25	M 24	T 25		M 24
M 25	T 26		T 25	F 26	S 25 *Trinity 26*	T 25 *Christmas*
T 26	F 27	S 26 *Trinity 13*	W 26	s 27	M 26	W 26
W 27	S 28	M 27	T 27		T 27	T 27
T 28		T 28	F 28	S 28 *Trinity 22*	W 28	F 28
F 29	S 29 *Trinity 9*	W 29	s 29 *Michael A.*	M 29	T 29	S 29
S 30	M 30	T 30		T 30	F 30	
	T 31	F 31	S 30 *Trinity 18*	W 31		S 30
						M 31

8/12 Easter Day 2 April

Dominical letter A for Common Years
Dominical letter BA for Leap Years (*in bold figures*)
Old style years 405, **416**, 489, **500**, 579, **584**, 663, 674, 747, 758, 769, 831, 842, 853, **864**, 926, 937, **948**, 1021, **1032**, 1111, **1116**, 1195, 1206, 1279, 1290, 1301, 1363, 1374, 1385, **1396**, 1458, 1469, **1480**, 1553, **1564**, 1643, **1648**, 1727, 1738

Leap years

JANUARY (Common)
S 1
·····
S 2
M3
T 4
W5
T 6 *Epiphany*
F 7
s 8
·····
S 9 *Epiph. 1*
M10
T 11
W12
T 13 *Hilary*
F 14
S 15
·····
S 16 *Epiph. 2*
M17
T 18
W19
T 20
F 21
S 22
·····
S 23 *Epiph. 3*
M24
T 25
W26
T 27
F 28
S 29
·····
S 30 *Septuag.*
M31

FEBRUARY (Common)
T 1
W2 *Purific. M.*
T 3
F 4
S 5
·····
S 6 *Sexages.*
M7
T 8
W9
T 10
F 11
S 12
·····
S 13 *Quinquag.*
M14
T 15 *Shrove Tu.*
W16 *Ash Wed.*
T 17
F 18
S 19
·····
S 20 *Quadrag.*
M21
T 22
W23 *Ember*
T 24
F 25 *Ember*
s 26 *Ember*
·····
S 27 *Lent 2*
M28
T 29

JANUARY (Leap)
S 1
M2
T 3
W4
T 5
F 6 *Epiphany*
S 7
·····
S 8 *Epiph. 1*
M9
T 10
W11
T 12
F 13 *Hilary*
S 14
·····
S 15 *Epiph. 2*
M16
T 17
W18
T 19
F 20
S 21
·····
S 22 *Epiph. 3*
M23
T 24
W25
T 26
F 27
S 28
·····
S 29 *Septuag.*
M30
T 31

FEBRUARY (Leap)
W1
T 2 *Purific. M.*
F 3
S 4
·····
S 5 *Sexages.*
M6
T 7
W8
T 9
F 10
S 11
·····
S 12 *Quinquag.*
M13
T 14 *Shrove Tu.*
W15 *Ash Wed.*
T 16
F 17
S 18
·····
S 19 *Quadrag.*
M20
T 21
W22 *Ember*
T 23
F 24 *Ember*
s 25 *Ember*
·····
S 26 *Lent 2*
M27
T 28
W29

MARCH
W1
T 2
F 3
S 4
·····
S 5 *Lent 3*
M6
T 7
W8
T 9
F 10
S 11
·····
S 12 *Lent 4*
M13
T 14
W15
T 16
F 17
S 18
·····
S 19 *Passion*
M20
T 21
W22
T 23
F 24
S 25 *Annunc.*
·····
S 26 *Palm*
M27
T 28
W29
T 30
F 31 *Good Fri.*

APRIL
S 1
·····
S 2 ***Easter Day***
M3
T 4
W5
T 6
F 7
s 8
·····
S 9 *Quasimodo*
M10
T 11
W12
T 13
F 14
S 15
·····
S 16 *Easter 2*
M17
T 18
W19
T 20
F 21
S 22
·····
S 23 *Easter 3*
M24
T 25
W26
T 27
F 28
S 29
·····
S 30 *Easter 4*

MAY
M1
T 2
W3
T 4
F 5
s 6
·····
S 7 *Rogation*
M8
T 9
W10
T 11 *Ascension*
F 12
S 13
·····
S 14 *Ascens. 1*
M15
T 16
W17
T 18
F 19
S 20
·····
S 21 *Whit Sun.*
M22
T 23
W24 *Ember*
T 25
F 26 *Ember*
s 27 *Ember*
·····
S 28 *Trinity*
M29
T 30
W31

Dominical letter A for Common Years
Dominical letter BA for Leap Years (*in bold figures*)
New style years   1589, **1600**, 1673, 1679, **1684**, 1741, 1747, **1752**, 1809, **1820**, 1893, 1899, 1961, **1972**, 2051,
2056

JUNE	JULY	AUGUST	SEPTEMBER	OCTOBER	NOVEMBER	DECEMBER
T 1 *Corpus C.*	S 1	T 1 *Lammas*	F 1	S 1 *Trinity 18*	W1	F 1
F 2	W2	W2	S 2	M2	T 2	S 2
S 3	....	T 3	....	T 3	F 3	....
....	S 2 *Trinity 5*	F 4	S 3 *Trinity 14*	W4	S 4	S 3 *Advent 1*
S 4 *Trinity 1*	M3	S 5	M4	T 5	....	M4
M5	T 4	....	T 5	F 6	S 5 *Trinity 23*	T 5
T 6	W5	S 6 *Trinity 10*	W6	S 7	M6	W6
W7	T 6	M7	T 7	....	T 7	T 7
T 8	F 7	T 8	F 8	S 8 *Trinity 19*	W8	F 8
F 9	S 8	W9	S 9	M9	T 9	S 9
S 10	....	T 10	....	T 10	F 10	....
....	S 9 *Trinity 6*	F 11	S 10 *Trinity 15*	W11	S 11 *Martin*	S 10 *Advent 2*
S 11 *Trinity 2*	M10	S 12	M11	T 12	....	M11
M12	T 11	....	T 12	F 13	S 12 *Trinity 24*	T 12
T 13	W12	S 13 *Trinity 11*	W13	S 14	M13	W13
W14	T 13	M14	T 14 *Exalt. C.*	....	T 14	T 14
T 15	F 14	T 15	F 15	S 15 *Trinity 20*	W15	F 15
F 16	S 15	W16	S 16	M16	T 16	S 16
S 17	....	T 17	....	T 17	F 17	....
....	S 16 *Trinity 7*	F 18	S 17 *Trinity 16*	W18	S 18	S 17 *Advent 3*
S 18 *Trinity 3*	M17	S 19	M18	T 19	....	M18
M19	T 18	....	T 19	F 20	S 19 *Trinity 25*	T 19
T 20	W19	S 20 *Trinity 12*	W20 *Ember*	S 21	M20	W20 *Ember*
W21	T 20	M21	T 21	....	T 21	T 21
T 22	F 21	T 22	F 22 *Ember*	S 22 *Trinity 21*	W22	F 22 *Ember*
F 23	S 22	W23	S 23 *Ember*	M23	T 23	S 23 *Ember*
S 24 *Nat. J. Bap.*	....	T 24	....	T 24	F 24	....
....	S 23 *Trinity 8*	F 25	S 24 *Trinity 17*	W25	S 25	S 24 *Advent 4*
S 25 *Trinity 4*	M24	S 26	M25	T 26	....	M25 *Christmas*
M26	T 25	....	T 26	F 27	S 26 *Trinity 26*	T 26
T 27	W26	S 27 *Trinity 13*	W27	S 28	M27	W27
W28	T 27	M28	T 28	....	T 28	T 28
T 29	F 28	T 29	F 29 *Michael A.*	S 29 *Trinity 22*	W29	F 29
F 30	S 29	W30	S 30	M30	T 30	S 30
	....	T 31		T 31		....
	S 30 *Trinity 9*					S 31
	M31					

8/13 Easter Day 3 April

Dominical letter B for Common Years
Dominical letter CB for Leap Years (*in bold figures*)
Old style years   421, 427, **432**, 511, **516**, 522, 595, 606, 617, 679, 690, 701, **712**, 763, 774, 785, **796**, 858, 869, **880**, 953, 959, **964**, 1043, **1048**, 1054, 1127, 1138, 1149, 1211, 1222, 1233, **1244**, 1295, 1306, 1317, **1328**, 1390, 1401, **1412**, 1485, 1491, **1496**, 1575, **1580**, 1586, 1659, 1670, 1681, 1743

Leap years						
JANUARY	FEBRUARY	JANUARY	FEBRUARY	MARCH	APRIL	MAY
F 1	M1	S 1	T 1	T 1	F 1 *Good Fri.*	S 1 *Easter 4*
S 2	T 2 *Purific. M.*		W2 *Purific. M.*	W2	S 2	M2
	W3	S 2	T 3	T 3		T 3
S 3	T 4	M3	F 4	F 4	S 3 *Easter Day*	W4
M4	F 5	T 4	S 5	S 5	M4	T 5
T 5	s 6	W5			T 5	F 6
W6 *Epiphany*		T 6 *Epiphany*	S 6 *Sexages.*	S 6 *Lent 3*	W6	S 7
T 7	S 7 *Sexages.*	F 7	M7	M7	T 7	
F 8	M8	s 8	T 8	T 8	F 8	S 8 *Rogation*
S 9	T 9		W9	W9	S 9	M9
	W10	S 9 *Epiph. 1*	T 10	T 10		T 10
S 10 *Epiph. 1*	T 11	M10	F 11	F 11	S 10 *Quasimodo*	W11
M11	F 12	T 11	S 12	S 12	M11	T 12 *Ascension*
T 12	S 13	W12			T 12	F 13
W13 *Hilary*		T 13 *Hilary*	S 13 *Quinquag.*	S 13 *Lent 4*	W13	S 14
T 14	S 14 *Quinquag.*	F 14	M14	M14	T 14	
F 15	M15	S 15	T 15 *Shrove Tu.*	T 15	F 15	S 15 *Ascens. 1*
S 16	T 16 *Shrove Tu.*		W16 *Ash Wed.*	W16	S 16	M16
	W17 *Ash Wed.*	S 16 *Epiph. 2*	T 17	T 17		T 17
S 17 *Epiph. 2*	T 18	M17	F 18	F 18	S 17 *Easter 2*	W18
M18	F 19	T 18	S 19	S 19	M18	T 19
T 19	S 20	W19			T 19	F 20
W20		T 20	S 20 *Quadrag.*	S 20 *Passion*	W20	S 21
T 21	S 21 *Quadrag.*	F 21	M21	M21	T 21	
F 22	M22	S 22	T 22	T 22	F 22	S 22 *Whit Sun.*
S 23	T 23		W23 *Ember*	W23	S 23	M23
	W24 *Ember*	S 23 *Epiph. 3*	T 24 *Matthias*	T 24		T 24
S 24 *Epiph. 3*	T 25 *Matthias*	M24	F 25 *Ember*	F 25 *Annunc.*	S 24 *Easter 3*	W25 *Ember*
M25	F 26 *Ember*	T 25	s 26 *Ember*	s 26	M25	T 26
T 26	s 27 *Ember*	W26			T 26	F 27 *Ember*
W27		T 27	S 27 *Lent 2*	S 27 *Palm*	W27	s 28 *Ember*
T 28	S 28 *Lent 2*	F 28	M28	M28	T 28	
F 29	M29	S 29	T 29	T 29	F 29	S 29 *Trinity*
S 30				W30	S 30	M30
		S 30 *Septuag.*		T 31		T 31
S 31 *Septuag.*		M31				

Easter Day 3 April

Dominical letter B for Common Years
Dominical letter CB for Leap Years (*in bold figures*)

New style years   1611, **1616**, 1695, 1763, **1768**, 1774, 1825, 1831, **1836**, **1904**, 1983, **1988**, 1994, 2067, 2078, 2089

JUNE	JULY	AUGUST	SEPTEMBER	OCTOBER	NOVEMBER	DECEMBER
W 1	F 1	M 1 *Lammas*	T 1	S 1	T 1	T 1
T 2 *Corpus C.*	S 2	T 2	F 2		W 2	F 2
F 3		W 3	S 3	S 2 *Trinity 18*	T 3	S 3
S 4	S 3 *Trinity 5*	T 4		M 3	F 4	
	M 4	F 5	S 4 *Trinity 14*	T 4	S 5	S 4 *Advent 2*
S 5 *Trinity 1*	T 5	S 6	M 5	W 5		M 5
M 6	W 6		T 6	T 6	S 6 *Trinity 23*	T 6
T 7	T 7	S 7 *Trinity 10*	W 7	F 7	M 7	W 7
W 8	F 8	M 8	T 8	S 8	T 8	T 8
T 9	S 9	T 9	F 9		W 9	F 9
F 10		W 10	S 10	S 9 *Trinity 19*	T 10	S 10
S 11	S 10 *Trinity 6*	T 11		M 10	F 11 *Martin*	
	M 11	F 12	S 11 *Trinity 15*	T 11	S 12	S 11 *Advent 3*
S 12 *Trinity 2*	T 12	S 13	M 12	W 12		M 12
M 13	W 13		T 13	T 13	S 13 *Trinity 24*	T 13
T 14	T 14	S 14 *Trinity 11*	W 14 *Exalt. C.*	F 14	M 14	W 14 *Ember*
W 15	F 15	M 15	T 15	S 15	T 15	T 15
T 16	S 16	T 16	F 16		W 16	F 16 *Ember*
F 17		W 17	S 17	S 16 *Trinity 20*	T 17	S 17 *Ember*
S 18	S 17 *Trinity 7*	T 18		M 17	F 18	
	M 18	F 19	S 18 *Trinity 16*	T 18	S 19	S 18 *Advent 4*
S 19 *Trinity 3*	T 19	S 20	M 19	W 19		M 19
M 20	W 20		T 20	T 20	S 20 *Trinity 25*	T 20
T 21	T 21	S 21 *Trinity 12*	W 21 *Ember*	F 21	M 21	W 21
W 22	F 22	M 22	T 22	S 22	T 22	T 22
T 23	S 23	T 23	F 23 *Ember*		W 23	F 23
F 24 *Nat. J. Bap.*		W 24	S 24 *Ember*	S 23 *Trinity 21*	T 24	S 24
S 25	S 24 *Trinity 8*	T 25		M 24	F 25	
	M 25	F 26	S 25 *Trinity 17*	T 25	S 26	S 25 *Christmas*
S 26 *Trinity 4*	T 26	S 27	M 26	W 26		M 26
M 27	W 27		T 27	T 27	S 27 *Advent 1*	T 27
T 28	T 28	S 28 *Trinity 13*	W 28	F 28	M 28	W 28
W 29	F 29	M 29	T 29 *Michael A.*	S 29	T 29	T 29
T 30	S 30	T 30	F 30		W 30	F 30
		W 31		S 30 *Trinity 22*		S 31
	S 31 *Trinity 9*			M 31		

8/14 Easter Day 4 April

Dominical letter C for Common Years
Dominical letter DC for Leap Years (*in bold figures*)
Old style years 443, 454, 527, 538, 549, 611, 622, 633, **644**, 706, 717, **728**, 801, **812**, 891, **896**, 975, 986, 1059, 1070, 1081, 1143, 1154, 1165, **1176**, 1238, 1249, **1260**, 1333, **1344**, 1423, **1428**, 1507, 1518, 1591, 1602, 1613, 1675, 1686, 1697, **1708**

Leap years						
JANUARY	FEBRUARY	JANUARY	FEBRUARY	MARCH	APRIL	MAY
T 1	S 1 *Septuag.*	F 1	M1	M1	T 1	S 1
F 2	M2 *Purific. M.*	S 2	T 2 *Purific. M.*	T 2	F 2 *Good Fri.*	
S 3	T 3		W3	W3	S 3	
	W4		T 4	T 4		S 2 *Easter 4*
	T 5	S 3	F 5	F 5		M3
S 4	F 6	M4	S 6	S 6	S 4 *Easter Day*	T 4
M5	S 7	T 5			M5	W5
T 6 *Epiphany*		w6 *Epiphany*			T 6	T 6
W7		T 7	S 7 *Sexages.*	S 7 *Lent 3*	W7	F 7
T 8	S 8 *Sexages.*	F 8	M8	M8	T 8	s 8
F 9	M9	S 9	T 9	T 9	F 9	
S 10	T 10		W10	W10	S 10	S 9 *Rogation*
	W11		T 11	T 11		M10
	T 12	S 10 *Epiph. 1*	F 12	F 12		T 11
S 11 *Epiph. 1*	F 13	M11	S 13	S 13	S 11 *Quasimodo*	W12
M12	S 14	T 12			M12	
T 13 *Hilary*		W13 *Hilary*			T 13	T 13 *Ascension*
W14		T 14	S 14 *Quinquag.*	S 14 *Lent 4*	W14	F 14
T 15	S 15 *Quinquag.*	F 15	M15	M15	T 15	S 15
F 16	M16	S 16	T 16 *Shrove Tu.*	T 16	F 16	
S 17	T 17 *Shrove Tu.*		w17 *Ash Wed.*	W17	S 17	S 16 *Ascens. 1*
	w18 *Ash Wed.*	S 17 *Epiph. 2*	T 18	T 18		M17
	T 19	M18	F 19	F 19		
S 18 *Epiph. 2*	F 20	T 19	S 20	S 20	S 18 *Easter 2*	T 18
M19	S 21	W20			M19	W19
T 20		T 21			T 20	T 20
W21		F 22	S 21 *Quadrag.*	S 21 *Passion*	W21	F 21
T 22	S 22 *Quadrag.*	S 23	M22	M22	T 22	S 22
F 23	M23		T 23	T 23	F 23	
S 24	T 24		w24 *Ember*	W24	S 24	S 23 *Whit Sun.*
	w25 *Ember*	S 24 *Epiph. 3*	T 25	T 25 *Annunc.*		M24
S 25 *Epiph. 3*	T 26	M25	F 26 *Ember*	F 26	S 25 *Easter 3*	T 25
M26	F 27 *Ember*	T 26	s 27 *Ember*	S 27	M26	w26 *Ember*
T 27	s 28 *Ember*	W27			T 27	T 27
W28		T 28	S 28 *Lent 2*	S 28 *Palm*	W28	F 28 *Ember*
T 29	S 29 *Lent 2*	F 29		M29	T 29	s 29 *Ember*
F 30		S 30		T 30	F 30	
S 31				W31		S 30 *Trinity*
		S 31 *Septuag.*				M31

Dominical letter C for Common Years
Dominical letter DC for Leap Years (*in bold figures*)
New style years   1627, 1638, 1649, 1706, 1779, 1790, 1847, 1858, 1915, **1920**, 1926, 1999, 2010, 2021, 2083,
2094

JUNE	JULY	AUGUST	SEPTEMBER	OCTOBER	NOVEMBER	DECEMBER
T 1	T 1	S 1 *Trinity 9*	W1	F 1	M1	W1
W2	F 2	M2	T 2	S 2	T 2	T 2
T 3 *Corpus C.*	S 3	T 3	F 3		W3	F 3
F 4		W4	S 4		T 4	S 4
S 5		T 5		S 3 *Trinity 18*	F 5	
	S 4 *Trinity 5*	F 6		M4	S 6	
	M5	S 7	S 5 *Trinity 14*	T 5		S 5 *Advent 2*
S 6 *Trinity 1*	T 6		M6	W6		M6
M7	W7		T 7	T 7	S 7 *Trinity 23*	T 7
T 8	T 8	S 8 *Trinity 10*	W8	F 8	M8	W8
W9	F 9	M9	T 9	S 9	T 9	T 9
T 10	S 10	T 10	F 10		W10	F 10
F 11		W11	S 11		T 11 *Martin*	S 11
S 12	S 11 *Trinity 6*	T 12		S 10 *Trinity 19*	F 12	
	M12	F 13	S 12 *Trinity 15*	M11	S 13	S 12 *Advent 3*
S 13 *Trinity 2*	T 13	S 14	M13	T 12		M13
M14	W14		T 14 *Exalt. C.*	W13	S 14 *Trinity 24*	T 14
T 15	T 15	S 15 *Trinity 11*	W15 *Ember*	T 14	M15	W15 *Ember*
W16	F 16	M16	T 16	F 15	T 16	T 16
T 17	S 17	T 17	F 17 *Ember*	S 16	W17	F 17 *Ember*
F 18		W18	S 18 *Ember*		T 18	S 18 *Ember*
S 19	S 18 *Trinity 7*	T 19		S 17 *Trinity 20*	F 19	
	M19	F 20	S 19 *Trinity 16*	M18	S 20	S 19 *Advent 4*
S 20 *Trinity 3*	T 20	S 21	M20	T 19		M20
M21	W21		T 21	W20	S 21 *Trinity 25*	T 21
T 22	T 22	S 22 *Trinity 12*	W22	T 21	M22	W22
W23	F 23	M23	T 23	F 22	T 23	T 23
T 24 *Nat. J. Bap.*	S 24	T 24	F 24	S 23	W24	F 24
F 25		W25	S 25		T 25	S 25 *Christmas*
S 26	S 25 *Trinity 8*	T 26		S 24 *Trinity 21*	F 26	
	M26	F 27	S 26 *Trinity 17*	M25	S 27	S 26
S 27 *Trinity 4*	T 27	S 28	M27	T 26		M27
M28	W28		T 28	W27	S 28 *Advent 1*	T 28
T 29	T 29	S 29 *Trinity 13*	W29 *Michael A.*	T 28	M29	W29
W30	F 30	M30	T 30	F 29	T 30	T 30
	S 31	T 31		S 30		F 31
				S 31 *Trinity 22*		

8/15 **Easter Day 5 April**

Dominical letter D for Common Years
Dominical letter ED for Leap Years (*in bold figures*)
Old style years   459, 470, 481, **492**, 543, 554, 565, **576**, 638, 649, **660**, 733, 739, **744**, 823, **828**, 834, 907, 918, 929, 991, 1002, 1013, **1024**, 1075, 1086, 1097, **1108**, 1170, 1181, **1192**, 1265, 1271, **1276**, 1355, **1360**, 1366, 1439, 1450, 1461, 1523, 1534, 1545, **1556**, 1607, 1618, 1629, **1640**, 1702, 1713, **1724**

Leap years						
JANUARY	FEBRUARY	JANUARY	FEBRUARY	MARCH	APRIL	MAY
W1	S 1	T 1	S 1 *Septuag.*	S 1 *Lent 2*	W1	F 1
T 2	F 2	F 2	M2 *Purific. M.*	M2	T 2	S 2
F 3	....	S 3	T 3	T 3	F 3 *Good Fri.*	....
S 4	S 2 *Septuag.*		W4	W4	S 4	S 3 *Easter 4*
	M3	....	T 5	T 5		M4
....	T 4	S 4	F 6	F 6	....	T 5
S 5	W5	M5	S 7	S 7	S 5 *Easter Day*	W6
M6 *Epiphany*	T 6	T 6 *Epiphany*			M6	T 7
T 7	F 7	W7			T 7	F 8
W8	S 8	T 8	S 8 *Sexages.*	S 8 *Lent 3*	W8	S 9
T 9	....	F 9	M9	M9	T 9	....
F 10	S 9 *Sexages.*	S 10	T 10	T 10	F 10	S 10 *Rogation*
S 11	M10	....	W11	W11	S 11	M11
....	T 11	S 11 *Epiph. 1*	T 12	T 12	....	T 12
S 12 *Epiph. 1*	W12	M12	F 13	F 13	S 12 *Quasimodo*	W13
M13 *Hilary*	T 13	T 13 *Hilary*	S 14	S 14	M13	T 14 *Ascension*
T 14	F 14	W14	....	....	T 14	F 15
W15	S 15	T 15	S 15 *Quinquag.*	S 15 *Lent 4*	W15	S 16
T 16	....	F 16	M16	M16	T 16	....
F 17	S 16 *Quinquag.*	S 17	T 17 *Shrove Tu.*	T 17	F 17	S 17 *Ascens. 1*
S 18	M17	....	W18 *Ash Wed.*	W18	S 18	M18
....	T 18 *Shrove Tu.*	S 18 *Epiph. 2*	T 19	T 19	....	T 19
S 19 *Epiph. 2*	W19 *Ash Wed.*	M19	F 20	F 20	S 19 *Easter 2*	W20
M20	T 20	T 20	S 21	S 21	M20	T 21
T 21	F 21	W21	....	....	T 21	F 22
W22	S 22	T 22	S 22 *Quadrag.*	S 22 *Passion*	W22	S 23
T 23	....	F 23	M23	M23	T 23	....
F 24	S 23 *Quadrag.*	S 24	T 24 *Matthias*	T 24	F 24	S 24 *Whit Sun.*
S 25	M24	....	W25 *Ember*	W25 *Annunc.*	S 25	M25
....	T 25 *Matthias*	S 25 *Epiph. 3*	T 26	T 26	....	T 26
S 26 *Epiph. 3*	W26 *Ember*	M26	F 27 *Ember*	F 27	S 26 *Easter 3*	W27 *Ember*
M27	T 27	T 27	S 28 *Ember*	S 28	M27	T 28
T 28	F 28 *Ember*	W28			T 28	F 29 *Ember*
W29	S 29 *Ember*	T 29		....	W29	S 30 *Ember*
T 30		F 30		S 29 *Palm*	T 30	....
F 31		S 31		M30		S 31 *Trinity*
				T 31		

Dominical letter D for Common Years
Dominical letter ED for Leap Years (*in bold figures*)
New style years   1643, 1654, 1665, **1676**, 1711, 1722, 1733, **1744**, 1795, 1801, 1863, 1874, 1885, **1896**, 1931,
1942, 1953, 2015, 2026, 2037, **2048**

JUNE	JULY	AUGUST	SEPTEMBER	OCTOBER	NOVEMBER	DECEMBER
M1	W1	S 1 *Lammas*	T 1	T 1	S 1 *Trinity 22*	T 1
T 2	T 2		W2	F 2	M2	W2
W3	F 3	S 2 *Trinity 9*	T 3	S 3	T 3	T 3
T 4 *Corpus C.*	S 4	M3	F 4		W4	F 4
F 5		T 4	S 5		T 5	S 5
S 6	S 5 *Trinity 5*	W5		S 4 *Trinity 18*	F 6	
	M6	T 6	S 6 *Trinity 14*	M5	S 7	S 6 *Advent 2*
S 7 *Trinity 1*	T 7	F 7	M7	T 6		M7
M8	W8	S 8	T 8	W7	S 8 *Trinity 23*	T 8
T 9	T 9		W9	F 9	M9	W9
W10	F 10	S 9 *Trinity 10*	T 10	S 10	T 10	T 10
T 11	S 11	M10	F 11		W11 *Martin*	F 11
F 12		T 11	S 12	S 11 *Trinity 19*	T 12	S 12
S 13	S 12 *Trinity 6*	W12		M12	F 13	
	M13	T 13	S 13 *Trinity 15*	T 13	S 14	S 13 *Advent 3*
S 14 *Trinity 2*	T 14	F 14	M14 *Exalt. C.*	W14		M14
M15	W15	S 15	T 15	T 15	S 15 *Trinity 24*	T 15
T 16	T 16		W16 *Ember*	F 16	M16	W16 *Ember*
W17	F 17	S 16 *Trinity 11*	T 17	S 17	T 17	T 17
T 18	S 18	M17	F 18 *Ember*		W18	F 18 *Ember*
F 19		T 18	S 19 *Ember*	S 18 *Trinity 20*	T 19	S 19 *Ember*
S 20	S 19 *Trinity 7*	W19		M19	F 20	
	M20	T 20	S 20 *Trinity 16*	T 20	S 21	S 20 *Advent 4*
S 21 *Trinity 3*	T 21	F 21	M21	W21		M21
M22	W22	S 22	T 22	T 22	S 22 *Trinity 25*	T 22
T 23	T 23		W23	F 23	M23	W23
W24 *Nat. J. Bap.*	F 24	S 23 *Trinity 12*	T 24	S 24	T 24	T 24
T 25	S 25	M24	F 25		W25	F 25 *Christmas*
F 26		T 25	S 26	S 25 *Trinity 21*	T 26	S 26
S 27	S 26 *Trinity 8*	W26		M26	F 27	
	M27	T 27	S 27 *Trinity 17*	T 27	S 28	S 27
S 28 *Trinity 4*	T 28	F 28	M28	W28		M28
M29	W29	S 29	T 29 *Michael A.*	T 29	S 29 *Advent 1*	T 29
T 30	T 30		W30	F 30	M30	W30
	F 31	S 30 *Trinity 13*		S 31		T 31
		M31				

8/16 Easter Day 6 April

Dominical letter E for Common Years
Dominical letter FE for Leap Years (*in bold figures*)
Old style years 402, 413, **424**, 475, 486, 497, **508**, 570, 581, **592**, 665, 671, **676**, 755, **760**, 766, 839, 850, 861, 923, 934, 945, **956**, 1007, 1018, 1029, **1040**, 1102, 1113, **1124**, 1197, 1203, **1208**, 1287, **1292**, 1298, 1371, 1382, 1393, 1455, 1466, 1477, **1488**, 1539, 1550, 1561, **1572**, 1634, 1645, **1656**, 1729, 1735, **1740**

Leap years

JANUARY
T 1 · W2 · T 3 · F 4 · S 5
S 6 *Epiphany* · M7 · T 8 · W9 · T 10 · F 11 · S 12
S 13 *Epiph. 1* · M14 · T 15 · W16 · T 17 · F 18 · S 19
S 20 *Epiph. 2* · M21 · T 22 · W23 · T 24 · F 25 · S 26
S 27 *Epiph. 3* · M28 · T 29 · W30 · T 31

FEBRUARY
F 1 · S 2 *Purific. M.*
S 3 *Septuag.* · M4 · T 5 · W6 · T 7 · F 8 · S 9
S 10 *Sexages.* · M11 · T 12 · W13 · T 14 · F 15 · S 16
S 17 *Quinquag.* · M18 · T 19 *Shrove Tu.* · W20 *Ash Wed.* · T 21 · F 22 · S 23
S 24 *Quadrag.* · M25 *Matthias* · T 26 · W27 *Ember* · T 28 · F 29 *Ember*

(Common years)

JANUARY
W1 · T 2 · F 3 · S 4
S 5 · M6 *Epiphany* · T 7 · W8 · T 9 · F 10 · S 11
S 12 *Epiph. 1* · M13 *Hilary* · T 14 · W15 · T 16 · F 17 · S 18
S 19 *Epiph. 2* · M20 · T 21 · W22 · T 23 · F 24 · S 25
S 26 *Epiph. 3* · M27 · T 28 · W29 · T 30 · F 31

FEBRUARY
S 1
S 2 *Septuag.* · M3 · T 4 · W5 · T 6 · F 7 · S 8
S 9 *Sexages.* · M10 · T 11 · W12 · T 13 · F 14 · S 15
S 16 *Quinquag.* · M17 · T 18 *Shrove Tu.* · W19 *Ash Wed.* · T 20 · F 21 · S 22
S 23 *Quadrag.* · M24 *Matthias* · T 25 · W26 *Ember* · T 27 · F 28 *Ember*

MARCH
S 1 *Ember*
S 2 *Lent 2* · M3 · T 4 · W5 · T 6 · F 7 · S 8
S 9 *Lent 3* · M10 · T 11 · W12 · T 13 · F 14 · S 15
S 16 *Lent 4* · M17 · T 18 · W19 · T 20 · F 21 · S 22
S 23 *Passion* · M24 · T 25 *Annunc.* · W26 · T 27 · F 28 · S 29
S 30 *Palm* · M31

APRIL
T 1 · W2 · T 3 · F 4 *Good Fri.* · S 5
S 6 ***Easter Day*** · M7 · T 8 · W9 · T 10 · F 11 · S 12
S 13 *Quasimodo* · M14 · T 15 · W16 · T 17 · F 18 · S 19
S 20 *Easter 2* · M21 · T 22 · W23 · T 24 · F 25 · S 26
S 27 *Easter 3* · M28 · T 29 · W30

MAY
T 1 · F 2 · S 3
S 4 *Easter 4* · M5 · T 6 · W7 · T 8 · F 9 · S 10
S 11 *Rogation* · M12 · T 13 · W14 · T 15 *Ascension* · F 16 · S 17
S 18 *Ascens. 1* · M19 · T 20 · W21 · T 22 · F 23 · S 24
S 25 *Whit Sun.* · M26 · T 27 · W28 *Ember* · T 29 · F 30 *Ember* · S 31 *Ember*

Easter Day 6 April

Dominical letter E for Common Years
Dominical letter FE for Leap Years (*in bold figures*)

New style years   1586, 1597, **1608**, 1670, 1681, **1692**, 1738, 1749, **1760**, 1806, 1817, **1828**, 1890, 1947, 1958, 1969, **1980**, 2042, 2053, **2064**

JUNE	JULY	AUGUST	SEPTEMBER	OCTOBER	NOVEMBER	DECEMBER
S 1 *Trinity*	T 1	F 1 *Lammas*	M1	W1	S 1	M1
M2	W2	S 2	T 2	T 2		T 2
T 3	T 3		W3	F 3	S 2 *Trinity 22*	W3
W4	F 4	S 3 *Trinity 9*	T 4	S 4	M3	T 4
T 5 *Corpus C.*	S 5	M4	F 5		T 4	F 5
F 6		T 5	S 6	S 5 *Trinity 18*	W5	S 6
S 7	S 6 *Trinity 5*	W6		M6	T 6	
	M7	T 7	S 7 *Trinity 14*	T 7	F 7	S 7 *Advent 2*
S 8 *Trinity 1*	T 8	F 8	M8	W8	S 8	M8
M9	W9	S 9	T 9	T 9		T 9
T 10	T 10		W10	F 10	S 9 *Trinity 23*	W10
W11	F 11	S 10 *Trinity 10*	T 11	S 11	M10	T 11
T 12	S 12	M11	F 12		T 11 *Martin*	F 12
F 13		T 12	S 13	S 12 *Trinity 19*	W12	S 13
S 14	S 13 *Trinity 6*	W13		M13	T 13	
	M14	T 14	S 14 *Trinity 15*	T 14	F 14	S 14 *Advent 3*
S 15 *Trinity 2*	T 15	F 15	M15	W15	S 15	M15
M16	W16	S 16	T 16	T 16		T 16
T 17	T 17		W17 *Ember*	F 17	S 16 *Trinity 24*	W17 *Ember*
W18	F 18	S 17 *Trinity 11*	T 18	S 18	M17	T 18
T 19	S 19	M18	F 19 *Ember*		T 18	F 19 *Ember*
F 20		T 19	S 20 *Ember*	S 19 *Trinity 20*	W19	S 20 *Ember*
S 21	S 20 *Trinity 7*	W20		M20	T 20	
	M21	T 21	S 21 *Trinity 16*	T 21	F 21	S 21 *Advent 4*
S 22 *Trinity 3*	T 22	F 22	M22	W22	S 22	M22
M23	W23	S 23	T 23	T 23		T 23
T 24 *Nat. J. Bap.*	T 24		W24	F 24	S 23 *Trinity 25*	W24
W25	F 25	S 24 *Trinity 12*	T 25	S 25	M24	T 25 *Christmas*
T 26	S 26	M25	F 26		T 25	F 26
F 27		T 26	S 27	S 26 *Trinity 21*	W26	S 27
S 28	S 27 *Trinity 8*	W27		M27	T 27	
	M28	T 28	S 28 *Trinity 17*	T 28	F 28	S 28
S 29 *Trinity 4*	T 29	F 29	M29 *Michael A.*	W29	S 29	M29
M30	W30	S 30	T 30	T 30		T 30
	T 31			F 31	S 30 *Advent 1*	W31
		S 31 *Trinity 13*				

8/17 Easter Day 7 April

Dominical letter F for Common Years
Dominical letter GF for Leap Years (*in bold figures*)
Old style years   418, 429, **440**, 513, **524**, 603, **608**, 687, 698, 771, 782, 793, 855, 866, 877, **888**, 950, 961, **972**, 1045, **1056**, 1135, **1140**, 1219, 1230, 1303, 1314, 1325, 1387, 1398, 1409, **1420**, 1482, 1493, **1504**, 1577, **1588**, 1667, **1672**, 1751

JANUARY	FEBRUARY	JANUARY	FEBRUARY	MARCH	APRIL	MAY
M 1	T 1	T 1	F 1	F 1 Ember	M 1	W 1
T 2	F 2 Purific. M.	W 2	S 2 Purific. M.	S 2 Ember	T 2	T 2
W 3	S 3	T 3			W 3	F 3
T 4		F 4			T 4	S 4
F 5	S 4 Septuag.	S 5	S 3 Septuag.	S 3 Lent 2	F 5 Good Fri.	
S 6 Epiphany	M 5		M 4	M 4	S 6	S 5 Easter 4
	T 6	S 6 Epiphany	T 5	T 5		M 6
S 7 Epiph. 1	W 7	M 7	W 6	W 6		T 7
M 8	T 8	T 8	T 7	T 7	S 7 *Easter Day*	W 8
T 9	F 9	W 9	F 8	F 8	M 8	T 9
W 10	S 10	T 10	S 9	S 9	T 9	F 10
T 11		F 11			W 10	S 11
F 12		S 12	S 10 Sexages.	S 10 Lent 3	T 11	
S 13 Hilary	S 11 Sexages.		M 11	M 11	F 12	
	M 12		T 12	T 12	S 13	S 12 Rogation
	T 13	S 13 Epiph. 1	W 13	W 13		M 13
S 14 Epiph. 2	W 14	M 14	T 14	T 14	S 14 Quasimodo	T 14
M 15	T 15	T 15	F 15	F 15	M 15	W 15
T 16	F 16	W 16	S 16	S 16	T 16	T 16 Ascension
W 17	S 17	T 17			W 17	F 17
T 18		F 18			T 18	S 18
F 19		S 19	S 17 Quinquag.	S 17 Lent 4	F 19	
S 20	S 18 Quinquag.		M 18	M 18	S 20	
	M 19		T 19 Shrove Tu.	T 19		S 19 Ascens. 1
	T 20 Shrove Tu.	S 20 Epiph. 2	W 20 Ash Wed.	W 20		M 20
S 21 Epiph. 3	W 21 Ash Wed.	M 21	T 21	T 21	S 21 Easter 2	T 21
M 22	T 22	T 22	F 22	F 22	M 22	W 22
T 23	F 23	W 23	S 23	S 23	T 23	T 23
W 24	S 24	T 24			W 24	F 24
T 25		F 25			T 25	S 25
F 26		S 26	S 24 Quadrag.	S 24 Passion	F 26	
S 27	S 25 Quadrag.		M 25	M 25 Annunc.	S 27	
	M 26		T 26	T 26		S 26 Whit Sun.
	T 27	S 27 Epiph. 3	W 27 Ember	W 27		M 27
S 28 Epiph. 4	W 28 Ember	M 28	T 28	T 28	S 28 Easter 3	T 28
M 29	T 29	T 29		F 29	M 29	W 29 Ember
T 30		W 30		S 30	T 30	T 30
W 31		T 31				F 31 Ember
				S 31 Palm		

Easter Day 7 April 8/17

Dominical letter F for Common Years
Dominical letter GF for Leap Years (*in bold figures*)
New style years 1602, 1613, **1624**, 1697, 1765, **1776**, 1822, 1833, **1844**, 1901, **1912**, 1985, **1996**, 2075, **2080**

JUNE	JULY	AUGUST	SEPTEMBER	OCTOBER	NOVEMBER	DECEMBER
S 1 *Ember*	M1	T 1 *Lammas*	S 1 *Trinity 13*	T 1	F 1	S 1 *Advent 1*
	T 2	F 2	M2	W2	S 2	M2
S 2 *Trinity*	W3	S 3	T 3	T 3		T 3
M3	T 4		W4	F 4	S 3 *Trinity 22*	W4
T 4	F 5	S 4 *Trinity 9*	T 5	S 5	M4	T 5
W5	S 6	M5	F 6		T 5	F 6
T 6 *Corpus C.*		T 6	S 7	S 6 *Trinity 18*	W6	S 7
F 7	S 7 *Trinity 5*	W7		M7	T 7	
S 8	M8	T 8	S 8 *Trinity 14*	T 8	F 8	S 8 *Advent 2*
	T 9	F 9	M9	W9	S 9	M9
S 9 *Trinity 1*	W10	S 10	T 10	T 10		T 10
M10	T 11		W11	F 11	S 10 *Trinity 23*	W11
T 11	F 12	S 11 *Trinity 10*	T 12	S 12	M11 *Martin*	T 12
W12	S 13	M12	F 13		T 12	F 13
T 13		T 13	S 14 *Exalt. C.*	S 13 *Trinity 19*	W13	S 14
F 14	S 14 *Trinity 6*	W14		M14	T 14	
S 15	M15	T 15	S 15 *Trinity 15*	T 15	F 15	S 15 *Advent 3*
	T 16	F 16	M16	W16	S 16	M16
S 16 *Trinity 2*	W17	S 17	T 17	T 17		T 17
M17	T 18		W18 *Ember*	F 18	S 17 *Trinity 24*	W18 *Ember*
T 18	F 19	S 18 *Trinity 11*	T 19	S 19	M18	T 19
W19	S 20	M19	F 20 *Ember*		T 19	F 20 *Ember*
T 20		T 20	S 21 *Ember*	S 20 *Trinity 20*	W20	S 21 *Ember*
F 21	S 21 *Trinity 7*	W21		M21	T 21	
S 22	M22	T 22	S 22 *Trinity 16*	T 22	F 22	S 22 *Advent 4*
	T 23	F 23	M23	W23	S 23	M23
S 23 *Trinity 3*	W24	S 24	T 24	T 24		T 24
M24 *Nat. J. Bap.*	T 25		W25	F 25	S 24 *Trinity 25*	W25 *Christmas*
T 25	F 26	S 25 *Trinity 12*	T 26	S 26	M25	T 26
W26	S 27	M26	F 27		T 26	F 27
T 27		T 27	S 28	S 27 *Trinity 21*	W27	S 28
F 28	S 28 *Trinity 8*	W28		M28	T 28	
S 29	M29	T 29	S 29 *Trinity 17*	T 29	F 29	S 29
	T 30	F 30	M30	W30	S 30	M30
S 30 *Trinity 4*	W31	S 31		T 31		T 31

8/18 Easter Day 8 April

Dominical letter G for Common Years
Dominical letter AG for Leap Years (*in bold figures*)
Old style years   445, 451, **456**, 535, **540**, 546, 619, 630, 641, 703, 714, 725, **736**, 787, 798, 809, **820**, 882, 893, **904**, 977, 983, **988**, 1067, **1072**, 1078, 1151, 1162, 1173, 1235, 1246, 1257, **1268**, 1319, 1330, 1341, **1352**, 1414, 1425, **1436**, 1509, 1515, **1520**, 1599, **1604**, 1610, 1683, 1694, 1705

Leap years						
JANUARY	FEBRUARY	JANUARY	FEBRUARY	MARCH	APRIL	MAY
S 1	W1	M1	T 1	T 1	S 1 *Palm*	T 1
M2	T 2 *Purific. M.*	T 2	F 2 *Purific. M.*	F 2 *Ember*	M2	W2
T 3	F 3	W3	S 3	S 3 *Ember*	T 3	T 3
W4	S 4	T 4			W4	F 4
T 5		F 5	S 4 *Septuag.*	S 4 *Lent 2*	T 5	S 5
F 6 *Epiphany*	S 5 *Septuag.*	s 6 *Epiphany*	M5	M5	F 6 *Good Fri.*	
S 7	M6		T 6	T 6	S 7	S 6 *Easter 4*
	T 7	S 7 *Epiph. 1*	W7	W7		M7
S 8 *Epiph. 1*	W8	M8	T 8	T 8	S 8 ***Easter Day***	T 8
M9	T 9	T 9	F 9	F 9	M9	W9
T 10	F 10	W10	S 10	S 10	T 10	T 10
W11	S 11	T 11			W11	W11
T 12		F 12	S 11 *Sexages.*	S 11 *Lent 3*	T 12	F 11
F 13 *Hilary*	S 12 *Sexages.*	s 13 *Hilary*	M12	M12	F 13	S 12
S 14	M13		T 13	T 13	S 14	
	T 14	S 14 *Epiph. 2*	W14	W14		S 13 *Rogation*
S 15 *Epiph. 2*	W15	M15	T 15	T 15	S 15 *Quasimodo*	M14
M16	T 16	T 16	F 16	F 16	M16	T 15
T 17	F 17	W17	S 17	S 17	T 17	W16
W18	S 18	T 18			W18	T 17 *Ascension*
T 19		F 19	S 18 *Quinquag.*	S 18 *Lent 4*	T 19	F 18
F 20	S 19 *Quinquag.*	S 20	M19	M19	F 20	S 19
S 21	M20		T 20 *Shrove Tu.*	T 20	S 21	
	T 21 *Shrove Tu.*	S 21 *Epiph. 3*	W21 *Ash Wed.*	W21		S 20 *Ascens. 1*
S 22 *Epiph. 3*	W22 *Ash Wed.*	M22	T 22	T 22	S 22 *Easter 2*	M21
M23	T 23	T 23	F 23	F 23	M23	T 22
T 24	F 24	W24	s 24 *Matthias*	S 24	T 24	W23
W25	s 25 *Matthias*	T 25			W25	T 24
T 26		F 26			T 26	F 25
F 27	S 26 *Quadrag.*	S 27	S 25 *Quadrag.*	S 25 *Passion*	F 27	S 26
S 28	M27		M26	M26	S 28	
	T 28	S 28 *Epiph. 4*	T 27	T 27		S 27 *Whit Sun.*
S 29 *Epiph. 4*	W29 *Ember*	M29	W28 *Ember*	W28	S 29 *Easter 3*	M28
M30		T 30		T 29	M30	T 29
T 31		W31		F 30		W30 *Ember*
				S 31		T 31

Easter Day 8 April 8/18

Dominical letter F for Common Years
Dominical letter GF for Leap Years (*in bold figures*)
New style years   1635, **1640**, 1703, **1708**, 1787, **1792**, 1798, 1849, 1855, **1860**, 1917, **1928**, 2007, **2021**, 2091

JUNE	JULY	AUGUST	SEPTEMBER	OCTOBER	NOVEMBER	DECEMBER
F 1 *Ember*	S 1 *Trinity 4*	W1 *Lammas*	S 1	M1	T 1	S 1
s 2 *Ember*	M2	T 2		T 2	F 2	
	T 3	F 3	S 2 *Trinity 13*	W3	S 3	S 2 *Advent 1*
S 3 *Trinity*	W4	S 4	M3	T 4		M3
M4	T 5		T 4	F 5	S 4 *Trinity 22*	T 4
T 5	F 6	S 5 *Trinity 9*	W5	s 6	M5	W5
W6	S 7	M6	T 6		T 6	T 6
T 7 *Corpus C.*		T 7	F 7	S 7 *Trinity 18*	W7	F 7
F 8	S 8 *Trinity 5*	W8	s 8	M8	T 8	s 8
S 9	M9	T 9		T 9	F 9	
	T 10	F 10	S 9 *Trinity 14*	W10	S 10	S 9 *Advent 2*
S 10 *Trinity 1*	W11	S 11	M10	T 11		M10
M11	T 12		T 11	F 12	S 11 *Trinity 23*	T 11
T 12	F 13	S 12 *Trinity 10*	W12	S 13	M12	W12
W13	S 14	M13	T 13		T 13	T 13
T 14		T 14	F 14 *Exalt. C.*	S 14 *Trinity 19*	W14	F 14
F 15	S 15 *Trinity 6*	W15	S 15	M15	T 15	S 15
s 16	M16	T 16		T 16	F 16	
	T 17	F 17	S 16 *Trinity 15*	W17	S 17	S 16 *Advent 3*
S 17 *Trinity 2*	W18	S 18	M17	T 18		M17
M18	T 19		T 18	F 19	S 18 *Trinity 24*	T 18
T 19	F 20	S 19 *Trinity 11*	W19 *Ember*	S 20	M19	W19 *Ember*
W20	S 21	M20	T 20		T 20	T 20
T 21		T 21	F 21 *Ember*	S 21 *Trinity 20*	W21	F 21 *Ember*
F 22	S 22 *Trinity 7*	W22	s 22 *Ember*	M22	T 22	s 22 *Ember*
S 23	M23	T 23		T 23	F 23	
	T 24	F 24	S 23 *Trinity 16*	W24	S 24	S 23 *Advent 4*
S 24 *Trinity 3*	W25	S 25	M24	T 25		M24
M25	T 26		T 25	F 26	S 25 *Trinity 25*	T 25 *Christmas*
T 26	F 27	S 26 *Trinity 12*	W26	S 27	M26	W26
W27	S 28	M27	T 27		T 27	T 27
T 28		T 28	F 28	S 28 *Trinity 21*	W28	F 28
F 29	S 29 *Trinity 8*	W29	s 29 *Michael A.*	M29	T 29	S 29
S 30	M30	T 30		T 30	F 30	
	T 31	F 31	S 30 *Trinity 17*	W31		S 30
						M31

191

8/19 Easter Day 9 April

Dominical letter A for Common Years
Dominical letter BA for Leap Years (*in bold figures*)
Old style years   467, 478, 551, 562, 573, 635, 646, 657, **668**, 730, 741, **752**, 825, **836**, 915, **920**, 999, 1010, 1083, 1094, 1105, 1167, 1178, 1189, **1200**, 1262, 1273, **1284**, 1357, **1368**, 1447, **1452**, 1531, 1542, 1615, 1626, 1637, 1699, 1710, 1721, **1732**

		Leap years				
JANUARY	FEBRUARY	JANUARY	FEBRUARY	MARCH	APRIL	MAY
S 1	T 1	S 1	W1	W1 *Ember*	S 1	M1
S 2	W2 *Purific. M.*	M2	T 2 *Purific. M.*	T 2	S 2 *Palm*	T 2
M3	T 3	T 3	F 3	F 3 *Ember*	M3	W3
T 4	F 4	W4	s 4	s 4 *Ember*	T 4	T 4
W5	S 5	T 5	S 5 *Septuag.*	S 5 *Lent 2*	W5	F 5
T 6 *Epiphany*	S 6 *Septuag.*	F 6 *Epiphany*	M6	M6	T 6	s 6
F 7	M7	S 7	T 7	T 7	F 7 *Good Fri.*	S 7 *Easter 4*
s 8	T 8	S 8 *Eph. 1*	W8	W8	s 8	M8
S 9 *Epiph. 1*	W9	M9	T 9	T 9	S 9 ***Easter Day***	T 9
M10	T 10	T 10	F 10	F 10	M10	W10
T 11	F 11	W11	S 11	S 11	T 11	T 11
W12	S 12	T 12	S 12 *Sexages.*	S 12 *Lent 3*	W12	F 12
T 13 *Hilary*	S 13 *Sexages.*	F 13 *Hilary*	M13	M13	T 13	S 13
F 14	M14	S 14	T 14	T 14	F 14	S 14 *Rogation*
S 15	T 15	S 15 *Epiph. 2*	W15	W15	S 15	M15
S 16 *Epiph. 2*	W16	M16	T 16	T 16	S 16 *Quasimodo*	T 16
M17	T 17	T 17	F 17	F 17	M17	W17
T 18	F 18	W18	s 18	s 18	T 18	T 18 *Ascension*
W19	S 19	T 19	S 19 *Quinquag.*	S 19 *Lent 4*	W19	F 19
T 20	S 20 *Quinquag.*	F 20	M20	M20	T 20	S 20
F 21	M21	S 21	T 21 *Shrove Tu.*	T 21	F 21	S 21 *Ascens. 1*
S 22	T 22 *Shrove Tu.*	S 22 *Epiph. 3*	W22 *Ash Wed.*	W22	S 22	M22
S 23 *Epiph. 3*	W23 *Ash Wed.*	M23	T 23	T 23	S 23 *Easter 2*	T 23
M24	T 24	T 24	F 24 *Matthias*	F 24	M24	W24
T 25	F 25 *Matthias*	W25	S 25	S 25 *Annunc.*	T 25	T 25
W26	S 26	T 26	S 26 *Quadrag.*	S 26 *Passion*	W26	F 26
T 27	S 27 *Quadrag.*	F 27	M27	M27	T 27	S 27
F 28	M28	S 28	T 28	T 28	F 28	S 28 *Whit Sun.*
S 29	T 29	S 29 *Epiph. 4*		W29	S 29	M29
S 30 *Epiph. 4*		M30		T 30	S 30 *Easter 3*	T 30
M31		T 31		F 31		W31 *Ember*

Dominical letter A for Common Years
Dominical letter BA for Leap Years (*in bold figures*)
New style years   1651, 1662, 1719, **1724** (German Protestant Style), 1730, 1871, 1882, 1939, **1944**, 1950,
2023, 2034, 2045

JUNE	JULY	AUGUST	SEPTEMBER	OCTOBER	NOVEMBER	DECEMBER
T 1	S 1	T 1 *Lammas*	F 1	S 1 *Trinity 17*	W1	F 1
F 2 *Ember*		W2	S 2	M2	T 2	S 2
s 3 *Ember*	S 2 *Trinity 4*	T 3		T 3	F 3	
	M3	F 4	S 3 *Trinity 13*	W4	S 4	S 3 *Advent 1*
S 4 *Trinity*	T 4	S 5	M4	T 5		M4
M5	W5		T 5	F 6	S 5 *Trinity 22*	T 5
T 6	T 6	S 6 *Trinity 9*	w6	S 7	M6	w6
W7	F 7	M7	T 7		T 7	T 7
T 8 *Corpus C.*	s 8	T 8	F 8	S 8 *Trinity 18*	W8	F 8
F 9		W9	S 9	M9	T 9	S 9
S 10	S 9 *Trinity 5*	T 10		T 10	F 10	
	M10	F 11	S 10 *Trinity 14*	W11	s 11 *Martin*	S 10 *Advent 2*
S 11 *Trinity 1*	T 11	S 12	M11	T 12		M11
M12	W12		T 12	F 13	S 12 *Trinity 23*	T 12
T 13	T 13	S 13 *Trinity 10*	W13	S 14	M13	W13
W14	F 14	M14	T 14 *Exalt. C.*		T 14	T 14
T 15	S 15	T 15	F 15	S 15 *Trinity 19*	W15	F 15
F 16		W16	S 16	M16	T 16	S 16
S 17	S 16 *Trinity 6*	T 17		T 17	F 17	
	M17	F 18	S 17 *Trinity 15*	W18	S 18	S 17 *Advent 3*
S 18 *Trinity 2*	T 18	S 19	M18	T 19		M18
M19	W19		T 19	F 20	S 19 *Trinity 24*	T 19
T 20	T 20	S 20 *Trinity 11*	w20 *Ember*	S 21	M20	w20 *Ember*
W21	F 21	M21	T 21		T 21	T 21
T 22	S 22	T 22	F 22 *Ember*	S 22 *Trinity 20*	W22	F 22 *Ember*
F 23		W23	s 23 *Ember*	M23	T 23	s 23 *Ember*
s 24 *Nat. J. Bap.*	S 23 *Trinity 7*	T 24		T 24	F 24	
	M24	F 25	S 24 *Trinity 16*	W25	S 25	S 24 *Advent 4*
S 25 *Trinity 3*	T 25	s 26	M25	T 26		M25 *Christmas*
M26	W26		T 26	F 27	S 26 *Trinity 25*	T 26
T 27	T 27	S 27 *Trinity 12*	W27	s 28	M27	W27
W28	F 28	M28	T 28		T 28	T 28
T 29	S 29	T 29	F 29 *Michael A.*	S 29 *Trinity 21*	W29	F 29
F 30		W30	s 30	M30	T 30	s 30
	S 30 *Trinity 8*	T 31		T 31		
	M31					S 31

8/20 **Easter Day 10 April**

Dominical letter B for Common Years
Dominical letter CB for Leap Years (*in bold figures*)
Old style years   410, 483, 494, 505, 567, 578, 589, **600**, 662, 673, **684**, 757, **768**, 847, **852**, 931, 942, 1015, 1026, 1037, 1099, 1110, 1121, **1132**, 1194, 1205, **1216**, 1289, **1300**, 1379, **1384**, 1463, 1474, 1547, 1558, 1569, 1631, 1642, 1653, **1664**, 1726, 1737, **1748**

Leap years						
JANUARY	FEBRUARY	JANUARY	FEBRUARY	MARCH	APRIL	MAY
F 1	M1	S 1	T 1	T 1	F 1	S 1 *Easter 3*
S 2	T 2 *Purific. M.*		W2 *Purific. M.*	W2 *Ember*	S 2	M2
	W3	S 2	T 3	T 3		T 3
S 3	T 4	M3	F 4	F 4 *Ember*	S 3 *Palm*	W4
M4	F 5	T 4	S 5	S 5 *Ember*	M4	T 5
T 5	S 6	W5			T 5	F 6
W6 *Epiphany*		T 6 *Epiphany*	S 6 *Septuag.*	S 6 *Lent 2*	W6	S 7
T 7	S 7 *Septuag.*	F 7	M7	M7	T 7	
F 8	M8	S 8	T 8	T 8	F 8 *Good Fri.*	S 8 *Easter 4*
S 9	T 9		W9	W9	S 9	M9
	W10	S 9 *Epiph. 1*	T 10	T 10		T 10
S 10 *Epiph. 1*	T 11	M10	F 11	F 11	S 10 *Easter Day*	W11
M11	F 12	T 11	S 12	S 12	M11	T 12
T 12	S 13	W12			T 12	F 13
W13 *Hilary*		T 13 *Hilary*	S 13 *Sexages.*	S 13 *Lent 3*	W13	S 14
T 14	S 14 *Sexages.*	F 14	M14	M14	T 14	
F 15	M15	S 15	T 15	T 15	F 15	S 15 *Rogation*
S 16	T 16		W16	W16	S 16	M16
	W17	S 16 *Epiph. 2*	T 17	T 17		T 17
S 17 *Epiph. 2*	T 18	M17	F 18	F 18	S 17 *Quasimodo*	W18
M18	F 19	T 18	S 19	S 19	M18	T 19 *Ascension*
T 19	S 20	W19			T 19	F 20
W20		T 20	S 20 *Quinquag.*	S 20 *Lent 4*	W20	S 21
T 21	S 21 *Quinquag.*	F 21	M21	M21	T 21	
F 22	M22	S 22	T 22 *Shrove Tu.*	T 22	F 22	S 22 *Ascens. 1*
S 23	T 23 *Shrove Tu.*		W23 *Ash Wed.*	W23	S 23	M23
	W24 *Ash Wed.*	S 23 *Epiph. 3*	T 24 *Matthias*	T 24		T 24
S 24 *Epiph. 3*	T 25 *Matthias*	M24	F 25	F 25 *Annunc.*	S 24 *Easter 2*	W25
M25	F 26	T 25	S 26	S 26	M25	T 26
T 26	S 27	W26			T 26	F 27
W27		T 27	S 27 *Quadrag.*	S 27 *Passion*	W27	S 28
T 28	S 28 *Quadrag.*	F 28	M28	M28	T 28	
F 29	M29	S 29		T 29	F 29	S 29 *Whit Sun.*
S 30				W30	S 30	M30
		S 30 *Epiph. 4*		T 31		T 31
S 31 *Epiph. 4*		M31				

Dominical letter B for Common Years
Dominical letter CB for Leap Years (*in bold figures*)
New style years   1583, 1594, 1605, 1667, 1678, 1689, 1735, 1746, 1757, 1803, 1814, 1887, 1898, 1955, 1966, 1977, 2039, 2050, 2061, **2072**

JUNE	JULY	AUGUST	SEPTEMBER	OCTOBER	NOVEMBER	DECEMBER
W 1 *Ember*	F 1	M 1 *Lammas*	T 1	S 1	T 1	T 1
T 2	S 2	T 2	F 2		W 2	F 2
F 3 *Ember*		W 3	S 3	....	T 3	S 3
S 4 *Ember*	....	T 4		S 2 *Trinity 17*	F 4	
	S 3 *Trinity 4*	F 5	....	M 3	S 5	....
....	M 4	S 6	S 4 *Trinity 13*	T 4		S 4 *Advent 2*
S 5 *Trinity*	T 5		M 5	W 5	....	M 5
M 6	W 6	....	T 6	T 6	S 6 *Trinity 22*	T 6
T 7	T 7	S 7 *Trinity 9*	W 7	F 7	M 7	W 7
W 8	F 8	M 8	T 8	S 8	T 8	T 8
T 9 *Corpus C.*	S 9	T 9	F 9		W 9	F 9
F 10		W 10	S 10	....	T 10	S 10
S 11	....	T 11		S 9 *Trinity 18*	F 11 *Martin*	
	S 10 *Trinity 5*	F 12	....	M 10	S 12	....
....	M 11	S 13	S 11 *Trinity 14*	T 11		S 11 *Advent 3*
S 12 *Trinity 1*	T 12		M 12	W 12	....	M 12
M 13	W 13	....	T 13	T 13	S 13 *Trinity 23*	T 13
T 14	T 14	S 14 *Trinity 10*	W 14 *Exalt. C.*	F 14	M 14	W 14 *Ember*
W 15	F 15	M 15	T 15	S 15	T 15	T 15
T 16	S 16	T 16	F 16		W 16	F 16 *Ember*
F 17		W 17	S 17	....	T 17	S 17 *Ember*
S 18	....	T 18		S 16 *Trinity 19*	F 18	
	S 17 *Trinity 6*	F 19	....	M 17	S 19	....
....	M 18	S 20	S 18 *Trinity 15*	T 18		S 18 *Advent 4*
S 19 *Trinity 2*	T 19		M 19	W 19	....	M 19
M 20	W 20	....	T 20	T 20	S 20 *Trinity 24*	T 20
T 21	T 21	S 21 *Trinity 11*	W 21 *Ember*	F 21	M 21	W 21
W 22	F 22	M 22	T 22	S 22	T 22	T 22
T 23	S 23	T 23	F 23 *Ember*		W 23	F 23
F 24 *Nat. J. Bap.*		W 24	S 24 *Ember*	....	T 24	S 24
S 25	....	T 25		S 23 *Trinity 20*	F 25	
	S 24 *Trinity 7*	F 26	....	M 24	S 26	....
....	M 25	S 27	S 25 *Trinity 16*	T 25		S 25 *Christmas*
S 26 *Trinity 3*	T 26		M 26	W 26	....	M 26
M 27	W 27	....	T 27	T 27	S 27 *Advent 1*	T 27
T 28	T 28	S 28 *Trinity 12*	W 28	F 28	M 28	W 28
W 29	F 29	M 29	T 29 *Michael A.*	S 29	T 29	T 29
T 30	S 30	T 30	F 30		W 30	F 30
		W 31		....		S 31
	....			S 30 *Trinity 21*		
	S 31 *Trinity 8*			M 31		

8/21 **Easter Day 11 April**

Dominical letter C for Common Years
Dominical letter DC for Leap Years (*in bold figures*)

Old style years 415, 426, 437, **448**, 499, 510, 521, **532**, 594, 605, **616**, 689, 695, **700**, 779, **784**, 790, 863, 874, 885, 947, 958, 969, **980**, 1031, 1042, 1053, **1064**, 1126, 1137, **1148**, 1221, 1227, **1232**, 1311, **1316**, 1322, 1395, 1406, 1417, 1479, 1490, 1501, **1512**, 1563, 1574, 1585, **1596**, 1658, 1669, **1680**

Leap years						
JANUARY	FEBRUARY	JANUARY	FEBRUARY	MARCH	APRIL	MAY
T 1	S 1 *Epiph. 4*	F 1	M1	M1	T 1	S 1
F 2	M2 *Purific. M.*	S 2	T 2 *Purific. M.*	T 2	F 2	
S 3	T 3		W3	W3 *Ember*	S 3	S 2 *Easter 3*
	W4	S 3	T 4	T 4		M3
S 4	T 5	M4	F 5	F 5 *Ember*	S 4 *Palm*	T 4
M5	F 6	T 5	S 6	S 6 *Ember*	M5	W5
T 6 *Epiphany*	S 7	w6 *Epiphany*			T 6	T 6
W7		T 7	S 7 *Septuag.*	S 7 *Lent 2*	W7	F 7
T 8	S 8 *Septuag.*	F 8	M8	M8	T 8	s 8
F 9	M9	S 9	T 9	T 9	F 9 *Good Fri.*	
S 10	T 10		W10	W10	S 10	S 9 *Easter 4*
	W11	S 10 *Epiph. 1*	T 11	T 11		M10
S 11 *Epiph. 1*	T 12	M11	F 12	F 12	S 11 **Easter Day**	T 11
M12	F 13	T 12	S 13	S 13	M12	W12
T 13 *Hilary*	S 14	W13 *Hilary*			T 13	T 13
W14		T 14	S 14 *Sexages.*	S 14 *Lent 3*	W14	F 14
T 15	S 15 *Sexages.*	F 15	M15	M15	T 15	S 15
F 16	M16	S 16	T 16	T 16	F 16	
S 17	T 17		W17	W17	S 17	S 16 *Rogation*
	W18	S 17 *Epiph. 2*	T 18	T 18		M17
S 18 *Epiph. 2*	T 19	M18	F 19	F 19	S 18 *Quasimodo*	T 18
M19	F 20	T 19	S 20	S 20	M19	W19
T 20	S 21	W20			T 20	T 20 *Ascension*
W21		T 21	S 21 *Quinquag.*	S 21 *Lent 4*	W21	F 21
T 22	S 22 *Quinquag.*	F 22	M22	M22	T 22	S 22
F 23	M23	S 23	T 23 *Shrove Tu.*	T 23	F 23	
S 24	T 24 *Shrove Tu.*		w24 *Ash Wed.*	W24	S 24	S 23 *Ascens. 1*
	w25 *Ash Wed.*	S 24 *Epiph. 3*	T 25	T 25 *Annunc.*		M24
S 25 *Epiph. 3*	T 26	M25	F 26	F 26	S 25 *Easter 2*	T 25
M26	F 27	T 26	S 27	S 27	M26	W26
T 27	S 28	W27			T 27	T 27
W28		T 28	S 28 *Quadrag.*	S 28 *Passion*	W28	F 28
T 29	S 29 *Quadrag.*	F 29		M29	T 29	S 29
F 30		S 30		T 30	F 30	
S 31				W31		S 30 *Whit Sun.*
		S 31 *Epiph. 4*				M31

Easter Day 11 April

Dominical letter C for Common Years
Dominical letter DC for Leap Years (*in bold figures*)

New style years 1599, 1610, 1621, **1632**, 1694, 1700 (*not* a leap year), 1751, 1762, 1773, **1784**, 1819, 1830, 1841, **1852**, 1909, 1971, 1982, 1993, **2004**, 2066, 2077, **2088**

JUNE	JULY	AUGUST	SEPTEMBER	OCTOBER	NOVEMBER	DECEMBER
T 1	T 1	S 1 *Trinity 8*	W 1	F 1	M 1	W 1
W 2 *Ember*	F 2	M 2	T 2	S 2	T 2	T 2
T 3	S 3	T 3	F 3		W 3	F 3
F 4 *Ember*		W 4	S 4		T 4	S 4
S 5 *Ember*	S 4 *Trinity 4*	T 5		S 3 *Trinity 17*	F 5	
	M 5	F 6	S 5 *Trinity 13*	M 4	S 6	S 5 *Advent 2*
S 6 *Trinity*	T 6	S 7	M 6	T 5		M 6
M 7	W 7		T 7	W 6	S 7 *Trinity 22*	T 7
T 8	T 8	S 8 *Trinity 9*	W 8	T 7	M 8	W 8
W 9	F 9	M 9	T 9	F 8	T 9	T 9
T 10 *Corpus C.*	S 10	T 10	F 10	S 9	W 10	F 10
F 11		W 11	S 11		T 11 *Martin*	S 11
S 12	S 11 *Trinity 5*	T 12		S 10 *Trinity 18*	F 12	
	M 12	F 13	S 12 *Trinity 14*	M 11	S 13	S 12 *Advent 3*
S 13 *Trinity 1*	T 13	S 14	M 13	T 12		M 13
M 14	W 14		T 14 *Exalt. C.*	W 13	S 14 *Trinity 23*	T 14
T 15	T 15	S 15 *Trinity 10*	W 15 *Ember*	T 14	M 15	W 15 *Ember*
W 16	F 16	M 16	T 16	F 15	T 16	T 16
T 17	S 17	T 17	F 17 *Ember*	S 16	W 17	F 17 *Ember*
F 18		W 18	S 18 *Ember*		T 18	S 18 *Ember*
S 19	S 18 *Trinity 6*	T 19		S 17 *Trinity 19*	F 19	
	M 19	F 20	S 19 *Trinity 15*	M 18	S 20	S 19 *Advent 4*
S 20 *Trinity 2*	T 20	S 21	M 20	T 19		M 20
M 21	W 21		T 21	W 20	S 21 *Trinity 24*	T 21
T 22	T 22	S 22 *Trinity 11*	W 22	T 21	M 22	W 22
W 23	F 23	M 23	T 23	F 22	T 23	T 23
T 24 *Nat. J. Bap.*	S 24	T 24	F 24	S 23	W 24	F 24
F 25		W 25	S 25		T 25	S 25 *Christmas*
S 26	S 25 *Trinity 7*	T 26		S 24 *Trinity 20*	F 26	
	M 26	F 27	S 26 *Trinity 16*	M 25	S 27	S 26
S 27 *Trinity 3*	T 27	S 28	M 27	T 26		M 27
M 28	W 28		T 28	W 27	S 28 *Advent 1*	T 28
T 29	T 29	S 29 *Trinity 12*	W 29 *Michael A.*	T 28	M 29	W 29
W 30	F 30	M 30	T 30	F 29	T 30	T 30
	S 31	T 31		S 30		F 31
				S 31 *Trinity 21*		

8/22 Easter Day 12 April

Dominical letter D for Common Years
Dominical letter ED for Leap Years (*in bold figures*)
Old style years 442, 453, **464**, 537, **548**, 627, **632**, 711, 722, 795, 806, 817, 879, 890, 901, **912**, 974, 985, **996**, 1069, **1080**, 1159, **1164**, 1243, 1254, 1327, 1338, 1349, 1411, 1422, 1433, **1444**, 1506, 1517, **1528**, 1601, **1612**, 1691, **1696**

Leap years

JANUARY	FEBRUARY
W 1	S 1
T 2	
F 3	S 2 *Epiph. 4*
S 4	M 3
	T 4
S 5	W 5
M 6 *Epiphany*	T 6
T 7	F 7
W 8	S 8
T 9	
F 10	S 9 *Septuag.*
S 11	M 10
	T 11
S 12 *Epiph. 1*	W 12
M 13 *Hilary*	T 13
T 14	F 14
W 15	S 15
T 16	
F 17	S 16 *Sexages.*
S 18	M 17
	T 18
S 19 *Epiph. 2*	W 19
M 20	T 20
T 21	F 21
W 22	S 22
T 23	
F 24	S 23 *Quinquag.*
S 25	M 24
	T 25 *Shrove Tu.*
S 26 *Epiph. 3*	W 26 *Ash Wed.*
M 27	T 27
T 28	F 28
W 29	S 29
T 30	
F 31	

JANUARY	FEBRUARY	MARCH	APRIL	MAY
T 1	S 1 *Epiph. 4*	S 1 *Quadrag.*	W 1	F 1
F 2	M 2 *Purific. M.*	M 2	T 2	S 2
S 3	T 3	T 3	F 3	
	W 4	W 4 *Ember*	S 4	S 3 *Easter 3*
S 4	T 5	T 5		M 4
M 5	F 6	F 6 *Ember*	S 5 *Palm*	T 5
T 6 *Epiphany*	S 7	S 7 *Ember*	M 6	W 6
W 7			T 7	T 7
T 8	S 8 *Septuag.*	S 8 *Lent 2*	W 8	F 8
F 9	M 9	M 9	T 9	S 9
S 10	T 10	T 10	F 10 *Good Fri.*	
	W 11	W 11	S 11	S 10 *Easter 4*
S 11 *Epiph. 1*	T 12	T 12		M 11
M 12	F 13	F 13	S 12 ***Easter Day***	T 12
T 13 *Hilary*	S 14	S 14	M 13	W 13
W 14			T 14	T 14
T 15	S 15 *Sexages.*	S 15 *Lent 3*	W 15	F 15
F 16	M 16	M 16	T 16	S 16
S 17	T 17	T 17	F 17	
	W 18	W 18	S 18	S 17 *Rogation*
S 18 *Epiph. 2*	T 19	T 19		M 18
M 19	F 20	F 20	S 19 *Quasimodo*	T 19
T 20	S 21	S 21	M 20	W 20
W 21			T 21	T 21 *Ascension*
T 22	S 22 *Quinquag.*	S 22 *Lent 4*	W 22	F 22
F 23	M 23	M 23	T 23	S 23
S 24	T 24 *Shrove Tu.*	T 24	F 24	
	W 25 *Ash Wed.*	W 25 *Annunc.*	S 25	S 24 *Ascens. 1*
S 25 *Epiph. 3*	T 26	T 26		M 25
M 26	F 27	F 27	S 26 *Easter 2*	T 26
T 27	S 28	S 28	M 27	W 27
W 28			T 28	T 28
T 29		S 29 *Passion*	W 29	F 29
F 30		M 30	T 30	S 30
S 31		T 31		
				S 31 *Whit Sun.*

Easter Day 12 April

Dominical letter D for Common Years
Dominical letter ED for Leap Years (*in bold figures*)
New style years   1626, 1637, **1648**, 1705, **1716**, 1789, 1846, 1857, **1868**, 1903, 1914, 1925, **1936**, 1998, 2009, **2020**, 2093, 2099

JUNE	JULY	AUGUST	SEPTEMBER	OCTOBER	NOVEMBER	DECEMBER
M 1	W 1	S 1 *Lammas*	T 1	T 1	S 1 *Trinity 21*	T 1
T 2	T 2		W 2	F 2	M 2	W 2
W 3 *Ember*	F 3	S 2 *Trinity 8*	T 3	S 3	T 3	T 3
T 4	S 4	M 3	F 4		W 4	F 4
F 5 *Ember*		T 4	S 5	S 4 *Trinity 17*	T 5	S 5
S 6 *Ember*	S 5 *Trinity 4*	W 5		M 5	F 6	
	M 6	T 6	S 6 *Trinity 13*	T 6	S 7	S 6 *Advent 2*
S 7 *Trinity*	T 7	F 7	M 7	W 7		M 7
M 8	W 8	S 8	T 8	T 8	S 8 *Trinity 22*	T 8
T 9	T 9		W 9	F 9	M 9	W 9
W 10	F 10	S 9 *Trinity 9*	T 10	S 10	T 10	T 10
T 11 *Corpus C.*	S 11	M 10	F 11		W 11 *Martin*	F 11
F 12		T 11	S 12	S 11 *Trinity 18*	T 12	S 12
S 13	S 12 *Trinity 5*	W 12		M 12	F 13	
	M 13	T 13	S 13 *Trinity 14*	T 13	S 14	S 13 *Advent 3*
S 14 *Trinity 1*	T 14	F 14	M 14 *Exalt. C.*	W 14		M 14
M 15	W 15	S 15	T 15	T 15	S 15 *Trinity 23*	T 15
T 16	T 16		W 16 *Ember*	F 16	M 16	W 16 *Ember*
W 17	F 17	S 16 *Trinity 10*	T 17	S 17	T 17	T 17
T 18	S 18	M 17	F 18 *Ember*		W 18	F 18 *Ember*
F 19		T 18	S 19 *Ember*	S 18 *Trinity 19*	T 19	S 19 *Ember*
S 20	S 19 *Trinity 6*	W 19		M 19	F 20	
	M 20	T 20	S 20 *Trinity 15*	T 20	S 21	S 20 *Advent 4*
S 21 *Trinity 2*	T 21	F 21	M 21	W 21		M 21
M 22	W 22	S 22	T 22	T 22	S 22 *Trinity 24*	T 22
T 23	T 23		W 23	F 23	M 23	W 23
W 24 *Nat. J. Bap.*	F 24	S 23 *Trinity 11*	T 24	S 24	T 24	T 24
T 25	S 25	M 24	F 25		W 25	F 25 *Christmas*
F 26		T 25	S 26	S 25 *Trinity 20*	T 26	S 26
S 27	S 26 *Trinity 7*	W 26		M 26	F 27	
	M 27	T 27	S 27 *Trinity 16*	T 27	S 28	S 27
S 28 *Trinity 3*	T 28	F 28	M 28	W 28		M 28
M 29	W 29	S 29	T 29 *Michael A.*	T 29	S 29 *Advent 1*	T 29
T 30	T 30		W 30	F 30	M 30	W 30
	F 31	S 30 *Trinity 12*		S 31		T 31
		M 31				

8/23 Easter Day 13 April

Dominical letter E for Common Years
Dominical letter FE for Leap Years (*in bold figures*)
Old style years   469, **480**, 559, **564**, 643, 654, 727, 738, 749, 811, 822, 833, **844**, 906, 917, **928**, 1001, **1012**, 1091, **1096**, 1175, 1186, 1259, 1270, 1281, 1343, 1354, 1365, **1376**, 1438, 1449, **1460**, 1533, **1544**, 1623, **1628**, 1707, 1718

Leap years						
JANUARY	FEBRUARY	JANUARY	FEBRUARY	MARCH	APRIL	MAY
T 1	F 1	W1	S 1	S 1	T 1	T 1
W2	S 2 *Purific. M.*	T 2			W2	F 2
T 3		F 3	S 2 *Epiph. 4*	S 2 *Quadrag.*	T 3	S 3
F 4	S 3 *Epiph. 4*	S 4	M3	M3	F 4	
S 5	M4		T 4	T 4	S 5	S 4 *Easter 3*
	T 5	S 5	W5 *Ember*	W5 *Ember*		M5
S 6 *Epiphany*	W6	M6 *Epiphany*	T 6	T 6	S 6 *Palm*	T 6
M7	T 7	T 7	F 7 *Ember*	F 7 *Ember*	M7	W7
T 8	F 8	W8	S 8 *Ember*	S 8 *Ember*	T 8	T 8
W9	S 9	T 9			W9	F 9
T 10		F 10	S 9 *Septuag.*	S 9 *Lent 2*	T 10	S 10
F 11	S 10 *Septuag.*	S 11	M10	M10	F 11 *Good Fri.*	
S 12	M11		T 11	T 11	S 12	S 11 *Easter 4*
	T 12	S 12 *Epiph. 1*	W12	W12		M12
S 13 *Epiph. 1*	W13	M13 *Hilary*	T 13	T 13	S 13 ***Easter Day***	T 13
M14	T 14	T 14	F 14	F 14	M14	W14
T 15	F 15	W15	S 15	S 15	T 15	T 15
W16	S 16	T 16			W16	F 16
T 17		F 17	S 16 *Sexages.*	S 16 *Lent 3*	T 17	S 17
F 18	S 17 *Sexages.*	S 18	M17	M17	F 18	
S 19	M18		T 18	T 18	S 19	S 18 *Rogation*
	T 19	S 19 *Epiph. 2*	W19	W19		M19
S 20 *Epiph. 2*	W20	M20	T 20	T 20	S 20 *Quasimodo*	T 20
M21	T 21	T 21	F 21	F 21	M21	W21
T 22	F 22	W22	S 22	S 22	T 22	T 22 *Ascension*
W23	S 23	T 23			W23	F 23
T 24		F 24	S 23 *Quinquag.*	S 23 *Lent 4*	T 24	S 24
F 25	S 24 *Quinquag.*	S 25	M24 *Matthias*	M24	F 25	
S 26	M25 *Matthias*		T 25 *Shrove Tu.*	T 25 *Annunc.*	S 26	S 25 *Ascens. 1*
	T 26 *Shrove Tu.*	S 26 *Epiph. 3*	W26 *Ash Wed.*	W26		M26
S 27 *Epiph. 3*	W27 *Ash Wed.*	M27	T 27	T 27	S 27 *Easter 2*	T 27
M28	T 28	T 28	F 28	F 28	M28	W28
T 29	F 29	W29		S 29	T 29	T 29
W30		T 30			W30	F 30
T 31		F 31				S 31
				S 30 *Passion*		
				M31		

Easter Day 13 April 8/23

Dominical letter E for Common Years
Dominical letter FE for Leap Years (*in bold figures*)
New style years 1653, 1659, **1664**, 1721, 1727, **1732**, 1800 (*not* a leap year), 1873, 1879, **1884**, 1941, **1952**, 2031, **2036**

JUNE	JULY	AUGUST	SEPTEMBER	OCTOBER	NOVEMBER	DECEMBER
S 1 *Whit Sun.*	T 1	F 1 *Lammas*	M 1	W 1	S 1	M 1
M 2	W 2	S 2	T 2	T 2		T 2
T 3	T 3		W 3	F 3	S 2 *Trinity 21*	W 3
W 4 *Ember*	F 4	S 3 *Trinity 8*	T 4	S 4	M 3	T 4
T 5	S 5	M 4	F 5		T 4	F 5
F 6 *Ember*		T 5	S 6	S 5 *Trinity 17*	W 5	S 6
S 7 *Ember*	S 6 *Trinity 4*	W 6		M 6	T 6	
	M 7	T 7	S 7 *Trinity 13*	T 7	F 7	S 7 *Advent 2*
S 8 *Trinity*	T 8	F 8	M 8	W 8	S 8	M 8
M 9	W 9	S 9	T 9	T 9		T 9
T 10	T 10		W 10	F 10	S 9 *Trinity 22*	W 10
W 11	F 11	S 10 *Trinity 9*	T 11	S 11	M 10	T 11
T 12 *Corpus C.*	S 12	M 11	F 12		T 11 *Martin*	F 12
F 13		T 12	S 13	S 12 *Trinity 18*	W 12	S 13
S 14	S 13 *Trinity 5*	W 13		M 13	T 13	
	M 14	T 14	S 14 *Trinity 14*	T 14	F 14	S 14 *Advent 3*
S 15 *Trinity 1*	T 15	F 15	M 15	W 15	S 15	M 15
M 16	W 16	S 16	T 16	T 16		T 16
T 17	T 17		W 17 *Ember*	F 17	S 16 *Trinity 23*	W 17 *Ember*
W 18	F 18	S 17 *Trinity 10*	T 18	S 18	M 17	T 18
T 19	S 19	M 18	F 19 *Ember*		T 18	F 19 *Ember*
F 20		T 19	S 20 *Ember*	S 19 *Trinity 19*	W 19	S 20 *Ember*
S 21	S 20 *Trinity 6*	W 20		M 20	T 20	
	M 21	T 21	S 21 *Trinity 15*	T 21	F 21	S 21 *Advent 4*
S 22 *Trinity 2*	T 22	F 22	M 22	W 22	S 22	M 22
M 23	W 23	S 23	T 23	T 23		T 23
T 24 *Nat. J. Bap.*	T 24		W 24	F 24	S 23 *Trinity 24*	W 24
W 25	F 25	S 24 *Trinity 11*	T 25	S 25	M 24	T 25 *Christmas*
T 26	S 26	M 25	F 26		T 25	F 26
F 27		T 26	S 27	S 26 *Trinity 20*	W 26	S 27
S 28	S 27 *Trinity 7*	W 27		M 27	T 27	
	M 28	T 28	S 28 *Trinity 16*	T 28	F 28	S 28
S 29 *Trinity*	T 29	F 29	M 29 *Michael A.*	W 29	S 29	M 29
M 30	W 30	S 30	T 30	T 30		T 30
	T 31			F 31	S 30 *Advent 1*	W 31
		S 31 *Trinity 12*				

8/24 **Easter Day 14 April**

Dominical letter F for Common Years

Dominical letter GF for Leap Years (*in bold figures*)

Old style years 401, 407, **412**, 491, **496**, 502, 575, 586, 597, 659, 670, 681, **692**, 743, 754, 765, **776**, 838, 849, **860**, 933, 939, **944**, 1023, **1028**, 1034, 1107, 1118, 1129, 1191, 1202, 1213, **1224**, 1275, 1286, 1297, **1308**, 1370, 1381, **1392**, 1465, 1471, **1476**, 1555, **1560**, 1566, 1639, 1650, 1661, 1723, 1734, 1745

Leap years						
JANUARY	FEBRUARY	JANUARY	FEBRUARY	MARCH	APRIL	MAY
M 1	T 1	T 1	F 1	F 1	M 1	W 1
T 2	F 2 *Purific. M.*	W 2	S 2 *Purific. M.*	S 2	T 2	T 2
W 3	S 3	T 3			W 3	F 3
T 4		F 4			T 4	S 4
F 5		S 5	S 3 *Epiph. 4*	S 3 *Quadrag.*	F 5	
S 6 *Epiphany*	S 4 *Epiph. 5*		M 4	M 4	S 6	
	M 5		T 5	T 5		S 5 *Easter 3*
	T 6	S 6 *Epiphany*	W 6	W 6 *Ember*		M 6
S 7 *Epiph. 1*	W 7	M 7	T 7	T 7	S 7 *Palm*	T 7
M 8	T 8	T 8	F 8	F 8 *Ember*	M 8	W 8
T 9	F 9	W 9	S 9	S 9 *Ember*	T 9	T 9
W 10	S 10	T 10			W 10	F 10
T 11		F 11			T 11	S 11
F 12		S 12	S 10 *Septuag.*	S 10 *Lent 2*	F 12 *Good Fri.*	
S 13 *Hilary*	S 11 *Septuag.*		M 11	M 11	S 13	
	M 12		T 12	T 12		S 12 *Easter 4*
	T 13	S 13 *Epiph. 1*	W 13	W 13		M 13
S 14 *Epiph. 2*	W 14	M 14	T 14	T 14	S 14 ***Easter Day***	T 14
M 15	T 15	T 15	F 15	F 15	M 15	W 15
T 16	F 16	W 16	S 16	S 16	T 16	T 16
W 17	S 17	T 17			W 17	F 17
T 18		F 18			T 18	S 18
F 19		S 19	S 17 *Sexages.*	S 17 *Lent 3*	F 19	
S 20	S 18 *Sexages.*		M 18	M 18	S 20	
	M 19		T 19	T 19		S 19 *Rogation*
	T 20	S 20 *Epiph. 2*	W 20	W 20		M 20
S 21 *Epiph. 3*	W 21	M 21	T 21	T 21	S 21 *Quasimodo*	T 21
M 22	T 22	T 22	F 22	F 22	M 22	W 22
T 23	F 23	W 23	S 23	S 23	T 23	T 23 *Ascension*
W 24	S 24	T 24			W 24	F 24
T 25		F 25			T 25	S 25
F 26		S 26	S 24 *Quinquag.*	S 24 *Lent 4*	F 26	
S 27	S 25 *Quinquag.*		M 25	M 25 *Annunc.*	S 27	
	M 26		T 26 *Shrove Tu.*	T 26		S 26 *Ascens. 1*
	T 27 *Shrove Tu.*	S 27 *Epiph. 3*	W 27 *Ash Wed.*	W 27		M 27
S 28 *Epiph. 4*	W 28 *Ash Wed.*	M 28	T 28	T 28	S 28 *Easter 2*	T 28
M 29	T 29	T 29		F 29	M 29	W 29
T 30		W 30		S 30	T 30	T 30
W 31		T 31				F 31
				S 31 *Passion*		

Easter Day 14 April

Dominical letter F for Common Years
Dominical letter GF for Leap Years (*in bold figures*)

New style years 1591, **1596**, 1675, 1686, 1743, **1748**, 1754, 1805, 1811, **1816**, 1895, 1963, **1968**, 1974, 2047, 2058, 2069

JUNE	JULY	AUGUST	SEPTEMBER	OCTOBER	NOVEMBER	DECEMBER
S 1	M1	T 1 *Lammas*	S 1 *Trinity 12*	T 1	F 1	S 1 *Advent 1*
S 2 *Whit Sun.*	T 2	F 2	M2	W2	S 2	M2
M3	W3	S 3	T 3	T 3		T 3
T 4	T 4		W4	F 4	S 3 *Trinity 21*	W4
W5 *Ember*	F 5	S 4 *Trinity 8*	T 5	S 5	M4	T 5
T 6	s 6	M5	F 6		T 5	F 6
F 7 *Ember*		T 6	S 7	S 6 *Trinity 17*	W6	S 7
s 8 *Ember*	S 7 *Trinity 4*	W7		M7	T 7	
	M8	T 8	S 8 *Trinity 13*	T 8	F 8	S 8 *Advent 2*
S 9 *Trinity*	T 9	F 9	M9	W9	S 9	M9
M10	W10	S 10	T 10	T 10		T 10
T 11	T 11		W11	F 11	S 10 *Trinity 22*	W11
W12	F 12	S 11 *Trinity 9*	T 12	S 12	M11 *Martin*	T 12
T 13 *Corpus C.*	S 13	M12	F 13		T 12	F 13
F 14		T 13	s 14 *Exalt. C.*	S 13 *Trinity 18*	W13	S 14
S 15	S 14 *Trinity 5*	W14		M14	T 14	
	M15	T 15	S 15 *Trinity 14*	T 15	F 15	S 15 *Advent 3*
S 16 *Trinity 1*	T 16	F 16	M16	W16	s 16	M16
M17	W17	S 17	T 17	T 17		T 17
T 18	T 18		W18 *Ember*	F 18	S 17 *Trinity 23*	W18 *Ember*
W19	F 19	S 18 *Trinity 10*	T 19	S 19	M18	T 19
T 20	S 20	M19	F 20 *Ember*		T 19	F 20 *Ember*
F 21		T 20	s 21 *Ember*	S 20 *Trinity 19*	W20	s 21 *Ember*
S 22	S 21 *Trinity 6*	W21		M21	T 21	
	M22	T 22	S 22 *Trinity 15*	T 22	F 22	S 22 *Advent 4*
S 23 *Trinity 2*	T 23	F 23	M23	W23	S 23	M23
M24 *Nat. J. Bap.*	W24	S 24	T 24	T 24		T 24
T 25	T 25		W25	F 25	S 24 *Trinity 24*	W25 *Christmas*
W26	F 26	S 25 *Trinity 11*	T 26	S 26	M25	T 26
T 27	S 27	M26	F 27		T 26	F 27
F 28		T 27	S 28	S 27 *Trinity 20*	W27	s 28
S 29	S 28 *Trinity 7*	W28		M28	T 28	
	M29	T 29	S 29 *Trinity 16*	T 29	F 29	S 29
S 30 *Trinity 3*	T 30	F 30	M30	W30	S 30	M30
	W31	S 31		T 31		

8/25 Easter Day 15 April

Dominical letter G for Common Years
Dominical letter AG for Leap Years (*in bold figures*)

Old style years   423, 434, 507, 518, 529, 591, 602, 613, **624**, 686, 697, **708**, 781, **792**, 871, **876**, 955, 966, 1039, 1050, 1061, 1123, 1134, 1145, **1156**, 1218, 1229, **1240**, 1313, **1324**, 1403, **1408**, 1487, 1498, 1571, 1582, 1593, 1655, 1666, 1677, **1688**, 1750

Leap years		JANUARY	FEBRUARY	MARCH	APRIL	MAY
JANUARY	FEBRUARY					
S 1	W1	M1	T 1	T 1	S 1 *Passion*	T 1
M2	T 2 *Purific. M.*	T 2	F 2 *Purific. M.*	F 2	M2	W2
T 3	F 3	W3	S 3	S 3	T 3	T 3
W4	S 4	T 4			W4	F 4
T 5		F 5			T 5	S 5
F 6 *Epiphany*	S 5 *Epiph. 5*	s 6 *Epiphany*	S 4 *Epiph. 5*	S 4 *Quadrag.*	F 6	
S 7	M6		M5	M5	S 7	
	T 7	S 7 *Epiph. 1*	T 6	T 6		S 6 *Easter 3*
S 8 *Epiph. 1*	W8	M8	W7	W7 *Ember*		M7
M9	T 9	T 9	T 8	T 8	S 8 *Palm*	T 8
T 10	F 10	W10	F 9	F 9 *Ember*	M9	W9
W11	S 11	T 11	S 10	S 10 *Ember*	T 10	T 10
T 12		F 12			W11	F 11
F 13 *Hilary*	S 12 *Septuag.*	s 13 *Hilary*	S 11 *Septuag.*	S 11 *Lent 2*	T 12	S 12
S 14	M13		M12	M12	F 13 *Good Fri.*	
	T 14	S 14 *Epiph. 2*	T 13	T 13	S 14	S 13 *Easter 4*
S 15 *Epiph. 2*	W15	M15	W14	W14		M14
M16	T 16	T 16	T 15	T 15	S 15 **Easter Day**	T 15
T 17	F 17	W17	F 16	F 16	M16	W16
W18	S 18	T 18	S 17	S 17	T 17	T 17
T 19		F 19			W18	F 18
F 20		S 20	S 18 *Sexages.*	S 18 *Lent 3*	T 19	S 19
S 21	S 19 *Sexages.*		M19	M19	F 20	
	M20		T 20	T 20	S 21	S 20 *Rogation*
	T 21	S 21 *Epiph. 3*	W21	W21		M21
S 22 *Epiph. 3*	W22	M22	T 22	T 22	S 22 *Quasimodo*	T 22
M23	T 23	T 23	F 23	F 23	M23	W23
T 24	F 24	W24	s 24 *Matthias*	S 24	T 24	T 24 *Ascension*
W25	s 25 *Matthias*	T 25			W25	F 25
T 26		F 26			T 26	S 26
F 27		S 27	S 25 *Quinquag.*	S 25 *Lent 4*	F 27	
S 28	S 26 *Quinquag.*		M26	M26	S 28	
	M27		T 27 *Shrove Tu.*	T 27		S 27 *Ascens. 1*
	T 28 *Shrove Tu.*	S 28 *Epiph. 4*	w28 *Ash Wed.*	W28		M28
S 29 *Epiph. 4*	W29 *Ash Wed.*	M29		T 29	S 29 *Easter 2*	T 29
M30		T 30		F 30	M30	W30
T 31		W31		S 31		T 31

Dominical letter G for Common Years
Dominical letter AG for Leap Years (*in bold figures*)
New style years 1607, 1618, 1629, 1691, 1759, 1770, 1781, 1827, 1838, 1900 (*not* a leap year), 1906, 1979, 1990, 2001, 2063, 2074, 2085, **2096**

JUNE	JULY	AUGUST	SEPTEMBER	OCTOBER	NOVEMBER	DECEMBER
F 1	S 1 *Trinity 3*	W 1 *Lammas*	S 1	M 1	T 1	S 1
S 2	M 2	T 2		T 2	F 2	
	T 3	F 3		W 3	S 3	S 2 *Advent 1*
S 3 *Whit Sun.*	W 4	S 4	S 2 *Trinity 12*	T 4		M 3
M 4	T 5		M 3	F 5		T 4
T 5	F 6	S 5 *Trinity 8*	T 4	S 6	S 4 *Trinity 21*	W 5
W 6 *Ember*	S 7	M 6	W 5		M 5	T 6
T 7		T 7	T 6		T 6	F 7
F 8 *Ember*	S 8 *Trinity 4*	W 8	F 7	S 7 *Trinity 17*	W 7	S 8
S 9 *Ember*	M 9	T 9	S 8	M 8	T 8	
	T 10	F 10		T 9	F 9	
S 10 *Trinity*	W 11	S 11	S 9 *Trinity 13*	W 10	S 10	S 9 *Advent 2*
M 11	T 12		M 10	T 11		M 10
T 12	F 13		T 11	F 12	S 11 *Trinity 22*	T 11
W 13	S 14	S 12 *Trinity 9*	W 12	S 13	M 12	W 12
T 14 *Corpus C.*		M 13	T 13		T 13	T 13
F 15	S 15 *Trinity 5*	T 14	F 14 *Exalt. C.*	S 14 *Trinity 18*	W 14	F 14
S 16	M 16	W 15	S 15	M 15	T 15	S 15
	T 17	T 16		T 16	F 16	
S 17 *Trinity 1*	W 18	F 17	S 16 *Trinity 14*	W 17	S 17	S 16 *Advent 3*
M 18	T 19	S 18	M 17	T 18		M 17
T 19	F 20		T 18	F 19	S 18 *Trinity 23*	T 18
W 20	S 21	S 19 *Trinity 10*	W 19 *Ember*	S 20	M 19	W 19 *Ember*
T 21		M 20	T 20		T 20	T 20
F 22	S 22 *Trinity 6*	T 21	F 21 *Ember*	S 21 *Trinity 19*	W 21	F 21 *Ember*
S 23	M 23	W 22	S 22 *Ember*	M 22	T 22	S 22 *Ember*
	T 24	T 23		T 23	F 23	
S 24 *Trinity 2*	W 25	F 24	S 23 *Trinity 15*	W 24	S 24	S 23 *Advent 4*
M 25	T 26	S 25	M 24	T 25		M 24
T 26	F 27		T 25	F 26	S 25 *Trinity 24*	T 25 *Christmas*
W 27	S 28	S 26 *Trinity 11*	W 26	S 27	M 26	W 26
T 28		M 27	T 27		T 27	T 27
F 29	S 29 *Trinity 7*	T 28	F 28	S 28 *Trinity 20*	W 28	F 28
S 30	M 30	W 29	S 29 *Michael A.*	M 29	T 29	S 29
	T 31	T 30		T 30	F 30	
		F 31	S 30 *Trinity 16*	W 31		S 30
						M 31

8/26 Easter Day 16 April

Dominical letter A for Common Years
Dominical letter BA for Leap Years (*in bold figures*)
Old style years   439, 450, 461, **472**, 523, 534, 545, **556**, 618, 629, **640**, 713, 719, **724**, 803, **808**, 814, 887, 898, 909, 971, 982, 993, **1004**, 1055, 1066, 1077, **1088**, 1150, 1161, **1172**, 1245, 1251, **1256**, 1335, **1340**, 1346, 1419, 1430, 1441, 1503, 1514, 1525, **1536**, 1587, 1598, 1609, **1620**, 1682, 1693, **1704**

Leap years		JANUARY	FEBRUARY	MARCH	APRIL	MAY
JANUARY	FEBRUARY					
S 1	T 1	S 1	W1	W1 *Ash Wed.*	S 1	M1
	W2 *Purific. M.*	M2	T 2 *Purific. M.*	T 2		T 2
S 2	T 3	T 3	F 3	F 3	S 2 *Passion*	W3
M3	F 4	W4	S 4	S 4	M3	T 4
T 4	S 5	T 5			T 4	F 5
W5		F 6 *Epiphany*	S 5 *Epiph. 5*	S 5 *Quadrag.*	W5	s 6
T 6 *Epiphany*	S 6 *Epiph. 5*	S 7	M6	M6	T 6	
F 7	M7		T 7	T 7	F 7	S 7 *Easter 3*
s 8	T 8	S 8 *Epiph. 1*	W8	W8 *Ember*	s 8	M8
	W9	M9	T 9	T 9		T 9
S 9 *Epiph. 1*	T 10	T 10	F 10	F 10 *Ember*	S 9 *Palm*	W10
M10	F 11	W11	S 11	s 11 *Ember*	M10	T 11
T 11	S 12	T 12			T 11	F 12
W12		F 13 *Hilary*	S 12 *Septuag.*	S 12 *Lent 2*	W12	s 13
T 13 *Hilary*	S 13 *Septuag.*	S 14	M13	M13	T 13	
F 14	M14		T 14	T 14	F 14 *Good Fri.*	S 14 *Easter 4*
S 15	T 15	S 15 *Epiph. 2*	W15	W15	S 15	M15
	W16	M16	T 16	T 16		T 16
S 16 *Epiph. 2*	T 17	T 17	F 17	F 17	S 16 ***Easter Day***	W17
M17	F 18	W18	S 18	S 18	M17	T 18
T 18	S 19	T 19			T 18	F 19
W19		F 20	S 19 *Sexages.*	S 19 *Lent 3*	W19	S 20
T 20	S 20 *Sexages.*	S 21	M20	M20	T 20	
F 21	M21		T 21	T 21	F 21	S 21 *Rogation*
S 22	T 22	S 22 *Epiph. 3*	W22	W22	S 22	M22
	W23	M23	T 23	T 23		T 23
S 23 *Epiph. 3*	T 24	T 24	F 24 *Matthias*	F 24	S 23 *Quasimodo*	W24
M24	F 25 *Matthias*	W25	S 25	S 25 *Annunc.*	M24	T 25 *Ascension*
T 25	S 26	T 26			T 25	F 26
W26		F 27	S 26 *Quinquag.*	S 26 *Lent 4*	W26	S 27
T 27	S 27 *Quinquag.*	S 28	M27	M27	T 27	
F 28	M28		T 28 *Shrove Tu.*	T 28	F 28	S 28 *Ascens. 1*
S 29	T 29 *Shrove Tu.*	S 29 *Epiph. 4*		W29	S 29	M29
		M30		T 30		T 30
S 30 *Epiph. 4*		T 31		F 31	S 30 *Easter 2*	W31
M31						

Dominical letter A for Common Years
Dominical letter BA for Leap Years (*in bold figures*)
New style years   1623, 1634, 1645, **1656**, 1702, 1713, **1724**, 1775, 1786, 1797, 1843, 1854, 1865, **1876**, 1911,
1922, 1933, 1995, 2006, 2017, **2028**, 2090

JUNE	JULY	AUGUST	SEPTEMBER	OCTOBER	NOVEMBER	DECEMBER
T 1	S 1	T 1 *Lammas*	F 1	S 1 *Trinity 16*	W1	F 1
F 2		W2	S 2	M2	T 2	S 2
S 3		T 3		T 3	F 3	
	S 2 *Trinity 3*	F 4		W4	S 4	S 3 *Advent 1*
S 4 *Whit Sun.*	M3	S 5	S 3 *Trinity 12*	T 5		M4
M5	T 4		M4	F 6		T 5
T 6	W5		T 5	S 7	S 5 *Trinity 21*	W6
W7 *Ember*	T 6	S 6 *Trinity 8*	W6		M6	T 7
T 8	F 7	M7	T 7		T 7	F 8
F 9 *Ember*	S 8	T 8	F 8	S 8 *Trinity 17*	W8	S 9
S 10 *Ember*		W9	S 9	M9	T 9	
	S 9 *Trinity 4*	T 10		T 10	F 10	S 10 *Advent 2*
S 11 *Trinity*	M10	F 11	S 10 *Trinity 13*	W11	S 11 *Martin*	M11
M12	T 11	S 12	M11	T 12		T 12
T 13	W12		T 12	F 13	S 12 *Trinity 22*	W13
W14	T 13	S 13 *Trinity 9*	W13	S 14	M13	T 14
T 15 *Corpus C.*	F 14	M14	T 14 *Exalt. C.*		T 14	F 15
F 16	S 15	T 15	F 15	S 15 *Trinity 18*	W15	S 16
S 17		W16	S 16	M16	T 16	
	S 16 *Trinity 5*	T 17		T 17	F 17	S 17 *Advent 3*
S 18 *Trinity 1*	M17	F 18	S 17 *Trinity 14*	W18	S 18	M18
M19	T 18	S 19	M18	T 19		T 19
T 20	W19		T 19	F 20	S 19 *Trinity 23*	W20 *Ember*
W21	T 20	S 20 *Trinity 10*	W20 *Ember*	S 21	M20	T 21
T 22	F 21	M21	T 21		T 21	F 22 *Ember*
F 23	S 22	T 22	F 22 *Ember*	S 22 *Trinity 19*	W22	S 23 *Ember*
S 24 *Nat. J. Bap.*		W23	S 23 *Ember*	M23	T 23	
	S 23 *Trinity 6*	T 24		T 24	F 24	S 24 *Advent 4*
S 25 *Trinity 2*	M24	F 25	S 24 *Trinity 15*	W25	S 25	M25 *Christmas*
M26	T 25	S 26	M25	T 26		T 26
T 27	W26		T 26	F 27	S 26 *Trinity 24*	W27
W28	T 27	S 27 *Trinity 11*	W27	S 28	M27	T 28
T 29	F 28	M28	T 28		T 28	F 29
F 30	S 29	T 29	F 29 *Michael A.*	S 29 *Trinity 20*	W29	S 30
		W30	S 30	M30	T 30	
	S 30 *Trinity 7*	T 31		T 31		S 31
	M31					

8/27 Easter Day 17 April

Dominical letter B for Common Years
Dominical letter CB for Leap Years (*in bold figures*)
Old style years   404, 466, 477, **488**, 561, **572**, 651, **656**, 735, 746, 819, 830, 841, 903, 914, 925, **936**, 998, 1009, **1020**, 1093, **1104**, 1183, **1188**, 1267, 1278, 1351, 1362, 1373, 1435, 1446, 1457, **1468**, 1530, 1541, **1552**, 1625, **1636**, 1715, **1720**

JANUARY	FEBRUARY	JANUARY	FEBRUARY	MARCH	APRIL	MAY
F 1	M1	S 1	T 1	T 1 *Shrove Tu.*	F 1	S 1 *Easter 2*
S 2	T 2 *Purific. M.*		W2 *Purific. M.*	W2 *Ash Wed.*	S 2	M2
	W3		T 3	T 3		T 3
S 3	T 4	S 2	F 4	F 4	S 3 *Passion*	W4
M4	F 5	M3	S 5	S 5	M4	T 5
T 5	S 6	T 4			T 5	F 6
W6 *Epiphany*		W5			W6	S 7
T 7	S 7 *Eph. 5*	T 6 *Epiphany*	S 6 *Eph. 5*	S 6 *Quadrag.*	T 7	
F 8	M8	F 7	M7	M7	F 8	S 8 *Easter 3*
S 9	T 9	S 8	T 8	T 8	S 9	M9
	W10		W9	W9 *Ember*		T 10
S 10 *Epiph. 1*	T 11	S 9 *Epiph. 1*	T 10	T 10	S 10 *Palm*	W11
M11	F 12	M10	F 11	F 11 *Ember*	M11	T 12
T 12	S 13	T 11	S 12	S 12 *Ember*	T 12	F 13
W13 *Hilary*		W12			W13	S 14
T 14	S 14 *Septuag.*	T 13 *Hilary*	S 13 *Septuag.*	S 13 *Lent 2*	T 14	
F 15	M15	F 14	M14	M14	F 15 *Good Fri.*	S 15 *Easter 4*
S 16	T 16	S 15	T 15	T 15	S 16	M16
	W17		W16	W16		T 17
S 17 *Epiph. 2*	T 18	S 16 *Epiph. 2*	T 17	T 17	S 17 ***Easter Day***	W18
M18	F 19	M17	F 18	F 18	M18	T 19
T 19	S 20	T 18	S 19	S 19	T 19	F 20
W20		W19			W20	S 21
T 21	S 21 *Sexages.*	T 20	S 20 *Sexages.*	S 20 *Lent 3*	T 21	
F 22	M22	F 21	M21	M21	F 22	S 22 *Rogation*
S 23	T 23	S 22	T 22	T 22	S 23	M23
	W24		W23	W23		T 24
S 24 *Epiph. 3*	T 25 *Matthias*	S 23 *Epiph. 3*	T 24 *Matthias*	T 24	S 24 *Quasimodo*	W25
M25	F 26	M24	F 25	F 25 *Annunc.*	M25	T 26 *Ascension*
T 26	S 27	T 25	S 26	S 26	T 26	F 27
W27		W26			W27	S 28
T 28	S 28 *Quinquag.*	T 27	S 27 *Quinquag.*	S 27 *Lent 4*	T 28	
F 29	M29	F 28	M28	M28	F 29	S 29 *Ascens. 1*
S 30		S 29		T 29	S 30	M30
				W30		T 31
S 31 *Eph. 4*		S 30 *Eph. 4*		T 31		
		M31				

Easter Day 17 April 8/27

Dominical letter B for Common Years
Dominical letter CB for Leap Years (*in bold figures*)

New style years **1588**, 1650, 1661, **1672**, 1718, 1729, **1740**, **1808**, 1870, 1881, **1892**, 1927, 1938, 1949, **1960**, 2022, 2033, **2044**

JUNE	JULY	AUGUST	SEPTEMBER	OCTOBER	NOVEMBER	DECEMBER
W 1	F 1	M 1 *Lammas*	T 1	S 1	T 1	T 1
T 2	S 2	T 2	F 2		W 2	F 2
F 3		W 3	S 3	S 2 *Trinity 16*	T 3	S 3
S 4	S 3 *Trinity 3*	T 4		M 3	F 4	
	M 4	F 5	S 4 *Trinity 12*	T 4	S 5	S 4 *Advent 2*
S 5 *Whit Sun.*	T 5	S 6	M 5	W 5		M 5
M 6	W 6		T 6	T 6	S 6 *Trinity 21*	T 6
T 7	T 7	S 7 *Trinity 8*	W 7	F 7	M 7	W 7
W 8 *Ember*	F 8	M 8	T 8	S 8	T 8	T 8
T 9	S 9	T 9	F 9		W 9	F 9
F 10 *Ember*		W 10	S 10	S 9 *Trinity 17*	T 10	S 10
S 11 *Ember*	S 10 *Trinity 4*	T 11		M 10	F 11 *Martin*	
	M 11	F 12	S 11 *Trinity 13*	T 11	S 12	S 11 *Advent 3*
S 12 *Trinity*	T 12	S 13	M 12	W 12		M 12
M 13	W 13		T 13	T 13	S 13 *Trinity 22*	T 13
T 14	T 14	S 14 *Trinity 9*	W 14 *Exalt. C.*	F 14	M 14	W 14 *Ember*
W 15	F 15	M 15	T 15	S 15	T 15	T 15
T 16 *Corpus C.*	S 16	T 16	F 16		W 16	F 16 *Ember*
F 17		W 17	S 17	S 16 *Trinity 18*	T 17	S 17 *Ember*
S 18	S 17 *Trinity 5*	T 18		M 17	F 18	
	M 18	F 19	S 18 *Trinity 14*	T 18	S 19	S 18 *Advent 4*
S 19 *Trinity 1*	T 19	S 20	M 19	W 19		M 19
M 20	W 20		T 20	T 20	S 20 *Trinity 23*	T 20
T 21	T 21	S 21 *Trinity 10*	W 21 *Ember*	F 21	M 21	W 21
W 22	F 22	M 22	T 22	S 22	T 22	T 22
T 23	S 23	T 23	F 23 *Ember*		W 23	F 23
F 24 *Nat. J. Bap.*		W 24	S 24 *Ember*	S 23 *Trinity 19*	T 24	S 24
S 25	S 24 *Trinity 6*	T 25		M 24	F 25	
	M 25	F 26	S 25 *Trinity 15*	T 25	S 26	S 25 *Christmas*
S 26 *Trinity 2*	T 26	S 27	M 26	W 26		M 26
M 27	W 27		T 27	T 27	S 27 *Advent 1*	T 27
T 28	T 28	S 28 *Trinity 11*	W 28	F 28	M 28	W 28
W 29	F 29	M 29	T 29 *Michael A.*	S 29	T 29	T 29
T 30	S 30	T 30	F 30		W 30	F 30
		W 31		S 30 *Trinity 20*		S 31
	S 31 *Trinity 7*			M 31		

8/28 Easter Day 18 April

Dominical letter D for Common Years
Dominical letter DC for Leap Years (*in bold figures*)
Old style years   409, **420**, 493, **504**, 583, **588**, 667, 678, 751, 762, 773, 835, 846, 857, **868**, 930, 941, **952**, 1025, **1036**, 1115, **1120**, 1199, 1210, 1283, 1294, 1305, 1367, 1378, 1389, **1400**, 1462, 1473, **1484**, 1557, **1568**, 1647, **1652**, 1731, 1742

Common Years

JANUARY	FEBRUARY
T 1	S 1 *Epiph. 4*
F 2	M 2 *Purific. M.*
S 3	T 3
S 4	W 4
M 5	T 5
T 6 *Epiphany*	F 6
W 7	S 7
T 8	S 8 *Epiph. 5*
F 9	M 9
S 10	T 10
S 11 *Epiph. 1*	W 11
M 12	T 12
T 13 *Hilary*	F 13
W 14	S 14
T 15	S 15 *Septuag.*
F 16	M 16
S 17	T 17
S 18 *Epiph. 2*	W 18
M 19	T 19
T 20	F 20
W 21	S 21
T 22	S 22 *Sexages.*
F 23	M 23
S 24	T 24
S 25 *Epiph. 3*	W 25 *Matthias*
M 26	T 26
T 27	F 27
W 28	S 28
T 29	S 29 *Quinquag.*
F 30	
S 31	

Leap years

JANUARY	FEBRUARY	MARCH	APRIL	MAY
F 1	M 1	M 1	T 1	S 1
S 2	T 2 *Purific. M.*	T 2 *Shrove Tu.*	F 2	S 2 *Easter 2*
S 3	W 3	W 3 *Ash Wed.*	S 3	M 3
M 4	T 4	T 4	S 4 *Passion*	T 4
T 5	F 5	F 5	M 5	W 5
W 6 *Epiphany*	s 6	s 6	T 6	T 6
T 7	S 7 *Epiph. 5*	S 7 *Quadrag.*	W 7	F 7
F 8	M 8	M 8	T 8	s 8
S 9	T 9	T 9	F 9	S 9 *Easter 3*
S 10 *Epiph. 1*	W 10	W 10 *Ember*	S 10	M 10
M 11	T 11	T 11	S 11 *Palm*	T 11
T 12	F 12	F 12 *Ember*	M 12	W 12
W 13 *Hilary*	S 13	S 13 *Ember*	T 13	T 13
T 14	S 14 *Septuag.*	S 14 *Lent 2*	W 14	F 14
F 15	M 15	M 15	T 15	S 15
S 16	T 16	T 16	F 16 *Good Fri.*	S 16 *Easter 4*
S 17 *Epiph. 2*	W 17	W 17	S 17	M 17
M 18	T 18	T 18	S 18 ***Easter Day***	T 18
T 19	F 19	F 19	M 19	W 19
W 20	S 20	S 20	T 20	T 20
T 21	S 21 *Sexages.*	S 21 *Lent 3*	W 21	F 21
F 22	M 22	M 22	T 22	S 22
S 23	T 23	T 23	F 23	S 23 *Rogation*
S 24 *Epiph. 3*	W 24 *Matthias*	W 24	S 24	M 24
M 25	T 25	T 25 *Annunc.*	S 25 *Quasimodo*	T 25
T 26	F 26	F 26	M 26	W 26
W 27	S 27	S 27	T 27	T 27 *Ascension*
T 28	S 28 *Quinquag.*	S 28 *Lent 4*	W 28	F 28
F 29		M 29	T 29	S 29
S 30		T 30	F 30	S 30 *Ascens. 1*
S 31 *Epiph. 4*		W 31		M 31

Easter Day 18 April 8/28

Dominical letter D for Common Years
Dominical letter DC for Leap Years (*in bold figures*)

New style years   1593, **1604**, 1677, 1683, **1688**, 1745, **1756**, 1802, 1813, **1824**, 1897, 1954, 1965, **1976**, 2049, 2055, **2060**

JUNE	JULY	AUGUST	SEPTEMBER	OCTOBER	NOVEMBER	DECEMBER
T 1	T 1	S 1 *Trinity 7*	W1	F 1	M1	W1
W2	F 2	M2	T 2	S 2	T 2	T 2
T 3	S 3	T 3	F 3		W3	F 3
F 4		W4	S 4		T 4	S 4
S 5	....	T 5		S 3 *Trinity 16*	F 5	
	S 4 *Trinity 3*	F 6	....	M4	s 6	....
....	M5	S 7	S 5 *Trinity 12*	T 5		S 5 *Advent 2*
S 6 *Whit Sun.*	T 6		M6	W6	....	M6
M7	W7	....	T 7	T 7	S 7 *Trinity 21*	T 7
T 8	T 8	S 8 *Trinity 8*	W8	F 8	M8	W8
W9 *Ember*	F 9	M9	T 9	S 9	T 9	T 9
T 10	S 10	T 10	F 10		W10	F 10
F 11 *Ember*		W11	S 11	....	T 11 *Martin*	S 11
S 12 *Ember*	....	T 12		S 10 *Trinity 17*	F 12	
	S 11 *Trinity 4*	F 13	....	M11	S 13	....
....	M12	S 14	S 12 *Trinity 13*	T 12		S 12 *Advent 3*
S 13 *Trinity*	T 13		M13	W13	....	M13
M14	W14	....	T 14 *Exalt. C.*	T 14	S 14 *Trinity 22*	T 14
T 15	T 15	S 15 *Trinity 9*	W15 *Ember*	F 15	M15	W15 *Ember*
W16	F 16	M16	T 16	S 16	T 16	T 16
T 17 *Corpus C.*	S 17	T 17	F 17 *Ember*		W17	F 17 *Ember*
F 18		W18	s 18 *Ember*	....	T 18	s 18 *Ember*
S 19	....	T 19		S 17 *Trinity 18*	F 19	
	S 18 *Trinity 5*	F 20	....	M18	S 20	....
....	M19	S 21	S 19 *Trinity 14*	T 19		S 19 *Advent 4*
S 20 *Trinity 1*	T 20		M20	W20	....	M20
M21	W21	....	T 21	T 21	S 21 *Trinity 23*	T 21
T 22	T 22	S 22 *Trinity 10*	W22	F 22	M22	W22
W23	F 23	M23	T 23	S 23	T 23	T 23
T 24 *Nat. J. Bap.*	S 24	T 24	F 24		W24	F 24
F 25		W25	S 25	....	T 25	s 25 *Christmas*
S 26	....	T 26		S 24 *Trinity 19*	F 26	
	S 25 *Trinity 6*	F 27	....	M25	S 27	....
....	M26	s 28	S 26 *Trinity 15*	T 26		S 26
S 27 *Trinity 2*	T 27		M27	W27	....	M27
M28	W28	....	T 28	T 28	S 28 *Advent 1*	T 28
T 29	T 29	S 29 *Trinity 11*	W29 *Michael A.*	F 29	M29	W29
W30	F 30	M30	T 30	S 30	T 30	T 30
	S 31	T 31		....		F 31
				S 31 *Trinity 20*		

8/29 Easter Day 19 April

Dominical letter D for Common Years
Dominical letter ED for Leap Years (*in bold figures*)
Old style years   425, **436**, 515, **520**, 526, 599, 610, 621, 683, 694, 705, **716**, 767, 778, 789, **800**, 862, 873, **884**, 957, 963, **968**, 1047, **1052**, 1058, 1131, 1142, 1153, 1215, 1226, 1237, **1248**, 1299, 1310, 1321, **1332**, 1394, 1405, **1416**, 1489, 1495, **1500**, 1579, **1584**, 1590, 1663, 1674, 1685, 1747

Leap years						
JANUARY	FEBRUARY	JANUARY	FEBRUARY	MARCH	APRIL	MAY
W1	S 1	T 1	S 1 *Epiph. 4*	S 1 *Quiquag.*	W1	F 1
T 2		F 2	M2 *Purific. M.*	M2	T 2	S 2
F 3		S 3	T 3	T 3 *Shrove Tu.*	F 3	
S 4	S 2 *Epiph. 4*		W4	W4 *Ash Wed.*	S 4	S 3 *Easter 2*
	M3		T 5	T 5		M4
S 5	T 4	S 4	F 6	F 6	S 5 *Passion*	T 5
M6 *Epiphany*	W5	M5	S 7	S 7	M6	W6
T 7	T 6	T 6 *Epiphany*			T 7	T 7
W8	F 7	W7			W8	F 8
T 9	S 8	T 8	S 8 *Epiph. 5*	S 8 *Quadrag.*	T 9	S 9
F 10		F 9	M9	M9	F 10	
S 11	S 9 *Epiph. 5*	S 10	T 10	T 10	S 11	S 10 *Easter 3*
	M10		W11	W11 *Ember*		M11
S 12 *Epiph. 1*	T 11	S 11 *Epiph. 1*	T 12	T 12	S 12 *Palm*	T 12
M13 *Hilary*	W12	M12	F 13	F 13 *Ember*	M13	W13
T 14	T 13	T 13 *Hilary*	S 14	S 14 *Ember*	T 14	T 14
W15	F 14	W14			W15	F 15
T 16	S 15	T 15	S 15 *Septuag.*	S 15 *Lent 2*	T 16	S 16
F 17		F 16	M16	M16	F 17 *Good Fri.*	
S 18	S 16 *Septuag.*	S 17	T 17	T 17	S 18	S 17 *Easter 4*
	M17		W18	W18		M18
S 19 *Epiph. 2*	T 18	S 18 *Epiph. 2*	T 19	T 19	S 19 ***Easter Day***	T 19
M20	W19	M19	F 20	F 20	M20	W20
T 21	T 20	T 20	S 21	S 21	T 21	T 21
W22	F 21	W21			W22	F 22
T 23	S 22	T 22	S 22 *Sexages.*	S 22 *Lent 3*	T 23	S 23
F 24		F 23	M23	M23	F 24	
S 25	S 23 *Sexages.*	S 24	T 24 *Matthias*	T 24	S 25	S 24 *Rogation*
	M24		W25	W25 *Annunc.*		M25
S 26 *Epiph. 3*	T 25 *Matthias*	S 25 *Epiph. 3*	T 26	T 26	S 26 *Quasimodo*	T 26
M27	W26	M26	F 27	F 27	M27	W27
T 28	T 27	T 27	S 28	S 28	T 28	T 28 *Ascension*
W29	F 28	W28			W29	F 29
T 30	S 29	T 29		S 29 *Lent 4*	T 30	S 30
F 31		T 29	F 30	M30		
			S 31	T 31		S 31 *Ascens. 1*

Easter Day 19 April 8/29
Dominical letter D for Common Years
Dominical letter ED for Leap Years (*in bold figures*)
New style years   1609, 1615, **1620**, 1699, 1767, **1772**, 1778, 1829, 1835, **1840**, **1908**, 1981, 1987, **1992**, 2071, **2076**, 2082

JUNE	JULY	AUGUST	SEPTEMBER	OCTOBER	NOVEMBER	DECEMBER
M1	W1	s 1 *Lammas*	T 1	T 1	S 1 *Trinity 20*	T 1
T 2	T 2		W2	F 2	M2	W2
W3	F 3	S 2 *Trinity 7*	T 3	S 3	T 3	T 3
T 4	S 4	M3	F 4		W4	F 4
F 5		T 4	S 5		T 5	S 5
s 6	S 5 *Trinity 3*	W5		S 4 *Trinity 16*	F 6	
	M6	T 6	S 6 *Trinity 12*	M5	S 7	S 6 *Advent 2*
S 7 *Whit Sun.*	T 7	F 7	M7	T 6		M7
M8	W8	s 8	T 8	W7	S 8 *Trinity 21*	T 8
T 9	T 9		W9	T 8	M9	W9
W10 *Ember*	F 10	S 9 *Trinity 8*	T 10	F 9	T 10	T 10
T 11	S 11	M10	F 11	S 10	W11 *Martin*	F 11
F 12 *Ember*		T 11	S 12		T 12	S 12
s 13 *Ember*	S 12 *Trinity 4*	W12		S 11 *Trinity 17*	F 13	
	M13	T 13	S 13 *Trinity 13*	M12	S 14	S 13 *Advent 3*
S 14 *Trinity*	T 14	F 14	M14 *Exalt. C.*	T 13		M14
M15	W15	S 15	T 15	W14	S 15 *Trinity 22*	T 15
T 16	T 16		W16 *Ember*	T 15	M16	W16 *Ember*
W17	F 17	S 16 *Trinity 9*	T 17	F 16	T 17	T 17
T 18 *Corpus C.*	s 18	M17	F 18 *Ember*	S 17	W18	F 18 *Ember*
F 19		T 18	s 19 *Ember*		T 19	s 19 *Ember*
S 20	S 19 *Trinity 5*	W19		S 18 *Trinity 18*	F 20	
	M20	T 20	S 20 *Trinity 14*	M19	S 21	S 20 *Advent 4*
S 21 *Trinity 1*	T 21	F 21	M21	T 20		M21
M22	W22	S 22	T 22	W21	S 22 *Trinity 23*	T 22
T 23	T 23		W23	T 22	M23	W23
W24 *Nat. J. Bap.*	F 24	S 23 *Trinity 10*	T 24	F 23	T 24	T 24
T 25	S 25	M24	F 25	S 24	W25	F 25 *Christmas*
F 26		T 25	S 26		T 26	S 26
S 27	S 26 *Trinity 6*	W26		S 25 *Trinity 19*	F 27	
	M27	T 27	S 27 *Trinity 15*	M26	S 28	S 27
S 28 *Trinity 2*	T 28	F 28	M28	T 27		M28
M29	W29	S 29	T 29 *Michael A.*	W28	S 29 *Advent 1*	T 29
T 30	T 30		W30	T 29	M30	W30
	F 31	S 30 *Trinity 11*		F 30		T 31
		M31		S 31		

8/30 Easter Day 20 April

Dominical letter E for Common Years
Dominical letter FE for Leap Years (*in bold figures*)
Old style years 447, 458, 531, 542, 553, 615, 626, 637, **648**, 710, 721, **732**, 805, **816**, 895, **900**, 979, 990, 1063, 1074, 1085, 1147, 1158, 1169, **1180**, 1242, 1253, **1264**, 1337, **1348**, 1427, **1432**, 1511, 1522, 1595, 1606, 1617, 1679, 1690, 1701, **1712**

Leap years

JANUARY	FEBRUARY
T 1	F 1
W2	S 2 *Purific. M.*
T 3	
F 4	....
S 5	S 3 *Epiph. 4*
....	M4
S 6 *Epiphany*	T 5
M7	W6
T 8	T 7
W9	F 8
T 10	S 9
F 11	....
S 12	S 10 *Epiph. 5*
....	M11
S 13 *Epiph. 1*	T 12
M14	W13
T 15	T 14
W16	F 15
T 17	S 16
F 18	....
S 19	S 17 *Septuag.*
....	M18
S 20 *Epiph. 2*	T 19
M21	W20
T 22	T 21
W23	F 22
T 24	S 23
F 25	....
S 26	S 24 *Sexages.*
....	M25 *Matthias*
S 27 *Epiph. 3*	T 26
M28	W27
T 29	T 28
W30	F 29
T 31	

JANUARY	FEBRUARY	MARCH	APRIL	MAY
W1	S 1	S 1	T 1	T 1
T 2			W2	F 2
F 3	....	....	T 3	S 3
S 4	S 2 *Epiph. 4*	S 2 *Quinquag.*	F 4	....
	M3	M3	S 5	S 4 *Easter 2*
....	T 4	T 4 *Shrove Tu.*	....	M5
S 5	W5	W5 *Ash Wed.*	S 6 *Passion*	T 6
M6 *Epiphany*	T 6	T 6	M7	W7
T 7	F 7	F 7	T 8	T 8
W8	S 8	S 8	W9	F 9
T 9	....	....	T 10	S 10
F 10	S 9 *Epiph. 5*	S 9 *Quadrag.*	F 11	....
S 11	M10	M10	S 12	S 11 *Easter 3*
....	T 11	T 11	....	M12
S 12 *Epiph. 1*	W12	W12 *Ember*	S 13 *Palm*	T 13
M13 *Hilary*	T 13	T 13	M14	W14
T 14	F 14	F 14 *Ember*	T 15	T 15
W15	S 15	S 15 *Ember*	W16	F 16
T 16	....	....	T 17	S 17
F 17	S 16 *Septuag.*	S 16 *Lent 2*	F 18 *Good Fri.*	....
S 18	M17	M17	S 19	S 18 *Easter 4*
....	T 18	T 18	....	M19
S 19 *Epiph. 2*	W19	W19	S 20 ***Easter Day***	T 20
M20	T 20	T 20	M21	W21
T 21	F 21	F 21	T 22	T 22
W22	S 22	S 22	W23	F 23
T 23	....	....	T 24	S 24
F 24	S 23 *Sexages.*	S 23 *Lent 3*	F 25	....
S 25	M24 *Matthias*	M24	S 26	S 25 *Rogation*
....	T 25	T 25 *Annunc.*	....	M26
S 26 *Epiph. 3*	W26	W26	S 27 *Quasimodo*	T 27
M27	T 27	T 27	M28	W28
T 28	F 28	F 28	T 29	T 29 *Ascension*
W29		S 29	W30	F 30
T 30		....		S 31
F 31		S 30 *Lent 4*		
		M31		

Easter Day 20 April

Dominical letter E for Common Years
Dominical letter FE for Leap Years (*in bold figures*)
New style years   1631, 1642, 1710, 1783, 1794, 1851, 1862, 1919, **1924**, 1930, 2003, 2014, 2025, 2087, 2098

JUNE	JULY	AUGUST	SEPTEMBER	OCTOBER	NOVEMBER	DECEMBER
S 1 *Ascens. 1*	T 1	F 1 *Lammas*	M1	W1	S 1	M1
M2	W2	S 2	T 2	T 2		T 2
T 3	T 3		W3	F 3	S 2 *Trinity 20*	W3
W4	F 4	S 3 *Trinity 7*	T 4	S 4	M3	T 4
T 5	S 5	M4	F 5		T 4	F 5
F 6		T 5	s 6	S 5 *Trinity 16*	W5	s 6
S 7	S 6 *Trinity 3*	W6		M6	T 6	
	M7	T 7	S 7 *Trinity 12*	T 7	F 7	S 7 *Advent 2*
S 8 *Whit Sun.*	T 8	F 8	M8	W8	s 8	M8
M9	W9	S 9	T 9	T 9		T 9
T 10	T 10		W10	F 10	S 9 *Trinity 21*	W10
W11 *Ember*	F 11	S 10 *Trinity 8*	T 11	S 11	M10	T 11
T 12	S 12	M11	F 12		T 11 *Martin*	F 12
F 13 *Ember*		T 12	S 13	S 12 *Trinity 17*	W12	s 13
s 14 *Ember*	S 13 *Trinity 4*	W13		M13	T 13	
	M14	T 14	S 14 *Trinity 13*	T 14	F 14	S 14 *Advent 3*
S 15 *Trinity*	T 15	F 15	M15	W15	S 15	M15
M16	T 16	s 16	T 16	T 16		T 16
T 17	T 17		W17 *Ember*	F 17	S 16 *Trinity 22*	W17 *Ember*
W18	F 18	S 17 *Trinity 9*	T 18	S 18	M17	T 18
T 19 *Corpus C.*	S 19	M18	F 19 *Ember*		T 18	F 19 *Ember*
F 20		T 19	s 20 *Ember*	S 19 *Trinity 18*	W19	s 20 *Ember*
S 21	S 20 *Trinity 5*	W20		M20	T 20	
	M21	T 21	S 21 *Trinity 14*	T 21	F 21	S 21 *Advent 4*
S 22 *Trinity 1*	T 22	F 22	M22	W22	S 22	M22
M23	W23	s 23	T 23	T 23		T 23
T 24 *Nat. J. Bap.*	T 24		W24	F 24	S 23 *Trinity 23*	W24
W25	F 25	S 24 *Trinity 10*	T 25	S 25	M24	T 25 *Christmas*
T 26	S 26	M25	F 26		T 25	F 26
F 27		T 26	s 27	S 26 *Trinity 19*	W26	S 27
s 28	S 27 *Trinity 6*	W27		M27	T 27	
	M28	T 28	S 28 *Trinity 15*	T 28	F 28	S 28
S 29 *Trinity 2*	T 29	F 29	M29 *Michael A.*	W29	S 29	M29
M30	W30	s 30	T 30	T 30		T 30
	T 31			F 31	S 30 *Advent 1*	W31
		S 31 *Trinity 11*				

8/31 Easter Day 21 April

Dominical letter F for Common Years
Dominical letter GF for Leap Years (*in bold figures*)
Old style years   463, 474, 485, 558, 569, **580**, 653, **664**, **748**, 827, 911, 922, 995, 1006, 1017, 1090, 1101, **1112**, 1185, **1196**, **1280**, 1359, 1443, 1454, 1527, 1538, 1549, 1622, 1633, **1644**, 1717, **1728**

Leap years

JANUARY	FEBRUARY
M1	T 1
T 2	F 2 Purific. M.
W3	S 3
T 4	
F 5	S 4 Epiph. 5
s 6 Epiphany	M5
	T 6
S 7 Epiph. 1	W7
M8	T 8
T 9	F 9
W10	S 10
T 11	
F 12	S 11 Epiph. 6
s 13 Hilary	M12
	T 13
S 14 Epiph. 2	W14
M15	T 15
T 16	F 16
W17	S 17
T 18	
F 19	S 18 Septuag.
S 20	M19
	T 20
S 21 Epiph. 3	W21
M22	T 22
T 23	F 23
W24	S 24
T 25	
F 26	S 25 Sexages.
S 27	M26
	T 27
S 28 Epiph. 4	W28
M29	T 29
T 30	
W31	

JANUARY	FEBRUARY	MARCH	APRIL	MAY
T 1	F 1	F 1	M1	W1
W2	S 2 Purific. M.	S 2	T 2	T 2
T 3			W3	F 3
F 4	S 3 Epiph. 4	S 3 Quinquag.	T 4	S 4
S 5	M4	M4	F 5	
	T 5	T 5 Shrove Tu.	s 6	S 5 Easter 2
S 6 Epiphany	w6	w6 Ash Wed.		M6
M7	T 7	T 7	S 7 Passion	T 7
T 8	F 8	F 8	M8	W8
W9	S 9	S 9	T 9	T 9
T 10			W10	F 10
F 11	S 10 Epiph. 5	S 10 Quadrag.	T 11	S 11
S 12	M11	M11	F 12	
	T 12	T 12	S 13	S 12 Easter 3
S 13 Epiph. 1	W13	W13 Ember		M13
M14	T 14	T 14	S 14 Palm	T 14
T 15	F 15	F 15 Ember	M15	W15
W16	S 16	s 16 Ember	T 16	T 16
T 17			W17	F 17
F 18	S 17 Septuag.	S 17 Lent 2	T 18	S 18
S 19	M18	M18	F 19 Good Fri.	
	T 19	T 19	S 20	S 19 Easter 4
S 20 Epiph. 2	W20	W20		M20
M21	T 21	T 21	S 21 *Easter Day*	T 21
T 22	F 22	F 22	M22	W22
W23	S 23	S 23	T 23	T 23
T 24			W24	F 24
F 25	S 24 Sexages.	S 24 Lent 3	T 25	S 25
S 26	M25	M25 Annunc.	F 26	
	T 26	T 26	S 27	S 26 Rogation
S 27 Epiph. 3	W27	W27		M27
M28	T 28	T 28	S 28 Quasimodo	T 28
T 29		F 29	M29	W29
W30		S 30	T 30	T 30 Ascension
T 31		S 31 Lent 4		F 31

Dominical letter F for Common Years
Dominical letter GF for Leap Years (*in bold figures*)
New style years   1585, 1647, 1658, 1669, **1680**, 1715, 1726, 1737, 1867, 1878, 1889, 1935, 1946, 1957, 2019, 2030, 2041, **2052**

JUNE	JULY	AUGUST	SEPTEMBER	OCTOBER	NOVEMBER	DECEMBER
S 1	M1	T 1 *Lammas*	S 1 *Trinity 11*	T 1	F 1	S 1 *Advent 1*
	T 2	F 2	M2	W2	S 2	M2
S 2 *Ascens. 1*	W3	S 3	T 3	T 3		T 3
M3	T 4		W4	F 4	S 3 *Trinity 20*	W4
T 4	F 5	S 4 *Trinity 7*	T 5	S 5	M4	T 5
W5	s 6	M5	F 6		T 5	F 6
T 6		T 6	S 7	S 6 *Trinity 16*	W6	S 7
F 7	S 7 *Trinity 3*	W7		M7	T 7	
s 8	M8	T 8	S 8 *Trinity 12*	T 8	F 8	S 8 *Advent 2*
	T 9	F 9	M9	W9	S 9	M9
S 9 *Whit Sun.*	W10	S 10	T 10	T 10		T 10
M10	T 11		W11	F 11	S 10 *Trinity 21*	W11
T 11	F 12	S 11 *Trinity 8*	T 12	S 12	M11 *Martin*	T 12
W12 *Ember*	S 13	M12	F 13		T 12	F 13
T 13		T 13	s 14 *Exalt. C.*	S 13 *Trinity 17*	W13	S 14
F 14 *Ember*	S 14 *Trinity 4*	W14		M14	T 14	
s 15 *Ember*	M15	T 15	S 15 *Trinity 13*	T 15	F 15	S 15 *Advent 3*
	T 16	F 16	M16	W16	S 16	M16
S 16 *Trinity*	W17	S 17	T 17	T 17		T 17
M17	T 18		W18 *Ember*	F 18	S 17 *Trinity 22*	W18 *Ember*
T 18	F 19	S 18 *Trinity 9*	T 19	S 19	M18	T 19
W19	S 20	M19	F 20 *Ember*		T 19	F 20 *Ember*
T 20 *Corpus C.*		T 20	s 21 *Ember*	S 20 *Trinity 18*	W20	s 21 *Ember*
F 21	S 21 *Trinity 5*	W21		M21	T 21	
S 22	M22	T 22	S 22 *Trinity 14*	T 22	F 22	S 22 *Advent 4*
	T 23	F 23	M23	W23	S 23	M23
S 23 *Trinity 1*	W24	S 24	T 24	T 24		T 24
M24 *Nat. J. Bap.*	T 25		W25	F 25	S 24 *Trinity 23*	W25 *Christmas*
T 25	F 26	S 25 *Trinity 10*	T 26	S 26	M25	T 26
W26	S 27	M26	F 27		T 26	F 27
T 27		T 27	s 28	S 27 *Trinity 19*	W27	s 28
F 28	S 28 *Trinity 6*	W28		M28	T 28	
S 29	M29	T 29	S 29 *Trinity 15*	T 29	F 29	S 29
	T 30	F 30	M30	W30	S 30	M30
S 30 *Trinity 2*	W31	S 31		T 31		T 31

8/32 Easter Day 22 April

Dominical letter G for Common Years
Dominical letter AG for Leap Years (*in bold figures*)
Old style years   406, 417, **428**, 501, **512**, **596**, 675, 759, 770, 843, 854, 865, 938, 949, **960**, 1033, **1044**, **1128**, 1207, 1291, 1302, 1375, 1386, 1397, 1470, 1481, **1492**, 1565, **1576**, **1660**, 1739

Leap years						
JANUARY	FEBRUARY	JANUARY	FEBRUARY	MARCH	APRIL	MAY
S 1	W1	M1	T 1	T 1	S 1 *Lent 4*	T 1
M2	T 2 *Purific. M.*	T 2	F 2 *Purific. M.*	F 2	M2	W2
T 3	F 3	W3	S 3	S 3	T 3	T 3
W4	S 4	T 4			W4	F 4
T 5		F 5	S 4 *Epiph. 5*	S 4 *Quinquag.*	T 5	S 5
F 6 *Epiphany*	S 5 *Epiph. 5*	s 6 *Epiphany*	M5	M5	F 6	
S 7	M6		T 6	T 6 *Shrove Tu.*	S 7	S 6 *Easter 2*
	T 7	S 7 *Epiph. 1*	W7	w7 *Ash Wed.*		M7
S 8 *Epiph. 1*	W8	M8	T 8	T 8	S 8 *Passion*	T 8
M9	T 9	T 9	F 9	F 9	M9	W9
T 10	F 10	W10	S 10	S 10	T 10	T 10
W11	S 11	T 11			W11	F 11
T 12		F 12	S 11 *Epiph. 6*	S 11 *Quadrag.*	T 12	S 12
F 13 *Hilary*	S 12 *Epiph. 6*	s 13 *Hilary*	M12	M12	F 13	
S 14	M13		T 13	T 13	S 14	S 13 *Easter 3*
	T 14	S 14 *Epiph. 2*	W14	W14 *Ember*		M14
S 15 *Epiph. 2*	W15	M15	T 15	T 15	S 15 *Palm*	T 15
M16	T 16	T 16	F 16	F 16 *Ember*	M16	W16
T 17	F 17	W17	S 17	s 17 *Ember*	T 17	T 17
W18	S 18	T 18			W18	F 18
T 19		F 19	S 18 *Septuag.*	S 18 *Lent 2*	T 19	S 19
F 20	S 19 *Septuag.*	S 20	M19	M19	F 20 *Good Fri.*	
S 21	M20		T 20	T 20	S 21	S 20 *Easter 4*
	T 21	S 21 *Epiph. 3*	W21	W21		M21
S 22 *Epiph. 3*	W22	M22	T 22	T 22	S 22 ***Easter Day***	T 22
M23	T 23	T 23	F 23	F 23	M23	W23
T 24	F 24	W24	s 24 *Matthias*	S 24	T 24	T 24
W25	s 25 *Matthias*	T 25			W25	F 25
T 26		F 26	S 25 *Sexages.*	S 25 *Lent 3*	T 26	S 26
F 27	S 26 *Sexages.*	S 27	M26	M26	F 27	
S 28	M27		T 27	T 27	S 28	S 27 *Rogation*
	T 28	S 28 *Epiph. 4*	W28	W28		M28
S 29 *Epiph. 4*	W29	M29		T 29	S 29 *Quasimodo*	T 29
M30		T 30		F 30	M30	W30
T 31		W31		S 31		T 31 *Ascension*

Easter Day 22 April 8/32

Dominical letter G for Common Years
Dominical letter AG for Leap Years (*in bold figures*)
New style years 1590, 1601, **1612**, 1685, **1696**, 1753, **1764**, 1810, 1821, **1832**, 1962, 1973, **1984**, 2057, **2068**

JUNE	JULY	AUGUST	SEPTEMBER	OCTOBER	NOVEMBER	DECEMBER
F 1	S 1 *Trinity 2*	W1 *Lammas*	S 1	M1	T 1	S 1
S 2	M2	T 2		T 2	F 2	
	T 3	F 3		W3	S 3	
	W4	S 4	S 2 *Trinity 11*	T 4		S 2 *Advent 1*
S 3 *Ascens. 1*	T 5		M3	F 5		M3
M4	F 6		T 4	s 6	S 4 *Trinity 20*	T 4
T 5	S 7	S 5 *Trinity 7*	W5		M5	W5
W6		M6	T 6		T 6	T 6
T 7		T 7	F 7	S 7 *Trinity 16*	W7	F 7
F 8	S 8 *Trinity 3*	W8	s 8	M8	T 8	s 8
S 9	M9	T 9		T 9	F 9	
	T 10	F 10		W10	S 10	
S 10 *Whit Sun.*	W11	S 11	S 9 *Trinity 12*	T 11		S 9 *Advent 2*
M11	T 12		M10	F 12		M10
T 12	F 13		T 11	S 13	S 11 *Trinity 21*	T 11
W13 *Ember*	S 14	S 12 *Trinity 8*	W12		M12	W12
T 14		M13	T 13		T 13	T 13
F 15 *Ember*	S 15 *Trinity 4*	T 14	F 14 *Exalt. C.*	S 14 *Trinity 17*	W14	F 14
s 16 *Ember*	M16	W15	s 15	M15	T 15	S 15
	T 17	F 17		T 16	F 16	
	W18	s 18	S 16 *Trinity 13*	W17	S 17	
S 17 *Trinity*	T 19		M17	T 18		S 16 *Advent 3*
M18	F 20		T 18	F 19		M17
T 19	S 21	S 19 *Trinity 9*	W19 *Ember*	S 20	S 18 *Trinity 22*	T 18
W20		M20	T 20		M19	W19 *Ember*
T 21 *Corpus C.*		T 21	F 21 *Ember*		T 20	T 20
F 22	S 22 *Trinity 5*	W22	s 22 *Ember*	S 21 *Trinity 18*	W21	F 21 *Ember*
S 23	M23	T 23		M22	T 22	s 22 *Ember*
	T 24	F 24		T 23	F 23	
	W25	S 25	S 23 *Trinity 14*	W24	S 24	
S 24 *Trinity 1*	T 26		M24	T 25		S 23 *Advent 4*
M25	F 27		T 25	F 26		M24
T 26	S 28	S 26 *Trinity 10*	W26	S 27	S 25 *Trinity 23*	T 25 *Christmas*
W27		M27	T 27		M26	W26
T 28		T 28	F 28		T 27	T 27
F 29	S 29 *Trinity 6*	W29	s 29 *Michael A.*	S 28 *Trinity 19*	W28	F 28
S 30	M30	T 30		M29	T 29	S 29
	T 31	F 31		T 30	F 30	
			S 30 *Trinity 15*	W31		S 30
						M31

8/33 Easter Day 23 April

Dominical letter A for Common Years
Dominical letter BA for Leap Years (*in bold figures*)
Old style years   444, 607, 691, 702, 786, 797, 881, **892**, **976**, 1139, 1223, 1234, 1318, 1329, 1413, **1424**, **1508**, 1671

Leap years						
JANUARY	FEBRUARY	JANUARY	FEBRUARY	MARCH	APRIL	MAY
S 1	T 1	S 1	W1	W1	S 1	M1
	W2 *Purific. M.*	M2	T 2 *Purific. M.*	T 2		T 2
S 2	T 3	T 3	F 3	F 3	S 2 *Lent 4*	W3
M3	F 4	W4	S 4	S 4	M3	T 4
T 4	S 5	T 5			T 4	F 5
W5		F 6 *Epiphany*	S 5 *Epiph. 5*	S 5 *Quinquag.*	W5	s 6
T 6 *Epiphany*	S 6 *Epiph. 5*	S 7	M6	M6	T 6	
F 7	M7		T 7	T 7 *Shrove Tu.*	F 7	S 7 *Easter 2*
s 8	T 8	S 8 *Epiph. 1*	W8	W8 *Ash Wed.*	s 8	M8
	W9	M9	T 9	T 9		T 9
S 9 *Epiph. 1*	T 10	T 10	F 10	F 10	S 9 *Passion*	W10
M10	F 11	W11	S 11	S 11	M10	T 11
T 11	S 12	T 12			T 11	F 12
W12		F 13 *Hilary*	S 12 *Epiph. 6*	S 12 *Quadrag.*	W12	S 13
T 13 *Hilary*	S 13 *Epiph. 6*	S 14	M13	M13	T 13	
F 14	M14		T 14	T 14	F 14	S 14 *Easter 3*
S 15	T 15	S 15 *Epiph. 2*	W15	W15 *Ember*	S 15	M15
	W16	M16	T 16	T 16		T 16
S 16 *Epiph. 2*	T 17	T 17	F 17	F 17 *Ember*	S 16 *Palm*	W17
M17	F 18	W18	S 18	s 18 *Ember*	M17	T 18
T 18	S 19	T 19			T 18	F 19
W19		F 20	S 19 *Septuag.*	S 19 *Lent 2*	W19	S 20
T 20	S 20 *Septuag.*	S 21	M20	M20	T 20	
F 21	M21		T 21	T 21	F 21 *Good Fri.*	S 21 *Easter 4*
S 22	T 22	S 22 *Epiph. 3*	W22	W22	S 22	M22
	W23	M23	T 23	T 23		T 23
S 23 *Epiph. 3*	T 24	T 24	F 24 *Matthias*	F 24	S 23 ***Easter Day***	W24
M24	F 25 *Matthias*	W25	S 25	S 25 *Annunc.*	M24	T 25
T 25	S 26	T 26			T 25	F 26
W26		F 27	S 26 *Sexages.*	S 26 *Lent 3*	W26	S 27
T 27	S 27 *Sexages.*	s 28	M27	M27	T 27	
F 28	M28		T 28	T 28	F 28	S 28 *Rogation*
S 29	T 29	S 29 *Epiph. 4*	W29	W29	S 29	M29
		M30		T 30		T 30
S 30 *Epiph. 4*		T 31		F 31	S 30 *Quasimodo*	W31
M31						

Easter Day 23 April 8/33

Dominical letter A for Common Years
Dominical letter BA for Leap Years (*in bold figures*)
New style years **1628**, **1848**, 1905, **1916**, **2000**, 2079

JUNE	JULY	AUGUST	SEPTEMBER	OCTOBER	NOVEMBER	DECEMBER
T 1 *Ascension*	S 1	T 1 *Lammas*	F 1	S 1 *Trinity 15*	W1	F 1
F 2	W2	W2	S 2	M2	T 2	S 2
S 3		T 3		T 3	F 3	
	S 2 *Trinity 2*	F 4		W4	S 4	
S 4 *Ascens. 1*	M3	S 5	S 3 *Trinity 11*	T 5		S 3 *Advent 1*
M5	T 4		M4	F 6		M4
T 6	W5		T 5	S 7	S 5 *Trinity 20*	T 5
W7	T 6	S 6 *Trinity 7*	W6		M6	W6
T 8	F 7	M7	T 7		T 7	T 7
F 9	S 8	T 8	F 8	S 8 *Trinity 16*	W8	F 8
S 10		W9	S 9	M9	T 9	S 9
	S 9 *Trinity 3*	T 10	T 10	T 10	F 10	
S 11 *Whit Sun.*	M10	F 11		W11	S 11 *Martin*	S 10 *Advent 2*
M12	T 11	S 12	S 10 *Trinity 12*	T 12		M11
T 13	W12		M11	F 13	S 12 *Trinity 21*	T 12
W14 *Ember*	T 13	S 13 *Trinity 8*	T 12	S 14	M13	W13
T 15	F 14	M14	W13		T 14	T 14
F 16 *Ember*	S 15	T 15	T 14 *Exalt. C.*		W15	F 15
S 17 *Ember*		W16	F 15	S 15 *Trinity 17*	T 16	S 16
	S 16 *Trinity 4*	T 17	S 16	M16	F 17	
S 18 *Trinity*	M17	F 18		T 17	S 18	S 17 *Advent 3*
M19	T 18	S 19	S 17 *Trinity 13*	W18		M18
T 20	W19		M18	T 19	S 19 *Trinity 22*	T 19
W21	T 20	S 20 *Trinity 9*	T 19	F 20	M20	W20 *Ember*
T 22 *Corpus C.*	F 21	M21	W20 *Ember*	S 21	T 21	T 21
F 23	S 22	T 22	T 21		W22	F 22 *Ember*
S 24 *Nat. J. Bap.*		W23	F 22 *Ember*	S 22 *Trinity 18*	T 23	S 23 *Ember*
	S 23 *Trinity 5*	T 24	S 23 *Ember*	M23	F 24	
S 25 *Trinity 1*	M24	F 25		T 24	S 25	S 24 *Advent 4*
M26	T 25	S 26	S 24 *Trinity 14*	W25		M25 *Christmas*
T 27	W26		M25	T 26	S 26 *Trinity 23*	T 26
W28	T 27	S 27 *Trinity 10*	T 26	F 27	M27	W27
T 29	F 28	M28	W27	S 28	T 28	T 28
F 30	S 29	T 29	T 28		W29	F 29
		W30	F 29 *Michael A.*	S 29 *Trinity 19*	T 30	S 30
	S 30 *Trinity 6*	T 31	S 30	M30		
	M31			T 31		S 31

8/34 Easter Day 24 April

Dominical letter B for Common Years
Dominical letter CB for Leap Years (*in bold figures*)
Old style years   455, 539, 550, 634, 645, 729, **740**, **824**, 987, 1071, 1082, 1166, 1177, 1261, **1272**, **1356**, 1519, 1603, 1614, 1698, 1709

Leap years						
JANUARY	FEBRUARY	JANUARY	FEBRUARY	MARCH	APRIL	MAY
F 1	M1	S 1	T 1	T 1	F 1	S 1 *Quasimodo*
S 2	T 2 *Purific. M.*		W2 *Purific. M.*	W2	S 2	M2
	W3	S 2	T 3	T 3		T 3
	T 4	M3	F 4	F 4		W4
S 3	F 5	T 4	S 5	S 5	S 3 *Lent 4*	T 5
M4	S 6	W5			M4	F 6
T 5		T 6 *Epiphany*			T 5	S 7
W6 *Epiphany*		F 7	S 6 *Epiph. 5*	S 6 *Quinquag.*	W6	
T 7	S 7 *Epiph. 5*	S 8	M7	M7	T 7	
F 8	M8		T 8	T 8 *Shrove Tu.*	F 8	S 8 *Easter 2*
S 9	T 9		W9	W9 *Ash Wed.*	S 9	M9
	W10	S 9 *Epiph. 1*	T 10	T 10		T 10
S 10 *Epiph. 1*	T 11	M10	F 11	F 11	S 10 *Passion*	W11
M11	F 12	T 11	S 12	S 12	M11	T 12
T 12	S 13	W12			T 12	F 13
W13 *Hilary*		T 13 *Hilary*	S 13 *Epiph. 6*	S 13 *Quadrag.*	W13	S 14
T 14	S 14 *Epiph. 6*	F 14	M14	M14	T 14	
F 15	M15	S 15	T 15	T 15	F 15	S 15 *Easter 3*
S 16	T 16		W16	W16 *Ember*	S 16	M16
	W17	S 16 *Epiph. 2*	T 17	T 17		T 17
S 17 *Epiph. 2*	T 18	M17	F 18	F 18 *Ember*	S 17 *Palm*	W18
M18	F 19	T 18	S 19	S 19 *Ember*	M18	T 19
T 19	S 20	W19			T 19	F 20
W20		T 20	S 20 *Septuag.*	S 20 *Lent 2*	W20	S 21
T 21	S 21 *Septuag.*	F 21	M21	M21	T 21	
F 22	M22	S 22	T 22	T 22	F 22 *Good Fri.*	S 22 *Easter 4*
S 23	T 23		W23	W23	S 23	M23
	W24	S 23 *Epiph. 3*	T 24 *Matthias*	T 24		T 24
S 24 *Epiph. 3*	T 25 *Matthias*	M24	F 25	F 25 *Annunc.*	S 24 ***Easter Day***	W25
M25	F 26	T 25	S 26	S 26	M25	T 26
T 26	S 27	W26			T 26	F 27
W27		T 27	S 27 *Sexages.*	S 27 *Lent 3*	W27	S 28
T 28	S 28 *Sexages.*	F 28	M28	M28	T 28	
F 29	M29	S 29		T 29	F 29	S 29 *Rogation*
S 30				W30	S 30	M30
		S 30 *Epiph. 4*		T 31		T 31
S 31 *Epiph. 4*		M31				

Dominical letter B for Common Years
Dominical letter CB for Leap Years (*in bold figures*)
New style years 1639, 1707, 1791, 1859, 2011

JUNE	JULY	AUGUST	SEPTEMBER	OCTOBER	NOVEMBER	DECEMBER
W 1	F 1	M 1 *Lammas*	T 1	S 1	T 1	T 1
T 2 *Ascension*	S 2	T 2	F 2	F 2	W 2	F 2
F 3		W 3	S 3		T 3	S 3
S 4	S 3 *Trinity 2*	T 4		S 2 *Trinity 15*	F 4	
	M 4	F 5	S 4 *Trinity 11*	M 3	S 5	S 4 *Advent 2*
S 5 *Ascens. 1*	T 5	S 6	M 5	T 4		M 5
M 6	W 6		T 6	W 5	S 6 *Trinity 20*	T 6
T 7	T 7	S 7 *Trinity 7*	W 7	T 6	M 7	W 7
W 8	F 8	M 8	T 8	F 7	T 8	T 8
T 9	S 9	T 9	F 9	S 8	W 9	F 9
F 10		W 10	S 10		T 10	S 10
S 11	S 10 *Trinity 3*	T 11		S 9 *Trinity 16*	F 11 *Martin*	
	M 11	F 12	S 11 *Trinity 12*	M 10	S 12	S 11 *Advent 3*
S 12 *Whit Sun.*	T 12	S 13	M 12	T 11		M 12
M 13	W 13		T 13	W 12	S 13 *Trinity 21*	T 13
T 14	T 14	S 14 *Trinity 8*	W 14 *Exalt. C.*	T 13	M 14	W 14 *Ember*
W 15 *Ember*	F 15	M 15	T 15	F 14	T 15	T 15
T 16	S 16	T 16	F 16	S 15	W 16	F 16 *Ember*
F 17 *Ember*		W 17	S 17		T 17	S 17 *Ember*
S 18 *Ember*	S 17 *Trinity 4*	T 18		S 16 *Trinity 17*	F 18	
	M 18	F 19	S 18 *Trinity 13*	M 17	S 19	S 18 *Advent 4*
S 19 *Trinity*	T 19	S 20	M 19	T 18		M 19
M 20	W 20		T 20	W 19	S 20 *Trinity 22*	T 20
T 21	T 21	S 21 *Trinity 9*	W 21 *Ember*	T 20	M 21	W 21
W 22	F 22	M 22	T 22	F 21	T 22	T 22
T 23 *Corpus C.*	S 23	T 23	F 23 *Ember*	S 22	W 23	F 23
F 24 *Nat. J. Bap.*		W 24	S 24 *Ember*		T 24	S 24
S 25	S 24 *Trinity 5*	T 25		S 23 *Trinity 18*	F 25	
	M 25	F 26	S 25 *Trinity 14*	M 24	S 26	S 25 *Christmas*
S 26 *Trinity 1*	T 26	S 27	M 26	T 25		M 26
M 27	W 27		T 27	W 26	S 27 *Advent 1*	T 27
T 28	T 28	S 28 *Trinity 10*	W 28	T 27	M 28	W 28
W 29	F 29	M 29	T 29 *Michael A.*	F 28	T 29	T 29
T 30	S 30	T 30	F 30	S 29	W 30	F 30
		W 31				S 31
	S 31 *Trinity 6*			S 30 *Trinity 19*		
				M 31		

8/35 Easter Day 25 April

Dominical letter C for Common Years
Dominical letter DC for Leap Years (*in bold figures*)
Old style years   482, 577, **672**, 919, 1014, 1109, **1204**, 1451, 1546, 1641, **1736**

Leap years						
JANUARY	FEBRUARY	JANUARY	FEBRUARY	MARCH	APRIL	MAY
T 1	S 1 *Epiph. 4*	F 1	M1	M1	T 1	S 1
F 2	M2 *Purific. M.*	S 2	T 2 *Purific. M.*	T 2	F 2	
S 3	T 3		W3	W3	S 3	
	W4	S 3	T 4	T 4		S 2 *Quasimodo*
S 4	T 5	M4	F 5	F 5	S 4 *Lent 4*	M3
M5	F 6	T 5	S 6	S 6	M5	T 4
T 6 *Epiphany*	S 7	w6 *Epiphany*			T 6	W5
W7		T 7	S 7 *Epiph. 5*	S 7 *Quinquag.*	W7	T 6
T 8	S 8 *Epiph. 5*	F 8	M8	M8	T 8	F 7
F 9	M9	S 9	T 9	T 9 *Shrove Tu.*	F 9	S 8
S 10	T 10		W10	W10 *Ash Wed.*	S 10	
	W11	S 10 *Epiph. 1*	T 11	T 11		S 9 *Easter 2*
S 11 *Epiph. 1*	T 12	M11	F 12	F 12	S 11 *Passion*	M10
M12	F 13	T 12	S 13	S 13	M12	T 11
T 13 *Hilary*	S 14	w13 *Hilary*			T 13	W12
W14		T 14	S 14 *Epiph. 6*	S 14 *Quadrag.*	W14	T 13
T 15	S 15 *Epiph. 6*	F 15	M15	M15	T 15	F 14
F 16	M16	S 16	T 16	T 16	F 16	S 15
S 17	T 17		W17	W17 *Ember*	S 17	
	W18	S 17 *Epiph. 2*	T 18	T 18		S 16 *Easter 3*
S 18 *Epiph. 2*	T 19	M18	F 19	F 19 *Ember*	S 18 *Palm*	M17
M19	F 20	T 19	S 20	S 20 *Ember*	M19	T 18
T 20	S 21	W20			T 20	W19
W21		T 21	S 21 *Septuag.*	S 21 *Lent 2*	W21	T 20
T 22	S 22 *Septuag.*	F 22	M22	M22	T 22	F 21
F 23	M23	S 23	T 23	T 23	F 23 *Good Fri.*	S 22
S 24	T 24		w24 *Matthias*	W24	S 24	
	W25 *Matthias*	S 24 *Epiph. 3*	T 25	T 25 *Annunc.*		S 23 *Easter 4*
S 25 *Epiph. 3*	T 26	M25	F 26	F 26	S 25 ***Easter Day***	M24
M26	F 27	T 26	S 27	S 27	M26	T 25
T 27	S 28	W27			T 27	W26
W28		T 28	S 28 *Sexages.*	S 28 *Lent 3*	W28	T 27
T 29	S 29 *Sexages.*	F 29		M29	T 29	F 28
F 30		S 30		T 30	F 30	S 29
S 31				W31		
		S 31 *Epiph. 4*				S 30 *Rogation*
						M31

Dominical letter C for Common Years
Dominical letter DC for Leap Years (*in bold figures*)
New style years 1582 (after 15 Oct.), 1666, 1734, 1886, 1943, 2038

JUNE	JULY	AUGUST	SEPTEMBER	OCTOBER	NOVEMBER	DECEMBER
T 1	T 1	S 1 *Trinity 6*	W1	F 1	M1	W1
W2	F 2	M2	T 2	S 2	T 2	T 2
T 3 *Ascension*	S 3	T 3	F 3		W3	F 3
F 4		W4	S 4		T 4	S 4
S 5	S 4 *Trinity 2*	T 5		S 3 *Trinity 15*	F 5	
	M5	F 6	S 5 *Trinity 11*	M4	s 6	S 5 *Advent 2*
S 6 *Ascens. 1*	T 6	S 7	M6	T 5		M6
M7	W7		T 7	W6	S 7 *Trinity 20*	T 7
T 8	T 8	S 8 *Trinity 7*	W8	T 7	M8	W8
W9	F 9	M9	T 9	F 8	T 9	T 9
T 10	S 10	T 10	F 10	S 9	W10	F 10
F 11		W11	S 11		T 11 *Martin*	S 11
S 12	S 11 *Trinity 3*	T 12		S 10 *Trinity 16*	F 12	
	M12	F 13	S 12 *Trinity 12*	M11	S 13	S 12 *Advent 3*
S 13 *Whit Sun.*	T 13	S 14	M13	T 12		M13
M14	W14		T 14 *Exalt. C.*	W13	S 14 *Trinity 21*	T 14
T 15	T 15	S 15 *Trinity 8*	W15 *Ember*	T 14	M15	W15 *Ember*
W16 *Ember*	F 16	M16	T 16	F 15	T 16	T 16
T 17	S 17	T 17	F 17 *Ember*	S 16	W17	F 17 *Ember*
F 18 *Ember*		W18	s 18 *Ember*		T 18	s 18 *Ember*
s 19 *Ember*	S 18 *Trinity 4*	T 19		S 17 *Trinity 17*	F 19	
	M19	F 20	S 19 *Trinity 13*	M18	S 20	S 19 *Advent 4*
S 20 *Trinity*	T 20	S 21	M20	T 19		M20
M21	W21		T 21	W20	S 21 *Trinity 22*	T 21
T 22	T 22	S 22 *Trinity 9*	W22	T 21	M22	W22
W23	F 23	M23	T 23	F 22	T 23	T 23
T 24 *Corpus C.*	S 24	T 24	F 24	S 23	W24	F 24
F 25		W25	S 25		T 25	s 25 *Christmas*
s 26	S 25 *Trinity 5*	T 26		S 24 *Trinity 18*	F 26	
	M26	F 27	S 26 *Trinity 14*	M25	S 27	S 26
S 27 *Trinity 1*	T 27	s 28	M27	T 26		M27
M28	W28		T 28	W27	S 28 *Advent 1*	T 28
T 29	T 29	S 29 *Trinity 10*	W29 *Michael A.*	T 28	M29	W29
W30	F 30	M30	T 30	F 29	T 30	T 30
	S 31	T 31		S 30		F 31
				S 31 *Trinity 19*		

9

Easter days according to Old Style, AD 400–1752

400	1 April	438	27 March	**476**	28 March	514	30 March	**552**	31 March	590	26 March
401	14 April	439	16 April	477	17 April	515	19 April	553	20 April	591	15 April
402	6 April	**440**	7 April	478	9 April	**516**	3 April	554	5 April	**592**	6 April
403	29 March	441	23 March	479	25 March	517	26 March	555	28 March	593	29 March
404	17 April	442	12 April	**480**	13 April	518	15 April	**556**	16 April	594	11 April
405	2 April	443	4 April	481	5 April	519	31 March	557	1 April	595	3 April
406	22 April	**444**	23 April	482	25 April	**520**	19 April	558	21 April	**596**	22 April
407	14 April	445	8 April	483	10 April	521	11 April	559	13 April	597	14 April
408	29 March	446	31 March	**484**	1 April	522	3 April	**560**	28 March	598	30 March
409	18 April	447	20 April	485	21 April	523	16 April	561	17 April	599	19 April
410	10 April	**448**	11 April	486	6 April	**524**	7 April	562	9 April	**600**	10 April
411	26 March	449	27 March	487	29 March	525	30 March	563	25 March	601	26 March
412	14 April	450	16 April	**488**	17 April	526	19 April	**564**	13 April	602	15 April
413	6 April	451	8 April	489	2 April	527	4 April	565	5 April	603	7 April
414	22 March	**452**	23 March	490	25 March	**528**	26 March	566	28 March	**604**	22 March
415	11 April	453	12 April	491	14 April	529	15 April	567	10 April	605	11 April
416	2 April	454	4 April	**492**	5 April	530	31 March	**568**	1 April	606	3 April
417	22 April	455	24 April	493	18 April	531	20 April	569	21 April	607	23 April
418	7 April	**456**	8 April	494	10 April	**532**	11 April	570	6 April	**608**	7 April
419	30 March	457	31 March	495	26 March	533	27 March	571	29 March	609	30 March
420	18 April	458	20 April	**496**	14 April	534	16 April	**572**	17 April	610	19 April
421	3 April	459	5 April	497	6 April	535	8 April	573	9 April	611	4 April
422	26 March	**460**	27 March	498	29 March	**536**	23 March	574	25 March	**612**	26 March
423	15 April	461	16 April	499	11 April	537	12 April	575	14 April	613	15 April
424	6 April	462	1 April	**500**	2 April	538	4 April	**576**	5 April	614	31 March
425	19 April	463	21 April	501	22 April	539	24 April	577	25 April	615	20 April
426	11 April	**464**	12 April	502	14 April	**540**	8 April	578	10 April	**616**	11 April
427	3 April	465	28 March	503	30 March	541	31 March	579	2 April	617	3 April
428	22 April	466	17 April	**504**	18 April	542	20 April	**580**	21 April	618	16 April
429	7 April	467	9 April	505	10 April	543	5 April	581	6 April	619	8 April
430	30 March	**468**	31 March	506	26 March	**544**	27 March	582	29 March	**620**	30 March
431	19 April	469	13 April	507	15 April	545	16 April	583	18 April	621	19 April
432	3 April	470	5 April	**508**	6 April	546	8 April	**584**	2 April	622	4 April
433	26 March	471	28 March	509	22 March	547	24 March	585	25 March	623	27 March
434	15 April	**472**	16 April	510	11 April	**548**	12 April	586	14 April	**624**	15 April
435	31 March	473	1 April	511	3 April	549	4 April	587	30 March	625	31 March
436	19 April	474	21 April	**512**	22 April	550	24 April	**588**	18 April	626	20 April
437	11 April	475	6 April	513	7 April	551	9 April	589	10 April	627	12 April

628	27 March	678	18 April	**728**	4 April	778	19 April	**828**	5 April	878	23 March
629	16 April	679	3 April	729	24 April	779	11 April	829	28 March	879	12 April
630	8 April	**680**	25 March	730	9 April	**780**	26 March	830	17 April	**880**	3 April
631	24 March	681	14 April	731	1 April	781	15 April	831	2 April	881	23 April
632	12 April	682	30 March	**732**	20 April	782	7 April	**832**	24 March	882	8 April
633	4 April	683	19 April	733	5 April	783	23 March	833	13 April	883	31 March
634	24 April	**684**	10 April	734	28 March	**784**	11 April	834	5 April	**884**	19 April
635	9 April	685	26 March	735	17 April	785	3 April	835	18 April	885	11 April
636	31 March	686	15 April	**736**	8 April	786	23 April	**836**	9 April	886	27 March
637	20 April	687	7 April	737	24 March	787	8 April	837	1 April	887	16 April
638	5 April	**688**	29 March	738	13 April	**788**	30 March	838	14 April	**888**	7 April
639	28 March	689	11 April	739	5 April	789	19 April	839	6 April	889	23 March
640	16 April	690	3 April	**740**	24 April	790	11 April	**840**	28 March	890	12 April
641	8 April	691	23 April	741	9 April	791	27 March	841	17 April	891	4 April
642	24 March	**692**	14 April	742	1 April	**792**	15 April	842	2 April	**892**	23 April
643	13 April	693	30 March	743	14 April	793	7 April	843	22 April	893	8 April
644	4 April	694	19 April	**744**	5 April	794	23 March	**844**	13 April	894	31 March
645	24 April	695	11 April	745	28 March	795	12 April	845	29 March	895	20 April
646	9 April	**696**	26 March	746	17 April	**796**	3 April	846	18 April	**896**	4 April
647	1 April	697	15 April	747	2 April	797	23 April	847	10 April	897	27 March
648	20 April	698	7 April	**748**	21 April	798	8 April	**848**	25 March	898	16 April
649	5 April	699	23 April	749	13 April	799	31 March	849	14 April	899	1 April
650	28 March	**700**	11 April	750	29 March	**800**	19 April	850	6 April	**900**	20 Aprll
651	17 April	701	3 April	751	18 April	801	4 April	851	22 March	901	12 April
652	1 April	702	23 April	**752**	9 April	802	27 March	**852**	10 April	902	28 March
653	21 April	703	8 April	753	25 March	803	16 April	853	2 April	903	17 April
654	13 April	**704**	30 March	754	14 April	**804**	31 March	854	22 April	**904**	8 April
655	29 March	705	19 April	755	6 April	805	20 April	855	7 April	905	31 March
656	17 April	706	4 April	**756**	28 March	806	12 April	**856**	29 March	906	13 April
657	9 April	707	27 March	757	10 April	807	28 March	857	18 April	907	5 April
658	25 March	**708**	15 April	758	2 April	**808**	16 April	858	3 April	**908**	27 March
659	14 April	709	31 March	759	22 April	809	8 April	859	26 March	909	16 April
660	5 April	710	20 April	**760**	6 April	810	31 March	**860**	14 April	910	1 April
661	28 March	711	12 April	761	29 March	811	13 April	861	6 April	911	21 April
662	10 April	**712**	3 April	762	18 April	**812**	4 April	862	19 April	**912**	12 April
663	2 April	713	16 April	763	3 April	813	27 March	863	11 April	913	28 March
664	21 April	714	8 April	**764**	25 March	814	16 April	**864**	2 April	914	17 April
665	6 April	715	31 March	765	14 April	815	1 April	865	22 April	915	9 April
666	29 March	**716**	19 April	766	6 April	**816**	20 April	866	7 April	**916**	24 March
667	18 April	717	4 April	767	19 April	817	12 April	867	30 March	917	13 April
668	9 April	718	27 March	**768**	10 April	818	28 March	**868**	18 April	918	5 April
669	25 March	719	16 April	769	2 April	819	17 April	869	3 April	919	25 April
670	14 April	**720**	31 March	770	22 April	**820**	8 April	870	26 March	**920**	9 April
671	6 April	721	20 April	771	7 April	821	24 March	871	15 April	921	1 April
672	25 April	722	12 April	**772**	29 March	822	13 April	**872**	30 March	922	21 April
673	10 April	723	28 March	773	18 April	823	5 April	873	19 April	923	6 April
674	2 April	**724**	16 April	774	3 April	**824**	24 April	874	11 April	**924**	28 March
675	22 April	725	8 April	775	26 March	825	9 April	875	27 March	925	17 April
676	6 April	726	24 March	**776**	14 April	826	1 April	**876**	15 April	926	2 April
677	29 March	727	13 April	777	30 March	827	21 April	877	7 April	927	25 March

928	13 April	978	31 March	**1028**	14 April	1078	8 April	**1128**	22 April	1178	9 April
929	5 April	979	20 April	1029	6 April	1079	24 March	1129	14 April	1179	1 April
930	18 April	**980**	11 April	1030	29 March	**1080**	12 April	1130	30 March	**1180**	20 April
931	10 April	981	27 March	1031	11 April	1081	4 April	1131	19 April	1181	5 April
932	1 April	982	16 April	**1032**	2 April	1082	24 April	**1132**	10 April	1182	28 March
933	14 April	983	8 April	1033	22 April	1083	9 April	1133	26 March	1183	17 April
934	6 April	**984**	23 March	1034	14 April	**1084**	31 March	1134	15 April	**1184**	1 April
935	29 March	985	12 April	1035	30 March	1085	20 April	1135	7 April	1185	21 April
936	17 April	986	4 April	**1036**	18 April	1086	5 April	**1136**	22 March	1186	13 April
937	2 April	987	24 April	1037	10 April	1087	28 March	1137	11 April	1187	29 March
938	22 April	**988**	8 April	1038	26 March	**1088**	16 April	1138	3 April	**1188**	17 April
939	14 April	989	31 March	1039	15 April	1089	1 April	1139	23 April	1189	9 April
940	29 March	990	20 April	**1040**	6 April	1090	21 April	**1140**	7 April	1190	25 March
941	18 April	991	5 April	1041	22 March	1091	13 April	1141	30 March	1191	14 April
942	10 April	**992**	27 March	1042	11 April	**1092**	28 March	1142	19 April	**1192**	5 April
943	26 March	993	16 April	1043	3 April	1093	17 April	1143	4 April	1193	28 March
944	14 April	994	1 April	**1044**	22 April	1094	9 April	**1144**	26 March	1194	10 April
945	6 April	995	21 April	1045	7 April	1095	25 March	1145	15 April	1195	2 April
946	22 March	**996**	12 April	1046	30 March	**1096**	13 April	1146	31 March	**1196**	21 April
947	11 April	997	28 March	1047	19 April	1097	5 April	1147	20 April	1197	6 April
948	2 April	998	17 April	**1048**	3 April	1098	28 March	**1148**	11 April	1198	29 March
949	22 April	999	9 April	1049	26 March	1099	10 April	1149	3 April	1199	18 April
950	7 April	**1000**	31 March	1050	15 April	**1100**	1 April	1150	16 April	**1200**	9 April
951	30 March	1001	13 April	1051	31 March	1101	21 April	1151	8 April	1201	25 March
952	18 April	1002	5 April	**1052**	19 April	1102	6 April	**1152**	30 March	1202	14 April
953	3 April	1003	28 March	1053	11 April	1103	29 March	1153	19 April	1203	6 April
954	26 March	**1004**	16 April	1054	3 April	**1104**	17 April	1154	4 April	**1204**	25 April
955	15 April	1005	1 April	1055	16 April	1105	9 April	1155	27 March	1205	10 April
956	6 April	1006	21 April	**1056**	7 April	1106	25 March	**1156**	15 April	1206	2 April
957	19 April	1007	6 April	1057	30 March	1107	14 April	1157	31 March	1207	22 April
958	11 April	**1008**	28 March	1058	19 April	**1108**	5 April	1158	20 April	**1208**	6 April
959	3 April	1009	17 April	1059	4 April	1109	25 April	1159	12 April	1209	29 March
960	22 April	1010	9 April	**1060**	26 March	1110	10 April	**1160**	27 March	1210	18 April
961	7 April	1011	25 March	1061	15 April	1111	2 April	1161	16 April	1211	3 April
962	30 March	**1012**	13 April	1062	31 March	**1112**	21 April	1162	8 April	**1212**	25 March
963	19 April	1013	5 April	1063	20 April	1113	6 April	1163	24 March	1213	14 April
964	3 April	1014	25 April	**1064**	11 April	1114	29 March	**1164**	12 April	1214	30 March
965	26 March	1015	10 April	1065	27 March	1115	18 April	1165	4 April	1215	19 April
966	15 April	**1016**	1 April	1066	16 April	**1116**	2 April	1166	24 April	**1216**	10 April
967	31 March	1017	21 April	1067	8 April	1117	25 March	1167	9 April	1217	26 March
968	19 April	1018	6 April	**1068**	23 March	1118	14 April	**1168**	31 March	1218	15 April
969	11 April	1019	29 March	1069	12 April	1119	30 March	1169	20 April	1219	7 April
970	27 March	**1020**	17 April	1070	4 April	**1120**	18 April	1170	5 April	**1220**	29 March
971	16 April	1021	2 April	1071	24 April	1121	10 April	1171	28 March	1221	11 April
972	7 April	1022	25 March	**1072**	8 April	1122	26 March	**1172**	16 April	1222	3 April
973	23 March	1023	14 April	1073	31 March	1123	15 April	1173	8 April	1223	23 April
974	12 April	**1024**	5 April	1074	20 April	**1124**	6 April	1174	24 March	**1224**	14 April
975	4 April	1025	18 April	1075	5 April	1125	29 March	1175	13 April	1225	30 March
976	23 April	1026	10 April	**1076**	27 March	1126	11 April	**1176**	4 April	1226	19 April
977	8 April	1027	26 March	1077	16 April	1127	3 April	1177	24 April	1227	11 April

Year	Date	Year	Date	Year	Date	Year	Date	Year	Date	Year	Date
1228	26 March	1278	17 April	1328	3 April	1378	18 April	1428	4 April	1478	22 March
1229	15 April	1279	2 April	1329	23 April	1379	10 April	1429	27 March	1479	11 April
1230	7 April	1280	21 April	1330	8 April	1380	25 March	1430	16 April	1480	2 April
1231	23 March	1281	13 April	1331	31 March	1381	14 April	1431	1 April	1481	22 April
1232	11 April	1282	29 March	1332	19 April	1382	6 April	1432	20 April	1482	7 April
1233	3 April	1283	18 April	1333	4 April	1383	22 March	1433	12 April	1483	30 March
1234	23 April	1284	9 April	1334	27 March	1384	10 April	1434	28 March	1484	18 April
1235	8 April	1285	25 March	1335	16 April	1385	2 April	1435	17 April	1485	3 April
1236	30 March	1286	14 April	1336	31 March	1386	22 April	1436	8 April	1486	26 March
1237	19 April	1287	6 April	1337	20 April	1387	7 April	1437	31 March	1487	15 April
1238	4 April	1288	28 March	1338	12 April	1388	29 March	1438	13 April	1488	6 April
1239	27 March	1289	10 April	1339	28 March	1389	18 April	1439	5 April	1489	19 April
1240	15 April	1290	2 April	1340	16 April	1390	3 April	1440	27 March	1490	11 April
1241	31 March	1291	22 April	1341	8 April	1391	26 March	1441	16 April	1491	3 April
1242	20 April	1292	6 April	1342	31 March	1392	14 April	1442	1 April	1492	22 April
1243	12 April	1293	29 March	1343	13 April	1393	6 April	1443	21 April	1493	7 April
1244	3 April	1294	18 April	1344	4 April	1394	19 April	1444	12 April	1494	30 March
1245	16 April	1295	3 April	1345	27 March	1395	11 April	1445	28 March	1495	19 April
1246	8 April	1296	25 March	1346	16 April	1396	2 April	1446	17 April	1496	3 April
1247	31 March	1297	14 April	1347	1 April	1397	22 April	1447	9 April	1497	26 March
1248	19 April	1298	6 April	1348	20 April	1398	7 April	1448	24 March	1498	15 April
1249	4 April	1299	19 April	1349	12 April	1399	30 March	1449	13 April	1499	31 March
1250	27 March	1300	10 April	1350	28 March	1400	18 April	1450	5 April	1500	19 April
1251	16 April	1301	2 April	1351	17 April	1401	3 April	1451	25 April	1501	11 April
1252	31 March	1302	22 April	1352	8 April	1402	26 March	1452	9 April	1502	27 March
1253	20 April	1303	7 April	1353	24 March	1403	15 April	1453	1 April	1503	16 April
1254	12 April	1304	29 March	1354	13 April	1404	30 March	1454	21 April	1504	7 April
1255	28 March	1305	18 April	1355	5 April	1405	19 April	1455	6 April	1505	23 March
1256	16 Aprll	1306	3 April	1356	24 April	1406	11 April	1456	28 March	1506	12 April
1257	8 April	1307	26 March	1357	9 April	1407	27 March	1457	17 April	1507	4 April
1258	24 March	1308	14 April	1358	1 April	1408	15 April	1458	2 April	1508	23 April
1259	13 April	1309	30 March	1359	21 April	1409	7 April	1459	25 March	1509	8 April
1260	4 April	1310	19 April	1360	5 April	1410	23 March	1460	13 April	1510	31 March
1261	24 April	1311	11 April	1361	28 March	1411	12 April	1461	5 April	1511	20 April
1262	9 April	1312	26 March	1362	17 April	1412	3 April	1462	18 April	1512	11 April
1263	1 April	1313	15 April	1363	2 April	1413	23 April	1463	10 April	1513	27 March
1264	20 April	1314	7 April	1364	24 March	1414	8 April	1464	1 April	1514	16 April
1265	5 April	1315	23 March	1365	13 April	1415	31 March	1465	14 April	1515	8 April
1266	28 March	1316	11 April	1366	5 April	1416	19 April	1466	6 April	1516	23 March
1267	17 April	1317	3 April	1367	18 April	1417	11 April	1467	29 March	1517	12 April
1268	8 April	1318	23 April	1368	9 April	1418	27 March	1468	17 April	1518	4 April
1269	24 March	1319	8 April	1369	1 April	1419	16 April	1469	2 April	1519	24 April
1270	13 April	1320	30 March	1370	14 April	1420	7 April	1470	22 April	1520	8 April
1271	5 April	1321	19 April	1371	6 April	1421	23 March	1471	14 April	1521	31 March
1272	24 April	1322	11 April	1372	28 March	1422	12 April	1472	29 March	1522	20 April
1273	9 April	1323	27 March	1373	17 April	1423	4 April	1473	18 April	1523	5 April
1274	1 April	1324	15 April	1374	2 April	1424	23 April	1474	10 April	1524	27 March
1275	14 April	1325	7 April	1375	22 April	1425	8 April	1475	26 March	1525	16 April
1276	5 April	1326	23 March	1376	13 April	1426	31 March	1476	14 April	1526	1 April
1277	28 March	1327	12 April	1377	29 March	1427	20 April	1477	6 April	1527	21 April

Year	Date	Year	Date	Year	Date	Year	Date	Year	Date	Year	Date
1528	12 April	1566	14 April	**1604**	8 April	1642	10 April	**1680**	11 April	1718	13 April
1529	28 March	1567	30 March	1605	31 March	1643	2 April	1681	3 April	1719	29 March
1530	17 April	**1568**	18 April	1606	20 April	**1644**	21 April	1682	16 April	**1720**	17 April
1531	9 April	1569	10 April	1607	5 April	1645	6 April	1683	8 April	1721	9 April
1532	31 March	1570	26 March	**1608**	27 March	1646	29 March	**1684**	30 March	1722	25 March
1533	13 April	1571	15 April	1609	16 April	1647	18 April	1685	19 April	1723	14 April
1534	5 April	**1572**	6 April	1610	8 April	**1648**	2 April	1686	4 April	**1724**	5 April
1535	28 March	1573	22 March	1611	24 March	1649	25 March	1687	27 March	1725	28 March
1536	16 April	1574	11 April	**1612**	12 April	1650	14 April	**1688**	15 April	1726	10 April
1537	1 April	1575	3 April	1613	4 April	1651	30 March	1689	31 March	1727	2 April
1538	21 April	**1576**	22 April	1614	24 April	**1652**	18 April	1690	20 April	**1728**	21 April
1539	6 April	1577	7 April	1615	9 April	1653	10 April	1691	12 April	1729	6 April
1540	28 March	1578	30 March	**1616**	31 March	1654	26 March	**1692**	27 March	1730	29 March
1541	17 April	1579	19 April	1617	20 April	1655	15 April	1693	16 April	1731	18 April
1542	9 April	**1580**	3 April	1618	5 April	**1656**	6 April	1694	8 April	**1732**	9 April
1543	25 March	1581	26 March	1619	28 March	1657	29 March	1695	24 March	1733	25 March
1544	13 April	1582¹	15 April	**1620**	16 April	1658	11 April	**1696**	12 April	1734	14 April
1545	5 April	1583	31 March	1621	1 April	1659	3 April	1697	4 April	1735	6 April
1546	25 April	**1584**	19 April	1622	21 April	**1660**	22 April	1698	24 April	**1736**	25 April
1547	10 April	1585	11 April	1623	13 April	1661	14 April	1699	9 April	1737	10 April
1548	1 April	1586	3 April	**1624**	28 March	1662	30 March	**1700**	31 March	1738	2 April
1549	21 April	1587	16 April	1625	17 April	1663	19 April	1701	20 April	1739	22 April
1550	6 April	**1588**	7 April	1626	9 April	**1664**	10 April	1702	5 April	**1740**	6 April
1551	29 March	1589	30 March	1627	25 March	1665	26 March	1703	28 March	1741	29 March
1552	17 April	1590	19 April	**1628**	13 April	1666	15 April	**1704**	16 April	1742	18 April
1553	2 April	1591	4 April	1629	5 April	1667	7 April	1705	8 April	1743	3 April
1554	25 March	**1592**	26 March	1630	28 March	**1668**	22 March	1706	24 March	**1742**	25 March
1555	14 April	1593	15 April	1631	10 April	1669	11 April	1707	13 April	1745	14 April
1556	5 April	1594	31 March	**1632**	1 April	1670	3 April	**1708**	4 April	1746	30 March
1557	18 April	1595	20 April	1633	21 April	1671	23 April	1709	24 April	1747	19 April
1558	10 April	**1596**	11 April	1634	6 April	**1672**	7 April	1710	9 April	**1748**	10 April
1559	26 March	1597	27 March	1635	29 March	1673	30 March	1711	1 April	1749	26 March
1560	14 April	1598	16 April	**1636**	17 April	1674	19 April	**1712**	20 April	1750	15 April
1561	6 April	1599	8 April	1637	9 April	1675	4 April	1713	5 April	1751	7 April
1562	29 March	**1600**	23 March	1638	25 March	**1676**	26 March	1714	28 March	**1752²**	29 March
1563	11 April	1601	12 April	1639	14 April	1677	15 April	1715	17 April		
1564	2 April	1602	4 April	**1640**	5 April	1678	31 March	**1716**	1 April		
1565	22 April	1603	24 April	1641	25 April	1679	20 April	1717	21 April		

1. See Table **10** for Easter days according to New Style after 1582.
2. Table **11** provides an English Calendar for 1752.

10

Easter days according to New Style, AD 1583–2100[1]

1583[2] 10 April	1618 15 April	1653 13 April	**1688** 18 April	1723 28 March	1758 26 March
1584 1 April	1619 31 March	1654 5 April	1689 10 April	**1724** 16 April	1759 15 April
1585 21 April	**1620** 19 April	1655 28 March	1690 26 March	1725 1 April	**1760** 6 April
1586 6 April	1621 11 April	**1656** 16 April	1691 15 April	1726 21 April	1761 22 March
1587 29 March	1622 27 March	1657 1 April	**1692** 6 April	1727 13 April	1762 11 April
1588 17 April	1623 16 April	1658 21 April	1693 22 March	**1728** 28 March	1763 3 April
1589 2 April	**1624** 7 April	1659 13 April	1694 11 April	1729 17 April	**1764** 22 April
1590 22 April	1625 30 March	**1660** 28 March	1695 3 April	1730 9 April	1765 7 April
1591 14 April	1626 12 April	1661 17 April	**1696** 22 April	1731 25 March	1766 30 March
1592 29 March	1627 4 April	1662 9 April	1697 7 April	**1732** 13 April	1767 19 April
1593 18 April	**1628** 23 April	1663 25 March	1698 30 March	1733 5 April	**1768** 3 April
1594 10 April	1629 15 April	**1664** 13 April	1699 19 April	1734 25 April	1769 26 March
1595 26 March	1630 31 March	1665 5 April	1700[3] 11 April	1735 10 April	1770 15 April
1596 14 April	1631 20 April	1666 25 April	1701 27 March	**1736** 1 April	1771 31 March
1597 6 April	**1632** 11 April	1667 10 April	1702 16 April	1737 21 April	**1772** 19 April
1598 22 March	1633 27 March	**1668** 1 April	1703 8 April	1738 6 April	1773 11 April
1599 11 April	1634 16 April	1669 21 April	**1704** 23 March	1739 29 March	1774 3 April
1600 2 April	1635 8 April	1670 6 April	1705 12 April	**1740** 17 April	1775 16 April
1601 22 April	**1636** 23 March	1671 29 March	1706 4 April	1741 2 April	**1776** 7 April
1602 7 April	1637 12 April	**1672** 17 April	1707 24 April	1742 25 March	1777 30 March
1603 30 March	1638 4 April	1673 2 April	**1708** 8 April	1743 14 April	1778 19 April
1604 18 April	1639 24 April	1674 25 March	1709 31 March	**1744** 5 April	1779 4 April
1605 10 April	**1640** 8 April	1675 14 April	1710 20 April	1745 18 April	**1780** 26 March
1606 26 March	1641 31 March	**1676** 5 April	1711 5 April	1746 10 April	1781 15 April
1607 15 April	1642 20 April	1677 18 April	**1712** 27 March	1747 2 April	1782 31 March
1608 6 April	1643 5 April	1678 10 April	1713 16 April	**1748** 14 April	1783 20 April
1609 19 April	**1644** 27 March	1679 2 April	1714 1 April	1749 6 April	**1784** 11 April
1610 11 April	1645 16 April	**1680** 21 April	1715 21 April	1750 29 March	1785 27 March
1611 3 April	1646 1 April	1681 6 April	**1716** 12 April	1751 11 April	1786 16 April
1612 22 April	1647 21 April	1682 29 March	1717 28 March	**1752** 2 April	1787 8 April
1613 7 April	**1648** 12 April	1683 18 April	1718 17 April	1753 22 April	**1788** 23 March
1614 30 March	1649 4 April	**1684** 2 April	1719 9 April	1754 14 April	1789 12 April
1615 19 April	1650 17 April	1685 22 April	**1720** 31 March	1755 30 March	1790 4 April
1616 3 April	1651 9 April	1686 14 April	1721 13 April	**1756** 18 April	1791 24 April
1617 26 March	**1652** 31 March	1687 30 March	1722 5 April	1757 10 April	**1792** 8 April

1. Information for Easter days from AD 2001 to AD 2100 has been kindly provided by Dr B. D. Yallop, Superintendent, HM Nautical Almanac Office, Royal Greenwich Observatory, Cambridge, whose NAO Technical Note no. 64 (April 1986) provides 'Algorithms for Calculating the Date of Easter'.
2. Gregory XIII's bull directed that ten days should be omitted after 4 Oct. 1582 and that Sunday, 17 Oct. should be treated as the eighteenth Sunday after Pentecost, which agrees with an Easter Day on 25 April. Table 8/35 should therefore be used for the period 15 Oct.–31 Dec. 1582 New Style.
3. 1700 NS was not a Leap Year.

1793 31 March	1845 23 March	1897 18 April	1949 17 April	2001 15 April	2053 6 April
1794 20 April	1846 12 April	1898 10 April	1950 9 April	2002 31 March	2054 29 March
1795 5 April	1847 4 April	1899 2 April	1951 25 March	2003 20 April	2055 18 April
1796 27 March	**1848** 23 April	1900[4] 15 April	**1952** 13 April	**2004** 11 April	**2056** 2 April
1797 16 April	1849 8 April	1901 7 April	1953 5 April	2005 27 March	2057 22 April
1798 8 April	1850 31 March	1902 30 March	1954 18 April	2006 16 April	2058 14 April
1799 24 March	1851 20 April	1903 12 April	1955 10 April	2007 8 April	2059 30 March
1800[4] 13 April	**1852** 11 April	**1904** 3 April	**1956** 1 April	**2008** 23 March	**2060** 18 April
1801 5 April	1853 27 March	1905 23 April	1957 21 April	2009 12 April	2061 10 April
1802 18 April	1854 16 April	1906 15 April	1958 6 April	2010 4 April	2062 26 March
1803 10 April	1855 8 April	1907 31 March	1959 29 March	2011 24 April	2063 15 April
1804 1 April	**1856** 23 March	**1908** 19 April	**1960** 17 April	**2012** 8 April	**2064** 6 April
1805 14 April	1857 12 April	1909 11 April	1961 2 April	2013 31 March	2065 29 March
1806 6 April	1858 4 April	1910 27 March	1962 22 April	2014 20 April	2066 11 April
1807 29 March	1859 24 April	1911 16 April	1963 14 April	2015 5 April	2067 3 April
1808 17 April	**1860** 8 April	**1912** 7 April	**1964** 29 March	**2016** 27 March	**2068** 22 April
1809 2 April	1861 31 March	1913 23 March	1965 18 April	2017 16 April	2069 14 April
1810 22 April	1862 20 April	1914 12 April	1966 10 April	2018 1 April	2070 30 March
1811 14 April	1863 5 April	1915 4 April	1967 26 March	2019 21 April	2071 19 April
1812 29 March	**1864** 27 March	**1916** 23 April	**1968** 14 April	**2020** 12 April	**2072** 10 April
1813 18 April	1865 16 April	1917 8 April	1969 6 April	2021 4 April	2073 26 March
1814 10 April	1866 1 April	1918 31 March	1970 29 March	2022 17 April	2074 15 April
1815 26 March	1867 21 April	1919 20 April	1971 11 April	2023 9 April	2075 7 April
1816 14 April	**1868** 12 April	**1920** 4 April	**1972** 2 April	**2024** 31 March	**2076** 19 April
1817 6 April	1869 28 March	1921 27 March	1973 22 April	2025 20 April	2077 11 April
1818 22 March	1870 17 April	1922 16 April	1974 14 April	2026 5 April	2078 3 April
1819 11 April	1871 9 April	1923 1 April	1975 30 March	2027 28 March	2079 23 April
1820 2 April	**1872** 31 March	**1924** 20 April	**1976** 18 April	**2028** 16 April	**2080** 7 April
1821 22 April	1873 13 April	1925 12 April	1977 10 April	2029 1 April	2081 30 March
1822 7 April	1874 5 April	1926 4 April	1978 26 March	2030 21 April	2082 19 April
1823 30 March	1875 28 March	1927 17 April	1979 15 April	2031 13 April	2083 4 April
1824 18 April	**1876** 16 April	**1928** 8 April	**1980** 6 April	**2032** 28 March	**2084** 26 March
1825 3 April	1877 1 April	1929 31 March	1981 19 April	2033 17 April	2085 15 April
1826 26 March	1878 21 April	1930 20 April	1982 11 April	2034 9 April	2086 31 March
1827 15 April	1879 13 April	1931 5 April	1983 3 April	2035 25 March	2087 20 April
1828 6 April	**1880** 28 March	**1932** 27 March	**1984** 22 April	**2036** 13 April	**2088** 11 April
1829 19 April	1881 17 April	1933 16 April	1985 7 April	2037 5 April	2089 3 April
1830 11 April	1882 9 April	1934 1 April	1986 30 March	2038 25 April	2090 16 April
1831 3 April	1883 25 March	1935 21 April	1987 19 April	2039 10 April	2091 8 April
1832 22 April	**1884** 13 April	**1936** 12 April	**1988** 3 April	**2040** 1 April	**2092** 30 March
1833 7 April	1885 5 April	1937 28 March	1989 26 March	2041 21 April	2093 12 April
1834 30 March	1886 25 April	1938 17 April	1990 15 April	2042 6 April	2094 4 April
1835 19 April	1887 10 April	1939 9 April	1991 31 March	2043 29 March	2095 24 April
1836 3 April	**1888** 1 April	**1940** 24 March	**1992** 19 April	**2044** 17 April	**2096** 15 April
1837 26 March	1889 21 April	1941 13 April	1993 11 April	2045 9 April	2097 31 March
1838 15 April	1890 6 April	1942 5 April	1994 3 April	2046 25 March	2098 20 April
1839 31 March	1891 29 March	1943 25 April	1995 16 April	2047 14 April	2099 12 April
1840 19 April	**1892** 17 April	**1944** 9 April	**1996** 7 April	**2048** 5 April	2100 28 March
1841 11 April	1893 2 April	1945 1 April	1997 30 March	2049 18 April	
1842 27 March	1894 25 March	1946 21 April	1998 12 April	2050 10 April	
1843 16 April	1895 14 April	1947 6 April	1999 4 April	2051 2 April	
1844 7 April	**1896** 5 April	**1948** 28 March	**2000**[5] 23 April	**2052** 21 April	

4. 1800 and 1900 were not Leap Years.
5. 2000 will be a Leap Year, 2100 will not.

11

The English calendar for 1752

In this year New Style was adopted in England. Eleven days were dropped out of the calendar in September, the day after Wednesday, 2 September, being called Thursday, 14 September. The year began with 1 January following 31 December 1751. The Dominical Letters for this year are three: since it was a Leap Year, the Letter for January and February was E, that from 1 March to 2 September was D, and that from 14 September to 31 December was A. Easter Day in 1752 was calculated according to Old Style; Easter Day for 1753 (Table 8/32) was calculated according to New Style.

Table 11
Easter Day 29 March

JANUARY	FEBRUARY	MARCH	APRIL	MAY	JUNE
W 1	S 1	S 1 *Lent 3*	W 1	F 1	M 1
T 2		M 2	T 2	S 2	T 2
F 3	S 2 *Sexages.*	T 3	F 3		W 3
S 4	M 3	W 4	S 4	S 3 *Rogation*	T 4
	T 4	T 5		M 4	F 5
S 5	W 5	F 6	S 5 *Easter 1*	T 5	S 6
M 6 *Epiphany*	T 6	S 7	M 6	W 6	
T 7	F 7		T 7	T 7 *Ascension*	S 7 *Trinity 2*
W 8	S 8	S 8 *Lent 4*	W 8	F 8	M 8
T 9		M 9	T 9	S 9	T 9
F 10	S 9 *Quinquag.*	T 10	F 10		W 10
S 11	M 10	W 11	S 11	S 10 *Ascens. 1*	T 11
	T 11 *Shrove Tu.*	T 12		M 11	F 12
S 12 *Epiph. 1*	W 12 *Ash Wed.*	F 13	S 12 *Easter 2*	T 12	S 13
M 13 *Hilary*	T 13	S 14	M 13	W 13	
T 14	F 14		T 14	T 14	S 14 *Trinity 3*
W 15	S 15	S 15 *Passion*	W 15	F 15	M 15
T 16		M 16	T 16	S 16	T 16
F 17	S 16	T 17	F 17		W 17
S 18	M 17	W 18	S 18	S 17 *Whit Sun.*	T 18
	T 18	T 19		M 18	F 19
S 19 *Epiph. 2*	W 19	F 20	S 19 *Easter 3*	T 19	S 20
M 20	T 20	S 21	M 20	W 20	
T 21	F 21		T 21	T 21	S 21 *Trinity 4*
W 22	S 22	S 22 *Palm*	W 22	F 22	M 22
T 23		M 23	T 23	S 23	T 23
F 24	S 23 *Lent 2*	T 24	F 24		W 24 *Nat. J. Bap.*
S 25	M 24	W 25 *Annunc.*	S 25	S 24 *Trinity*	T 25
	T 25 *Matthias*	T 26		M 25	F 26
S 26 *Septuag.*	W 26	F 27 *Good Fri.*	S 26 *Easter 4*	T 26	S 27
M 27	T 27	S 28	M 27	W 27	
T 28	F 28		T 28	T 28 *Corpus C.*	S 28 *Trinity 5*
W 29	S 29	S 29 ***Easter Day***	W 29	F 29	M 29
T 30		M 30	T 30	S 30	T 30
F 31		T 31			
				S 31 *Trinity 1*	

Table 11

Easter Day 29 March

JULY	AUGUST	SEPTEMBER	OCTOBER	NOVEMBER	DECEMBER
W 1	S 1	T 1	S 1 *Trinity 17*	W 1	F 1
T 2	W 2	Eleven days	M 2	T 2	S 2
F 3		omitted	T 3	F 3	
S 4	S 2 *Trinity 10*	T 14	W 4	S 4	S 3 *Advent 1*
	M 3	F 15	T 5		M 4
S 5 *Trinity 6*	T 4	S 16	F 6	S 5 *Trinity 22*	T 5
M 6	W 5		S 7	M 6	W 6
T 7	T 6			T 7	T 7
W 8	F 7	S 17 *Trinity 15*	S 8 *Trinity 18*	W 8	F 8
T 9	S 8	M 18	M 9	T 9	S 9
F 10		T 19	T 10	F 10	
S 11	S 9 *Trinity 11*	W 20	W 11	S 11	S 10 *Advent 2*
	M 10	T 21	T 12		M 11
S 12 *Trinity 7*	T 11	F 22	F 13	S 12 *Trinity 23*	T 12
M 13	W 12	S 23	S 14	M 13	W 13
T 14	T 13			T 14	T 14
W 15	F 14	S 24 *Trinity 16*	S 15 *Trinity 19*	W 15	F 15
T 16	S 15	M 25	M 16	T 16	S 16
F 17		T 26	T 17	F 17	
S 18	S 16 *Trinity 12*	W 27	W 18	S 18	S 17 *Advent 3*
	M 17	T 28	T 19		M 18
S 19 *Trinity 8*	T 18	F 29 *Michael A.*	F 20	S 19 *Trinity 24*	T 19
M 20	W 19	S 30	S 21	M 20	W 20
T 21	T 20			T 21	T 21
W 22	F 21		S 22 *Trinity 20*	W 22	F 22
T 23	S 22		M 23	T 23	S 23
F 24			T 24	F 24	
S 25	S 23 *Trinity 13*		W 25	S 25	S 24 *Advent 4*
	M 24		T 26		M 25 *Christmas*
S 26 *Trinity 9*	T 25		F 27	S 26 *Trinity 25*	T 26
M 27	W 26		S 28	M 27	W 27
T 28	T 27			T 28	T 28
W 29	F 28		S 29 *Trinity 21*	W 29	F 29
T 30	S 29		M 30	T 30	S 30
F 31			T 31		
	S 30 *Trinity 14*				S 31
	M 31				

12

Dates of adoption of the Gregorian calendar in Europe[1]

From 1582 until 1700 the difference between the Julian and Gregorian calendars was ten days. In Italy, Poland, Spain and Portugal the day after Thursday 4 October 1582 was declared to be Friday 15 October 1582; the ten suppressed days (listed below) were 5–14 October. The year 1700 was a leap year in the Gregorian calendar but a common year in the Julian, so the discrepancy increased to 11 days; in 1800 the gap became 12 days and 13 days in 1900; the year 2000 is a leap year in both calendars. The suppressed days have been listed whenever possible, but when territories changed hands by force or treaty, calendars changed without a formal declaration of suppressed days.

State, etc.	Date	Days suppressed
Albania	1913	
Alsace		
Catholic	1584	
Protestant	1648	
Artois/Picardy	1582	22–31 Dec.
Austria[2]	1584	7–16 Jan.
Brixen and Salzburg	1583	6–15 Oct.
Styria	1583	15–24 Dec.
Baltic States		
Courland		
adopts Gregorian	1617	
reverts to Julian	1795	
Estonia	1918	1–13 Feb.[3]

1. Much of the information in this table has been kindly supplied by Professor Gordon Campbell, University of Leicester.
2. Except Brixem, Salzburg and Styria.
3. Estonia followed the Swedish calendar until 1721 and then the Russian one.

State, etc.	Date	Days suppressed
Livonia		
Polish calendar until	1629	
Swedish calendar	1629–1721	
Russian calendar from	1721	
adopts Gregorian	1918	1–13 Feb.
Lithuania		
adopts Gregorian	1586	
reverts to Julian	1795	
Bohemia	1584	7–16 Jan.
Bulgaria	1916	1–13 April
Denmark (incl. Iceland)	1700	18–28 Feb.
England and Wales	1752	3–13 Sep.
France	1582	10–19 Dec.
Germany (Catholic)	1583–5	
Bishoprics		
Augsburg	1583	14–23 Feb.
Eichstadt	1583	6–15 Oct.
Freising	1583	6–15 Oct.
Cologne	1583	3–12 Nov.
Mainz	1583	12–21 Nov.
Munster	1583	18–27 Nov.
Paderborn	1585	17–26 June
Ratisbon/Regensburg	1583	6–15 Oct.
Trier	1583	5–14 Oct.
Würzburg	1583	5–14 Nov.
Duchies		
Bavaria	1583	6–15 Oct.
Cleves	1583	18–27 Nov.
Jülich	1583	3–12 Nov.
Westphalia	1584	2–11 July
Margraviates		
Baden	1583	17–26 Nov.
Lusatia	1584	7–16 Jan.
Prussia	1612	23 Aug.–1 Sep.
Germany (Protestant)	1700	18–28 Feb.
Greece		
Civil calendar	1923	16–28 Feb.
Church calendar	1924	10–22 March

State, etc.	Date	Days suppressed
Hungary	1587	22–31 Oct.
Ireland	1752	3–13 Sep.
Italy	1582	5–14 Oct.
Florence and Pisa adopt		
1 January New Year	1750	
Liège	1583	11–20 Feb.
Lorraine	1582	10–19 Dec.
Luxembourg	1582	22–31 Dec.
Moravia	1584	7–16 Jan.
Norway	1700	18–28 Feb.
Poland	1582	5–14 Oct.[4]
Portugal	1582	5–14 Oct.
Rumania	1924	1–13 Oct.[5]
Russia	1918	1–13 Feb.
Savoy	1582	22–31 Dec.
Scotland	1752	3–13 Sep.
adopts 1 January New Year	1600	
Silesia	1584	13–22 Jan.
Slovakia	1587	22–31 Oct.
Spain	1582	15–24 Oct.
Spanish Netherlands		
Brabant (inc. Antwerp)	1583	22–31 Dec.
Flanders	1582	22–31 Dec.
Hainaut	1582	22–31 Dec.
Limburg	1582	22–31 Dec.
Namur	1582	22–31 Dec.
Strasbourg		
bishopric	1583	12–21 Nov.
city	1682	19–28 Feb.
Sweden (incl. Finland)		
Court		
adopts Gregorian calendar	1590	
reverts to Julian	1604	
Country	1753	18–28 Feb.

4. Some authorities give the date 1585, with the suppression of 22–31 December, while Orthodox Poland continued to use the Greek calendar.
5. Some authorities give 1919, with 19–31 January suppressed.

State, etc.	Date	Days suppressed
Switzerland[6]		
Catholic Cantons		
Freiburg, Lucerne, Schwyz		
Solothurn, Ury, Zug	1584	12–21 Jan.
Unterwalden	1584	
Protestant Cantons		
Zürich, Berne, Basel,		
Schaffhausen	1701	1–11 Jan.
Mixed Cantons		
Appenzell (divided 1597)		
Inner Appenzell	1584 (confirmed 1590)	
Outer Appenzell		
adopts Gregorian	1584	
reverts to Julian	1597	
adopts Gregorian	1798 (Christmas)	
Glarus		
Catholic communes	1701	1–11 Jan.
Protestant communes	1798	
Territories allied to one canton		
Grisons		
Catholic communes	1623–4	
Protestant communes	1783–1812	
Mixed communes	c. 1650–1750	
Valese[7]	1622	
St Gall		
Principality	1584	
City	1724	
Togenburg	1724	
Berne		
Bishopric (Catholic)	1584	12–21 Jan.

6. We are indebted to Professor André Dubois for his help in elucidating the extremely complex series of changes affecting Switzerland and for directing attention to H. Gutzwiller, 'Die Einführung des Gregorianschen Kalenders in der Eidgenossenschaft in Konfessioneller, Volkskundlicher, Staatsrechtlicher und Wirtschaftpolitischer Schau', *Zeitschrift für Schweizerische Kirchengeschichte*, 72 (1978), 54–73 and H. Kläui, 'Grundlagen der Zeitrechnung und Einführung des Gregorianischen Kalenders in der Alten Eidgenossenschaft', *Schweizerische Gesselschaft für Familienforschung, Jahrbuch 1985*, 3–22.
7. Regions subject to St Moritz and Monthey; the remainder adopted the Gregorian calendar on 11 March 1655.

State, etc.	Date	Days suppressed
Neuchâtel		
Protestant	1701	1–11 Jan.
Catholic (Solothurn)	1584	12–21 Jan.
Geneva	1701	12–21 Jan.
Biel	1701	12–21 Jan.
Territories subject to several cantons:		
Baden		
Protestant communes	1701	1–11 Jan.
Catholic communes	1585	
St Gall		
Rheinthal	1585	
Sargans	1584	
Thurgau		
Catholics	1584/5	
Protestants	Retain Julian for festivals	
Uznach	1584	
Gaster	1584	
Ticino	1584	
Mulhouse	1701	
Transylvania	1590	15–24 Dec.
Turkey	1925[8]	
United Provinces		
Friesland	1701	2–12 Jan.
Gelderland (Catholic inc. Nijmegen)	1582	22–31 Dec.
Gelderland (Protestant inc. Zutphen)	1700	1–11 July
Groningen		
adopts Gregorian	1583	1–10 March
reverts to Julian	24 June 1594	
adopts Gregorian	1701	1–11 Jan.
Holland	1582	22–31 Dec.
Overijssel	1701	1–11 Jan.
Utrecht	1700	1–11 Dec.

8. Until 1917 the Ottoman calendar was exactly 584 years behind the Julian calendar and the new year began on 1 March. In 1917 thirteen days were suppressed to bring the dates (but not the years) into line with the Gregorian calendar. The discrepancy of 584 years was resolved when the Ottoman year 1341 became 1925.

State, etc.	Date	Days suppressed
Zeeland	1582	22–31 Dec.
Yugoslavia		
Bosnia, Croatia, Dalmatia,		
Herzogovina, Slovenia	1919	15–27 Jan.
Montenegro	1916	
Serbia	1919	19–31 Jan.

13

The French Revolutionary calendar

Suggestions about replacing the Gregorian calendar in France had attracted some attention in the years immediately prior to the revolution (e.g. from Pierre Sylvain Maréchal in his *Almanach des honnêtes gens*, 1788). Advocates were anxious to replace all calculations of time with Christian associations, striking a blow against the clergy, and many spoke of 'the first year of liberty'. In 1793 the National Convention appointed Charles Gilbert Romme, president of the committee of public instruction, to carry out the reform, assisted, among others, by the mathematicians, Gaspard Monge and Joseph Louis Lagrange. Their proposals were accepted in September and became law on 5 October 1793, with the start of the calendar back-dated to 22 September 1792, because it was both the day of the equinox that year and the day the Republic was proclaimed.

The calendar year of 365 days was divided into twelve months of thirty days, and each month into three *décades* of ten days, the last day of each *décade* being assigned as a day of rest. The five days out of the 365 remaining were set aside for national festivals and holidays (*Sans-culottides*), taken altogether at the end of the year, i.e. from 17 to 21 September. Leap years were treated in the same fashion, but began in 1795, not 1796 as in the Gregorian calendar. The poet of the reforming committee, Fabre d'Églantine, was responsible for the names of the months, which reflected seasonal events or attributes. Days were assigned numerical names in sequence: *Primedi, Duodi*, etc., with the day of rest being *Décadi*. But the new system only lasted thirteen years, being discontinued on 1 January 1806.

	AN II 1793–1794	AN III 1794–1795	AN IV 1795–1796	AN V 1796–1797	AN VI 1797–1798	AN VII 1798–1799	AN VIII 1799–1800	AN IX 1800–1801
1 Vendémiaire	22 Sep. 1793	22 Sep. 1794	23 Sep. 1795	22 Sep. 1796	22 Sep. 1797	22 Sep. 1798	23 Sep. 1799	23 Sep. 1800
1 Brumaire	22 Oct. 1793	22 Oct. 1794	23 Oct. 1795	22 Oct. 1796	22 Oct. 1797	22 Oct. 1798	23 Oct. 1799	23 Oct. 1800
1 Frimaire	21 Nov. 1793	21 Nov. 1794	22 Nov. 1795	21 Nov. 1796	21 Nov. 1797	21 Nov. 1798	22 Nov. 1799	22 Nov. 1800
1 Nivôse	21 Dec. 1793	21 Dec. 1794	22 Dec. 1795	21 Dec. 1796	21 Dec. 1797	21 Dec. 1798	22 Dec. 1799	22 Dec. 1800
1 Pluviôse	20 Jan. 1794	20 Jan. 1795	21 Jan. 1796	20 Jan. 1797	20 Jan. 1798	20 Jan. 1799	21 Jan. 1800	21 Jan. 1801
1 Ventôse	19 Feb. 1794	19 Feb. 1795	20 Feb. 1796	19 Feb. 1797	19 Feb. 1798	19 Feb. 1799	20 Feb. 1800	20 Feb. 1801
1 Germinal	21 March 1794	21 March 1795	21 March 1796	21 March 1797	21 March 1798	21 March 1799	22 March 1800	22 March 1801
1 Floréal	20 April 1794	20 April 1795	20 April 1796	20 April 1797	20 April 1798	20 April 1799	21 April 1800	21 April 1801
1 Prairial	20 May 1794	20 May 1795	20 May 1796	20 May 1797	20 May 1798	20 May 1799	21 May 1800	21 May 1801
1 Messidor	19 June 1794	19 June 1795	19 June 1796	19 June 1797	19 June 1798	19 June 1799	20 June 1800	20 June 1801
1 Thermidor	19 July 1794	19 July 1795	19 July 1796	19 July 1797	19 July 1798	19 July 1799	20 July 1800	20 July 1801
1 Fructidor	18 Aug. 1794	18 Aug. 1795	18 Aug. 1796	18 Aug. 1797	18 Aug. 1798	18 Aug. 1799	19 Aug. 1800	19 Aug. 1801
1 Sans-culottides	17 Sep. 1794	17 Sep. 1795	17 Sep. 1796	17 Sep. 1797	17 Sep. 1798	17 Sep. 1799	18 Sep. 1800	18 Sep. 1801
6 Sans-culottides		22 Sep. 1795				22 Sep. 1799		

	AN XIV 1805
1 Vendémiaire	23 Sep. 1805
1 Brumaire	23 Oct. 1805
1 Frimaire	22 Nov. 1805
1 Nivôse	22 Dec. 1805

	AN X 1801–1802	AN XI 1802–1803	AN XII 1803–1804	AN XIII 1804–1805
1 Vendémiaire	23 Sep. 1801	23 Sep. 1802	24 Sep. 1803	23 Sep. 1804
1 Brumaire	23 Oct. 1801	23 Oct. 1802	24 Oct. 1803	23 Oct. 1804
1 Frimaire	22 Nov. 1801	22 Nov. 1802	23 Nov. 1803	22 Nov. 1804
1 Nivôse	22 Dec. 1801	22 Dec. 1802	23 Dec. 1803	22 Dec. 1804
1 Pluviôse	21 Jan. 1802	21 Jan. 1803	22 Jan. 1804	22 Jan. 1805
1 Ventôse	20 Feb. 1802	20 Feb. 1803	21 Feb. 1804	20 Feb. 1805
1 Germinal	22 March 1802	22 March 1803	22 March 1804	22 March 1805
1 Floréal	21 April 1802	21 April 1803	21 April 1804	21 April 1805
1 Prairial	21 May 1802	21 May 1803	21 May 1804	21 May 1805
1 Messidor	20 June 1802	20 June 1803	20 June 1804	21 June 1805
1 Thermidor	20 July 1802	20 July 1803	20 July 1804	20 July 1805
1 Fructidor	19 Aug. 1802	19 Aug. 1803	19 Aug. 1804	19 Aug. 1805
1 Sans-culottides	18 Sep. 1802	18 Sep. 1803	18 Sep. 1804	18 Sep. 1805
6 Sans-culottides		23 Sep. 1803		

Index

Index

Index

privy seal office, xi, 46
Protestant calendar, viii, 63
Provence, 8

quarter-days, English and Scottish, 59

railway time-tables, 16
receipt rolls, 22
regnal years, 4, 10, 11, 21–2, 32–45, 61, 104,
    109
return days, 99–101
Richard I, king, 21, 94, 96–7
Roman calendar, 15, 145–6
    Easter, 147–54
Russia, 18, 19

St John the Baptist, Nativity, as quarter-day,
    59
Saints' days, viii, 15, 59–95
Salisbury calendar, 62, 83n, 95
Scotland, beginning of year in, 14
    James VI of, 39n, 72n
    quarter-days in, 59n
    rulers of, 47
September, beginning of year in, 3, 4
Shetland, 14
signet office, xi
Society of Friends, calendar, xv
Spain, 2, 9, 14
Star Chamber, 106
statutes, 96–7, 102–9

summer time, 17
Sweden, 5n
Switzerland, adoption of Gregorian calendar,
    239–40

Terms, law, viii, 98–105, 112–43
Trinity, *see* Terms

universities, calendars of, 62, 66n, 67n, 95

Venice, beginning of year in, 8

Wales, rulers of, 47
wardrobe account rolls, 22n
watermarks, xvii
weather, xv
week, 15n; *see also* days
Whitby, Synod of, 2, 20
Whit-Sunday, as Scottish quarter-day, 59n
Worcester calendar, 62
World War I, 17n
World War II, 17

year, beginning of the, 8–14; *see also* Leap
    year, New Year's Day, pontifical year,
    regnal year
year books, 104
York calendar, 62, 95
    Scandinavian rulers of, 25–6

zone standard time, 17

246